Portraits of Influential Chinese Educators

CERC Studies in Comparative Education

1. Mark Bray & W.O. Lee (eds.) (2001): *Education and Political Transition: Themes and Experiences in East Asia*. Second edition. ISBN 962-8093-84-3. 228pp. HK$200/US$32.

2. Mark Bray & W.O. Lee (eds.) (1997): *Education and Political Transition: Implications of Hong Kong's Change of Sovereignty*. ISBN 962-8093-90-8. 169pp. [Out of print]

3. Philip G. Altbach (1998): *Comparative Higher Education: Knowledge, the University, and Development*. ISBN 962-8093-88-6. 312pp. HK$180/US$30.

4. Zhang Weiyuan (1998): *Young People and Careers: A Comparative Study of Careers Guidance in Hong Kong, Shanghai and Edinburgh*. ISBN 962-8093-89-4. 160pp. HK$180/US$30.

5. Harold Noah & Max A. Eckstein (1998): *Doing Comparative Education: Three Decades of Collaboration*. ISBN 962-8093-87-8. 356pp. HK$250/US$38.

6. T. Neville Postlethwaite (1999): *International Studies of Educational Achievement: Methodological Issues*. ISBN 962-8093-86-X. 86pp. HK$100/US$20.

7. Mark Bray & Ramsey Koo (eds.) (2004): *Education and Society in Hong Kong and Macao: Comparative Perspectives on Continuity and Change*. Second edition. ISBN 962-8093-34-7. 323pp. HK$200/US$32.

8. Thomas Clayton (2000): *Education and the Politics of Language: Hegemony and Pragmatism in Cambodia, 1979-1989*. ISBN 962-8093-83-5. 243pp. HK$200/US$32.

9. Gu Mingyuan (2001): *Education in China and Abroad: Perspectives from a Lifetime in Comparative Education*. ISBN 962-8093-70-3. 252pp. HK$200/US$32.

10. William K. Cummings, Maria Teresa Tatto & John Hawkins (eds.) (2001): *Values Education for Dynamic Societies: Individualism or Collectivism*. ISBN 962-8093-71-1. 312pp. HK$200/US$32.

11. Ruth Hayhoe & Julia Pan (eds.) (2001): *Knowledge Across Cultures: A Contribution to Dialogue Among Civilizations*. ISBN 962-8093-73-8. 391pp. HK$250/US$38.

12. Robert A. LeVine (2003): *Childhood Socialization: Comparative Studies of Parenting, Learning and Educational Change*. ISBN 962-8093-61-4. 299pp. HK$200/US$32.

13. Mok Ka-Ho (ed.) (2003): *Centralization and Decentralization: Educational Reforms and Changing Governance in Chinese Societies*. ISBN 962-8093-58-4. 230pp. HK$200/US$32.

14. W.O. Lee, David L. Grossman, Kerry J. Kennedy & Gregory P. Fairbrother (eds.) (2004): *Citizenship Education in Asia and the Pacific: Concepts and Issues*. ISBN 962-8093-59-2. 313pp. HK$200/US$32.

15. Alan Rogers (2004): *Non-Formal Education: Flexible Schooling or Participatory Education?* ISBN 962-8093-30-4. 316pp. HK$200/US$32.

16. Peter Ninnes & Meeri Hellstén (eds.) (2005): *Internationalizing Higher Education: Critical Explorations of Pedagogy and Policy*. ISBN 962-8093-37-1. 231pp. HK$200/US$32.

17. Ruth Hayhoe (2006): *Portraits of Influential Chinese Educators*. ISBN 978-962-8093-40-3. 398pp. HK$250/US$38.

Order through bookstores or from:

Comparative Education Research Centre
Faculty of Education, The University of Hong Kong, Pokfulam Road, Hong Kong, China.
Fax: (852) 2517 4737; E-mail: cerc@hkusub.hku.hk; Website: www.hku.hk/cerc

The list prices above are applicable for order from CERC, and include sea mail postage. For air mail postage, please contact CERC for the amount.

No.7 in the series and Nos. 13-15 are co-published by Kluwer Academic Publishers and the Comparative Education Research Centre of the University of Hong Kong. Kluwer Academic Publishers publishes hardback versions. No.16 onwards are co-published with Springer.

CERC Studies in Comparative Education 17

Portraits of Influential Chinese Educators

Ruth Hayhoe

Comparative Education Research Centre
The University of Hong Kong

Springer

Comparative Education Research Centre
Faculty of Education
The University of Hong Kong
Pokfulam Road, Hong Kong, China

© Comparative Education Research Centre
First published 2006

ISBN 978 962 8093 40 3

Cover design by Vincent Lee.
Type-setting, layout and index by Emily Mang.

Permission to use the photos has been granted by the author. Selected photos of Xie Xide are reproduced with permission from Shanghai Scientific & Technical Publishers.

Contents

Dedication

This book is lovingly dedicated to the memory of Professor Li Bingde who passed away on May 2, 2005, and thus was not able to hold it in his hands. It is also dedicated to all of the influential educators, and their families and students, who were tireless in responding to questions and providing details to ensure its accuracy. Finally, it is dedicated to the people of China, who have so much to be proud of in their educators and educational traditions.

Acknowledgements

Without the active cooperation of each of the influential educators, and the assistance of their doctoral students and family members, this book could never have been written. In the case of Professor Liu Fonian, who is presented in chapter eleven, health did not permit him to be interviewed, and I am grateful to Professor Jin Yiming, his former student and biographer, for the valuable insights he provided in an interview. Thanks are also due to Professor Ding Gang, Dean of Education at the East China Normal University, for his encouragement and assistance in many aspects of the work. In addition, I wish to thank Dr. Julia Pan, a joint member of the Ontario Institute for Studies in Education and the Institute for Environmental Studies at the University of Toronto, for her passionate commitment to the project, and the great help she provided in liaising with many of the influential educators over the years. My sincere appreciation also goes to Professor Anthony Sweeting for his careful reading of the entire manuscript, his constructive suggestions, and his thought-provoking foreword.

Almost all of the photographs in this book are either personal photographs belonging to the author, or have been entrusted to her by the influential educators for the purpose of using them in this book. The second, third and fourth photos in chapter six about Xie Xide have been taken, with permission, from the *Selected Works of Xie Xide* (Shanghai: Shanghai Scientific & Technical Publishers).

Finally, special thanks are due to Ms. Emily Mang for the meticulous care and professionalism that are evident in the book's layout and index.

A Note about Romanization and Terminology

This book has largely used the Hanyu pinyin form of Romanization, which has been officially used in China since the 1950s, and widely used elsewhere since 1978. However, in the case of certain well-known names, such as Chiang Kai-shek and Sun Yat Sen, the commonly used spelling has been retained. In the case of names of Christian universities before 1949, the form of Romanization used before 1949 has been kept, since this is how the universities are best known. Thus Yenching, rather than Yanjing, Ginling, rather than Jinling, Hangchow Christian University rather than Hangzhou Christian University. In the case of China's best-known contemporary universities, two have chosen to re-instate the Romanization used for their names before 1949, and I have followed their chosen usage. Thus I use Tsinghua University, rather than Qinghua University, and Peking University rather than Beijing University.

A few words about short-forms may also be helpful. The Chinese language lends itself to abbreviation, and a widely used abbreviation for universities is "da" from "daxue" (university). For convenience, and because it conveys a pleasant sense of familiarity, I have used Beida for Peking University, Wuda for Wuhan University, Zheda for Zhejiang University, Xiada for Xiamen University, Kangda for the Anti-Japanese Resistance University. In other cases, initials are the popularly used shortform, such as ECNU for the East China Normal University, HUST for the Huazhong University of Science and Technology, NENU for the Northeast Normal University.

Another needed note relates to the name of China's capital. Beijing was called Beiping while the Nationalist government had its capital in Nanjing ("jing" meaning capital in Chinese). To avoid confusion, I have used Beijing throughout the book. However, this change in name during the Nationalist period explains the name of Beiping University. It was a different institution from Peking University. Beijing Normal University was also called Beiping Normal University during the Nationalist period, but I have used the name Beijing Normal University consistently.

Map of China

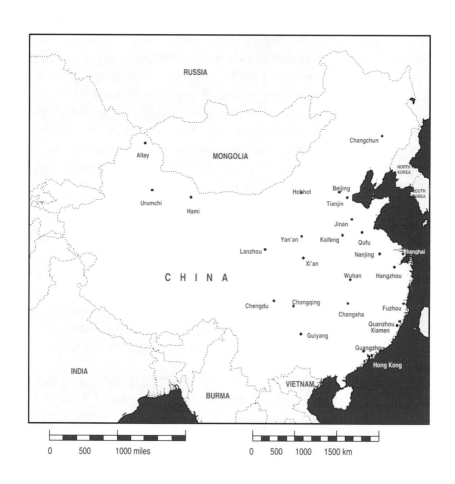

Foreword

Portraits, whether graphic or verbal, have distinct purposes and values. Through deliberate selection, they seek to reveal and, thereby, to illuminate. In their literary form, selection of content and style ensures that they do not presume to achieve the status of fully-fledged biographies. Even so, a carefully brush-stroked, multi-layered and richly textured pen-portrait is capable of revealing much about both character and circumstance. And what it reveals is likely to be different from and far more profound than any insights permitted by other miniatures, such as simple snapshots or polemical caricatures. Professor Ruth Hayhoe has produced a whole gallery of valuable portraits in the present book.

For a book in the present series, however, a key question remains. How and why may pen-portraits of eleven influential educators, from a single country and within roughly the same time frame, contribute significantly to the literature of comparative education? My own answer to this question is simple. This particular gallery makes its important contribution in two main ways and for a number of good reasons.

The 'How?' part of the question clearly involves process, especially methodological process. A portrait typically involves both foreground and background features. Some of the most effective portraits seem to encourage their observers to recognize interplay between foreground and background.

In the present book, the introductory chapter provides the reader with important background information and ideas, methodological, cultural, and historical. Many of these are revisited in the concluding chapter. These are, however, certainly not the only instances in which an outline of background factors plays an important part in facilitating readers' understanding. In each of the portrait-chapters, more specific background factors interact with a foreground that includes the individual subject's life-choices, struggles, ideas, and achievements.

This foreground emerges from an application of the "narrative approach" that is currently becoming a widely accepted alternative to the conventional linear, causation-oriented, and law-deriving methods that have dominated the social sciences for so long. Focusing upon the range of stories that help give meaning to an individual's life – combining such narratives as those related to an individual's private life, career, family life, and links with institutions, as well as with contemporary local, regional, national, and international developments – accentuates and adds depth to the foreground. Such an approach also encourages consideration of various dialogues and their contribution towards the stimulation of ideas. In the foreground, relevant dialogues include those between the subject of the portrait and members of his/her family, his/her colleagues, and, particularly as far as the generation of data and insights are concerned, between the subject-as-interviewee and the author/portrait-painter, who acted as interviewer. Moreover, the qualitative, more subjective, narrative approach provides grounds for comparisons that transcend the merely numerical.

Background features include broad, macro-level ones, some of which are derived from a sense of dialogue between civilizations. Thus, in the introductory chapter, an outline of two millennia of Chinese philosophical traditions serves as important context within which to view the lives and thoughts of the eleven educators who feature in the gallery-chapters. A similar function is performed by an identification of the main turning points in the development of education in twentieth century China. And, as noted above, in the gallery-chapters themselves, more specific contextual factors, such as those concerning the individual's family and the institutions s/he attended as learner and teacher (which typically assume a quasi-familial role) provide a background that puts the foreground in even sharper, clearer perspective. Moreover, issues related to background and the links between background and foreground, like those concerned entirely with foreground, certainly provoke interesting comparisons, both implicit and explicit.

The 'Why?' part of the key question identified above is appropriately answered by reference to end products. In this case, the portraits themselves have their own intrinsic value. Each provides and, together, all provide highly nutritious food for thought. At least some of that thought is likely to involve comparisons – intra-book comparisons between the eleven individuals portrayed (eight men and three women) and 'external' comparisons with educators from other societies and other times. Despite differences in personalities, socio-economic status, age, and gender, the educators portrayed all became, often after struggles and hardships, not only successful, prominent, and influential in their own fields, but also people who were, in the best senses of the terms, "noble" and "cultivated" – in the classic Chinese sense, people of *xiuyang*.

The gallery as a whole and the individual portraits stimulate myriad comparisons, at various different levels of focus. Some of these may be considered *micro*-level, involving personalities, family-links, gender, and schooling, for example. Others seem to involve a higher, perhaps a *meso*-level, such as comparisons of institutional affiliations, as well as of the actual historical fates of the institutions, and comparisons of influences, from within China and from outside, on the development of an individual educator's ideas. And some operate at the highest, *macro*-level, involving attempts to understand characteristics of different cultures. It is at this level, at least as much as it is at the levels of greater detail, that *Portraits* makes significant contributions towards the literature of comparative education and, especially, comparative studies of education in China.

Earlier publications by other writers have focused largely on the minutiae of educational practice and on formally promulgated educational policy, often expressed in slogans and associated with the names of paramount political leaders. They have typically adopted the positivist, objectivist, value-free approaches to comparative education. The new work, with its fresh approach, illuminates questions concerning attitudes, values, ideas, and subjective experience. At the macro-level, it shows that the traditional Chinese "Way of the Scholar", which was, to a great extent, endorsed by all eleven of the educators portrayed in the book, has much relevance for educators in other parts of the world. In doing so, it effectively distinguishes between the Confucian concern for the extended self, which tolerates the co-existence of facts with values, and a major philosophical tradition of the West, which includes the rationalism and idealism of Plato, the dualism of Kant, and the focus on causes and laws of the Enlightenment. Many active workers in the field of comparative education will be pleased to note the consonance of the Chinese *Way of the Scholars* not only with "Western" pragmatism and existentialism, but also with the counter-Enlightenment rhetoric of much post-modernist and post-structuralist thought. Indeed, some will be happy to infer that the typically Chinese capacity to tolerate, accommodate, and even integrate the mundane and the heavenly, as well as to incorporate other apparent ambiguities in both daily life and in educational practice, is compatible with the post-rationalist attractions of chaos theory.

Thus, the *Portraits* as a whole and its separate sketches have valuable lessons for people interested in comparative education, around the world. One of the most important of these is that the study of comparative education does not benefit from being confined to largely quantitative comparisons of educational systems associated exclusively with different nation-states, but that it does benefit from the comparison of qualitative, subjective, and humanist aspects. A more content-specific one emphasizes the growing importance of China in and for the present and future of the global community. It makes clear that this importance not only relates to the political economy, but especially to philosophical heritage and, even more specifically to the synaptic rewards of dialogue between the traditions and typical thought-patterns of different cultures. And a third is that pen-portraits, like most other forms, tend, in their construction, also to involve at least the glimmer of a self-portrait. This is true of the present book, which has been created by a person uniquely qualified by experience, interests, and abilities to do so and a person who, in doing so, has proved that she, herself, is a scholar with *xiuyang*.

Anthony Sweeting
Department of History and
Comparative Education Research Centre
The University of Hong Kong

Chapter One

Creating the Portraits –
An Interpretive Framework

This book is being written in order to sketch out portraits of eleven influential educators in contemporary China. My purpose in writing the book is to make possible a subjective account of some of the important educational ideas and values of Chinese culture, through the lives of educators who have lived through a century of dramatic change, suffered greatly but remained true to their calling. The life experiences which they chose to share with me express their personal understanding of their educational mission, and the meaning of their lives. The ways in which they lived their lives, and their educational ideas give insights into the treasures of a civilization very different from that of Europe and North America. In this period of dialogue among civilizations, Chinese educational thought and practice constitutes a global heritage, with much to offer to educators around the world. This book undertakes to communicate aspects of this heritage within a comparative perspective.

In order to set a context for these portraits of influential educators, this introductory chapter will provide a background for readers. I begin with some comments on the dialogue of civilizations, and the opportunities it has opened up for global appreciation of Eastern thought. Then I will consider the use of narrative method in social science research, and the new possibilities for making use of this approach in understanding Chinese education.

The rest of the chapter will focus on the traditions of Chinese educational thought and practice, in Confucian and Daoist philosophy, and in the Buddhist influences which interacted with these two Chinese thought systems. It would be impossible to give a comprehensive picture of such a vast subject in one chapter, but the basic information provided

1

here should assist the reader in understanding the philosophical and spiritual resources that have been available to Chinese educators over this century of tumultuous change. The chapter concludes with a brief overview of the major educational transitions which have framed the lives of these educators.

The Dialogue of Civilizations

It is one of the wrenching ironies of the move into the 21st century that the year 2001 should have been both the year of the 9/11 terrorist attack on New York and the United Nations' year of Dialogue among Civilizations. The decision to give 2001 this designation had been made in 1998, at the proposal of the Islamic Republic of Iran. The stated purpose was to encourage a focus on human cultural and spiritual dimensions, and on the interdependence of humankind and its rich diversity.[1] A further elaboration of purpose by UNESCO put forward the aim of "acquiring a better understanding of the long-term processes that are the mainspring of the memory of people." It also called for "an analysis of the basic concepts of heritage, identity and creativity as they take shape..."[2]

The beginning of this dialogue among civilizations can be traced back to the early 1990s. The collapse of the Soviet Union in the autumn of 1991 led to a reconsideration of the framework of the social sciences, which was explicitly secular, and tended to privilege political and economic factors in characterizing the varieties of modern society. This was certainly the case in my field of comparative education where societies tended to be characterized as capitalist or socialist, economically developed or developing. Comparative research was geared towards understanding how education contributed to development within this framework. The underlying dynamic was rooted in an embrace of European enlightenment thought in one or other of its major trajectories; educational patterns or practices of other civilizations were then judged by the degree to which they presented a barrier to modern development, whether socialist or capitalist, or were able to provide implicit forms of support for it.

---

[1] http://www.unesco.org/dialogue2001/en/background.htm Paragraph 2.
[2] *Ibid.*

The end of the Cold War has brought in its train a new set of conflicts and geopolitical uncertainties that have been summed up in Harvard professor Samuel Huntington's haunting phrase, "The Clash of Civilizations." While many aspects of Huntington's argument have been challenged, and some proven wrong, no-one has contested the important call that he gives at the end of his 1993 article for "a more profound understanding of the basic religious and philosophical assumptions underlying other civilizations and the ways in which people in those civilizations see their interests."[3] As a political scientist imbued with a realist approach to global politics, Huntington saw this as necessary to the West, if it was to maintain its leadership of the global community. However, others have seen this in a somewhat different light, as an opportunity for the West to learn from other civilizations, and to explore ways in which it might move beyond the patterns of the enlightenment heritage, which have dominated the past several centuries.

One of the most prominent of these voices belongs to another Harvard professor, Tu Wei-ming, who has dedicated several decades to writing and teaching on Confucian philosophy. His purpose has been to clarify and make explicit what Confucianism could offer to a Western world that is finally prepared to listen. In a thoughtful piece entitled "Beyond the Enlightenment Mentality," Tu identifies the core values of the Enlightenment as liberty, equality, human rights, the dignity of the individual, respect for privacy, government by the people and due process of law.[4] He summarizes these values in the concepts of progress, reason and individualism, and notes the human potential for global transformation that has become evident as modernization has carried them around the world.

At the same time, Tu identifies what he describes as the dark side of the Enlightenment, with progress, reason and individualism being developed into self-interest, expansionism, domination, manipulation and control. He sees the need for a rethinking of the enlightenment heritage that may broaden its scope, deepen its moral sensitivity and creatively transform its genetic constraints. His long-term vision is the

---

[3] Samuel Huntington, "The Clash of Civilizations?" in *Foreign Affairs*, Vol. 72, No. 3, 1993, p.49.

[4] Tu Wei-Ming, "Beyond the Enlightenment Mentality," in Mary Evelyn Tucker and John Berthrong (eds.) *Confucianism and Ecology: The Interrelation of Heaven, Earth and Humans* (Cambridge, Mass.: Centre for the Study of World Religions, Harvard University, 1998), pp.3-21.

development of enlightenment values into a worldview for the human community as a whole.

Tu calls for a new vision of human community, which he suggests may draw upon Christianity, Judaism, and Islam, but also bring in Eastern religions such as Confucianism, Daoism and Buddhism, as well as indigenous traditions. He finds two points in the basic tenets of Confucianism, which could be a first step in the kind of dialogue needed for such a transformation. The first is the new golden rule: "Do not do unto others what you would not want others to do to you." The second is the positive Confucian principle: "In order to establish myself, I have to help others to enlarge themselves."[5] He envisions an inclusive sense of community, based on the communal critical self-consciousness of reflective minds as an ethico-religious goal, as well as a philosophical ideal.

Tu's work complements and carries forward a rich literature on Confucian thought in Western languages which has been developed over the century, but has been seen more as an academic exercise in preserving and ordering classical knowledge than as an important resource for the West. One of the reasons for this lies in the general disregard for spiritual or religious knowledge in the social sciences, with their focus on political, social and economic aspects of modernization, as mentioned above. There has been very little readiness to listen to spiritual lessons that might come from other civilizations, or indeed to the rich spiritual heritage of the West itself, which was seen as inevitably eroding in face of the secularizing tendencies of modernization. The other reason lies in the fate of Confucian thought and ideas in China itself over the 20th century.

In a chapter on "Confucian Traditions in East Asian Modernity," William Theodore de Bary comments on what has been overlooked and misunderstood in much of the discussion about Confucianism. After the May 4th Movement of 1919, which has often been described as the "Chinese Enlightenment," Confucianism came to be regarded as a major obstacle to modernity by both Marxists and liberal modernizers. It was criticized for its tendency to hierarchy, rigidity, conformism, and suppression of creativity. Then the remarkable success of East Asian societies such as Taiwan, Singapore, South Korea and Hong Kong in the 1960s and 1970s led to a reconsideration of the relationship between Confucianism and modern development, and a literature emerged that credited Con-

---

[5] *Ibid.* p.5.

fucianism with giving East Asian peoples the motivation, discipline and skills necessary to engage in essential processes of modernization.

De Bary makes the point that both of these views of Confucianism and its educational implications misrepresent the actual character and enduring values of the forms of Confucian education that had been widespread among Chinese people for a millennium or more. He notes how the traditional Chinese state rarely intervened in education at the local level, limiting itself to control over the imperial examinations, used to select a scholar elite to rule. If there were tendencies to conformity, hierarchy, discipline and rigidity, it may have been at this level. However, education at the local level fitted into the neo-Confucian perception of a proper human order, grounded in values such as self-reliance, individual responsibility, family cooperation and local self-governance.

While there was considerable variety and change over time in the most basic level primers for study, the mid-level texts arranged as a core curriculum for all young people, the *Four Books* and *Five Classics*, were used from the 12th century to the early part of the 20th century. These texts had been selected in the 11th century, and provided with commentaries by the Song neo-Confucian scholar Zhu Xi, in the 12th century. Could it be, asks Professor de Bary, that their lasting popularity was a reflection of their intrinsic cultural merits? He goes on to comment on the marked eclecticism and diversity of research orientations among Chinese and Japanese scholars of the 19th century, suggesting that this core curriculum did not constrain openness to new ideas in this crucial century of change, but rather provided individuals with a strong foundation in their own learning, from which to branch out into many different areas of specialization, and bring in the new scientific knowledge from the West that was so essential to modernization.

Far from imposing a kind of conformism and subordination to the state, Confucian learning was "learning for one's self", in de Bary's judgement. "*The Four Books* with Zhu Xi's commentary gave the individual a sense of self-worth and self-respect not to be sacrificed for any short-term utilitarian purpose; a sense of place in the world not to be surrendered to any state or party; a sense of how one could cultivate one's individual powers to meet the social responsibilities that the enjoyment of learning always brought with it – powers and responsibilities not to be defaulted on. Moreover it gave a sense of educational process through discursive learning in dialogue among teachers and students which allowed different understandings of traditional teachings to emerge." [6]

All of the scholars whose portraits are included in this volume had a degree of exposure to these classical texts and to this Confucian approach to learning in their early years, though they grew up in times of drastic change and lived through wars, revolutions and radical political movements. One of the factors that drew me to these scholars was a sense of wonderment, at how they had persisted in their devotion to education, and made remarkable contributions in their older years, after overcoming immense difficulties. Most made the point in their interviews with me that only after Deng Xiaoping's accession to power in 1978 were they finally able to focus all of their energies on their educational mission. In a certain sense the ways in which they lived their lives, and built their contributions to education, are a continuing testimony to the possibilities of the Confucian tradition, and the ways in which it may have relevance beyond East Asia in this period of dialogue among civilizations.

But how are we to explore and understand this? How are we to look at their lives over time, and to learn from them some of the values of this rich civilization? Much of the research done on Chinese educational development over the twentieth century has focused on the changing political scene and the ways in which educational policy and practice were used as an instrument for economic modernization and nation building. There is detailed documentation of successive reform efforts, policy documents, legislation, institutional development, statistical data right down to the level of the village on questions such as educational participation rates and the achievement of literacy. However, there is little understanding of how education has been perceived from within, of the subjective experience of education in individual lives. There are also few accounts of the ideas of specific educators, particularly after 1949, when such political figures as Mao Zedong and Deng Xiaoping were widely quoted in the educational literature, and little opportunity was given for professional educators to assert their views.

The Western literature on Chinese education has tended to be concerned with an accurate, objective presentation of educational

---

[6] William Theodore de Bary, "Confucian Education in Premodern Asia," in Tu Wei-ming (ed.), *Confucian Traditions in East Asian Modernity* (Cambridge: Harvard University Press, 1996), p.33.

developments, and an understanding of the relationship between education and socio-economic or political development. To a considerable degree this literature has been shaped by the canons of enlightenment rationality, and its patterns of social science research. It is thus important for me to say something about my reasons for attempting to adopt narrative method in this study, and my hopes for the kinds of understanding and contribution to dialogue that could result.

Narrative Method in Social Science Research

Alasdair MacIntyre's influential book *After Virtue* explored the dilemma of modern life in terms of the emergence of morality as a category, separate from scientific knowledge, set against lives that had been lived within an integrated understanding of knowledge and virtue before Immanuel Kant introduced a dualism between facts and values. "In a world of secular rationality, religion could no longer provide a shared background and foundation for moral discourse and action: and the failure of philosophy to provide what religion could no longer furnish was an important cause of philosophy losing its central cultural role and becoming a marginal, narrowly academic subject."[7] This in turn led to the social sciences becoming dominated by objectivist studies of human society that focused on what could be observed, measured and patterned, rather than the inner meaning of human lives.

MacIntyre suggests that "conversations in particular... and human actions in general" might be viewed as "enacted narratives." ... "It is because we understand our own lives in terms of the narratives that we live out that the form of narrative is appropriate for understanding the action of others. Stories are lived before they are told."[8] He goes on to make the point that "the other aspect of narrative selfhood is correlative: I am not only accountable, I am one who can always ask others for an account, who can put others to the question. I am part of their story, as they are part of mine. The narrative of any one life is part of an interlocking set of narratives." [9]

---

[7] Alasdair MacIntyre, *After Virtue: A Study in Moral Theory* (Notre Dame, Indiana: University of Indiana Press, 1984), p.50.

[8] *Ibid.* p.211.

[9] *Ibid.* p.218.

Donald Polkinghorne provides a comprehensive overview of the scholarly challenges that have come forth in recent years to a world of social sciences that had come to be dominated by Max Weber's commitment to value neutrality. He notes how "Weber defended a dualism of understanding in which the personal decision pertaining to private world-orientations was separated from a scientism or instrumentalism in the sphere of rational, inter-subjectively valid information."[10] From William Dilthey's concept of understanding, as against explanation, through the work of Roland Barthes, Jerome Bruner, Maurice Merleau-Ponty, on to Noam Chomsky and Karl Sheibe, Polkinghorne traces these challenges. He provides an overview of how narrative has come to be used in the fields of history, literature and psychology. Most interesting is his discussion of the healing character of narrative within psychology – the importance to human well-being of the ability to "create a narrative that is coherent and satisfying and that will serve as a justification for one's present condition and situation."[11]

Polkinghorne goes on to say that "in the understanding of human existence – both human lives and organizational 'lives' – narrative has a central role." [12] "According to a narrative theory of human existence, a study needs to focus its attention on existence as it is lived, experienced, and interpreted by the human person."[13] This in turn leads to a different conception of time from that which has dominated the social sciences. "In the objective view of reality constructed by the formal science of the Enlightenment, the world was pictured as space filled with meaningless objects that moved through a time plane which made up the present moment."[14] In narrative understanding, however, one is dealing with multiple layers of time – time past, in memory, time present, in attention, and time future, in expectation. Thus the person or institution in a narrative study is seen as an unfolding story, rather than a fixed entity in time and space; the person is also seen in relationship with his or her family, colleagues, institution, and also with the researcher. Furthermore, the person is seen over time, looking both backward and forward.

---

[10] Donald E. Polkinghorne, *Narrative Knowing and the Human Sciences* (Albany: State University of New York Press, 1988), p.41.

[11] *Ibid.* p.106.

[12] *Ibid.* p.123.

[13] *Ibid.* p.125.

[14] *Ibid.* p.126.

Jean Clandinin and Michael Connelly note that "temporality" is a key term in their narrative work. "We are ... not only concerned with life as it is experienced in the here and now but also with life as it is experienced on a continuum – people's lives, institutional lives, lives of things. Just as we found our own lives embedded within a larger narrative of social science inquiry, the people, schools, and educational landscapes we study undergo day-by-day experiences that are con-textualized within a longer-term historical narrative." [15] Clandinin and Connelly end their first chapter with what they called a 'working concept' of narrative inquiry as a way of understanding experience. "It is a collaboration between researcher and participants, over time, in a place or a series of places, and in social interaction with milieus ... Simply stated, ... narrative inquiry is stories lived and told."[16]

Several core points come out of this literature on narrative that I will try to elaborate in terms of the way in which the eleven portraits of Chinese educators in this book have been constructed. The first is the point that people's lives are lived in inter-relation with others, and they cannot be seen as isolated entities but as members of a family, of one or several institutions, of a community, of a nation. A particular charac-teristic of the lives of scholars in modern China has been the fact that many have been associated with one university throughout their lifetime, and their personal narrative has been intertwined with the narrative of their institution over a very long period of time. For both individual scholars, and university institutions, the new directions in education, introduced by Deng Xiaoping in 1978, constituted a crucial turning-point. For the first time since the Communist Revolution of 1949, they were given space and time to reflect on their own life-stories.

Likewise, institutions finally had the opportunity to reconstruct their stories. Almost every university in China produced an institutional history in the period between 1978 and the late 1980s, recovering details of their histories which had been submerged under the Soviet-style reorganization of 1952, and in some cases regarded as dangerous during the traumatic decade of the Cultural Revolution. These institutional histories charted the development of modern institutions from the late 19th century, how they evolved from different traditional institutions in

---

[15] Jean Clandinin and Michael F. Connelly, *Narrative Inquiry: Experience and Story in Qualitative Research* (San Francisco: Jossey-Bass Inc., 2000), p.19.
[16] *Ibid.* p.20.

varying regions, how they had been influenced by external models, those introduced by scholars returning from study in Japan, Europe or North America, and those brought by missionaries from Europe, Canada and the USA. The generation of scholars who had been educated before 1949 and in many cases had studied abroad, came to be treasured for their living links to a past that had so long been repudiated in the revolutionary narrative of self-sufficiency and independence that had consumed people during the Cultural Revolution.

The second point of importance is the fact that narrative research takes place in a relationship between researcher and participants. The fact that I was able to hold lengthy interviews with each of the educators, whose life-story is told in this volume, came about as a result of a relationship built up over a long period of time, between my first experience of living in China in 1980 to 1982, when I worked as a foreign expert at Fudan University in Shanghai, and the time I spent in Hong Kong from 1997 to 2002, leading a new institute for teacher education.

Over those five years, I found time to sit down with these scholars and listen to their stories, either in Hong Kong, or during my frequent trips to the Mainland. Four of them came to Hong Kong and were interviewed by me there, as well as in Shanghai, Nanjing and Beijing. The others were interviewed entirely on their home ground, the various cities of China where they live. The fact that these are spread from Xiamen in the Southeast to Lanzhou in the Northwest, Changchun in the Northeast, Wuhan in Central China, and the cities of Nanjing, Shanghai and Beijing in the East, shows how broad and deep were the links I had formed with the Chinese educational community during my twenty-four years of teaching, research and project work with China.

I am deeply touched and honored by the fact that each of them, distinguished and revered figures within contemporary Chinese education as they are, was willing to share their life-story with me. I am also aware that the nature of this sharing, the way in which the story was told and the kinds of details that were revealed, reflected the character of our relationship and the degree of trust and understanding that had developed over time. With some of these elder scholars, my links went back over many years, with others they were more tenuous.

My purpose has been to probe the links between their educational work and influence and their own life experience. On a deeper level, I wanted to explore and understand how the living of their lives illustrates some of the values and perspectives of the Confucian tradition. As far as possible, I will introduce some of their major writings and educational achievements, but it would be beyond the scope of this book to provide a comprehensive account of their educational theories in fields such as higher education, comparative education, moral education, educational sociology, curriculum and learning theory. Rather it is the nexus between their creation of a literature in these fields since 1978 and their own life experiences that will be the focus.

Working on this project of collecting their life-stories has made me deeply aware of my own life-story, in turn, and has indeed been the catalyst for a memoir about my own life with Hong Kong and China over a 35 year period.[17] The probing of my own life experiences, and the ways in which they shaped my educational ideas and research questions, has reminded me of how impossible it would be for another, no matter how close, to fully interpret one's life. All I can present in these portraits is the picture these educators have given to me, at a particular time in history, in a relationship shaped by our past interactions, as well as our future expectations and hopes. In each case, the particular threading of past, present and future is somewhat different.

In the case of Xie Xide, for example, our relationship went back to the early 1980s, when I was a foreign expert at Fudan University and she was vice-president responsible for international affairs. In the years between 1980 and the late 1990s, our paths crossed on a number of occasions, and this shared memory shaped the two lengthy afternoon interviews, which took place in a Shanghai hospital where she was recuperating from an operation for breast cancer in the autumn of 1998. Her untimely death in February of 2000 left me feeling deeply bereft.

In the case of Wang Chengxu, our first meeting had taken place in London in 1983, while I was a doctoral student at the University of London Institute of Education, and he was returning to visit the country where he had done graduate work several decades earlier in the 1930s and 1940s. It was a wonderful opportunity for me to meet one of the luminaries in the field from China, just as I was starting my research on Chinese education. I invited him and a colleague for dinner in the dining room of the William Goodenough House, our pleasant graduate residence, and made the most of that opportunity to learn. While I was

---

[17] Ruth Hayhoe, *Full Circle: A Life with Hong Kong and China* (Toronto: Women's Press, Hong Kong: Comparative Education Research Centre, The University of Hong Kong, 2004).

aware of Professor Wang's work over the subsequent years, it was to be the spring of 2001 before I met him again at Zhejiang University in Hangzhou, when I visited to fulfill my duties as a recently appointed advisory professor.

Their lives were evolving over the period from 1978 to the early 21st century, as was mine, and it was in the interface between their evolving experience in educational leadership, research and teaching and my development as a scholar and as the head of an educational institution, that their stories emerged and were related to me. My readiness to undertake this kind of research was also an essential part of the context.

During my doctoral studies under Brian Holmes at the University of London Institute of Education, my approach to research had been shaped by principles of objectivity and value neutrality, a key aspect of Holmes' 'Problem Approach' to comparative education. After completing my doctorate, however, I moved forward with new research on Chinese higher education within a value explicit approach, using the literature of the stimulating group of scholars who call themselves the World Order Models Project. Their scholarly efforts towards visioning preferred futures made possible a framework characterized by openness to multiple civilizations and cultural heritages, as sources of value in this quest. I thus tried to sketch out a picture of mutually respectful relations between universities in China and various western countries, in which learning took place both ways. The various projects of collaboration and activities of exchange and development were then evaluated against this ideal model.[18]

A second innovation in my research was what might be described as a narrative approach to understanding the roles of Chinese universities in different regions, different disciplinary areas and with distinctive historical traditions and external cultural relationships. As I studied the development of higher education policy in the post Cultural Revolution period and visited about 100 universities in the six major regions of the country, it was interesting to see how they responded differently to the new opportunities opening up to them. I came to see each institution as having a personality and identity of its own, rather than as a cog in a huge system of higher education.

---

[18] Ruth Hayhoe, *China's Universities and the Open Door* (Toronto: OISE Press, New York: M.E.Sharpe, 1989).

Gradually I collected many of their institutional histories, which were published in the 1980s, and was fascinated to see how the process of writing their institution's history constituted a kind of exercise in identity formation, and a healing process after the wounds of the Cultural Revolution. My research sought to understand the coming of age of modern Chinese universities in terms of the cultural dimension. I attempted to analyze past conflicts in relation to deep rooted cultural differences between Chinese and Western views of knowledge, not only the more obvious stresses brought about by drastic changes in political system and economic development model. I also ventured to sketch out a preferred future for Chinese universities as institutions that could contribute not only to the scientific and technological knowledge needed for rapid economic growth, but also to the social knowledge that could ensure justice with growth, and the cultural authenticity that could root this justice firmly within Chinese civilization.[19]

In the field trips I took to all different parts of China from 1985 to 1994, I interviewed dozens of university administrators as well as university scholars, and their views and insights were often represented in my writing. Seldom, however, did I identify them by name, since there were many sensitive issues under consideration. It was still too close to the difficult days of the Cultural Revolution for people to feel free to share their views with complete frankness. It is thus wonderful to have reached the point where it is possible to sketch out the portraits of eleven influential educators by name, and to be certain that none of them feel any sense of threat in opening up the story of their lives to an international readership.

In writing their stories, I am thus also sketching out the story of their institution. Most have been closely associated with one institution since the early1950s. My main sources for these brief sketches of 'their' universities are the institutional histories I have collected over the years. My approach to interpreting the stories of these institutions is, however, rooted in the perspectives I have developed over two decades of research on modern Chinese higher education.

---

[19] Ruth Hayhoe, *China's Universities 1895-1995: A Century of Cultural Conflict* (New York: Garland, 1996, Hong Kong: Comparative Education Research Centre, The University of Hong Kong, 1999, Chapter Seven.)

China's Educational Traditions

As I have approached the writing of this section on China's educational traditions, I have found myself nearly paralyzed at the thought of trying to sketch out the main characteristics of a subject so rich and so thoroughly studied, that there are probably thousands of volumes one could draw upon. I have also reflected on my own relationship to the Chinese classics, and how my thinking has changed over time, as I pursued my research into the development of modern Chinese universities.

My first degree was in Western classical studies and included the reading of much of our traditional philosophy and poetry in Greek and Latin, including Homer's *Iliad*, the *Apology* of Socrates, Plato's *Republic*, the *Aeneid* of Virgil and many other texts. My studies of Chinese, however, were undertaken mainly on an informal basis, with a private teacher, and never gave me the opportunity for a rigorous exposure to the learning of classical Chinese. A natural interest arising from my own education drew me to informal studies of the classics at certain times, including a fascinating experience I had as a foreign expert living in Shanghai in the early 1980s and teaching English at Fudan University. My decision to audit a class in the philosophy department led me to meet a self-educated classical scholar, who had his own collection of classical texts and led me through a traditional pedagogical experience of reading the *Great Learning* and parts of the *Mencius*, two of the *Four Books* of Confucius.

Later, as I became more and more absorbed in the literature on modern Chinese education, both that written by scholars within China and abroad, I was strongly influenced by a prevailing attitude of criticism towards the Confucian educational heritage. It was seen as a major barrier to modernization, a set of ideas and patterns that had to be completely rooted out if China was to move towards democracy, scientific understanding and greater personal freedoms. Emphasis was put upon the way it fostered conformity and subordination to hierarchy, its tendency to encourage rote learning, and the ease with which it became a tool in the hands of political authority to legitimate the repression of dissent.

Then there was a sudden turnaround in these views, as scholars sought to explain the remarkable economic achievements of post-Confucian East Asian societies, such as Japan and the "four little dragons," South Korea, Taiwan, Hong Kong and Singapore.[20] A more positive picture of Confucianism emerged, suggesting a Confucian ethic that paralleled Max Weber's famous theory of the Protestant ethic and the spirit of capitalism. An essay review I wrote in 1991 reflected my personal struggle to come to terms with this shift in thinking.[21]

Only as I got to know an older generation of scholars better and better, through my collaborative projects in China, did I come to realize how their approaches to education were deeply rooted in views of the human person, views of the learning process, views of society, views of the natural environment, that owed much to China's philosophical traditions. This was increasingly evident to me, in spite of the fact that debates about educational policy and educational reform were almost always phrased within the prevailing Marxist-Leninist-Maoist orthodoxy. This new realization drew me to delve into the rich literature on Confucian thought that exists in English, including the work of William Theodore de Bary, Benjamin Schwartz, Tu Wei-ming, Julia Ching, Roger Ames, David Hall, Robert Neville and others.

One of the features of Chinese educational philosophy that I have found most striking is the connection between knowledge and action, the belief that experience is the fundamental basis of knowledge. Another side of this is the view that knowledge can only finally be demonstrated as true or valid through its expression in action, not merely through logical argument or critical testing. Since this book is more about the life experiences of the ten educators than their theories or writings, it seems important to set a context for their lives through an overview of the Confucian tradition. Many of these scholars had some exposure to traditional forms of schooling, and most were influenced by the values and beliefs of parents, who had been steeped in these traditions.

To provide some sort of structure for this overview, I will take the elegant framework provided by de Bary, in his probing volume, *East Asian Civilizations – A Dialogue in Five Stages.*[22] I will first attempt to sketch out the classical traditions of Confucian education, as they took form from the life time of Confucius, in the 5th century BCE, up to the

---

[20] Ezra Vogel, *The Four Little Dragons: The Spread of Industrialization in East Asia* (Cambridge, Mass.: Harvard University Press, 1991).

[21] Ruth Hayhoe, "The Confucian Ethic and the Spirit of Capitalism," in *Curriculum Inquiry*, Vol. 22, No. 4, (Winter, 1992), pp.425-431.

[22] William Theodore de Bary, *East Asian Civilizations – A Dialogue in Five Stages* (Cambridge, Mass.: Harvard University Press, 1988).

beginnings of the Tang dynasty when Buddhism came to dominate Chinese educational thought and practice. Then I look at the main ideas of Daoism and Buddhism, and their educational legacy. Subsequently I turn to neo-Confucian values and ideas of education, as set in place by the Cheng brothers and Zhu Xi in the 12th century CE, a curriculum that was to remain a core orientation of Chinese education right up to the early part of the 20th century. This is the third stage in de Bary's brilliant overview. From here I deviate from the structure of de Bary's dialogue, and tell the story of Wang Yangming, the neo-Confucian educator of the 15th-16th centuries, whose philosophy of knowledge and action underlay many of the efforts of progressive educators in the 1920s and 1930s. His life-story, as told by Tu Wei-ming and Julia Ching, provides an example of an influential educator in the Chinese tradition.

The Confucian Tradition or the Way of the Scholars

The first point that needs to be made before summing up an educational tradition that arose in the 6th century BCE, and developed into a mainstream influence in Chinese society and culture is that the English term Confucianism itself is somewhat of a misnomer. The Chinese phrase, *Rujia*, has much broader connotations and is sometimes translated as the "Way of the Scholars." Suffice it to say that there was a clearly defined tradition and set of texts, originating with Confucius, and a lineage that passed this down through Mencius, Xun Zi, and Dong Zhongshu, to name just a few of the major figures in this educational tradition.

Confucius, or the Master Kung, lived from 551 to 479 BCE, in the final years of what is called the Spring and Autumn Period (770-476 BCE) and just before the beginning of the Warring States (475-221 BCE). He lived in the state of Lu in Northeastern China, holding some minor official positions, advising kings and rulers and taking on a large number of disciples. The book most closely associated with Confucius, *The Analects*, is a collection of conversations between the master and his disciples, concerning human life, the family, government, and the good society. Confucius was known as a preserver and transmitter of the classics, and was thought to have had a role in collating what were known as the *Six Classics – The Book of Odes, The Book of Rites, The Book of Music, The Book of Documents* (History), *The Book of Changes* and *The Spring and Autumn Annals*. He is thought to have had a particularly close association with the last of these classical texts.

Mencius, often regarded as the next great figure in the Confucian tradition, lived from 385 to 304 BCE, and is known best through his book, *The Mencius*, which presents him in conversation with the King Hui of Liang, covering a large range of topics relating to good governance, and meeting the needs of the people. Mencius is particularly known for his strong faith in the inherent goodness of humankind, and the tendency of the human heart to feel sympathy for all those who may be suffering or in need. Schwartz notes his central belief that the achievement of a good society depends wholly on the inherent moral intentionality of good men.[23]

Xun Zi or the Master Xun, the third important figure in the Confucian lineage, lived from 325 to 238 BCE, and is best known for a view that is often set in contrast to that of Mencius – the human tendency to evil. Xun Zi felt that the only way to curb the boundless desires of human beings and confine them within proper limits was to create and impose a clear system of rules of behavior, laws and institutions.[24] Education played a key role in this and de Bary suggests that he was the first to conceive of a full blown educational program and to define a classical curriculum.

De Bary outlines his educational philosophy as follows: "Education continues till death, and only then does it cease... To pursue it is to be a man, to give it up is to become a beast. *The Book of Documents* is the record of government affairs, the *Odes* the repository of correct sounds, and the *Rites* the great basis of law and the foundation of precedents. Therefore learning reaches its completion with the rites, for they may be said to represent the highest point of the way and its power. The reverence and order of the *Rites*, the fitness and harmony of *Music*, the breadth of the *Odes* and *Documents*, the subtlety of the *Spring and Autumn Annals* – these encompass all that is between heaven and earth."[25]

Finally, Dong Zhongshu, who was the leading scholar in the time of Emperor Wu of the Western Han Dynasty (206-24 BCE) and lived from 179-104 BCE was a key figure in establishing the classics as the basis of public instruction. The *Five Classics* which were laid out at this time basically followed the original identified by Confucius himself, with the

---

[23] Benjamin I. Schwartz, *The World of Thought in Ancient China* (Cambridge, Mass.: The Bellknap Press of Harvard University Press, 1985), p.262.
[24] *Ibid.* p.295.
[25] de Bary, *East Asian Civilizations*, pp.10-11.

exception of *The Book of Music* which had been destroyed along with all others in the campaign of the Qin Emperor (221-206 BCE) against Confucianism, and was the only one for which no version had been hidden and preserved through that difficult period.

While many other important figures were involved in the development of this educational tradition, which dominated Chinese culture up to the Tang dynasty (618-907 CE) when Buddhism brought great changes, these four are key figures in the development of Confucianism, or the "Way of the Scholars." *The Five Classics* also persisted as the most important and influential common readings for all those who aspired to scholarship and who participated in the increasingly sophisticated system of selecting scholar-officials to lead the government through the civil service examination system. Although there were differences in emphasis among these four sage leaders, it was their common adherence to the classical teachings and commitment to nurturing good governance and human flourishing (to use a phrase of Tu Wei-ming) that made them a kind of lineage of the Way (*Daotong*).

What were the core values and ideas of Confucianism over this period? How was society and government perceived? What was the view of the human person? How was knowledge understood and the process of learning encouraged? Most scholars who attempt to address these fundamental questions find that the Chinese educational tradition is fundamentally opposite to that of Europe, and that comparisons can be helpful in drawing attention to the core values.

In considering Confucian views of the good society, Benjamin Schwartz notes how the ideal family is "the ultimate source of all those values which humanize the relations of authority and hierarchy which must exist in any civilized society."[26] He notes how different this is from the views of Plato who saw the family as devoted to pursuing its own particularistic economic goals and having a limited familial morality. One of the reasons for this fundamental difference, Schwartz suggests, is the character and size of the Greek city state, small enough for a limited form of democracy to emerge among male citizens. The size and scope of the Chinese empire was quite different, of course.

While Plato saw the family as likely to encourage narrow self interest, for Confucius "it is precisely in the family that humans learn those virtues which redeem the society" and that "authority comes to be

---

[26] Schwartz, *The World of Thought in Ancient China*, p.70.

accepted and exercised, not through reliance on physical coercion but through the binding power of religious, moral sentiments based on kinship ties."[27] The rites or ceremonies established by the classics, the *li*, hold together an entire normative order, which is derived from the relations of the ideal family.

The Confucian view of knowledge can also be seen in striking contrast to that of Plato. For Confucius, says Schwartz, knowledge begins with "the empirical cumulative knowledge of masses of particulars and then includes the ability to link these particulars first to one's own experiences and then ultimately with the underlying 'unity' that binds this thought together."[28] For Plato, by contrast, knowledge was achieved through mathematical reasoning and the perception of eternal abstract forms, something achieved by philosopher kings through a rigorous process of deductive logic. While Plato thought it was essential to rise above the chaos of ordinary human experience, "Confucius does not rise from the chaos of the world of particulars to a world of eternal forms, since, in his view, the way (*dao*) remains indissolubly linked to the empirical world."[29]

As for the human person, Confucius called for a lifelong pursuit of love or humanheartedness (*ren*), a personal cultivation that involves achieving inner equanimity and outer integrity and responsibility to society. It was distinctive for men and for women, and for members of the four major classes of society, scholars, farmers, craftspeople and merchants, with only males of the scholar class having access to positions of leadership. Over time, however, the civil service examinations opened up opportunity to boys of all four classes, who devoted themselves to learning. In the concept of the human person and leadership, probably Confucius and Plato were closer than in their views of knowledge and the good society. "In both the Republic and in Confucius, what brings about the good society is the government of good men," notes Schwartz, yet there were enormous differences in the methods of producing the "best men."[30]

Whereas Plato's thought lay at the root of the forms of rationalism and linear logic that culminated in the dualism of Immanuel Kant, briefly

---

[27] *Ibid.*
[28] *Ibid.* p.89.
[29] *Ibid.* p.94.
[30] *Ibid.* p.87.

noted earlier in this chapter, the Chinese knowledge tradition developed very differently. There was a continuing emphasis on knowledge as a process of absorbing and interacting with experience, and human development as a way of harmonizing the self with heaven, human society and the world of nature. Two scholars who have done much to develop a philosophical exploration of Confucian thought in contrast to European traditions, Roger Ames and David Hall, comment that pragmatism and existentialism in Western philosophy probably come closest to Confucian ways of knowing. They note the dominant Western absorption in the issue of causation, and a belief in "laws which define the structure of the world and the relation of the human mind to that structure." [31] They suggest this strand reached its full development with Immanuel Kant and the articulation of the separate value spheres of art, morality and science.

By contrast, "the explanation of the social, political and cosmological processes in terms of the interaction of complementary contrasts is fundamental to the Chinese tradition."[32] "(W)hen the question was of the place of the human being in his or her broader social or cosmological context, there was among the Chinese a concern to relegate causal thinking to the sphere of everyday life [where they were very successful with technological innovation] and to pursue the correlative mode of understanding with respect to the larger issues of cultural life. By the same token, they never tolerated a complete separation between facts and values, but ensured the integration of technological developments into the sphere of concrete social praxis…to insure the continuance of that valuational matrix pervading the established correlative construction."[33]

The parallels between Deweyan pragmatism and the Wang Yangming school of neo-Confucianism will be explored later in this chapter, but here I will turn to an earlier book by Hall and Ames which gives profound insights into Confucianism as a way of thinking and living, through a close examination of Confucius' own interpretation of the stages of his life. This book may be particularly relevant, given that

---

[31] David Hall and Roger Ames, *Anticipating China: Thinking Through the Narratives of Chinese and Western Culture* (Albany, State University of New York Press, 1995). p.80.

[32] *Ibid.* p.130.

[33] *Ibid.* p.132.

this overview of Confucianism is designed to stimulate reflection on the life-stories of contemporary Chinese educators.

In a much-quoted account of his life in the *Analects,* Confucius depicted its six phases in the following way:

At fifteen, my heart and mind were set on learning.

At thirty I took my stance.

At forty I was no longer of two minds.

At fifty I understood Heaven's place for me.

At sixty my ear was attuned.

At seventy I could give my heart-and-mind free reign without overstepping the mark.[34]

In Confucianism, the human being is primarily a maker of meaning, and the primary meaning made is related to the self-conscious appropriation of the world of experience. "What it means to be human is contingent, being ever redefined by man himself in the emergence of new circumstances."[35] For Confucius the formation of an ethical vision is not a rationalization process, but a matter of remaining open to the experience of authoritative humanity or *ren* ... [36] "The authoritative person is perpetually self-surpassing, to be evaluated in open-ended qualitative terms rather than in terms of "completion."[37] And so "I took my stance." I began that journey, says Confucius, at the age of thirty.

Being "no longer of two minds" suggests that human development is not a matter of considering alternatives and weighing different possibilities but of growing into a kind of focus on those fields of possibility where one engages in the fullest and most fruitful way with society, with nature, with heaven itself. The fully developed person is a model of personal and socio-political order, both a source of continuity and a ground for creativity in the influences one has on others, suggest Hall and Ames.[38] At age 40 Confucius felt he had reached this place.

Understanding "Heaven's place for me" (*tian ming*) at age fifty suggests a profound sense of clarity about his life. *Tian ming* is often translated as destiny, or the mandate of heaven, but Hall and Ames point out that this is a very European concept, carrying notions of transcen-

---

[34] This translation is adapted from David Hall and Roger Ames, *Thinking Through Confucius* (Albany: State University of New York Press, 1987).

[35] *Ibid.* p.97.

[36] *Ibid.* p.104.

[37] *Ibid.* p.115.

[38] *Ibid.* p.192.

dence and the sense of a moral imperative that are absent in Chinese thought. Rather they suggest that Heaven (*tian*) designates the process itself of the natural and human worlds arising spontaneously, and *ming* (place or destiny) the conditions or possibilities of a particular phenomenon which provide the context for its arising.[39] They suggest parallels to the Western existentialist tradition. "In the immanent cosmos of Confucius, one accomplishes this same project of bonding by achieving a quality of integration into the world which dissolves the distinction between part and whole, and makes of one a peculiar focus of meaning and value in the field of existing things."[40]

Contemporary Chinese philosopher Li Zehou interprets *tian ming* in relation to the ability of the human person to make decisions for their own life in face of the fortuity of unexpected circumstances. One thus knows and accepts one's own limits, is never disappointed, and does not seek for what is beyond one's grasp.[41]

At sixty Confucius felt he had reached the point where his ear was attuned to Heaven and he was able to communicate its message through his teaching. The word sage (*sheng*) in Chinese has a picture of a large ear, beside a mouth, and over the word for king. Although Confucius never claimed sagehood himself, he simply stated. "I learn without relenting and teach without tiring of it."[42] Hall and Ames suggest that music and the aesthetic world are the best way of understanding this: "It is distinctly aesthetic rightness that provides the fundamental meaning for the Confucian notion of *yi* (rightness). Rightness as aesthetic harmony is a function of concrete, immediate, pre-cognitive choices made by the creator or appreciator of a given harmony."[43]

Finally, at seventy, Confucius felt he had reached the point where the self-discipline of a life of listening, learning and teaching brought his inner self, his *xin* or heart-and-mind, into perfect harmony with Heaven, the natural world and human society, such that there was no more striving. "I could give my heart and mind free rein, without overstepping the mark."

---

[39] *Ibid*. p.209.

[40] *Ibid*. p.243.

[41] Li Zehou, *Lunyu jindu* [Contemporary Reading of the Analects] (Hefei: Anhui Art Press, 1998), p.53.

[42] Hall and Ames, *Anticipating China*, p.258.

[43] *Ibid*. p.266.

This brief overview cannot begin to do justice to the rich qualities of Confucian thought and understanding which are explored in great depth in the work of William Theodore de Bary, David Hall, Roger Ames, Julia Ching, Tu Wei-ming and many others. However, I think readers will note the ways in which it resonates with aspects of narrative knowing, outlined earlier in this chapter. Two concepts stand out. The first is correlation, a way of understanding lives lived in changing contexts, with evolving relationships. The second is coherence, the healing power of an inner understanding of the meaning of the different phases of a life.

Daoism and Buddhism in the Chinese Educational Tradition

In his beautifully elaborated *Dialogue in Five Stages* de Bary calls stage two "The Buddhist age," and marks the time frame as beginning in China's Tang dynasty (618-907 CE), when the influence of Buddhism, introduced from India a few centuries earlier, was at its peak. Since Daoism is often regarded as the Chinese philosophical tradition which paved the way for the acceptance and transformation of Buddhism, I will provide a brief overview of the key figures and educational ideas associated with both in this section.

The two names closely associated with Daoism are Lao Zi, or the Master Lao, and Zhuang Zi, the Master Zhuang. Lao Zi was thought to have lived in the 6th century BCE, contemporary with and somewhat earlier than Confucius. There is a celebrated story of Confucius' paying a visit to the older philosopher, when he was a young man. However, almost nothing is known about the life of Lao Zi, and his famous text, the *Dao De Jing* or Classic of the Way[44] is thought to be a compilation of several writers.[45] Zhuang Zi, a famous disciple or successor of Lao Zi, is more clearly known as a historical figure, who lived from 369-289 BCE, around the same time as Mencius, and a little bit earlier than Aristotle in Greece. He was thought to have worked as a minor official but was better known as a recluse. His classic, simply called the *Zhuang Zi*,[46] is also thought to be a compilation. While both of these early texts remain vital parts of the Chinese philosophical tradition, later Daoist writings had less

---

[44] Lao Tzu, *Tao Te Ching* (Trans. D.C. Lau) (Harmondsworth: Penguin Books, 1982).

[45] Schwartz, *The World of Thought in Ancient China*, p.187.

[46] *Chuang Tzu: Taoist Philosopher and Chinese Mystic* (Trans. Herbert Giles) (London: Unwin Paperbacks, 1980).

impact, being developed mainly in association with popular religion and the quest for immortality, rather than as philosophical enquiry.

No one can be sure when the first Buddhist influences reached China from India, but it is likely this was in the first or second centuries of the Common era. Before long, Chinese thinkers sought out Buddhist scriptures, and a wide range of texts was translated into Chinese. The impetus for this pro-active interest in Buddhist thought and religion seems to have been linked mainly to the influences of Daoism. It would be impossible to name all of the important figures involved in the introduction of Buddhism to China, but one name should be mentioned. That is the Chinese Buddhist monk Xuan Zang (596-664 CE), who made an epic voyage across Western China and Central Asia to study the original texts of Buddhism in India. He stayed for a number of years, and on return devoted the rest of his life to translating 75 volumes of Buddhist teaching into Chinese.[47]

It was during the great Tang dynasty (618-907 CE), a period when China was more open to the world than at any other time in its history, that Buddhism flourished, becoming a dominant force in education, literature, the arts, and every arena of society. This was a period when Confucianism had less influence, while Daoism flourished alongside of Buddhism, giving it support.

Daoist ideas are in some ways best understood as a kind of polar opposite to Confucianism, the other side of the Chinese character. De Bary expresses the relationship in this way: "To the solemn, rather pompous gravity and burden of social responsibility of Confucianism, Daoism opposes a carefree flight from respectability and the con-ventional duties of society; in place of the stubborn Confucian concern for things human and mundane, it holds out a vision of other, transcendental worlds of the spirit. Where the Confucian philosophers are often prosaic and dull, moralistic and commonsensical, the early Daoist writings are all wit and paradox, mysticism and poetic vision. As the two streams of thought developed in later ages, Confucianism has represented the mind of the Chinese scholar-gentleman in his ... study, being a good family man, a conscientious bureaucrat and a sober, responsible citizen. Daoism has represented the same gentleman in his ... mountain retreat, seeking surcease from the cares of official life, perhaps

---

[47] Wm Theodore de Bary, Wing-Tsit Chan and Burton Watson (eds.), *Sources of Chinese Tradition* (New York: Columbia University Press, 1960), pp.303-306.

a little drunk but more likely intoxicated by the beauties of nature or of the world of the spirit."[48]

What were the core values of Daoism? How was society and government perceived? How was knowledge advanced, and how was the human person viewed? The overarching value of Daoist thought seems to be one of attachment to nature, which runs spontaneously, without deliberate planning. The ideal society would be one which operates according to the principles of nature, through minimal planning or intervention, and maximum space for nature's principles and patterns to exert themselves. Non-action (*wuwei*) is the means whereby everything gets done in the best possible way, the way of nature. The Daoist view of knowledge is equally paradoxical, involving intense observation of nature and its processes, on the one hand, and a distrust of written texts, and formal compilations of knowledge on the other.

It is perhaps in its view of the human person that Daoism departs farthest from Confucian views. While Confucianism privileges the male, and affirms male authority in the natural hierarchy of family and empire, Daoism privileges the female, as the symbol of the principles of non-action and spontaneity. Schwartz makes the following comment about the mysterious female in Daoism: "She ... represents the nonassertive, the uncalculating, the non-deliberative, non-purposive processes of generation and growth – the processes by which the 'empty' gives rise to the full; the quiet gives rise to the active and the 'one' gives rise to the many. The female is the epitome of *wuwei*."[49] While Daoism never had enough social or political influence to affect the role of women significantly in traditional Chinese society, the Tang dynasty was known as being a time when women had greater social, intellectual and artistic freedom than at any other period. Under the influences of Buddhism, they also had the opportunity for forms of study outside of home and family that had not been available in earlier dynasties.

Buddhism had similarities to Daoism, yet was principally a psychological rather than philosophical understanding of human life and society. Of the two main schools of Buddhism, Hinayana and Mahayana, it was the latter, which appealed to Chinese thinkers with its emphasis on "the resplendent personal attributes of the Buddha and the compassionate help of the bodhisattvas. All beings were now assured that

---

[48] *Ibid*. p.48.
[49] Schwartz, *The World of Thought in Ancient China*, p.200.

they possessed the seeds of Buddhahood and that with the aid of the bodhisattvas, they could bring these seeds to fruition – a prospect far more attractive to most people than the difficult ascent to Nirvana via the Eightfold Path," writes de Bary, [50] contrasting the attractions of the Mahayana school to the more severe demands of the Hinayana.

A number of distinctive schools of Buddhism developed in China, but here we will consider only broad parameters of the Buddhist view of human society, of knowledge, and of the human person, as these are relevant to understanding Chinese traditions of education. A contemporary Buddhist writer gives the following depiction of the ideal society and how education contributes to its development: "The Buddhist tradition of education, right from its inception, has concentrated all its energies to found a society where there are neither cultural nor social identities among its members. Men and women, irrespective of their stations of life, when bound together by unity and concord give rise to a homogeneous society."[51] Both religious and lay-persons understand that castes and classes and every other type of identity are man-made, and practice the democracy of interdependence and mutual respect.

De Bary's depiction of the Buddhist age shows how Buddhist emphasis on democratic equality made itself felt in a new emphasis on public discussion and the cooperation of ordinary people in consensus building. He also notes how Buddhism shed its Indian garments and adapted to many aspects of Chinese culture, carrying these in turn to Korea and Japan.

The Buddhist view of knowledge puts emphasis on the *Dharma* or teaching of the Buddha, and all followers are expected to listen to and meditate on that knowledge. The scriptures, however, are not a finite canon, but an ever-growing body of knowledge and wisdom, with new texts being developed within Chinese Buddhism, in addition to those translated from India. Furthermore, the study of Confucian and Daoist texts was also encouraged in Buddhist monasteries and nunneries during the Tang dynasty and later. The development of women's orders within Buddhism provided what may have been the first opportunity in Chinese history for women to pursue formal studies in an institutional

---

[50] de Bary, *East Asian Civilizations*, p.23.
[51] Henry Weerasinghe, *Education for Peace: The Buddha's Way* (Ratmalana, Sri Lanka: Aarvodaya Book Publishing Services, 1992), pp.49-50.

setting, rather than in the family.[52]

The human person, in Buddhist thinking, does not have an unchanging soul or a persisting identity. Rather, personality implies "a bundle of mere physical and psychical elements conditioned into a certain conventional shape ... an ever-expanding, ever changing and ever-renewing phenomenon."[53] Perhaps the most striking aspect of the Buddhist view of the person in the Chinese context was its insistence on celibacy for those who were to be its teachers and preachers, a point of striking difference from Confucianism. For Confucianism, one can only become fully human within the family, living out the rites that express appropriate relationships within family and society. Celibacy was unacceptable to a Confucian view of humanity, which emphasized filial piety and saw the nurturing of the next generation as the most important element in that piety. For all of its other accommodations to Chinese society, however, Buddhism continued to inspire men and women to separate themselves from family, and live out their lives in celibate communities.

Much more could be said about the Buddhist contribution to Chinese culture, with the impact of many of its ideas being felt in literature, poetry and painting, and the Chinese language itself. Many scholars have regarded it as one of three ways of thought in traditional China, along with Confucianism and Daoism.[54] After its predominant influence during the Tang, however, it retreated to a less dominant, though still influential position in Chinese education and society, in face of the revival of Confucianism in the Song dynasty (920-1279 CE). Thus we now turn to what de Bary called the third stage in the dialogue of East Asian Civilizations, that of Neo-Confucianism.

Neo-Confucianism in China's Educational Tradition

Towards the end of the Tang dynasty, Confucian thought began to reassert itself, in face of increasing problems in the ruling imperial house,

---

[52] Kathryn Tsai, "The Chinese Buddhist Monastic Order for Women: The First Two Centuries," in Richard Guisso and Stanley Johannesen (eds.) *Women in China: Current Directions in Historical Research* (Lewiston, New York: Edwin Mellen Press, 1982), pp.1-20.

[53] Henry Weerasinghe, *Education for Peace*, p.30.

and the fact that Buddhism and Daoism had had little to say on core issues of good government and societal development. One of the most famous voices, criticizing Buddhist influences and calling for a revival of Confucian learning was Han Yu (786-824 CE), whose brilliant essays initiated a revival of interest in Confucian thought.[55] There are too many scholars and reformers involved in bringing about the neo-Confucian revival of the Song dynasty to mention in detail, but three names are probably of greatest importance: the brothers Cheng Hao (1032-1085 CE) and Cheng Yi (1033-1107 CE) and Zhu Xi (1130-1200 CE).

The Cheng brothers identified two chapters in the *Book of Rites*, one of the *Five Classics*, as having particular importance and authority in the Confucian canon. They believed that *The Great Learning* had been written by Confucius' disciple Zeng Zi, and that *The Doctrine of the Mean* had been written by another disciple of Confucius, Zi Si. These two texts passed on the essence of Confucian thought, and they were grouped together with the *Analects* and the *Mencius* to become *The Four Books* of Confucianism. Thus *The Four Books* and *Five Classics* (*Rites, History, Change, Odes,* and *Spring and Autumn Annals*) became the central curriculum of the neo-Confucian school and dominated Chinese education up to the 20th century.[56]

Zhu Xi subsequently wrote detailed annotations for each of the *Four Books*, so that they could be effectively used in education. De Bary notes how he tried to achieve the utmost clarity, precision and economy of expression. Using philosophical language carefully, he nevertheless wrote as if to reach the widest possible audience, not just the learned elite."[57] In 1212 CE, the Director of Education approved the *Four Books*, with Zhu Xi's commentaries, for use in education and in the civil service examinations. Reforms in the civil service examinations, and the ordering of that knowledge which would be tested through the examinations also led to a strengthening of the meritocratic features of the governmental system, with opportunity being opened up to all young males who set themselves to study and prepare for the various levels of examination, from local to provincial and metropolitan.

---

[55] de Bary, *Sources of Chinese Tradition*, pp.371-379.
[56] Limin Bai, *Shaping the Ideal Child: Children and their Primers in Late Imperial China* (Hong Kong: Chinese University of Hong Kong Press, 2005), p.34.
[57] De Bary, *East Asian Civilizations*, p.52.

What were the views of knowledge, society and the human person within this school of principle (*lixue*), which was to dominate Chinese education up to the late Ming dynasty (1368-1644 CE)? De Bary talks of Neo-Confucian learning as "learning for the self" and Tu Wei-ming provides a picture of the self in relationship which he sees as the defining view of the human person within this school of thought: "the self in Neo-Confucian thought, instead of being the private possession of an isolated individual, is an open system. It is a dynamic center of organismic relationships and a concrete personal path to the human community as a whole."[58]

The Neo-Confucian approach to knowledge was rationalist and secular, involving a painstakingly cumulative study of the classical texts, and all other accumulated bodies of knowledge, in order to understand the basic principles of both the natural and the social world. The phrase often used for this, drawn from *The Great Learning*, is the "extension of things" (*gewu*). This approach to knowledge did not discount the studies of subjects such as engineering, agriculture and mathematics, although these were not made a part of the examination curriculum. They were undertaken under the sponsorship of scholar-officials for specific purposes of governmental works or improved facilities for the people's welfare. The other form of knowledge which was highly valued is sometimes called "learning of the mind-and-heart" (*xinxue*), and involved intense development of the inner self through meditation, self-discipline and a reflection on one's behavior and responsibilities within the family and society.

The neo-Confucian view of society is often seen as a rather conservative one, supporting and reaffirming the imperial order and the rule of scholar-officials, and emphasizing the education of all to find their appropriate place within the social order. Their acceptance of that place was then shown through adherence to the various rituals that gave visual form to a society of harmony and order. While law and punishment had its place, there was a profound belief in the humanizing power of education at all levels, and the possibilities of a harmonious society governed by scholar-officials of integrity, who had the responsibility of reprimanding the Emperor himself, should he stray from the paths laid out in the classical texts.

---

[58] Tu Wei-ming, *Confucian Thought: Selfhood as Creative Transformation* (Albany: State University of New York Press, 1985), p.131.

After just over three hundred years, the Song dynasty gave way to the Yuan dynasty, when China was ruled by Mongol emperors for nearly a century, then the Ming dynasty which lasted from 1368 to 1644. Throughout all of this period The *Four Books* and *Five Classics*, which Zhu Xi had so lovingly ordered and annotated, remained the core curriculum, even though the civil service examinations were halted during the Yuan dynasty. In spite of the emphasis on humanistic and social knowledge, there continued to be remarkable developments of traditional science in many areas. It was only with the fall of the Ming, and the emergence of the Manchu or Qing dynasty (1644-1911 CE), that China began to fall behind scientific developments in the West. It was in the later part of this dynasty, that the kinds of conservativism, ridigity and conformity in education and the civil service developed, which lead many to believe China's weakness and humiliation in face of the Western powers in the 19th and 20th centuries was a result of its Confucian heritage.

While the Confucian classics were formally removed from the school curriculum in China with the Revolution of 1911, and there was a further backlash against persisting Confucian educational influences with the May 4th Movement of 1919, there can be little doubt that many of the intellectuals and political leaders who built up a modern system of schools and universities continued to be influenced by aspects of Confucian thought. As they struggled to develop forms of education that would nurture democratic thinking in young people, and encourage them to take an interest in science rather than focusing only on subjects that would open up bureaucratic careers, they were greatly influenced by European and American educational ideas. Quite a number of Chinese educators studied with John Dewey at Columbia University, and Dewey's two-year visit to China that began on the eve of the May 4th movement in 1919, contributed to the particularly strong influence of Dewey's educational thought in China. Some of those who studied with Dewey were also stimulated to explore their own progressive educational traditions, a process that took them back to the great Ming neo-Confucian educator, Wang Yangming.

In this last section on China's educational traditions, I will attempt to tell the story of Wang Yangming's life, a story which I believe has been a reference point for many of China's educators in the 20th century, including some of those whose life-stories will be told later in this book. The core concept which has defined his progressive philosophy of education is the "unity of knowledge and action" (*zhixing heyi*).

Wang Yangming and China's Progressive Tradition of Education

Wang Yangming was born to a prominent scholar-official family in 1472 CE. His father had a remarkable career, set firmly within the orthodox neo-Confucian traditions established by Zhu Xi a few centuries earlier. Yangming himself, however, had a rather different experience of educational development and government service, a life which he himself described as one of "a hundred deaths and a thousand sufferings."[59] I believe this personal depiction of his own life, so different from Confucius' serene outline of the six stages of progress in his life, has great resonance for our influential educators of the 20th century. They have all gone through deep periods of suffering and persecution, before finally reaching a phase of life when they were able to contribute richly to the educational reforms of the 1980s and 1990s.

Yangming's education followed the common patterns of young boys of the period, with studies of the core curriculum, *The Four Books* and *The Five Classics*, and participation in the civil service examinations at local, provincial and metropolitan level. At the age of 20, he was successful in passing the provincial level examinations and gaining a *juren* degree. It took three tries, however, to pass the metropolitan examinations, and he finally attained the *jinshi* degree at the age of 28.

Before starting his examination studies, Yangming was married at the age of 16. Over all of these years, up till his first official appointment in 1499, he pursued education in many different areas, not limited to the knowledge needed for the examinations. He was a great lover of literature, and wrote poetry that was much admired from an early age. He was also a calligrapher, who developed a distinctive style which was later recognized as highly original. He had a longstanding interest in military affairs, greatly admiring Ma Yuan, a general of the Eastern Han period (25-220 CE), as a scholar-general who combined the art of learning with that of war. He thus undertook rigorous studies in archery, horsemanship and military strategy. In addition he took a great deal of interest in both Buddhism and Daoism. One story recounts that on his wedding night he spent a night and day in meditation with a Daoist priest, and had to be fetched the next morning.[60]

---

[59] Tu Wei-ming, *Neo-Confucian Thought in Action: Wang Yang-ming's Youth (1472-1509)* (Berkeley: University of California Press, 1976), p.4.

[60] *Ibid.* p.45.

Yangming's official career began with a minor official appointment in 1499, and within one year he had written a policy document to the Emperor relating to the frontier which was widely circulated and admired. After only three years in government service, he chose to give up his official career and go into retreat in order to follow studies in both Buddhism and Daoism. It was during this period of time that he made an important life decision – to embrace Confucian philosophy as his main life's direction, while putting Daoism and Buddhism into a secondary place. One of the stories associated with this decision tells how he stopped one day to talk with a Chan (Zen) Buddhist monk, who had been sitting in quietude for three years. He asked him about his family, and the monk replied, "My mother is still alive." "Are you ever homesick for her?" asked Yangming. The monk replied, "It is impossible to eliminate these thoughts."[61]

On the basis of this experience, Yangming came to the conclusion that "the intimate feeling for one's mother is so intrinsically rooted in human nature that to suppress it is more than difficult, it is both undesirable and unnatural." He embraced a Confucian ethic of life, which meant devotion to family and its demands, as well as respon-sibility for government and society. His thinking and writing continued to be enriched, however, by his studies of Buddhism and Daoism. Scholars have noted how his poetry reflects a "Chan-like subtlety and sharpness" while one of his major texts, the *Instructions for Practical Living*, contains forty or more Buddhist expressions and stories. Tu Wei-ming comments on this vital decision and turning-point in his life in the following way: "In Confucian symbolism individual freedom is not attained by cutting of one's given bonds. Instead, one finds one's selfhood in the network of these bonds."[62]

After a couple of years in retreat, Yangming returned to government service in 1504, and was given a prestigious posting as a relatively young scholar-official to travel to Shandong province and supervise the civil service examinations there at the provincial level. This was his first appointment as an examiner, and 75 candidates were admitted to the *juren* degree. He also took the opportunity to carry out a pilgrimage, writing a number of poems about Confucius on the sacred Mount Tai. In addition he wrote some model essays for the examinations

---

[61] *Ibid.* p.61.
[62] *Ibid.* p.70.

on issues of statecraft and official-Emperor relations. In these essays, he emphasized the responsibility of scholar-officials to remonstrate with the Emperor, if there be any misconduct against the Confucian way, and never to submit to imperial orders without discrimination.[63] This was a principle on which he was to be severely tested in his own career, just two years later.

In 1505, Yangming served as a junior secretary in the Division of Military Appointments, and it was in this year that he began to accept disciples of his own, at the age of 33. This commitment to teaching, in addition to his bureaucratic responsibilities, was an effort to create a more meaningful world within the petty concerns that occupied him in his daily tasks, Tu suggests. One year later, in 1506, Yangming faced a severe test, when his memorial to the Emperor on behalf of two senior officials who had been unjustly imprisoned resulted in his own imprisonment. This was followed by a public flogging and banishment to the remote southwestern province of Guizhou, where he was given a minor official position in charge of a small dispatch station.

Tu describes the temptations facing him in these harsh circum-stances – to withdraw into a life of retreat as a Buddhist monk, or to abandon his responsibilities to family and state in other ways. In the end he accepted the exile, and worked in remote isolation for several years, finally being given the position of head of the Lung Kang Academy. During the years between 1506 and 1510, he pursued studies of Confucianism, focusing on the inner life of the mind-and-heart, rather than the external studies of principle (*li*), the "extension of things," in Zhu Xi's system. Disciples flocked to study with him in this remote location, taking up his new learning of the mind-and-heart (*xinxue*), with its conviction that all the knowledge needed for sageliness could be found in the self.

Yangming's study program involved four stages: first, forming a resolution to adopt the Confucian way (*lizhi*), second, engaging in diligent study such that the whole personality is transformed (*qinxue*), third, reviewing one's mistakes and correcting them (*gaiguo*) and finally, reproving one another within the community so that each one improves (*zeshan*). The questions asked in this final aspect of learning come directly from *The Analects* of Confucius: "Whether in dealing with others I have not been honest, whether in intercourse with friends I have not been

---

[63] *Ibid*. p.82.

faithful, and whether I have not studied and practiced the precepts that have been handed down to me."[64]

In 1510, Yangming completed his period of exile, and was made a magistrate in Jiangxi, then transferred to serve in various posts in Nanjing and Beijing.[65] In 1517 he was given responsibility as governor of the border regions of three provinces in the southeast, Jiangxi, Guangdong and Fujian, with a specific focus on pacifying bandits in the region. With the death of his father in 1522, he spent three years in mourning, as required by Confucian rituals, and subsequently lived in virtual retirement until 1527, when, at the age of 55 he was called upon to undertake another military campaign against rebels in Guangxi, the southwestern province neighboring Guizhou, where he had passed his years in exile. By 1528, he managed to pacify two counties, and put in place village schools and other measures to support the people. He died on January 9, 1529, while on his return journey back home for a period of sick leave. His last words were as follows: "My heart is full of brightness; what more can I say?" [66]

Wang Yangming is often regarded as the greatest of the neo-Confucian scholars, an educator with a large number of disciples, a writer of the famous *Instructions for Practical Living* as well as of hundreds of poems, reports and essays, and a teacher who opened up a new stream of creativity in Confucian thought. Deeply influenced by Buddhism and Daoism, much of his thinking and writing was lively and unconventional. He gave particular importance to the power of the subjective mind, and the value of practical personal knowledge, arising from reflection on experience, as against the stores of bookish knowledge, which had been painstakingly accumulated through the "extension of things," the other important thread of the Confucian knowledge tradition.

Why have I told his story in such detail here? Largely because I believe his life provides a picture of the patterns of life that are seen less as personal choices, than as the way life is to be lived by Chinese intellectuals steeped in the Confucian tradition. The first point is that a Confucian philosophy by no means commits one to a life of conformity and stereotype, but to a life of creative thought, writing and teaching,

---

[64] *Ibid.* p.145.
[65] Julia Ching, *To Acquire Wisdom – The Way of Wang Yang-ming* (New York and London: Columbia University Press, 1976), p.32.
[66] *Ibid.* p.34.

combined with social responsibility, that may come at a very high cost. Secondly, family and community are integral to the Confucian intellectual, and although there may be times of retreat into quiet isolation, a fulfilled life is one lived in relationship to family, community and nation. The integration of knowledge from deep within oneself and action that arises from and transforms that knowledge was the keystone of Wang Yangming's life, and the secret he passed on to his disciples and followers over the subsequent centuries.

All of the eleven influential educators whose stories will be told in this volume have lived lives that expressed many of the same values and concerns – a profound commitment to family and community, a readiness to make sacrifices for the sake of principles they had embraced, and a continuous stream of creative energy that enabled them to adapt to rapidly changing circumstances in their society and nation. Eight of them were men, and three were women. Thus the question arises, what about women intellectuals, and the Confucian way? Was there any place in Confucian philosophy for women who chose to commit themselves to education and scholarship? How did the views of knowledge encouraged within Confucian thought appeal to women?

In answering these questions, we first have to note the dominant stereotype of Confucianism as repressive to women and the Confucian social and political order as one in which women were allowed to function only within home and family. They were given no opportunity to participate in the kinds of formal education that prepared young men for the civil service examinations. We have already noted how the spread of Buddhism during the Tang dynasty in China provided an alternative to family life for women who chose to become Buddhist nuns, and how their studies often went beyond Buddhism to embrace Confucian and Daoist texts as well.

With the restoration of Confucianism to dominance in Chinese society and government in the Song dynasty, women's responsibilities to and within the family were reaffirmed, and a separate set of women's classics were formalized, with an emphasis on moral development, rather than extensive learning.[67] The fact that women were confined within a separate sphere from the world of men, sometimes called the

---

[67] Bettine Birge, "Chu Hsi and Women's Education," in William Theodore de Bary and John Chaffee (eds.), *Neo-Confucian Education: The Formative Stage* (Berkeley: University of California Press, 1989), pp.325-367.

"inner chambers," and were expected to demonstrate their piety through the famous "three followings," of father, husband and son in different phases of their lives, has given rise to a persistent image of women as victims of the rigidity of Confucian patriarchy.

Recent historical research, however, has attempted to reconstruct the way in which literate women understood their lives and the Confucian world of scholarship, in the 16th and 17th centuries. This was a period of relative economic prosperity during the late Ming dynasty, particularly in the region known as Jiangnan on China's Eastern coast. Dorothy Ko's path-breaking book, *Teachers of the Inner Chambers*, explores the lives and writings of many women of this period and region, showing the communities of learning they formed, within the family, with other women in their neighborhoods, and in some cases, public communities with extensive publications of poetry, drama, essays and other works that gained considerable attention. She shows the roles they found for themselves as writers, teachers, scholars and organizers of women's literary activity. She also shows how their experience of marriage and family sometimes gave them opportunities for involvement in the public sphere alongside of their husbands, and how many had extensive experiences of travel.

Ko provides a detailed biographical account of one outstanding woman scholar and poet, Shen Yixiu, and her relationship with her husband, daughters, friends and colleagues, including the poetry society she organized and the many works she authored or edited, which have survived up to the present.[68] Here we can see the possibilities that were open to women within a Confucian social order, as well as the constraints. Here we also see how limiting is the stereotype of Confucian learning as rigid, conformist, tending to rote memorization and dedicated to the past.

Ko points out how it was because Confucianism was an evolving system of thought, that women were able to find relatively satisfying roles for themselves within its broad parameters. This was the period when the teachings of Wang Yangming were having a wide impact, leading to a radical re-interpretation of the Confucian canon, away from the "dry rationality and scholastic orientation" of the Confucian main-

---

[68] Dorothy Ko, *Teachers of the Inner Chambers: Women and Culture in Seventeenth Century China* (Stanford: Stanford University Press, 1994), Chapter Five.

stream, and towards greater "intuitiveness, spontaneity, and expression of emotion." [69]

The final point I would like to make in this overview of China's educational traditions relates to the possibilities of Confucian epistemology, broadly understood, in this time of dialogue among civilizations, and growing interest on the part of the West in understanding what Chinese civilization might contribute to global education. A recent book by Hall and Ames lays out an exciting set of possibilities in its very title: *The Democracy of the Dead: Dewey, Confucius and the Hope for Democracy in China*. Here Hall and Ames go beyond their comparative analysis of Chinese and European philosophy and epistemology, in the two books cited earlier, to point out the many areas of resonance between Deweyan pragmatism, with its emphasis on learning from experience, and learning within the community, and the Confucian tradition.

Here is how they define the Confucian way of knowing: "Confucianism is not an isolatable doctrine or the commitment to a certain belief structure, but is, in fact, the continuing narrative of a specific community of people, the center of an ongoing "way" or *dao* of thinking and living."[70] Later in the book, they point out parallels with Deweyan ideas of democracy, which they see as quite distinct from the European-based emphasis on the individual and rights-based liberalism. In Dewey's vision, they suggest, "the individual is *particular* but not *discrete*. Individuals are unique elements in a community where members serve in mutually satisfying ways to enrich the experiencing of one another. Interactive, participatory behavior is the mark of a viable democratic community, and this provides the context within which an individual is constituted."[71]

These shared features of Confucian and pragmatist thought are set against the essentialist categories that have been associated with the European enlightenment. "Universal laws of nature, scientific principles or logical categories, do not best serve to define us at the levels of personal, social and political existence. Our cultural narratives tell us who we are," state Hall and Ames.[72] This brings us back to the discussion

---

[69] *Ibid*. p.18.

[70] David L. Hall and Roger T. Ames, *The Democracy of the Dead: Dewey, Confucius and the Hope for Democracy in China* (Chicago and Lasalle, Illinois: Open Court, 1999), p.31.

[71] *Ibid*. p.127.

[72] *Ibid*. p.151.

of narrative knowing in the early part of this chapter, and the reasons for attempting a narrative understanding of the lives of our eleven influential educators.

One more connection that might be made at this point is the obvious link here with much of the literature on women's ways of knowing, that tends to emphasize the integration of subjective and objective in learning, the importance of context and relationship in understanding, and a discomfort with aspects of the fact/value dichotomy in European dualism. This causes one to reflect on the fascinating contradiction between the obvious constraints on women's development imposed by Confucian social categories and political theory, as against the confluence between Confucian epistemology and some aspects of feminist thought.

Conclusion: A Context for the Educators' Lives

This chapter has covered three main topics – the dialogue of civilizations, narrative approaches to research in the social sciences, and China's educational traditions. In this conclusion I return to the main focus of the book – the lives of eleven influential educators in modern China, and the institutions, which nurtured these lives over the 20th century. The overview of Confucian thought above should help us to understand them as inheritors of a rich educational tradition, going back two millennia. Of course we also need to understand them in the context of the dramatic changes that came about in Chinese society and education over the 20th century, as they lived out their lives as educators. Many aspects of the evolving story of Chinese educational development will emerge in the telling of their stories. Here I will only sketch out the briefest of frameworks to assist the reader who may not be familiar with the turns and twists of China's development over the century.[73]

The first definitive turning-point for education in 20th century China was the Revolution of 1911, in which the Qing or Manchu government was overthrown and a nascent republican system established. The main external influence on China's modern education development before

---

[73] A set of references for the research publications over this period would constitute a volume in itself. However, the main developments of each period have been covered in R. Hayhoe, *China's Universities 1895-1995,* especially chapters two, three, four and seven.

1911 had been that of Japan, with proponents of constitutional monarchy hoping for a moderate set of reforms, which would preserve aspects of the classical heritage. From 1912 European patterns and values exerted considerable influence, and subsequently American ones, particularly during and after the visit of John Dewey from 1919 to 1921. With the May Fourth movement of 1919, Confucian educational ideas were subject to vigorous criticism, and there were wide-ranging debates over liberal, pragmatist and Marxist ideas for a fully modern educational system. The year 1928 was the next political turning point, with the establishment of a government under the Nationalist or Guomindang party, and efforts to unify the country and modernize the economy.

The Japanese invasion in 1937, two years before the outbreak of the Second World War, was a tremendous setback for China's development. The war-time years from 1937 to 1945 were a kind of crucible for modern education, with many universities making an epic trip to establish themselves in the hinterland during the Japanese occupation of China's coastal regions. With the end of the Second World War, Civil War broke out between the Nationalist government and the Chinese Communist Party, culminating in a successful Communist Revolution in 1949, and the withdrawal of the Nationalists to Taiwan.

The two decades that followed the Communist Revolution were to be almost as traumatic for Chinese intellectuals as had been the years of war and revolution, due to the series of political movements that were launched against them by the radical faction within the new Communist government. In 1952, the whole education system, particularly higher education, was reorganized under the guidance of experts from the Soviet Union. In 1956, Mao launched the Hundred Flowers Movement, and invited intellectuals to give free expression to any criticisms they might have of the new regime. This was followed by an Anti-Rightist Movement in 1957, which resulted in a number of renowned intellectuals being sent into exile. The subsequent Great Leap Forward of 1958 saw a rejection of Soviet patterns, and an effort to expand educational provision more quickly than the economy could support. Severe damage was done to the quality of university programs, though there were some positive outcomes in the application of science to local development needs.

The early sixties is often described as a period of retrenchment, and the Sixty Articles for Higher Education, adopted in 1961, again emphasized academic standards. However this moderate period was not to last long, with the Cultural Revolution breaking out in 1966. It was marked by violence against intellectuals and few positive outcomes have been identified at the higher education level. Only with the death of Mao in 1976, and the subsequent rise to power of Deng Xiaoping in 1977 to 1978, was there a period free from political turmoil, when the influential educators profiled in this book finally had time and space to make their contribution to educational development.

The campaign of educational modernization launched by Deng Xiaoping in 1978 was consolidated in a major educational reform document of 1985, which gave considerable autonomy to universities. The Tiananmen tragedy of 1989 was a serious setback to educational development, but by 1993 there was a new reform document, which showed the government's commitment to further enhancing university autonomy and providing significant funding for the upgrading of university programs. The 21/1 project, announced in this document, created the opportunity for universities to compete for entry into a leading group of 100 institutions which were to be funded to achieve world-class standing in the 21st century. All of the universities associated with the influential educators were successful in gaining entry to this group of elite institutions. In 1999, the Ministry of Education announced a plan for national key bases in humanities and social sciences, and all of the eight bases in diverse fields of education were awarded to institutions affiliated with the eleven influential educators.[74]

The lives of these eleven educators can be grouped into four distinct time periods. Four were born in the early years of the republic, between 1912 and 1916, and so can remember the May Fourth movement, and had already begun their university careers in the 1930s. Two were born in 1920 and 1921, just after the May Fourth Movement, and thus were absorbed in higher education studies during the period of the Second World War and the Civil War. Another four were born between 1928 and 1930, and so were undergoing secondary education during the wartime period, and completed their higher education in the early years of the new Communist regime. Finally, the last was born in 1941, at the end of the Second World War, and experienced the Communist Revolution as a primary school student, following her secondary studies in the early years after the Revolution.

---

[74] Yang Rui, and King Hau Au Yeung, "China's Plan to Promote Research in the Humanities and Social Sciences," in *International Higher Education*, No. 27, Spring, 2002.

The fifteen institutions which frame the lives of these influential educators represent the whole spectrum of modern universities established in China over the 20th century. Four were well-known national universities, Peking University (Beida), Tsinghua University, Zhejiang University (Zheda), Wuhan University (Wuda) and Henan University, with roots going back to the early 20th century. Two were private universities in the pre-1949 era, established by patriotic individuals eager to contribute to China's modern development: Fudan University in Shanghai and Xiamen University (Xiada) in the southeastern city of Xiamen or Amoy. Two were former American missionary universities, which had been developed into provincial level universities with a strong emphasis on education after 1949: Nanjing Normal University, on the campus of Ginling Women's College, and Hangzhou University, a successor to Hangchow Christian University. Three were publicly established normal universities with roots going back before 1949 – Beijing Normal University, Northwest Normal University in the city of Lanzhou, and Northeast Normal University in the city of Changchun. Finally, two were new universities established after 1949: The Huazhong University of Science and Technology (HUST) in the central city of Wuhan and East China Normal University (ECNU) in Shanghai. There is also a brief profile of the Anti-Japanese Resistance University (Kangda), an important institution for training leaders during the liberation struggle.

My narrative account of each of these influential educators begins with a sketch of the institution or institutions which set the context for their lives, and then allows their story to emerge, from family, childhood and early education, up through their studies and the phases of their educational careers over this tumultuous century. While the focus of most of the research literature on Chinese education has been on understanding change, this book probes the continuities that have persisted through these dramatic changes. The portraits that emerge reveal deep-rooted cultural dimensions of Chinese educational thought and practice, as expressed in the life experiences and ideas of these influential educators.

The interviews on which the portraits are based took place between the autumn of 1997 and the spring of 2001. After each chapter was drafted, a copy was sent to each of the educators for comment and feedback.[75] Most were meticulous in giving me detailed factual cor-rections, as well as providing further background material for me to consider incorporating into the portrait.[76] The process of finalizing these portraits has thus also been one of dialogue and a deepening of our relationship. Each of the educators is pleased to know that their life-story and contributions to education in China may serve to inspire others and enrich global educational dialogue in the 21st century.

---

[75] The exception was Xie Xide, who passed away in February of 2000. The draft material had been sent to her, but she was sadly unable to respond.
[76] In some cases the chapter had been first translated into Chinese by one of their doctoral students.

Chapter Two

Wang Chengxu –
A Leading Figure in Comparative Education

Wang Chengxu was born in 1912 in the small county of Jiangyin, in southern Jiangsu province, a coastal province stretching north from the city of Shanghai. He has been one of the most influential figures in comparative education in China, and it is fascinating to note that the other outstanding scholar of comparative education, Gu Mingyuan, was born in the same county 17 years later in 1929.[1] They were not destined to meet each other, however, until 1978. In their early education, both benefited from the progressive educational ethos that had marked this province as a leading center for educational reform from the beginning of the century. This becomes evident as Wang Chengxu tells the story of his early life and school experiences later in this chapter.

First, however, we will sketch out the story of the two institutions where Wang studied and where he spent much of his life as a teacher and scholar. He began his studies at Zhejiang University (Zheda) in 1932, and returned from higher studies in England to teach there in 1947. After 1949, he moved to Hangzhou University, teaching there until 1998, when Hangzhou University was merged with Zheda, bringing his life full circle.

My first meeting with Professor Wang took place in London, England, in November of 1983, when he was visiting the University of London Institute of Education, where he had studied in the 1930s and 1940s. It was nearly twenty years later when I met him again in Hangzhou in April of 2001. I had the privilege of spending two days at Zhejiang University listening to his story, and meeting with students and scholars in the field of education. Over the years since our first meeting the volume of scholarship he had produced was remarkable, given the

---

[1] See Chapter Nine.

43

fact that he was already over sixty five years old when Deng Xiaoping
came to power in 1978.

Wang Chengxu and Zhu Bo have dinner with Ruth Hayhoe and
Pauline Chan at a student dining room in Mecklenburgh Square, London.

Hangzhou and the Story of Two Universities

The city of Hangzhou is one of the most beautiful in China, with the
famous West Lake where poets such as Su Dongpo of the Song dynasty
(960-1279 CE) wrote their poetry. Capital of the Chinese empire during a
part of the Song dynasty, it has long been known for its gardens, the
scenery around the Lake, its silks and tea. "Above is Heaven, below the
cities of Suzhou and Hangzhou" [2] goes a popular Chinese phrase
suggestive of the aura that surrounds Hangzhou and the nearby canal
city of Suzhou.

As I write this chapter I hold in my hands the histories of the two
universities where Wang studied and taught over his long career –
Zhejiang University and Hangzhou University. The stories of these two
institutions are interwoven in fascinating ways over the hundred years
and more that their histories can be traced back. The defining year, in
which each took their identity within socialist China, was 1952 when
Zhejiang University was shaped within the Soviet model of the
polytechnical university to be a major institution focusing on the
engineering sciences. Meanwhile the campus of Hangzhou Christian
University, one of the 13 American missionary institutions, was given to
a newly established provincial college for teacher education. Wang

---

[2] *Shang you tiantang, xia you Suhang.*

Chengxu spent many years as a student and then a professor at Zhejiang University, between 1932 and 1952, and then moved to the newly established Zhejiang Teachers College in 1952. In 1958 he saw this institution take the name Hangzhou University and develop into one of the most respected comprehensive universities at the provincial level in China. Thirty years later, in 1997, it was merged with Zhejiang University.

Here I would like to introduce these two universities by selecting a few elements from the colorful story of each, so that the reader can understand the intellectual and social context in which Wang lived out his life as a student and scholar. I begin with Zhejiang University, which traces its history back to the year 1897, and the establishment of the Qiu Shi Academy in the city of Hangzhou by Lin Qi, a progressive scholar-official of the Qing government. Lin Qi felt that none of the six traditional academies or *shuyuan* in Hangzhou was promoting the kinds of knowledge needed to bring about reform, and he gained the support of his superiors to establish this new higher institution.[3] Its name, which means "seeking truth," comes from a phrase in the Hanshu, "Seek Truth through Facts" (*shishi qiushi*). This phrase was destined to become one of the most widely quoted phrases in China's modernization efforts after 1978 because it was a favorite of Deng Xiaoping.

The Qiu Shi Academy was given a beautiful site in a former Buddhist temple, and opened its doors to students in the New Year of 1897. By May of that year 30 students had enrolled.[4] Its curriculum focused on practical areas of knowledge such as shipbuilding, mining, agriculture and manufacturing, reflecting the concern of self-strengthening reformers of the period. All of the students had already passed lower levels of the traditional civil service examination, and so had considerable knowledge in the classics and the humanities. In 1898 the student body expanded to admit another 60 students, and more in subsequent years. In 1903, its name was changed to Zhejiang Higher School (*gaodeng xuetang*), following the general trends of reform in education at the time.[5] By 1907 there were 319 students and 29 teaching staff.[6] Over the years up to the 1911 Revolution, this was one of the most

---

[3] Zhejiang daxue xiaoshi bianxiezu, *Zhejiang daxue jianshi* [A Brief History of Zhejiang University] (Hangzhou: Zhejiang daxue chubanshe, 1996), p.5.
[4] *Ibid.* p.7.
[5] *Ibid.* p.10.
[6] *Ibid.* pp.11-12.

prominent modern institutions in the province, and its students were actively involved in progressive movements and various kinds of community action.

Between 1914 and 1927, however, Zhejiang Higher School ceased to enroll students, and two specialist colleges in agriculture and engineering took over similar kinds of education for the province. With the death of Sun Yat Sen in 1925, and the successful Northern Expedition of the Nationalist revolutionary forces in 1927, a new era in higher education was about to begin under a Nationalist government based in Nanjing. The most prominent intellectual of the period, Cai Yuanpei, had spent eight years of study in Germany and France over the years between 1907 and 1916, when he returned to take up the Chancellorship of Peking University.[7] A member of the Nationalist party, he was appointed minister of education by the new government in 1927, and he tried to put in place a university district system modeled on France's higher education system.[8]

Cai's two major concerns were to assure the autonomy of China's newly developing universities from political party manipulation, and to make provision for their rational geographical distribution throughout the country. Under the scheme he tried to initiate in 1927, there were to be four universities named after Sun Yat Sen, all called Zhongshan University after Sun's birthplace. One was to be in Canton, in the south, a second in Wuhan in central China, a third in Hangzhou, and a fourth in Nanjing, the new national capital. Under this stimulus the educational authorities in Zhejiang province established a new university, built on the foundations of the Zhejiang Higher School and the specialist schools of engineering and agriculture that had succeeded it. By 1928, it became clear that the university-district system could not be effectively implemented, and this new institution took the name National Zhejiang University, a public university at the national level.[9]

While the emphasis had been on the applied sciences needed for modernization in the earlier curriculum, a faculty of arts and sciences became the core of National Zhejiang University, with the objectives of

---

[7] Chapter Eight, p.233

[8] Allen B. Linden, "Politics and Education in Nationalist China: The Case of the University Council 1927-1928," in *The Journal of Asian Studies*, Vol. XXVII, No. 4 (August, 1968), pp.763-776.

[9] *Zhejiang daxue jianshi*, pp.23-26.

encouraging new ideas and freedom of thought, promoting scientific methods of study and research, and undertaking educational research that would transform approaches to teaching in primary and secondary schools throughout the province. It thus had a department of education, as well as departments of Chinese, history, foreign languages, political science, economics, mathematics, physics, chemistry and biology. There was also a stated commitment to turning out bright graduates with great mental flexibility, who would serve their community well.[10]

National Zhejiang University had several presidents in its early years, with Guo Renyuan, taking up the position in 1933. He was a professor of psychology, educated in the United States, and having an outstanding academic reputation. He was also a strong Nationalist Party (Guomindang) loyalist, determined to keep students and professors under firm political control. In the turbulent situation of the times, with Japanese aggression beginning in the early 1930s, and a series of student movements urging the government to resist Japan, the campus became a center of radical struggle. The saga of how students rebelled against Guo Renyuan and demanded his resignation, leading to a visit from President Chiang Kai-shek himself to the campus in January of 1936, makes for an exciting episode in the university's history.[11] The subsequent appointment of the distinguished scientist Zhu Kezheng to take over the presidency in the spring of 1936 was an important new beginning. Zheda became known as one of the top three or four universities in the country for its academic excellence and courageous spirit. And next to Cai Yuanpei, Zhu is probably the most revered of the pre-1949 university presidents.[12]

A specialist in geology and meteorology, Zhu was first and foremost an outstanding scientist. He was also a man of principle, who would not allow himself to be manipulated by external political forces. He had a vision for the university which led him to attract scholars of the highest caliber, and provide conditions for them to work unhindered. He was also open to students, and handled their concerns and activism in a balanced and wise way, gaining their trust and even adulation.

Located near China's East Coast, Zhejiang University was one of the first that had to move inland, in face of the Japanese invasion that

---

[10] *Ibid*. p.28.
[11] *Ibid*. pp.33-36.
[12] See Chapter Four, pp.124, 133.

began in 1937. The epic story of its move to three different hinterland locations between 1937 and 1945 has been celebrated in the film "Wandering University" (*Liuwang daxue*). Throughout that difficult period, Zhu led the university, maintained morale, and ensured that teaching and research continued at the highest possible level, in spite of the war-time exigencies. In 1938, the phrase *Qiu Shi*, which had been the name of the predecessor academy founded in 1897, was chosen by Zhu as the motto for Zheda. He gave it the English translation, "Faith of Truth". The two values which lay at the heart of Zheda's work, in his view, were sincerity (*cheng*) and diligence (*qin*).[13]

In 1945 the university moved back to Hangzhou after the defeat of Japan. Zhu continued to lead it up to the success of the Communist Revolution in 1949. In spite of his seniority in Nationalist government circles as president of a major national university, he refused to move to Taiwan. He was appointed vice-president of the Chinese Academy of Sciences by the new regime, and remained a revered figure up to his death in 1974. A full chapter of the university's history is devoted to a description of Zhu's style of leadership and achievements as a university president,[14] which were emulated by many later university leaders.

Zheda entered a new phase of its history after the Revolution of 1949, as the new Chinese leadership decided on an all-out emulation of the Soviet Union in higher education. In 1952 they carried out a wide-reaching reorganization of the whole system of higher education, which sought to bring about a geographical rationalization along the lines of the six major military districts the country had been divided into: North China, the Northeast, East China, the Northwest, the Central South and the Southwest. Each major region was to have at least one national comprehensive university, focusing on the arts and sciences, one polytechnical university, one normal university for teachers, and a range of specialized institutions under various national ministries. Geographical rationalization along Soviet lines dictated a concentration of the most prestigious institutions in one or two major cities in each region. The intention was to ensure that the new higher education system would produce the specialized personnel needed for socialist construction in every sector of society.

---

[13] *Zhejiang daxue jianshi*, p.155.
[14] *Ibid.* Chapter Five, pp.151-169.

In this situation, Zhejiang University had the misfortune of being located in a provincial capital, which could not compete with the larger cities of Shanghai and Nanjing for the opportunity of having one of the few national comprehensive universities in the East China Region. East China encompassed the five eastern provinces of Shandong, Zhejiang, Jiangsu, Fujian and Jiangxi. Shanghai was its undisputed center, as an independent municipality having the same status as a province under the new regime. Before 1949, Fudan University had nothing like the academic reputation of Zhejiang University, yet its geographical location in the city of Shanghai gave it the opportunity to become the region's leading comprehensive university.

Shandong University in the North, Nanjing University in Jiangsu and Xiamen University in the South were also developed as comprehensive universities within the region. Zhejiang University, however, was compelled to become a polytechnical university, focusing on the engineering sciences. The faculties of medicine, agriculture and law became specialist institutes in their specific fields under the Soviet model. The faculties of arts and education formed the basis for a new provincial-level institution for teacher education, Zhejiang Teachers College.

Many of Zheda's famous professors in mathematics and the physical sciences were transferred to institutes of the Chinese Academy of Science in Beijing or to Fudan University in Shanghai, a loss long mourned by the university. One of these figures, the famous mathematician Su Buqing, was to become president of Fudan University in 1978. Su was invited to write a preface for the Zheda history in 1994, where he commented on the dynamic leadership of Zhu Kezheng, and the productive years he spent as professor, department head and provost over the twenty-year period before his move to Fudan in 1952.[15] A lengthy list of famous professors in all of the fields transferred out of the university in 1951 and 1952 is provided in the university history. Twenty-three of them were later honored with the title of academician, indicating how great was the loss the university sustained.[16] The other major national university which suffered a similar loss was Tsinghua University, whose story is told in chapter eight.

In 1958, when Zhejiang University was transferred to provincial authorities at the time of the Great Leap Forward, it established a number

---

[15] *Ibid.* just before p.1. See Chapter Six, pp.174-186, for Fudan's story.
[16] *Ibid.* pp.325-326.

of programs in basic sciences in an attempt to rebuild the strength it had had in these areas before 1949. Many other engineering universities took a similar step, only to have these programs .closed down with the retrenchment of 1961. In the case of Zhejiang University, however, its then president, Zhou Rongxi, insisted that Zheda should not go back under the management of the Ministry of Higher Education in Beijing, but stay under provincial jurisdiction, which it did until after the Cultural Revolution. As a result, he was able to maintain the basic science programs, which gave Zheda an advantage in the reform period after 1978.[17]

In 1998, the reorganization of 1952 was reversed, when Zhejiang University (Zheda) became the lead institution in a merger which brought the universities of agriculture, medicine, political science and law back into its fold. These specialized institutions largely concurred with the move back into the mother institution. For Hangzhou University (Hangda), however, which had developed from Zhejiang Teachers College into a distinguished provincial-level comprehensive university with a prominent faculty of education, there was reluctance about losing the identity it had built since the early 1950s. Wang Chengxu had spent the longest part of his career at Hangda, so his story is linked to its story.

Hangzhou University claims a history that also goes back also to the Qiu Shi Academy established in 1897, since the faculty of arts of Zhejiang University was moved out to form the Zhejiang Teachers College in the reorganization of 1952, as noted above. The other major institution whose college of arts and sciences was given to the new institution was Hangchow Christian University, one of 13 American missionary universities. Zhejiang Teachers College thus inherited both of these traditions. It was also give the beautiful campus of Hangchow Christian University, which had been purchased for the Hangchow Presbyterian College in 1911, the year of the Nationalist Revolution.[18] The history of this institution can thus help us understand the ethos of the new college for teachers founded in 1952, and destined to become Hangzhou University in 1958.

---

[17] This point was noted by Zhu Jiusi, "Liushi de Huigu" in Zhu Jiusi, *Jingzheng yu zhuanhua* [Struggle and Transformation] (Wuhan: Huazhong Keji Daxue Chubanshe, 2000), p.6.

[18] Jessie Lutz, *China and the Christian Colleges 1850-1950* (Ithaca and London: Cornell University Press, 1971), p.110.

Hangchow Christian University traced its roots back to 1844, when American Presbyterian missionaries founded the Ningbo Boys Academy in the coastal city of Ningbo, east of Hangzhou in Zhejiang province. Their purpose was to train Chinese ministers and assistants for their mission work. In 1867, the academy was moved to Hangzhou, the provincial capital, and in 1880 the energetic missionary, Junius Judson, took over responsibility for it. He was determined to raise its academic standards and broaden its curriculum, so that it could become a fully-fledged high school.[19] By 1897 it was known as Hangchow Presbyterian College, and had about 50 students enrolled in a 6-year course. Laboratories for the teaching of physics and chemistry had been built.

With the Boxer Rebellion of 1900, the lives of many missionaries were endangered and the Hangzhou missionaries moved to Shanghai for safe haven, closing down the school for a year. In 1910, a second group of American Presbyterian missionaries, from the southern United States, joined in support of the college, and a permanent site was acquired in 1911 in a central part of Hangzhou, near the West Lake. The name was changed to Hangchow Christian College in 1914, and it was incorporated under the law of the District of Columbia to give bachelor level degrees in 1920.[20] By 1925 it had a student body of about 148 and a teaching staff of 15-20 at the college level.[21] In these years, the college mainly served the families of Chinese Christians in Zhejiang province, and about 75% of students were Christian.[22]

This situation was to change in the later 1920s, as nationalism swept over China and there were strong pressures on the Christian colleges and universities to register with the new Nationalist government, which was set up in 1928 after the successful Northern Expedition, when Nationalist party forces moved up to Nanjing from Canton in the south. In face of intense anti-foreign feelings, many of the missionaries departed or withdrew to safe havens in 1927 and Hangchow Christian College was closed for a year. It reopened in 1928 and quickly moved to register with the new Nationalist government, under the agreement that all religious instruction was to be voluntary, and the board of trustees would have a

---

[19] *Ibid.* p.27.
[20] *Ibid.* p.110.
[21] *Ibid.* p.162.
[22] *Ibid.* p.165.

majority of Chinese in its membership.[23]

It took some time to meet the fairly stringent government require-ments, but it was finally registered as Hangchow Christian College, since it did not have the three colleges needed to gain recognition as a university. Its college of arts had departments of Chinese, English, political science, economics, education, and philosophy, while its college of sciences had departments of mathematics, chemistry, biology and engineering. By 1932 there were nearly 600 students enrolled, and students took part actively in some of the protest movements designed to prod their government into resistance against Japan throughout the 1930s.

With the full-scale Japanese invasion of Eastern China in 1937, it was impossible to continue the work of teaching and research. After some efforts to move inland, it was decided rather to establish a presence in Shanghai and continue classes in cooperation with two other Christian universities there, St. John's and the University of Shanghai.

After the war was over, the campus in Hangzhou was recovered and the college re-established. A new department of engineering, established during the war, was raised to the level of a college in 1948, and so it finally gained the title of Hangchow Christian University in that year.[24] The heritage it brought to the newly established Zhejiang Teachers College in 1952 was thus far more than a historic campus – it included a rich tradition of study in the humanities, sciences and social sciences, with particular strengths in the areas of Chinese language and literature, as well as Chinese history.

The newly established Zhejiang Teachers College had a relatively low status within the new system of education when Wang moved there in 1952, in spite of the rich academic traditions it had inherited. It was a provincial level institution, responsible for training secondary school teachers for the province. [25] Humanities professors from Zheda and Hangchow Christian University, as well as science professors from the latter, formed the nucleus for this newly established teachers college, ensuring high standards in the subject areas of importance to the

---

[23] *Ibid*. p.264.

[24] *Ibid*. p.409.

[25] Two other sub-degree institutions were made part of the merger, a college for the teaching of Russian and a sub-degree teachers college. See Hangzhou daxue xiaoshi bianji weiyuanhui, *Hangzhou daxue xiaoshi 1897-1997* [An Institutional History of Hangzhou University] (Published by Hangzhou University, 1997), pp.54-55.

secondary school curriculum. Its lowly status within the new Soviet defined system of higher education thus belied the actual quality of its programs and the scholarship of its faculty.

This may have been the reason behind the decision to change its name and status to Hangzhou University in 1958. Between 1957 and 1958 there had been a strong backlash around the country against the imposition of the highly specialized and sectorally oriented Soviet model of higher education, with its strong emphasis on engineering sciences and its top down approach to leadership and the training of personnel. Many provinces created comprehensive institutions of their own in this year, calling them either normal universities or comprehensive universities, and in many cases involving the merger of small specialized institutions into these new provincial universities. Colleges of traditional Chinese medicine were also created in most provinces of China in this year. It was a movement to assert local control and emphasize local culture in face of the over-centralization and top-down control that had been imposed under the Soviet model.[26]

In the case of Zhejiang province, provincial authorities decided to create a local comprehensive university with places for 2000 students in response to the call for a massive expansion in higher education places that was part of Mao Zedong's Great Leap Forward. A secondary school campus was initially selected for the project, but within a matter of months it became clear that there simply were not adequate resources for such an ambitious initiative. At that point, provincial authorities suddenly thought of the idea of upgrading Zhejiang Teachers College to the status of a provincial comprehensive university, and giving it the name Hangzhou University. It thus became a comprehensive university of the arts and science with a large and distinguished faculty of education that focused on the training of teachers for secondary schools throughout the province.[27] This made it an unusual institution within the dominant Soviet ethos of the period, which had limited comprehensive universities to departments in the arts and sciences only, and made them quite distinct from normal universities for the training of teachers.

---

[26] Ruth Hayhoe, *China's Universities 1895-1995: A Century of Cultural Conflict* (Hong Kong: Comparative Education Research Centre, The University of Hong Kong, 1999), pp.93-96.

[27] *Hangzhou daxue xiaoshi*, pp.83-85.

Hangzhou University was, in fact, unique as a comprehensive university with high academic standards and a significant focus on teacher education. It also established its own departments of political science and economics in 1958, marking a determination to integrate these fields into its ethos rather than bow to the leadership of the specialist institutes of economics and finance, political science and law controlled from Beijing under the Soviet model. The university history defines its ethos in the following way: "a new type of comprehensive university, with social sciences as its core and humanities and natural sciences complementing each other."[28]

Naturally, Hangzhou University went through all of the same traumas as other higher institutions in the upheavals of the Cultural Revolution of 1966. Beginning in 1978, however, with Deng Xiaoping's policy of four modernizations and of opening up to the world, it was able to move forward quickly into the top ranks of provincial-level universities. Zhejiang province took justifiable pride in its reputation and accomplishments. Due to its excellent location and resources, it was able to attract good students and high caliber faculty. Little wonder that there was not much enthusiasm for the idea of merging with a national university of engineering sciences, when this idea began to be entertained in the mid-1990s. In the end, however, it proved impossible to resist the pressures of a national movement towards mergers.

China's famous 21/1 project, which refers to the idea of having 100 world class universities in the 21st century, was first launched in 1993,[29] and developed into a plan whereby the central government devoted considerable resources to those institutions which were able to get parallel funding from their provincial authorities to enter this top league. Given the prevailing politics and the difficulty of getting a provincial-level institution into this league of 100 top institutions, Zhejiang provincial authorities calculated that Hangzhou University's only choice was to join the merger with Zhejiang University. This would bring back into Zheda the rich heritage of humanities and social sciences that had been developed by both institutions since the turn of the century. Hangzhou University thus took part in the merger of 1998, as we have seen above. At the advanced age of 86, still an active scholar and teacher,

---

[28] *Ibid.* p.85.
[29] *The Outline for Educational Reform and Development in China was* adopted at the Fourth National Conference on Higher Education in 1993.

Wang Chengxu thus found he had returned to the university where he had received his own undergraduate education in the early 1930s!

At this point, we leave the story of the two universities which provide the context for Wang's life in education and turn to the man himself, beginning with his early years within the family and local community.

Growing up in Jiangsu – Wang Chengxu's Early Years

Wang was born in 1912, in the small county of Jiangyin in southern Jiangsu province, not far from the city of Wuxi.[30] He grew up in the county town of San Jia Li, now called Nan Sha Zhen. His grand father had tried the *xiucai* examinations, the lowest level within the traditional civil service examinations, but did not pass. His father was educated in a traditional *sishu* or private school, and owned a small piece of land, which he farmed for a living. He described his mother as "very traditional" but noted that she was able to read some characters. There were six children in the family and he was the oldest. The two following him died at a young age, and the next younger was born sixteen years later in 1928, followed by two more.

Wang described his family as an "education family," noting that his parents put great emphasis on their children's education and that his uncle was a teacher. He spoke proudly of the fact that the brother born in 1928 had also studied at Zhejiang University, after the 1949 Revolution, had then gone to Northeast China to work in the field of virology in the Jilin Academy of Sciences, and had won many prizes for his work. His youngest brother, born in 1930, is a primary school teacher.

Wang began his own education at the age of six, studying at a traditional private school or *sishu*, where he was taught by his uncle to read the *Four Books* of Confucius in the old style. A year later, at the age of 7, he entered a modern style primary school, which had been set up in an old run-down temple. Up till now, he has the greatest regard for the principal who started up this school. In spite of its humble circumstances, he was able to attract good teachers, due to his own love for education.

---

[30] All of the material in this section is based on two 2-hour interviews with Professor Wang Chengxu in Hangzhou on April 14 and 15, 2001. Additional material is drawn from an unpublished document about his life and achievements, which he gave me on that day.

The teacher for English and mathematics was a graduate of Ginling University, one of the American missionary institutions. The teacher of physical education was a patriot who became a revolutionary martyr in 1927, when Chiang Kai-shek persecuted many suspected of Communist leanings.

There were five grades in this primary school, and Wang started to learn English in the fourth grade. He loved his studies there, finding the teaching methods very lively. The teachers were close to their students, with class sizes of only about thirty, and often they organized various learning expeditions for the students. The school was inexpensive, being a public one, and many children came to school from nearby villages, since there were only about 80 families in the town itself. This was a fairly early period in the development of modern schooling in China, yet the province of Jiangsu, and especially southern Jiangsu, was one of the most progressive regions, and Wang's description of the school reflects what is known about education in Jiangsu at the time.

After the completion of his first five years of primary schooling, Wang had to leave the town and go to a boarding school in a town about ten kilometers from his home. He entered a primary school patterned after Japanese influences, which had dominated China's modern schooling in the period from 1902 up to the 1911 Revolution. The Liangfeng higher primary school had three grades, and here Wang was able to complete his final years of primary education between 1923 and 1925. The focus of his studies was on Chinese, mathematics and English. The mathematics teacher was a friend of his father, and kept a close eye on him, as he had to live in the school as a boarder and could not go home very often. The school was not free, but his family was able to afford the modest fees charged.

On completion of primary schooling, Wang went on to a lower secondary school in the same town for another three years. He felt these years laid an important foundation for his life. The principal was a graduate of the Nanjing Higher School (later to become Nanjing University), and he benefited from several excellent teachers. He particularly remembers his English teacher, who had been a student at St John's University in Shanghai when the May 30th Movement broke out in 1925, and had left St John's to attend the private Guanghua University because of the restraints put on student activism.[31] He also remembered

---

[31] Chapter Eleven, p.338.

the excellent quality of the textbooks used in teaching, which were published by the Commercial Press in Shanghai.

In 1928, Wang graduated from lower secondary school. He was 16 years old, and expected that he would have to go to work in order to help his family, who were struggling financially. They asked him to consider working for a relative who had a shop selling cotton cloth. He loved study so much that he still looked for a way to continue, and took the entry examination for the normal school (*shifan xuexiao*), an upper secondary program of three years for training primary school teachers for the burgeoning modern primary schools. These schools were free, due to a government commitment to developing primary education.

The most famous of these normal schools, Xiao Zhuang, had been established by Tao Xingzhi near Nanjing.[32] Tao had studied with John Dewey at Columbia during the First World War, and became famous on his return to China.[33] It was Wang's greatest desire to study at Xiao Zhuang under Tao, but Nanjing was too far away. He therefore applied to take the examinations of the Number Three normal school in the nearer city of Wuxi. It was considered to be one of the four best normal schools of the time. Thus everyone in his home-town was excited, when he was successful in gaining entry.

During his three years of study at the Wuxi Number Three Normal School, Wang was again most impressed by the quality and qualifications of his teachers. The English teacher was a graduate of Ginling, the American missionary university in Nanjing. Wang knew he was fortunate to have classes in English as most of the normal schools were not able to provide them. His teachers of mathematics and chemistry were graduates of National Central University, the leading national university in Nanjing. He particularly remembers the two teachers responsible for classes in education, Wu Bai'ang, a graduate of Dongnan University, the precursor to National Central University in Nanjing, and Zhang Zhongyou, a graduate of Nanjing Higher Normal School. Zhang had been a student at Nanjing Higher Normal School when John Dewey visited there in 1919 and 1920, and had been responsible to prepare the record of his lectures in English, while another teacher did the translation

---

[32] Chapter Ten, p.300.
[33] Barry Keenan, *The Dewey Experiment in China* (Cambridge, Mass.: Council on East Asian Studies, Harvard University, 1977), pp.81-99.

into Chinese.[34] Wang revelled in all that he was able to learn over the years from 1928 to 1931.

In 1931, Wang graduated first in his class. There was a rule that students with excellent results could go directly into the education department of National Central University without examination, after one year's teaching experience in a primary school. Wang taught for a year in the experimental primary school attached to Wuxi's normal school, practicing the project method at fourth grade level. He was responsible for teaching Chinese, mathematics and all other subjects except English, art and physical education, where there were specialist teachers. He was also the grade tutor. By this time, he was already steeped in progressive ideas of pedagogy. He was enthusiastic in trying out progressive approaches to teaching Chinese and mathematics, devising projects where the children could learn through activity. He felt this year of practical experience was extremely valuable, a genuine opportunity for him to try out Western approaches to teaching and adapt them to the Chinese environment.

In 1932, Wang was expecting to enter National Central University in Nanjing, but the university was engulfed in a wave of student activism against the president who had been appointed by the Nationalist government, with the result that no new students were enrolled in that year. At this critical juncture, when he had lost the opportunity for the university education he had been counting on, two of his teachers at the Wuxi normal school came to his rescue. Wu Bai'ang and Zhang Zhongyou gave him a letter and sent him to meet the famous educator Zheng Xiaocang at Zhejiang University in Hangzhou. This was a portentous meeting for the young Wang, and Zheng was to become a kind of model and mentor for many years thereafter.

Zheng had graduated from Zhejiang Higher School in 1912, and gone to the US for studies at the University of Wisconsin and Columbia University, where he received bachelor and masters degrees in education, studying with John Dewey among others. In 1918, he returned to China and first taught at Nanjing Higher Normal School, where he helped to arrange aspects of Dewey's visit in 1919 and 1920. Subsequently he taught in Dongnan University's department of education[35] and also spent

---

[34] Chapter Ten, p.299.
[35] Dongnan University was later renamed National Central University.

some time as principal of Zhejiang provincial girls secondary school.[36] From 1928 onwards, he was a professor and director of the department of education at Zhejiang University. It was there Wang met him in 1932.

Zheng opened the letter Wang had brought from his two teachers in Wuxi, and agreed to allow him to study "on trial" (*jiedu*) for a year. Wang's two teachers in Wuxi then arranged some loans to help him pay for his studies, which he was able to repay after he graduated. He had also saved money himself through writing articles for publication during his years of study at Wuxi Normal School and his year as a primary school teacher. The first article he had written for publication was in memory of a female cousin, the daughter of his father's brother, who had died after being cruelly mistreated by a stepmother.

Another way in which he had saved money was by working for the summer for Wang Yunwu, the famous editor-in-chief of the Commercial Press in Shanghai. It was a very special experience for this young student from a village background to live in Shanghai for the summer and work at the Commercial Press office opposite the Dongfang Library. His job was to assist in the development of a new type of Chinese dictionary, which devised an approach to categorizing Chinese characters by their "four corners," a method he still uses now, in writing Chinese on the computer. Many years later, when he was a graduate student in London, England, Wang was delighted to receive Wang Yunwu on a visit to England and take him around the British Museum. He was also proud and pleased that Wang Yunwu had mentioned his work during that Shanghai summer in his published diary.

Wang began his studies at Zhejiang University in the autumn of 1932, never imagining that seventy years later, in 2002, he would still be an active scholar at the same university, after extremes of change, and difficulties which could be compared with the hundred deaths and thousand sufferings of Wang Yangming.[37] Likewise the university had been dismantled, reorganized, integrated into a macro system of planning and then released to recover its history and identity, and embrace once again the wide array of disciplines and fields that had made it one of China's proudest institutions in the 1930s.

---

[36] *Hangzhou daxue xiaoshi*, pp.387-389.
[37] Chapter One, p.31.

University Education and Early Career

During his first year at Zhejiang University, Wang was excited to have the opportunity of learning from five famous professors in different fields of education at Zheda. He wanted to be sure to take courses with each of them, since he expected to be moving on to National Central University the following year. He thus studied sociology of education with Meng Xiancheng, [38] educational psychology with Huang Yuyi, [39] comparative education with Zhuang Zexuan, primary education with Yu Ziyi, and educational statistics with Shen Youjian. When he was not able to move to National Central University the following year, as planned, Professor Zheng Xiaocang found him a scholarship and made it possible for him to stay permanently at Zhejiang University. His family also found assistance for him through a local family loan arrangement.

The department of education was located within a college of arts and sciences, and the curriculum was very broad. The dean, Shao Peizi, had studied economics at Stanford University, but was also very familiar with education in Japan and Europe. In the first year all students were expected to cover a wide range of subjects, and he took courses in Chinese, chemistry, mathematics, physics and biology, as well as the five courses in education. In the second year he focused on educational courses, and he remembers how many of these were taught in English, using American textbooks. He particularly remembers the textbook used for comparative education by Isaac Kandel, a famous scholar in the field at Columbia University. He also appreciated three books of Zhuang Zexuan, who was a specialist both in the history of education and comparative education. His book entitled *Comparative Theory on Education around the World* (Geguo jiaoyu bijiaolun) had been published in 1928, four years before Kandel's famous text, and was the first Chinese textbook in the field.

Wang was particularly excited by his studies of comparative education, and delighted at the resources available in the Zhejiang University library for this subject, which included educational yearbooks and compilations from London, Geneva and New York. By his third year he found himself able to do research and write articles about education in different countries, including Mexico, Poland, Turkey and the Soviet Union. He contributed a number of articles to the *Journal of Education*

---

[38] Chapter Eleven, pp.338-339.

[39] Huang had studied at Smith College in the United States.

(Jiaoyu zazhi) and *China's Educational Circles* (Zhonghua jiaoyu jie). This was not only a stimulating learning experience, but also enabled him to earn money that was badly needed for his studies, as the remuneration for such articles was quite high. He also gained experience with journal editing through assisting Professor Yu Ziyi with the education supplement to the *Journal of Primary Education* (Xiaoxue jiaoyu). These experiences of writing and editing as an undergraduate were extremely valuable to him in later years.

In Wang's third year at Zhejiang University, the winter and spring of 1935, the campus was convulsed with student protests over Japan's invasion of China, and the occupation of China's Northeastern provinces. There had been strong student protests also in 1931 at the time of Japan's initial incursions, but Wang had been a teacher at the experimental school in Wuxi at the time and had not participated. Now he was fully aware of the seriousness of the national situation, and joined with fellow students in planning protest activities. Students of Peking University and Tsinghua University had gone to Nanjing to petition Chiang Kai-shek and the national government to take a strong stand against Japan, but students at Zhejiang University were prevented from going to Nanjing by then president, Guo Renyuan. Wang commented in retrospect that Guo may have been a good psychologist, but he was repressive towards students. They thus went on strike for four months, and the president of the student association took a particularly strong stand. In the end, they succeeded in forcing President Guo to resign. Chiang Kai-shek himself came to the campus in January of 1936, to persuade the students to return to class. Finally, with the appointment of the famous geologist, Zhu Kezheng, as president in the spring of 1936, the university returned to normalcy.

Wang was intensely involved in the protests. He found his respect and appreciation for his teacher and mentor, Zheng Xiaocang, who was head of the department of education, increased further over this time. Zheng supported the students in their struggle against the government and determination to resist the Japanese incursions.

On graduation in 1936, Wang stayed on at the university as an assistant lecturer. His fiancée, Zhao Dunyi, had been a classmate in the department of education at Zheda. She took up a teaching job in a secondary school in Songjiang, just south of Shanghai, where her father worked. With the full-scale invasion of Japan in 1937, the university had no alternative but to move inland, first to Jiande, in the western part of

Zhejiang province, then later to Jiangxi, further south and west, and finally to Guangxi, in the southwest. Wang took part in the first phase of the move, and arranged to bring his fiancée, her mother and her grandparents along with them. By January of 1938, however, he decided to go to Shanghai with his fiancée, in order to prepare for examinations that were being held to select young scholars for study abroad on Boxer indemnity scholarships. [40] Wang taught in a secondary school from January to June, and took the examinations in May of 1938. He knew there was only one place for education, and had little expectation that he would be able to win it. When the results were announced in August of 1938, he was preparing to join the university in Guangxi. What a surprise to learn that he had succeeded in winning that one and only scholarship in his field! The results were posted in the newspaper, and Professor Meng Xiancheng came in person to let him know of his success.

Studies in England, 1938 to 1947

There were twenty young scholars in the group who went to England that September of 1938, four in the humanities and social sciences, 16 in various areas of science, including two in physics who were later to become famous for their work on China's atomic program. They set out together by ship from Hong Kong, arriving in Marsailles and then going on to Paris and London by train. Wang reached London in October of

1938, just a year before the outbreak of the Second World War. His fiancée joined him a year later, arriving in August of 1939, and they were married in Switzerland.

Wang Chengxu with his fiancée, Zhao Dunyi. Engagement photo taken in Shanghai in 1938, before he left for Europe.

---

[40] The British had kept indemnity funds paid by the Chinese government after the Boxer Rebellion of 1900 to be used for scholarships for Chinese students studying in England, and there were parallel programs in the United States and France. See Chapter Eight, p.238.

He pursued his studies in the University of London Institute of Education, which was then in the University's Senate House and had about 100 students. He first took a teacher's diploma program, which involved teaching practice as well as academic studies, something he welcomed as an opportunity to get to know schools in England better, even though he was already a qualified teacher. After completing the diploma, he followed with a Master of Education which he completed in 1941. In that year he moved to Nottingham with the university, in order to avoid the bombardments in London, and began studying for the doctorate. He also found the opportunity to teach courses in Chinese history in Nottingham University's department of adult education, as a way of supporting himself. Many of the students were sponsored by the British army. Meanwhile his wife took courses in the department of child development of the University of London Institute of Education,

Professor Fred Clarke, who was director of the Institute of Education, supervised his doctoral thesis, which was to focus on 19th century philosophical thought and its relevance for education, particularly the work of Jeremy Bentham and John Stuart Mill. Wang also got to know Professor Joseph Lauwerys, and visited him on several occasions in his country home. Wang was particularly drawn to the history of the workers' movement in England, and its links with the University of London. He noted that the University of London developed as a secular institution, influenced by socialist values. Given the war-time conditions, and his deep concern for his own country, Wang was never able to complete his doctorate. However, many years later he published an influential history of the University of London in Chinese, which owed much to his studies over these years.[41]

In 1946, Wang felt honored to have a visit from Zhu Kezheng, the president of Zhejiang University, in London, and also from his professor, Zheng Xiaocang. Both urged him to return to Zhejiang University as soon as possible, even though it would mean a delay in the completion of his doctoral thesis. He obtained permission to complete the thesis back in China and submit it later, and returned to China in 1947, a three and a half month journey by ship. He remarked that he had never considered staying abroad long term, in spite of the difficult circumstances he knew

---

[41] It was published by Hunan Education Press in 1995, a timely publication for Chinese educational leaders who were looking to models for the reform of higher education in China after 1978.

he would find on return. There was no anguished consideration but rather a sense of the rightness of returning, a sense that this was how his life had to be lived. His oldest son had been born in London, and he and his wife and child now returned to Hangzhou. A second son was born not long after their return to China.

While he was still in England, in January of 1946, he had the opportunity of attending a meeting of European ministers of education in London to discuss postwar education, which included a delegation from China. He accompanied the delegation to Paris as their secretary, and participated in the inaugural meeting of UNESCO. His connection with the London Institute and Joseph Lauwerys, one of the leading figures in the founding of UNESCO, proved extremely valuable to the Chinese delegation. This was a moment he looked back on with much nostalgia, as it was to be followed by a long period of isolation from contacts with Western Europe.

An Educational Career under Socialism – Adjusting to Dramatic Change

Wang arrived back in Hangzhou in the spring of 1947, and had four years of teaching in the department of education at Zhejiang University. Appointed a full professor, and head of the department of education from 1948, he lectured in comparative and international education. All thought of completing his thesis had to be set aside, given the turbulent conditions of Civil War. Wang decided to focus on Soviet education, recognizing the widespread interest in Soviet achievements, and organized an exhibition of pictures about Soviet education. In 1948, UNESCO organized a conference on basic education in the Far East. It was convened in Nanjing, and Wang was a member of the Chinese delegation. He also translated a UNESCO volume on basic education into Chinese for the occasion. [42]

In the spring of 1949, the People's Liberation Army reached Hangzhou, and the city and university were liberated. Wang was fully prepared, and in fact had a Communist Party member living in his home, a man from his home county of Jiangyin. After the revolution, he continued to teach in the education department of Zhejiang University, and in 1951 he led students down to the countryside of Anhui province

---

[42] The book was published by the Commercial Press in Shanghai.

to join in the land reform movement for some months. On returning from the countryside, he learned about the reorganization of academic faculties and departments which was underway, resulting in Zhejiang University becoming a polytechnical university, and the establishment of Zhejiang Teachers College as a new institution.

In spite of these organizational changes, his teaching work continued as normal. He was now made head of the department of education at Zhejiang Teachers College, with many of the same staff members as before. A year later he was appointed associate provost, and he served in these leadership roles up to 1958, when Hangzhou University was founded on the basis of Zhejiang Teachers College.

How did he feel about the Soviet model of education that had been imposed? Wang noted how the thought reform movement launched in 1952 was strongly anti-American, something he felt was not surprising after the outbreak of the Korean war. He had already began to study Russian while in London, and now applied himself to it seriously, such that he was later to be able to do considerable translation from Russian into Chinese. In 1952, he began to use Ivan Kairov's works in his teaching, and he noted how much of the content of Kairov's edited book, which was widely used in China, was actually rather European, though adapted to the purposes and demands of Communist thought and the Communist system.

Wang was hesitant to express criticism of the teaching materials and patterns of education in the early 1950s, when the Soviet influence predominated. However, he did note that one simply had to accept what came down from above. The teaching timetable was extremely demanding and complex, with five hours of classes every morning, and little adjustment made to local Chinese conditions. Still he was delighted to be able to buy lots of books, including books by and about older Russian reformers in education. He also found the work of the education department extremely demanding, as all students in the teachers college had to have classes in education, mainly using Kairov's work as a textbook. This meant the department was always extremely busy. In a sense he felt not much had changed – educational theory and content was still largely Western, as it had been in the 1930s and 1940s, but simply from a different West, the Soviet Union. Not only was educational theory mainly derived from the Soviet Union over this period, but also political education was being done under Soviet auspices, bringing a certain coherence to the overall situation.

In 1956, Mao called for a hundred flowers to blossom and a hundred schools of thought to contend, and many intellectuals expressed their criticism of the new Communist system. Did Wang take part in this critical movement? "Yes" was his brief answer. He commented that it was a frightening time, but worse in Shanghai than in Hangzhou, since criticism there focused on famous older educators such as Tao Xingzhi and Chen Heqin, also, of course, on John Dewey, who had taught many of these Chinese progressive educators. He felt he was fortunate that the leaders in the Zhejiang Teachers College were restrained, and he suffered less than many others, though he had spoken out. In 1958 came the Great Leap Forward and the accompanying educational revolution. He was again sent down to the countryside. In the great famine that followed, times were extremely difficult, and he remembered his salary having been cut. Overall, however, he felt he suffered less than most.

Wang did not have much to say about the creation of Hangzhou University in 1958, as a major provincial comprehensive university, having a strong faculty of education. One of the reasons for its establishment has been discussed in the early part of this chapter – the determination of provincial level authorities to have their own intellectual institutions in the face of the centralizing tendencies of the Soviet model that had been imposed in 1952. For Wang, it marked the end of his administrative leadership, as department head and associate provost, and the beginning of a period of time in which he focused strongly on scholarship, and on what he could bring to the new institution from his wealth of experience in London and Nottingham, and his years of research on education in England. With the end of the Great Leap Forward, and the decision to restore a kind of academic normalcy to universities in the Sixty Articles passed in 1961, Wang became excited about the possibilities of introducing a range of Western texts to Chinese students of education.

In 1960, he participated in discussion about a fifteen year plan for education, and offered to help prepare a new series of textbooks which would introduce the ideas and writings of Western educators from the Greek and Roman period forward. A three-volume set of texts was prepared, under the title *Selected Educational Essays from Western Capitalist Countries* [Zichan jieji guojia jiaoyu lunzhu xuan]. Volume one covered the ancient period, volume two the recent period and volume three the contemporary period. In this project, Wang worked closely with colleagues at East China Normal University in Shanghai, and at Nanjing

Normal University. Among the writers whose work was translated for this three-volume text were Plato, Aristotle, Quintillian, Comenius, Owen, Disterweg, Erasmus, Montaigne and Rabelais. The contemporary volume included scholars such as Skinner, Whitehead, O'Connor and Neil. Some of the translation was done from Soviet texts, as that was all that was available.

In 1963, Wang began to teach courses on foreign education, for the first time since comparative education had been dropped from the syllabus in 1952, and the focus on Soviet theories and texts had begun. The new set of textbooks had not yet been published, but he was delighted to introduce a wide range of materials he had collected from Soviet journals and from the material he had brought back from England. It was a time of openness and exploration, of hope and new directions. He was also working on two other projects at this time, the translation of selected essays from John Dewey, along with a professor at East China Normal University, and a set of translations from educational writers of the Italian Renaissance. The latter project was never completed, while the translated essays from John Dewey were published only after 1978.

The three-volume collection of translations from Western capitalist countries did not come out until 1979, and Wang was expecting to see a new edition appear in the spring of 2001 when I visited him. This time the title was to be, simply, *Selected Educational Works from Western Countries* [Xifang guojia jiaoyu lunzhu xuan]. The one work of translation he was able to complete and publish before the Cultural Revolution was Percy Nunn's *Education: Its Data and Principles.*[43] Nunn had been Director of the University of London Institute of Education when Wang studied there.

The outbreak of the Cultural Revolution in 1966 brought an end to all the efforts Wang had made over the fourteen year period since he had had left Zhejiang University, and worked to build up the field of education in Zhejiang Teachers College and Hangzhou University. Over the years from 1952 to 1958, he had embraced the Soviet model, improved his Russian, and worked hard to develop an approach to pedagogy based on Soviet texts. Subsequently, he had gone back into the rich materials collected during his eight years in London, as well as drawing on the historical and philosophical understanding of European thought developed over that time, to prepare an extensive collection of

---

[43] It had been first published in 1930, with a revised edition in 1949.

translations from Plato and Aristotle up to the 19th and 20th centuries. Wang preferred to draw a veil over the violent years of strife and rebellion that followed.

During that period, he stayed on the campus, along with many other older professors, while all younger teachers were sent to the countryside. For the first two months, the older professors were required to live in the student dormitories, study the works of Mao Zedong, make thorough criticism of the past, and acknowledge or confess whatever in their past might be seen as suspect. It was 1972 before the first group of "worker-peasant-soldier" students were recruited for study at Hangda – they had been recommended from their work units, with no entry examinations required. Over this period of time, Wang felt fortunate that his wife was able to stay with him on the campus, as well as his older son. She was an ordinary person, he explained, who did not become a target of political attack. His younger son was sent to do agricultural labor in Jiangyin county in Jiangsu, where he had been born. After working on the farm for some time, he had managed to find a job in a nearby town.

Wang's home was ransacked by the Red Guards, but they put all of his precious collection of books in the Foreign Languages Department for safe keeping, and he was able to recover them a few years later. He and his wife never recovered the jewellery taken from them at the same time, but neither felt that was important. They were thankful to be safe. Wang took the opportunity to focus on his translation projects between 1974 and 1978. Some further work for the Contemporary education volume, in the three volume collection on education from capitalist countries, was done over these years. He also did further work on John Dewey, organizing a group of younger scholars to work on various translations.

In 1978, Wang visited Beijing Normal University in order to collaborate with Gu Mingyuan. Gu was seventeen years younger, and had studied in the Soviet Union in the 1950s.[44] These two scholars have done most to develop the field of comparative education in China in the period since 1978. They had both been born in Jiangyin county, Jiangsu province, yet this was the first time they had met.

---

[44] Gu's story is told in Chapter Nine of this book.

Spring Time for Educational Science

This is the term Wang used to describe the situation after Deng Xiaoping came to power and China was launched into a movement of reform and opening up. It was only then, when he was already 66 years old, that he was able to dedicate his efforts without reservation to his chosen field of comparative education, the field he had discovered at Zhejiang University forty five years earlier. He described himself as being "like a monk with three heads and six arms." He simply wanted to do everything at once!

In April of 1979 a national meeting was held to set out a long-term plan for educational research, and the Ministry of Education's higher education bureau began to organize the writing of teaching materials in comparative education at certain universities. Wang was well prepared for this as a year earlier he had met with Gu Mingyuan and other scholars interested in the field at Beijing Normal University, and begun to discuss its development. In October of 1979, a second national comparative education meeting was held in Shanghai, where the Comparative Education Research Society was formally established. The speed of this development showed how much pent-up interest and energy there was for comparative studies in education. Wang was at the forefront of this.

He was already familiar with the field as it had developed in the West, particularly up to the end of the Second World War. In 1980, he wrote an influential article which was included in the first book to be published in the field in socialist China, *Comparative Education*, co-edited with Zhu Bo and Gu Mingyuan.[45] The article was entitled "Considering comparative education in China from the perspective of the development of comparative education abroad." In it he took up four main issues: periods in the development of the field; the nature of comparative education; the countries of interest for China in comparative education; and the issue of comparability.

On the first issue, Wang agreed with George Bereday's simple yet flexible framework, with period one being the 19th century, period two the 20th century up to the end of the Second World War, and period three the post-war era. On the nature of comparative education, Wang felt it had two notable characteristics. First, it always considers more than one country and more than one culture, so must involve comparative

---

[45] Wang Chengxu, Zhu Bo, Gu Mingyuan (eds.) *Bijiao jiaoyu* [Comparative Education] (Beijing: People's Education Press, 1982). See also Chapter Nine, p.290.

understanding. Second, it has always been cross-disciplinary, including philosophy, history, economics and sociology as major disciplinary perspectives and methodologies. On the issue of which countries China should give close attention to, Wang made his recommendation on the basis of the needs of China's four modernizations, and the experience and qualifications of those who would teach the new courses in the field. The countries of priority, he felt, were the USA, the USSR, England, France, Germany and Japan. Others could be added if practically possible, and gradually it would be worthwhile to include some Third World countries as well. The textbook thus covered these six countries. Wang explored the issue of comparability in an initial way in this essay, but only later was he able to come to grips with it. Wang's other major project at this time was the translation of Edmund King's *Other Schools and Ours* into Chinese, which was published in the late 1980s.

Wang Chengxu with Edmund King at the University of London after he was made an Honorary Fellow of the Institute of Education in 1993

In the early 1990s, Wang launched a major project within the national 8th five-year plan for educational research, which allowed him to explore the issue of comparability in depth. This was a three-volume history of education in China and abroad.[46] Up till that time, the study of Chinese educational history and foreign educational history had always been two separate subjects. For this major project Wang gathered together a group of thirty scholars from both sides of the divide. The

---

[46] Zhang Ruifan and Wang Chengxu (eds.) *Zhongwai jiaoyu bijiaoshi gang* [An Outline of Comparative Chinese and Western History of Education] (Jinan: Shandong Education Press, 1997.) Three volumes.

project came out in three substantive volumes, covering ancient history, recent history and the modern period. The approach to comparison draws on the metaphor of weaving, with the vertical thread or warp (*jing*) being primary, and referring to historical time periods, and the horizontal thread or woof (*wei*) being secondary and relating to the nature of the context.

This comparative study focused on identifying and analyzing problems in education, which might have common features across different societies. China's own history was its primary reference point, but careful attention was also given to parallel developments and turning points in education around the world. It was a first for modern China, to have a study integrating China's own history of education with world educational history. Intense debates and discussions were stimulated by this work, as the reform of China's education system moved apace. Wang also initiated new translation projects in the context of a new phase of international collaboration and dialogue that was emerging.

In November of 1983, Wang and Zhu Bo, a comparative education scholar from South China Normal University, traveled to England to renew links with the University of London and visit other universities around the country. That was my first encounter with the two professors, as I was working on my doctorate at the University of London, and met them there. They also visited UNESCO in Paris, and met with Michel Debeauvais and others from the Francophone Comparative Education Society. Two years later, Wang received funding from the Luce Foundation which enabled him to spend a year at the University of Southern California with Professor Stanley Rosen, also to visit many other universities and community colleges. A particular benefit of this visit was getting to know Professor Burton Clark, whose work became a major focus for translation. In the early 1990s, Wang visited England again, and developed close relations with the University of Sussex.

Over the years, he also had the opportunity to host a number of distinguished scholars in the field at Hangzhou University. Edmund King visited in 1983, Keith Lewin and Angela Little in 1986, and Burton Clark in 1987 and on subsequent occasions. In spite of extensive travels abroad and visits, also increasingly intensive work in guiding doctoral students in comparative education and higher education, Wang was able to oversee a remarkable series of translations from the literature of higher education over these years. It was a time of dramatic reform and upgrading for Chinese universities, with a series of major projects supported by the World Bank. These translated works brought a rich flow of information, analysis and reflection on higher education in Europe, USA and around the world, to the attention of scholars and policy-makers in China.

The list of translated works he organized includes Cardinal Newman, *The Idea of a University* (1873), Abraham Flexner, *Universities: American, English, German* (1930), Ortega y Gasset, *Mission of the University* (1944), Robert Hutchins, *The Higher Learning in America* (1962), John Brubacher, *On the Philosophy of Higher Education* (1977), Derek Bok, *Beyond the Ivory Tower* (1982), Leo Goedegebuure and Frans Van Vught, *Comparative Policy Studies in Higher Education* (1994), Clark Kerr, *Higher Education Cannot Escape History* (1994) and Burton Clark, *The Higher Education System* (1983), *Places of Enquiry (1995)*, and *Creating the Entreprenurial University* (1998). What is remarkable about this list is how well chosen are these works, in terms of scholarship that has influenced foundational understanding of university development in North America and Europe. In the required course for all higher education students at the University of Toronto, most of these same works appear, showing an interesting consonance of views on their importance. In addition, Wang has translated a number of important policy documents from the United Kingdom, including the 1988 Education Act which had a dramatic effect on curriculum development and management for schools around the country, and the 1992 and 1994 White Papers, also the 1987 White Paper on higher education.

When asked what considerations were most important in his work of translation, Wang made reference to the famous Chinese translator of the late 19th and early 20th century, Yan Fu. His brilliant translations of works on politics, economics, sociology and philosophy into elegant classical Chinese had a wide intellectual impact in the late 19th and early 20th centuries.[47] They included writings of J.S. Mill, Herbert Spencer, Thomas Huxley, Edward Jencks and Adam Smith, as well as other British social thinkers. Wang noted how Yan Fu had internalized the ideas of the works he was translating, and only then was he able to express them effectively in Chinese. Deep understanding is needed for this kind of translation, and it can never be mechanical, he said.

---

[47] Benjamin Schwartz, *In Search of Wealth and Power: Yen Fu and the West* (London: England, and Cambridge, Mass.: The Belknap Press of Harvard University Press, 1983). See also Chapter Eight, p.232.

Wang felt that his early efforts to translate John Dewey's *Democracy and Education* (1915) and Herbert Spencer's *Education: Intellectual, Moral, Physical* (1880) had been crucially helpful. His visits to the UK and the USA were also important, as he visited many schools and universities, and saw for himself the changes underway. Through his steady and dedicated work in translation, Wang effectively provided China with a stream of ideas and analyses from the international community that could feed into ongoing reforms in higher education and other areas over the 1980s and 1990s.

The graduate students whom he nurtured also became important actors in the reform movement at both the provincial and national level. In 2001, he told me that 11 students had already completed doctoral theses under his guidance and another seven were in progress. These doctoral holders are now teaching in universities throughout the country, including Beijing University of Science and Technology, Harbin Normal University, Shenyang Normal University, Suzhou University, Xiamen University and Zhejiang University itself, where three are teaching. One of his doctoral graduates, Zhang Jiwei is vice director of the educational bureau of Zhejiang province and two others are presidents of institutions in Zhejiang, Xu Hui of the Zhejiang Teachers University, and Lin Zhengfan of Hangzhou Normal College.

What about his family? Wang's wife of over fifty years, Zhao Dunyi, is still at his side, supporting him in his ongoing work of scholarship and teaching. His older son, Wang Zhongwei, is a researcher at Zhejiang Provincial Museum, while his younger son, Wang Zhongming is a professor of industrial and organizational psychology and executive dean of the school of management at Zhejiang University. The whole family remains close and supportive, as he continues his scholarly work into his nineties!

Conclusion: A Life that Bridged China and the Anglophone World

Wang Chengxu's life story, as he shared it with me in our two afternoons of discussion in April of 2001, reveals a person deeply rooted in his own culture and civilization who reached out eagerly for new ideas in education and new experiences. His passion to learn enabled him to find his way first into a teacher training school that was accessible, since it charged no fees, then into university, and finally on a scholarship to

England during the dark days of Japan's invasion of China. Passing the years of the Second World War doing graduate studies in England, he had no thought but to return to China and to Zhejiang University once it became possible. There he rapidly shifted his interests to Soviet education, as China's revolution approached, leaving unfinished his doctoral research on the socialist ideals that shaped the early history of the University of London.

Wang Chengxu on the beautiful campus of the former Hangzhou University, now Zhejiang University in April of 2001

In the early years of socialist higher education in China, Wang accepted leadership roles as well as devoting himself to teaching and scholarship, but from 1958 he gave himself entirely to his chosen work of translating valuable educational texts from Europe and North America and pioneering the field of comparative education. This choice may have been linked to the tumultuous political movements of the time, but he drew a veil over the difficulties he must have suffered. The tremendous value of his cumulative work over the years became evident after Deng Xiaoping launched the reform movement in 1978.

In no way did his creativity and openness to learn flag in the subsequent years, as can be seen in the enormous energy he brought to travel abroad, building links with universities in England and USA, and the launching of a huge program of translation in the 1980s and 1990s. The fact that he has been able to share these experiences in education with his wife of a lifetime and his sons and their families has been another important aspect of his sense of fulfillment. The reader may judge how far these life patterns illustrate some of the qualities of

Confucian learning, and the Confucian sense of self, family and community that have been depicted in chapter one.

If any one greatest achievement should be highlighted in these concluding lines, I would suggest it is the three-volume work in comparative education, which Wang co-edited with Zhang Ruifan. This set of books roots comparative education in the history of education around the world, and its declared purpose is to "start with feet firmly on Chinese soil and look out to educational developments around the world."[48] For a very long period comparative education had meant surveys and overviews of education abroad, which were intended to stimulate reform at home. Yet the missing link was precisely what Wang's life work tried to establish – a deep connection between the understanding of Chinese educational history and that of Europe, which could lead to lasting and effective reform.

Volume one in the series begins with the dawn of civilization in the ancient middle east, then proceeds to a comparison of the thought of Confucius and Socrates, Xun Zi and Plato, and then the ancient school systems of China and Europe. Subsequent chapters compare the traditional curriculum, the emergence of academies and universities in the 12th century, the rise of neo-Confucianism and the Protestant Reformation and aspects of enlightenment thought in China and Europe. Volumes two and three carry forward the comparison into the 19th and 20th centuries.

While there can be little doubt about the balance of power and influence of European and Chinese educational ideas over the late 19th and 20th centuries, what is so important about this mammoth work for China is the way it puts contemporary and recent educational problems and dilemmas into the perspective of long history. China may have received and absorbed many progressive ideas in education from abroad over the past century, but these have to be understood in relation to its own rich heritage of educational thought and practice. As we move into the 21st century and China is increasingly expected to play a leadership role in the global community, the cultural and educational resources that are brought to this task will represent a kind of synthesis of Chinese and Western thought. Wang Chengxu's visionary intellectual leadership had laid a foundation for the communication of this knowledge and understanding.

---

[48] Zhang Ruifan and Wang Chengxu (eds.) *Zhongwai jiaoyu bijiaoshi gang*, Vol. 1, p.3.

Chapter Three

Li Bingde –
Pioneer of Learning Theory and Educational Experimentation

Li Bingde was born in 1912 in the city of Luoyang, Henan province, an area that might be described as China's cultural heartland. The province is in from the coast and just south of Hebei which surrounds the capital city of Beijing. Henan's ancient capital, Kaifeng, housed the imperial palaces of the Northern Song dynasty (from 960-1127 CE), and there are many cultural and archaeological treasures throughout this large agriculturally rich province, including the famous Shaolin monastery.

Li was the oldest son of a father who had some education, though he had neither land nor any other form of wealth. The province of Henan was less progressive in matters of education than Jiangsu, where Wang Chengxu was born. Nevertheless, the history of Henan University, where Li Bingde was educated, and began his career as a university scholar in the 1930s, tells us something about the spirit of this place. An overview of the university's development will be given in the first part of this chapter.

The second university which is important for understanding the context of Li's life is Northwest Normal University in Lanzhou, a major city of China's Northwest region. Li was assigned to go and work there by the newly established Communist government, on his return to China from Europe in 1949. These two institutions, Henan University and Northwest Normal University, provided the context for a life in education that has spanned more than ninety years.

My personal links to Professor Li Bingde have been more extensive than those I had with Professor Wang Chengxu, and so my own story is somewhat intertwined in this account. In 1986, I was invited to plan a program for joint doctoral training in education between the Ontario

Institute for Studies in Education (OISE), University of Toronto, and Beijing Normal University, along with other normal universities in China that had doctoral programs in education. As the leading scholar in education for Northwest China, and the only doctoral supervisor in the region, Li Bingde emerged as an important partner in this program. One of his students at Northwest Normal University was the first to come to Canada under the program in 1990, and I first met Li on a trip to Lanzhou in the spring of that year. Many subsequent visits were made as the project developed and several outstanding doctoral students and scholars came to Canada to study, while OISE students also spent time at Northwest Normal University. The collaboration was to last for 12 years. I was aware from the beginning how Li Bingde's guidance and support brought a special depth and educational richness to our collaborative activities, as he freely shared with us the wisdom and experience of a remarkable life in education.

The Story of Two Institutions: Henan University and Northwest Normal University

In 1912, the first year after the Qing imperial government had been overthrown by the revolutionary forces associated with Dr. Sun Yat Sen, the provincial government of Henan, then located in the city of Kaifeng, decided to establish a school for the study of foreign languages. It took as its model the Tsinghua School founded with American Boxer Indemnity funds in Beijing in 1911,[1] and the Nanyang secondary school in Shanghai. The curriculum was strongly oriented towards Western subjects, and included study of English, French and German. Entering students were graduates of upper primary schools, with good standards in mathematics and Chinese.

The institutional history of Henan University, which describes this initiative, comments how the province of Henan was a center of classical Chinese culture and history, but had tended to lag behind provinces such as Jiangsu in terms of the development of modern education. This language school was the initiative of one or two forward-looking members of the government who wanted to ensure opportunities for

---

[1] See Chapter Eight, p.238.

talented young people from Henan to study abroad.[2]

Considerable detail is provided about the principal of the new school, Lin Boxiang, a graduate of the famous Zhongguo Gongxue in Wusong, near Shanghai, where scholars such as Hu Shi had studied. Lin had returned to Henan in 1908 with a commitment to developing modern education for the province. He made great efforts to recruit excellent teachers, including an American teacher of English and a German woman teacher of German. By 1923, there were more than 40 teachers, some with graduate degrees from abroad, and others who had studied at reputable modern universities in cities such as Shanghai and Beijing. Two of the principals who succeeded Lin were scholars who had returned from Japan and the United States.

While the school was intended to focus on modern languages, and prepare students for study abroad, it was a full academic secondary school covering mathematics, physics, chemistry, history, geography and Chinese as well as foreign languages. Science subjects, world history and geography were taught in English, German or French, to ensure students gained good standards in these languages and were prepared for study abroad. Between 1912 and 1923, 261 students graduated, out of a total of 662 enrolled. Eighty-one of these students went abroad for further studies, while many others entered universities in different parts of China.[3] This was clearly an important institution, which gave a chance to talented young people from Henan province to enter the world of modern higher education.

Just nine years after the language school was founded, the provincial assembly of Henan province passed a motion to establish a modern university. That was 1921. The following year, the famous Christian warlord, Feng Yuxiang, became governor of Henan province. A strong supporter of education, he managed to chase out a number of other warlords and confiscate their funds. Then he asked Beijing for permission to use this money for the new university. The name he chose for the university, Zhongzhou (Central Continent) University, expressed well Henan's sense of itself as the heartland of Chinese culture. In March of 1923 a formal inauguration ceremony was held for the new university, which had been established on the foundation laid by the school for

---

[2] *Henan daxue xiaoshi* [An Institutional History of Henan University] (Kaifeng: Henan daxue xiaoshi bianji shi, 1985), p.1.

[3] *Ibid*, p.10.

foreign languages. There were two faculties, arts and sciences, and the famous philosopher Feng Youlan was the first dean of the faculty of arts.

In May of 1927, the new university's campus suffered some destruction as a result of civil disorder and the struggle among warlords vying for power at the time of the Northern Expedition. By June, however, the reform-oriented warlord, Feng Yuxiang, reasserted control over the province and forces affiliated with the Northern Expedition entered Kaifeng. When a new Nationalist government was installed in Nanjing the following year, Feng cooperated with it and agreed to the establishment of a new university at the national level in Kaifeng on the foundation laid by Zhongzhou University. Two specialist training colleges in agriculture and law were merged into the new institution, and it was given the name Guoli (national) Zhong Shan University. This impetus to create a series of universities in honor of Sun Yat Sen and named after his home town of Zhong Shan did not last, however, as has been seen with the founding of Zhejiang University (Zheda) in Hangzhou.[4] Nor was any financial support provided by the new national government.

By the end of 1929, therefore, the university took the name Henan University and became known as a provincially established public university. A golden era followed, with student numbers in degree programs growing to 595 by 1935, in colleges of arts, sciences, law, agriculture and medicine.[5] New buildings were built that reflected pride in Chinese traditions and openness to Western ideas. These included an impressive entry gate, and a huge ceremonial hall, which remains a monument to the vision of educators and scholars of that period. The intellectual atmosphere was lively, with many important academic visitors, journals encouraging lively scholarly debates and active participation by students and faculty in the various progressive movements against the Japanese and other foreign imperialist threats over this time.

There were also many famous professors. One of them, Li Lianfang, had studied in Japan. On return to Henan province, he had headed the provincial bureau of education for a time, then later become dean of the faculty of arts and head of the department of education at Henan University. He also established an educational experimental district in

---

[4] Chapter Two, p.46.
[5] *Henan daxue xiaoshi*, pp.32-34.

Kaifeng, where ideas of the noted Belgian educator, Ovide Decroly, were applied to studies of the process of education.

With the Japanese invasion of China in 1937, Henan University was swept into the vortex of war. Its location not far south from Beijing meant that by the end of 1937, it had begun its life of wandering, with different colleges moving one by one to sites farther inland, where they could avoid the invading Japanese soldiers and continue their educational programs. The first moves were to the West of the province, later ones farther into the Northwest. By 1942, Henan province was in such a state of disarray, that the only way the university could survive was with national assistance. A vice-minister of education in the Nationalist government, who happened to be a former president of Henan University, visited one of the refugee campuses and arranged for university finances to be taken over by the National government.

This allowed the university to survive and to make a significant contribution during the difficult war-time years.[6] The faculty of medicine established a hospital in a remote mountainous area, the faculty of education established schools for rural children, and the faculty of agriculture disseminated knowledge about agricultural science.[7] Efforts were also made to initiate studies in engineering, with the result that a college of engineering was founded right after the war in 1946.

Over one thousand students graduated during the war years. Once Henan University had become a national university and could enroll students through a joint national enrollment process, it proved highly competitive, with 120 students selected from 3000 applicants in 1943. After the war, major efforts were made to restore the campus that had been occupied by the Japanese, and further build the university's academic reputation. The liberation of Henan province by the Communist forces in June of 1948 introduced a completely new era. It was not, however, to be beneficial for Henan University's development.

The reorganization of colleges and departments under Soviet influence in 1952 had a devastating effect on Henan province in terms of educational resources and status. Henan University was to suffer losses that could never be recovered, due to its geographical location, and the place it was given within the new socialist system of higher education. Kaifeng, where it was located, was no longer the provincial capital under

---

[6] *Ibid.* p.45.
[7] *Ibid.* pp.46-47.

the new regime. This role was taken over by the city of Zhengzhou, and major new developments in higher education were located there. Henan University was thus even more disadvantaged than Zhejiang University in Hangzhou. While Zheda lost its status as a national comprehensive university, it remained in the provincial capital of an important province and was given significant resources as a polytechnical university.[8]

Henan province was the most northerly of the six provinces in the newly demarcated Central South Region, running from Henan down through Hubei, Hunan, Guangdong and Guangxi. The center of the region was Wuhan, the capital of Hubei province, with its strategic position on the Yangzi River. Wuhan was made a center of the Central South Region, and the locus for a large number of major universities, including a new university of engineering sciences, the Huazhong University of Science and Technology (HUST), the already well established Wuhan University (Wuda),[9] a new normal university, and a range of specialized institutions in various fields of medicine, engineering, law, economics and agriculture.

By contrast, not a single national level university or institute was located in Henan province. Rather, Henan University was called upon to transfer many of its precious resources to these new institutions in Wuhan, and was itself downgraded to a lowly teachers college. Its engineering faculty became part of the Wuhan Institute of Hydraulics and its economics department was integrated within the Central South Institute of Finance and Economics in Wuhan. Its medical and agricultural colleges became independent institutions at the provincial level.

If Zhejiang University had felt a great sense of loss in 1952, Henan University suffered far greater devastation. This is described in a diplomatic way in its institutional history, yet the sense of trauma at the loss of its proud academic heritage is palpable.[10] Even its college of basic sciences was moved away to the nearby city of Xin Xiang. All that was left on its beautiful campus was the Kaifeng Teachers College, combining the former colleges of arts and education to train secondary school

---

[8] See Chapter Two, pp.48-49.

[9] Chapter Four profiles HUST and Wuda. See also R. Hayhoe, *China's Universities 1895-1995: A Century of Cultural Conflict* (Hong Kong: Comparative Education Research Centre, The University of Hong Kong, 1999), pp.154, 167-171.

[10] *Henan daxue xiaoshi*, pp.82-83.

teachers in history, geography, Chinese literature, and foreign languages.[11]

Only after Deng Xiaoping came to power in 1978 was Henan University able to begin the arduous task of recovering its historical heritage and rebuilding some of the strengths for which it had been famous in the 1930s and 1940s. In 1984 its original name was restored. In 1992, while I was doing research on higher education reforms in the region, I had the opportunity of visiting its campus. I was stunned by the beauty and grace of its historic buildings, which integrated Western and Chinese architectural features in striking ways. I was also impressed by the energy and passion that was being brought to bear on restoring its once proud reputation in classical Chinese history, Chinese literature, education and related areas

In October of that year I met Professor Li Bingde for the second time, when he visited us at the University of Toronto in order to present a paper at a conference on "Knowledge Across Cultures." While speaking at the conference, he had made reference to his studies and early career as a professor at this beloved institution in the late 1930s and 1940s, and I had responded by noting how unfairly this university had been treated in the reorganization of higher education in 1952. This comment struck a deep chord in his own memories and feelings, although by this time he had already spent more than forty years at Northwest Normal University in Lanzhou. " Much later, he told me how amazed he had been to discover my familiarity with Henan University and its fate after 1949.

We now turn to a brief historical overview of Northwest Normal University, where Li devoted a lifetime of professional work in the period after 1949. This was also where he brought up his five children, and where his family became recognized as an "education family." Li had not chosen to work in this rather remote part of the Northwest, but once assigned to go there by the new regime in 1950, he had embraced it as his own.

Northwest Normal University published its institutional history in 1989, with a title noting its founding in 1939. Once one opens the volume, however, one discovers that its history is actually traced back to 1902, when a teacher education school was added to the imperial university that had been founded in 1898, later to become Peking University. In

---

[11] *Ibid*. p.84.

1908, this school for teachers became independent, and from 1912 it was called the Beijing Higher Teachers School. The principal of this school between 1912 and 1919, Chen Baoquan, had studied in Japan, and was committed to training teachers for modern schools along similar lines to those followed in Japan, an important model for China at the time.[12]

In 1922, with educational reforms that reflected growing American influence on China's modern schools, Beijing Higher Teachers School was renamed Beijing Normal University,[13] and several parallel institutions in other parts of the country also became normal universities. The new president, Fan Yuanlian, had been minister of education for several brief periods between 1912 and 1919 and had supported the idea of fairer geographical distribution of higher education by the establishment of educational districts. He had studied in Japan, and had pioneered efforts to send young women to Japan for study at an early period. He had also visited England, and participated in negotiations over the use of Boxer Indemnity funds for scholarships for Chinese students studying in England.[14]

In 1931 Beijing Women's Normal University was merged with Beijing Normal University, consolidating the model of an institution with education and the training of teachers as its focus, as well as departments in all the main school subjects, Chinese, English, history, geography, mathematics, physics, chemistry, biology, and physical education. The pattern has changed little right up to the 1980s and 1990s in China. Both institutions were active in political movements and progressive in their outlook, and considerable detail is given in the Northwest Normal institutional history about students' participation in various anti-Japanese demonstrations, also about early activities of the Chinese Communist party on their campuses.

With the Japanese invasion of 1937, Beijing Normal University moved inland, joining the Northwest United University in Xi'an for a period of time. Northwest United University was composed of Beiyang Engineering University of Tianjin, founded in 1895 as China's first modern higher institution, National Beiping University and Beijing

---

[12] Wang Minghan, Heng Jun (eds.), *Xibei shifan daxue xiaoshi 1939-1989* [An Institutional History of Northwest Normal University] (Xining: Qinghai People's Press, 1989), p.3.

[13] See Chapter Nine, pp.263-264.

[14] *Xibei shifan daxue xiaoshi*, p.4.

Normal University, in combination with Northwest University in Xi'an, an institution whose history went back to 1912. In 1938 Northwest United moved to several different locations in southern Shaanxi province, due to the Nationalist government's concern about the Communist revolutionary base in Yan'an in Northern Shaanxi province. In 1939, the Normal College decided to move to Lanzhou, where it was given a big welcome by local authorities, who saw it as "an important force for raising the cultural level of the region."[15] A spacious campus on the outskirts of the city of Lanzhou was provided by provincial authorities.

Northwest Normal's institutional history gives a proud record of the achievements of the university over the war years, with the publication of many journals and books and extensive curricular development. There were particular strengths in Chinese history and literature, also in the field of education, including the psychology of education, educational philosophy, secondary education and teaching methodologies. The national government gave them responsibility for leading educational developments in the provinces of Henan, Shaanxi, Gansu, Qinghai, Ningxia and Suiyuan, now a part of Inner Mongolia, in an urgent effort to maintain and develop a national education system during the war years. There was also a research institute in teacher education attached to the university, where nine professors carried out research on educational issues and taught courses to a group of 16 graduate students.

During the war there was an intense struggle among students and staff who supported the Nationalist government and those supporting the Communist cause, a struggle that reflected the tension of the region, with the revolutionary base areas gradually gaining a foothold, and Nationalist forces straining to retain control. With the end of the war, most of the coastal universities moved back to their home cities. The staff and students of the former Beijing Normal University hoped to move back to Beijing, and their president, Li Jianxun, flew to the war-time capital of Chongqing to discuss the move with government officials. He was initially told that the university would now be located in Shijiazhuang, a city south of Beijing in Hebei province. After protestation, the Nationalist government finally allowed them to move back to Beijing, but only in late 1946 did they get back the status of university.[16] About 300 students and many staff moved back, leaving behind in Lanzhou a

---

[15] *Xibei shifan daxue xiaoshi*, p.8.
[16] *Ibid.* pp.9-10.

well-established institution, which continued to develop and contribute to the region.

After 1949, Northwest Normal College was managed by an educational bureau responsible for the whole Northwest region of China, including three provinces, Shaanxi, Gansu and Qinghai and two autonomous regions, Ningxia and Xinjiang. When this regional education bureau was dissolved in 1954, Northwest Normal came under the direct control of the Ministry of Education in Beijing up till 1956. This gave it the status of the leading institution for teacher education in the Northwest region. Early in 1956, however, it was handed over to provincial authorities, and renamed Gansu Normal College.[17] By this time it had nearly 2000 students, and a teaching staff of 257, including 38 professors, and 34 associate professors.[18]

The institutional history gives no explanation for the decision to downgrade Northwest Normal to a second-tier institution managed by provincial authorities. However, this happening became part of the lore of the institution, a historical loss which was greatly regretted by staff and students. Around the same time, Shaanxi Normal University in the larger city of Xi'an, was able to move from provincial to national level affiliation and take over the role of the leading university for teacher education in the Northwest of China. As with most of the other changes of the 1950s, this reflected its geographic advantage. Xi'an was the most important city in the Northwest and had a concentration of national-level higher institutions, parallel to the situation of Wuhan in the Central South Region. This decision did not reflect the history or traditional prestige of the two institutions, since Shaanxi Normal University was newly established after 1949.

No wonder I had been puzzled in 1986, when negotiating the major project for joint doctoral programs in education with Beijing Normal University, to discover that the only doctoral program in education in the Northwest region of China resided in a provincial-level institution in Gansu, not in the national-level Shaanxi Normal University in Xi'an. In spite of the greater national prominence and higher levels of funding enjoyed by Shaanxi Normal University, the presence of one outstanding scholar in the field of education, Professor Li Bingde, meant that

---

[17] *Ibid.* p.40.
[18] *Ibid.* p.41.

Northwest Normal maintained its leadership in graduate education into the 1990s.

From 1956 up to the end of the Cultural Revolution in 1976, Gansu Normal College endured political movements that brought serious disruption to academic life, as happened throughout China. Only after the end of the Cultural Revolution in 1976, could it take back its historic name of Northwest Normal, while still remaining under the administration of the province of Gansu. Before long it was given special responsibility for the training of minority teachers from Tibetan, Hui Muslim and many other diverse backgrounds, for the two autonomous regions, Ningxia and Xinjiang, and the many autonomous prefectures and countries of the Northwest region. [19] To some extent this counterbalanced the more prominent role of Shaanxi Normal University in Xi'an, which was responsible for mainstream teacher education for the whole region. In 1988 Northwest Normal was upgraded to university status.

In the 12 years of our cooperation with Northwest Normal University, we found it a wonderful partner. It was one of seven normal universities linked in a network with the Ontario Institute for Studies in Education, for the joint training of doctoral students in education. The project was funded by the Canadian International Development Agency and had been under negotiation from 1986. It was finally approved for startup in April of 1989. The timing was problematic, since the sudden death of a beloved leader, Hu Yaobang, and the celebration of the 70th anniversary of the May 4th movement, led to the June 4th tragedy on Tiananmen Square that spring.

As a result, educational collaboration and exchange at the national level was largely put on hold for a year or two. Ironically, this meant that the two provincial-level universities in our project, Northwest Normal and Nanjing Normal, were able to move ahead more quickly than the national-level universities. Northwest Normal was actually the first to participate actively in our project, sending one of Li Bingde's doctoral students to Toronto in the autumn of 1990, and several more in subsequent years, also receiving several Canadian doctoral students and assisting them in research.

It did not take me long to discover that the moving force behind the collaboration was one outstanding educator, Li Bingde, whose story is the focus of this chapter. He had been president from 1980 to 1983, and

---

[19] *Ibid.* p.157.

his subsequent "retirement years" were filled to the brim with teaching, research, writing and project work. This introduction to Northwest Normal University can thus be brought to a close with the story of Li's visit to Canada in 1992.

That October we had organized a conference for our project of collaboration under the title "Knowledge Across Cultures: Universities East and West." We had invited all of the older educators who were doctoral supervisors responsible for our project on the Chinese side, as well as numerous other scholars from China, India, Africa, Europe and the Middle East. Li was the oldest of those invited, and in making travel arrangements we were dismayed to learn that no travel insurance program would cover the health of visitors aged 80 or over! Fortunately, Northwest Normal University's international office assured us that they would be pleased to take responsibility for Professor Li's health during his trip to Canada. As it turned out, he proved to be one of the healthiest and most active of the core group who came from our partner universities.

At the conference itself Li Bingde gave an inspiring plenary address, which provided an overview of China's educational traditions back to the time of Confucius, showing how much openness and diversity had characterized Chinese thought up until the adoption of a closed door policy during the last imperial dynasty, the Qing (1644 to 1911 CE). Li felt China reached a nadir in the Opium Wars of 1840 and the 1850s. The subsequent period he characterized as a "half-open door" with numerous episodes in which Chinese leaders and educators had blindly copied Western or Soviet educational ideas and patterns, and failed to build upon the rich foundations of their own civilization. Only with the declaration of an open door by Deng Xiaoping in 1978, had it become possible for Chinese educators to "follow a new route" and foster "cultural multiplicity" in the global environment, through active efforts to build upon and transform China's own culture.[20]

Li had come to Canada that October with a mission – to ensure that the young scholars in the field of education at Northwest Normal University would be able to get ongoing support. He wanted to see them

---

[20] Li Bingde, "A Brief Overview of Sino-Western Exchange Past and Present," in Ruth Hayhoe and Julia Pan (eds.), *Knowledge Across Cultures: A Contribution to Dialogue among Civilizations* (Hong Kong: Comparative Education Research Centre, The University of Hong Kong, 2001), pp.289-294.

develop careers in education that would support the improvement of education in China's poorest rural schools as well reaching out into active participation in the international community of educational scholarship. This was a challenging vision, and Li saw our project as crucial to its fulfillment. After delivering his speech to a plenary session of the conference, he took me aside and pleaded with me to ask CIDA for a second project to build on the results of the first one.

Our project was still relatively young at the time, having three more years to run until 1995, but Li wanted assurance that his young people would not be abandoned when that time came. I was taken by surprise and replied that I planned to take a sabbatical after completing the project, since I had found project work extraordinarily taxing on top of my responsibilities for teaching and research. Li's response was simple and direct, but it still rings in my ears: "I have never had a sabbatical in the whole of my scholarly career!" A statement like this from an 80-year-old had to be the last word. I meekly set myself to gather information about potential follow-up projects, and was successful in landing a second major grant for collaborative research between two Canadian universities and six universities in different regions of China.

Li Bingde (far right) with Ruth Hayhoe, Wang Fengxian and then doctoral student, Wang Jiayi, at the conference on Knowledge Across Cultures, October 1992.

About 15 of the original doctoral students and visiting scholars were the key collaborators with Canadian and international scholars in a wide range of educational research projects which made a direct contribution to improving education in rural and minority settings, as well as the education of women. There were also significant academic research results, which were published in refereed journals and books. The remarkable individual who had done most to make this possible was Li Bingde.

What had gone into the development of this influential educator? Which of his life experiences were most important in his development? What facets of the Chinese educational heritage can be seen in his life and work? How had he integrated his experience of European educational thought and practice into that heritage?

In many ways, Li's life parallels that of Wang Chengxu, which was profiled in chapter two of this volume. The two were born in the same year, educated over a similar period in different regions of China, had exposure to education in England and continental Europe, one during the Second World War, the other directly after. Both had returned to serve their people with remarkable devotion, though in different educational fields and different geographical regions. While Wang focused on the translation of important Western educational works into Chinese, seeking to ensure they could be understood in relation to the Chinese education heritage, Li had the ambition of building an approach to educational development that was rooted in Chinese culture, yet empirically based in extensive educational experimentation.

Growing up in Henan

The young Li Bingde grew up in a very poor family, the eldest of four children. His father had no land, no established profession and no house. He managed to eke out a living by doing part-time jobs as an accountant. His father loved to study, and had received a traditional education in a local private school or *sishu*. He often told Li how he had loved to read, and hoped to study the *Four Books* in depth, but this had been impossible, since he had to go out and earn a living at an early age. At that time he had put all of his books in one place and cried, because he was not able to continue his studies. He had a deep desire for his sons to gain the education he had been denied. Li's mother came from a peasant family. Li described her as "illiterate, but a very good person, warm and kind."

Li's father loved study so much that he turned his home into a kind of private school where he could teach his own children and other children in the neighborhood, during hard times when he was out of work. Li noted how two of his own daughters had studied with his father during the harsh days of the Sino-Japanese War, when regular education was widely disrupted. No wonder then that Li himself felt a tremendous responsibility for the education of his three younger brothers, and now takes as much pride in their achievements as his own and those of his children. One brother is a professor of medicine, while two are professors of engineering. Two had the opportunity of studying in the United States, while he was doing his studies in Europe. Behind these achievements, he felt, lay the passion of a father who loved books, but was prevented from study by the difficult circumstances of his life.

Li started primary school at age seven, in 1919, the year of the May 4th Movement. When he began his studies, the school was a reformed *sishu*, or private school of a traditional type. His family was not well off, but fortunately this school only required a payment of three yuan at the end of each year. Five years later, in 1924, he entered a public primary school nearby, where no fees were required. Li was able to walk to school from his home, and he did so well in school that he was allowed to continue to lower secondary school. His memory of these early years of education was that conditions were extremely poor, and the quality of his teachers was low. There were no textbooks for studying Chinese in the primary school, but there were basic texts for physics, chemistry and mathematics in Chinese at the lower secondary level.

School was often interrupted for weeks at a time, due to warlord violence and disruption, something noted earlier where the context of Henan University is described. During these periods when the school was closed, Li remembers studying with his father, his younger brothers and other neighborhood children at home. Father taught him to read the *Four Books*, as well as two of the *Five Classics*, the *Classic of History* and the *Book of Odes.* He later realized how valuable were these experiences of traditional education, which laid a foundation on which his education in the new disciplines of knowledge introduced from the West could be built.

On completion of lower secondary education, Li faced a challenge. He longed to continue his education, but there was no upper secondary school in Luoyang, even though it was a medium sized city. The costs of pursuing upper secondary education elsewhere were completely beyond the means of his family. Furthermore, he felt a tremendous sense of responsibility for the education of his three younger brothers. The one ray of hope was the possibility of a scholarship, and he managed to find enough money to travel to Kaifeng, the provincial capital, and take the examinations for entry into the preparatory school for Henan University, a three-year upper secondary school. He was successful, and because this was a provincial government school the fees were only six yuan a term.

Many difficult questions faced him, nevertheless. How was he to cover his living costs while studying? How could he afford trips home to help his family, given it cost more than three yuan each way on the train? How would he contribute to the education of his younger brothers? At first, he had to borrow money from relatives of his father, but within a very short time of enrolling in this school he was able to find a job teaching English in a private secondary school in Kaifeng. This paid 12 yuan a month. In addition, he did tutoring. After gaining entry to the university program, a few years later, he was successful in winning a scholarship from the Henan provincial government. It provided 200 yuan a year, a magnificent sum for an aspiring young scholar. All this meant that he was not only able to throw himself into his own studies with a passion, but also send money to his family for the education of his younger brothers.

The year was 1928, the same year that the new Nationalist government established itself in Nanjing. Li moved to Kaifeng, and began his studies in the province's top secondary school. In taking the entrance examinations, he had not been able to understand what was the difference between humanities (*wen*) and sciences (*li*), as these were modern terms he had not come across in his earlier education. By chance, he stumbled into the arts stream on the advice of a friend. Once he had entered the school, he was simply dazzled by the number of books in the library. He had never dreamed so many books existed, and he felt as if his eyes were being opened on a new world.

His teacher of English had been born in the United States, and could speak only English and the Ningpo dialect, which he was unable to understand. For the first two classes, he did not understand a word of the English used as the medium of instruction. This spurred him to give his best efforts to the study of English, making extensive use of his dictionary. He was rewarded with a mark of 70 on his first exam, while many other students failed. He also worked hard in mathematics and other subjects. The pressure to succeed was enormous, as failure in any two subjects meant one would be expelled from the school. As it turned out, 28 of the 170 students enrolled failed to pass into the second year, but Li was among the successful ones.

After two years of secondary study, Li gained entrance to Henan University in the class of 1930. He chose English language and literature as his major field, and education as his minor field. He felt there would be no difficulty for him to study Chinese literature, history and philosophy on his own, and so did not select these choices for a major. After his first year, he made the further decision to make education his major. He felt this was not only a subject area but a profession, and he was increasingly drawn to education as his life work. Furthermore, he felt no matter how successful he was in his studies of English, he would never be able to outdo those who were native speakers of the language!

His memories of his university studies at Henan University in its golden years, between 1930 and 1934, are rich and stimulating. The professor who remains most vivid in his memory was another American-returned scholar, Tai Shuangqiu, who had Ph.D. from Columbia University. Tai had been teaching at the private Daxia (Utopia) University in Shanghai, but decided to leave there in 1933, due to increasing disruption by the Japanese and the temporary closure of the university.

The course taught by Professor Tai, which remains most vivid in Li's memory, was entitled "The problem of a way forward for Chinese education" (*Zhongguo jiaoyu chulu de wenti*). In this course Tai used newspapers and other contemporary materials, as well as loaning many relevant books to students to read. Li felt it was a course not only about the future of Chinese education, but about the future of China as a nation. Tai was deeply patriotic, and like his friend Tao Xingzhi, whom he had known at Columbia, he adopted the habit of wearing a traditional Chinese cotton robe, to affirm his cultural identity. While lecturing for one hour each week on the subject of China's future, and how government corruption and incompetence could be overcome through education, his tears would flow freely. These tears, Li felt, caused him to dedicate his whole life to the cause of education in China.

Educator in Nationalist China

In 1934, Li graduated from Henan University with excellent grades. He was confident in what he could contribute to his chosen field of education, and knew he was one of a very few people with a university degree in the field. He thus hoped to get a job as principal of a provincial-level secondary school, where he knew the salary would be excellent. However, it was not long before he discovered that such positions were available only to those with good connections or *guanxi*; qualifications alone were not enough. Undaunted by this, Li went on to consider other possibilities. One of his professors at Henan University had been Li Lianfang, whose educational experiments were adapting the method of efficient learning developed by Belgian educator Ovide Decroly to the Chinese context. He was able to secure a position as principal of a rural primary school in one of the experimental districts included in Li Lianfang's major research program.

Li describes how he approached this first job full of confidence. After all it was a rural primary school with only three grades, located in the countryside about three miles from the city of Kaifeng. Now that he was a university graduate, it should be easy to run a primary school, he thought. He went to see Li Lianfang to ask about how the classrooms should

Li Bingde with his wife Zheng Mengfen, a fellow student at Henan University, in 1937.

be prepared and organized for the experimental work to be done, only to discover this was just the beginning. The teachers had to be trained to participate in experimental work, and the research demands were rigorous. There were three books to explain the experimental plan, and various sets of teaching aids had to be prepared for its implementation. The purpose was to have children reading a larger amount and more quickly than was normally expected, cutting one year out of four from the normal learning trajectory.

Li became very animated in describing his first professional job to me some sixty two years later! He talked about how he had been visited by the famous adult educator, Huang Yanpei, who wrote an article about this experimental work in education for the *Dongfang Zazhi* [Eastern Miscellany]. He also talked about how much he had learned from Li Lianfang, a scholar who was rigorous, careful and restrained. He did not engage in the kinds of rhetoric of Tai Shuangqiu, whom he admired for different reasons.[21] Li also spoke proudly of the role Li Lianfang had

---

[21] Li Bingde, "Yige laonian jiaoshi de xinsheng" [The heart-cry of a senior teacher] in *Jiaoyu yanjiu* [*Educational Research*] No. 8, 2002, pp.48-54. In this article, Li

played after the Revolution of 1949, when he was made Vice-Bureau Chief of the Central South Regional Bureau of Education and a member of the prestigious Chinese People's Political Consultative Conference at the national level. Sadly, he was to die in the dark days of the Cultural Revolution.

After two years as a rural school principal, Li's eye was caught one day by a newspaper announcement in the *Da Gong Bao,* a newspaper widely read by intellectuals,[22] advertising an attractive program offered by Yenching University in Beijing, an American missionary university. The program was supported by the Rockefeller Foundation and offered scholarships for five rural teachers to study two years of a Masters Degree Program, and then be given a third year of study in the United States. The obligation of successful applicants was then to work for two years at the Ding Xian experimental center for rural development in Hebei province, under the leadership of James Yan Yangchu.[23] Parallel programs were being supported at Nankai University in development economics, at Ginling University in agriculture, and at the Peking Union Medical College in medicine.[24]

When Li's eye fell upon this notice, his heart leapt with excitement. After all educational experimentation was his chosen field, and here was an opportunity to learn more, gain a higher educational qualification and work at the premier site for rural educational experimentation in China at the time. He applied to the program immediately and was chosen as one of five successful candidates. He made the move to Beijing in the autumn of 1936, two years after graduating from Henan University. He was paid what he felt to be a princely salary at the time, 600 yuan a year, with an additional 300 yuan per year for travel! An important consideration in accepting this opportunity was that the salary would enable him to give more help to his three younger brothers, who were by this time pursuing their studies at secondary school and university.

In the first year of his studies at Yenching University, Li managed to complete all of the course work for the Masters degree, and then

---

describes what he learned from Tai Shuangqiu and Li Lianfang, and then reflects on his own relationship with his students.

[22] See Chapter Nine, p.268.

[23] Charles Hayford, *To the People: James Yen and Village China* (New York: Columbia University Press, 1990), pp.117-142.

[24] Mary Brown Bullock, *An American Transplant: The Rockefeller Foundation and Peking Union Medical College* (Berkeley: University of California Press, 1980).

pursue ambitious plans to travel to as many of the various experimental educational sites as possible. He started with Liang Shuming's rural education site in Zouping county, Shandong province, then proceeded to Ding Xian in Hebei province, where James Yan Yangchu worked, and on to Jiangsu and Shanghai, where Tao Xingzhi had experimental sites.[25] From there he traveled southward to Guangxi and Guangdong, and finally to Hong Kong.

In observing and reflecting on these different cases of rural experimental work in education, Li felt that Liang Shuming's efforts were entirely based on traditional Chinese ideas, Yan Yangchu's were drawn from his work in France and from Western thinking, while Tao Xingzhi was most successful in integrating Western and Chinese ideas. Li felt that all three were linking their educational work with broader political change, and there was genuine educational value in what they were doing. This was in important contrast to the empty talk of some of the American returned Chinese scholars who had taught him at Henan University.

The Marco Polo Bridge [*Lu Gou Qiao*] incident of July 7, 1937, caused all of Li's plans for continued study and work to come crashing down. This was the formal beginning of Japanese hostilities in China, and Beijing and the Northeast became a zone of war and occupation. It was impossible for him to return to Beijing and complete the second year of his scholarship, which was intended to precede the year of study in the United States. Rather he returned to Kaifeng, first continuing his work in rural education experimentation and then finding a position in the provincial normal school, where he trained teachers for modern primary schools from 1938 to 1941. It was a difficult time, with the Sino-Japanese War underway, but satisfying because of his passionate commitment to education. In May of 1941 he took a job as inspector of schools for the educational bureau of Hubei province, the province bordering on Henan to the south.

At the end of that year Li decided to accept a position as associate professor in the education department of Henan University. Even though it meant a cut in salary from 380 to 260 yuan, he was delighted to fulfill a longstanding dream of teaching in the university. The university was forced to move farther and farther inland, as Japanese forces advanced, and Li and his family joined in the moves. One of the heroic stories of

---

[25] Li Bingde, "Yige laonian jiaoshi de xinsheng," p.50.

this period relates to the birth of a fourth child and only son to Li and his wife, during a difficult journey of several days through mountainous terrain.[26]

With the end of the war in 1945, Henan University moved back to its campus in Kaifeng, and worked to restore normal conditions, though the continued Civil War made this difficult. Li had always had an openness to new ideas and opportunities and his eye was once again caught by a new possibility. The Ministry of Education of the Nationalist government was offering 100 places at full funding for study abroad, and another 1000 places for self-funded study abroad. He took the required examinations, and was offered funding for study in Switzerland at the University of Lausanne. At around the same time two of the three brothers whom he had helped in their studies gained scholarships for study in the United States, one in medicine, the other in engineering.

Li set off alone, leaving his family behind. Li's wife, Zheng Mengfen, had been a classmate at Henan University, and had worked with him in the educational experimental district after graduation. Their marriage was thus based on a shared passion for education. Later she was principal of the Henan Number One primary school for many years, including the first year of Li's absence in Europe. In 1948, she was selected by the Henan provincial assembly as one of five provincial delegates to the Nationalist government's Control Yuan, and the only woman delegate.[27] She thus worked in Nanjing for a number of months prior to the 1949 Revolution.

---

[26] Li Bingde, "Henan daxue de banqianji," in *Zong Heng*, No. 2, 1996; also in Li Bingde, *Li Bingde jiaoyu wenxuan* [Selected education essays by Li Bingde] (Beijing: Jiaoyu keuxue chubanshe, 1997, pp.379-380.

[27] Li explained in the Nationalist governmental system in a detailed letter to me (February 2, 2005), It had a Control Yuan (Jianchayuan) in addition to the Legislative, Judicial, Executive and Examinations Yuan. While legislators were popularly elected on the basis of population size, each province was given five seats in the Control Yuan, and delegates were selected by their provincial assembly. It was mandated that one of the five delegates must be a woman. Li noted that this body was something like the US Senate, except that it had no legislative power.

Li Bingde (seated far left) and his wife Zheng Mengfen (seated, holding their only son on her knee), also three daughters (two standing, one seated beside Li), with Zhu Deming and wife (centre back), their son (standing) and two young daughters (sitting in front). [28]

Li spent his first year abroad at the University of Lausanne, living with a family and taking every opportunity to visit local schools, and learn from observation. He reveled in the freedom to explore all aspects of the society in which he found himself, as well as attending lectures and using the library. While at Lausanne, he had the opportunity of hearing weekly lectures by the famous psychologist, Jean Piaget, who visited Lausanne from Geneva, where he was dean of the Institut Jean Jacques Rousseau. He found it stimulating to listen to these lectures, although his comprehension in French was somewhat limited.

During his years of university study in China, Li had learned American theories of educational psychology, studying the works of scholars such as Thorndike and Gates, and he now saw this as an opportunity to get a European perspective. His deeper interest, however, was in educational experimentation, and his decision to move to Geneva

[28] The occasion for this very special photograph was a reunion of the two families in Kaifeng in 1947, after the difficult war years. Li Bingde and his wife wanted to thank Zhu Deming, professor of medicine at Henan University, and his wife, also a doctor. Professor Zhu had delivered their son, Li Chong'an, in a peasant's hut during their difficult journey as the university moved inland to escape the Japanese invaders.

and the Institut Jean Jacques Rousseau the following year had less to do with Piaget's presence there, than with the vice-dean, Robert Dottrens, who was renowned for his educational experimentation. After a second year in Geneva, Li proceeded to the University of Paris for four months, and also traveled to many parts of Europe to observe schools and learn about educational experiments that were going on. During his three years in Europe, he visited Italy, Holland, England and Belgium, in addition to his periods of stay in Switzerland and France.[29]

A Career in Education under Socialism

Why did Li decide to return to China in September of 1949, just before the new Communist-led government was established in October of that year, asked a young colleague interviewing him in the mid-1990s. For younger Chinese in a period when so many Chinese students and scholars abroad had chosen not to return, this was a loaded question. Li's answer was simple and direct. "It was not lofty Communist ideals, nor was it a high-level sense of political responsibility. It was simply a sense of love for China." In fact, suggested the interviewer, "the storm waves in his heart had not been calmed, as he had experienced so many years of war and violence, under the warlords and during a ten-year Civil War. He had also experienced what it was like to be a Chinese abroad at a time when China was despised and pitied in the international community."[30]

Li traveled by sea from France back to China in August of 1949, arriving first in Hong Kong, then taking another ship up to Tianjin, and arriving in Beijing just after the new People's Republic had been celebrated on October 1st, 1949. For eight months he studied at the Huabei University, one of the revolutionary institutions, which was to be renamed People's University the following year. There he met many other scholars in the social sciences and humanities who were receiving a re-education that would prepare them to serve the new regime, including Tai Shuangqiu, his former professor at Henan University.

---

[29] The details of Li's life and career were shared with the author in a series of interviews, held in Lanzhou at the Northwest Normal University on the following dates: May 8, May 12, 1998; June 8, 2000.

[30] Xu Jifuo, "Li Bingde jiaoshou zhuanlue, in Li Bingde, *Li Bingde jiaoyu wenxuan* [Selected educational essays of Li Bingde] (Beijing: Jiaoyu keuxue chubanshe, 1997), p.393.

The study of Marxism-Leninism was something entirely new to Li, but he was happy to have this opportunity to learn and understand the theories that were to guide China's socialist development. Most of all, he hoped for a peaceful and stable situation for China's new phase of development, after all the conflict and disruption of the past decades. Li also noted, with a humorous twinkle in his eyes, that two of his brothers, one an engineer and the other a specialist in medicine, who had returned from USA at around the same time, were not required to participate in this special political study program.

By June of 1950, Li was thinking about how he would take up his work as an educator under the new regime, and had been approached by the provost of Furen University, a Catholic University in Beijing, to see if he would take up a position as professor there. [31] Just as he was deliberating this possibility, he was invited to a lunch at the Ministry of Education, along with 20 other scholars who had returned from the USA and Europe. After lunch, each was given his work assignment, with more than 10 being sent to universities in the Northeast of China, and three to the Northwest. The one other scholar in Education, Professor Zhu Bo, a specialist in comparative education, had gone abroad from Yunnan province in southwest China. The third was a scholar in the fine arts, returning from France. All three were sent to Xi'an where the Bureau of Education for Northwest China was to assign them to specific institutions. Zhu Bo was sent to Shaanxi Normal College in Xi'an, while Li and the scholar of fine arts were sent to the more remote Northwest Normal College in Lanzhou.

Li commented on the logic of this assignment. Zhu Bo had come from the south, while Li was from Henan, north of the Yangzi River. Therefore the bureau felt he could better adapt to the rigors of a more remote city in the Northwest! There was no discussion of this decision, but Li accepted his assignment with alacrity, and set off for Lanzhou in the summer of 1950. His wife and five children joined him by the end of the year, after she had spent some months in political study at Huabei University.

Li was immediately appointed professor and provost at Northwest Normal College, and set himself to learn as much as possible about the Soviet ideas that were now to guide educational development under socialism. He commented on the fact that many Soviet experts were

---

[31] Chapter Nine, pp.267-269.

appointed to work at Beijing Normal University, which was the major center for training teachers in the fields of education and psychology for teachers colleges throughout China. No Soviet experts were posted to Northwest Normal College, but several visited, accompanied by an official from the Ministry of Education, to monitor the teaching and research and give advice.

Li also remembered attending a lecture by Ivan Kairov in Beijing in 1956, in which he gave an overview of his theory of pedagogy, found in the textbook which was then widely used in translation throughout China. Li made the comment that Kairov had spoken with great authority on that occasion, holding up his volume as the most advanced theory of education, indeed one that had reached near perfection. Li also remembered the image of Kairov standing in the lecture hall, a tall and imposing man, quite heavy, with a shock of white hair. He was reminded of Piaget's lectures in Geneva.

As for Kairov's theories, Li had noted from the beginning that the book was actually a compilation, with contributions from other authors, including Zankov. While Kairov had presented it as a complete and final work in 1956, Li noted how one year later Zankov came out with new findings, relating to ways of speeding up the processes of children's learning, which showed it was actually still a work in progress.

Overall, Li felt the early fifties was not an easy period for educators like himself. He had no regrets about leaving behind the chaos and conflict of the pre-revolutionary period, yet he missed the lively debates among scholars adhering to different visions of education, and drawing upon diverse theoretical approaches that had characterized education in the Nationalist period. Now Soviet ideas reigned supreme and were not to be questioned, while much that he had learned previously was criticized. In particular John Dewey's ideas were attacked, as were those of Tao Xingzhi, an educator whom Li had admired for the way he had integrated ideas learned in America with a Chinese progressive philosophy of education. It was a complete "about-turn" and Li found that difficult to adjust to. Still, he did his best, carrying forward his responsibilities as the senior professor of education in this rather remote college, and nurturing a similar passion for education in his five children.

The Anti-Rightist Movement of 1957 spelled disaster for Li, as he was singled out as a Rightist. He was removed from his position as provost of the university, and his professorial salary was downgraded by two levels, from 283 yuan to 208 yuan, still a respectable salary for academics of that time. This was a difficult setback, but the Rightist label was to be removed only two years later, in 1959.

More disturbing he felt, was the next "about turn" which came in 1958, the first Education Revolution, when the ideas of Kairov and the Soviet model were criticized and rejected, in favor of a revolutionary approach to education that was supposed to open much wider opportunities to the rural masses. This rejection of the Soviet model left Li feeling a deep sense of crisis, as another foreign model was withdrawn before it could take root in Chinese soil. He saw it as one more example of a pattern seen throughout the century of embracing a foreign model wholeheartedly, and then rejecting it, before there was time for reflection and integration within China's own educational heritage.

The Cultural Revolution of 1966 carried forward the revolutionary rhetoric in far more extreme forms, and now Li, in his mid-fifties, faced criticism and attack from students and younger colleagues, suffered from being held by Red Guards in a student dormitory for a period of time, and had his home ransacked four times.

Li had little to say about all that he and his family suffered over this time. Rather he focused on his experience from 1969 to 1972, when he was assigned to teach in Northwest Normal's attached primary school, and he threw his whole heart and soul into carrying out experimental work in the teaching of mathematics and English to young children.[32] His only son, Li Chong'an, now vice-chairman of the Central Committee of the China Democratic League, told me how vividly he remembers the enthusiasm with which his father went to work each day over those difficult years, armed with creative teaching aids for his experiments in mathematics and language education. Li Chong'an was in his early twenties at the time.

The Years since 1978: Harmony as the Watchword

For Li, the rise of Deng Xiaoping to power in 1978, and the subsequent period of reform and opening up, finally made possible a space for his work as a professional educator. He was already sixty-six years old. In 1979 he was accepted into the Communist Party, and from 1980 to 1983 he was president of Northwest Normal College. Over the years of his presidency he made great efforts to strengthen its academic and pro-

---

[32] Li Bingde, "Yige laonian jiaoshi de xinsheng," pp.50-51.

fessional profile, and help it establish relations with universities in North America and Europe, which would be mutually beneficial. While his leadership over this period was valuable and important, it has been his scholarship and mentorship of younger scholars which has made the greatest impact, both in the Northwest and nationwide.

Li had his own thoughtful assessment of what had made possible this new era of openness and experimentation, a time when it was finally possible for educators to consider diverse ideas from different schools of thought, and work to integrate foreign and indigenous values and patterns. He gave tremendous credit to Deng Xiaoping, and felt that his personal life experience as a young worker and revolutionary in France in the 1920s, and later in the Soviet Union, had opened his mind to understanding the challenges of development under both capitalism and socialism. By contrast, Li felt that Mao Zedong had been a good fighter, willing to suffer for China's liberation, yet he simply did not know how to run a country. Thus he had a tendency to hold on to power and manage everything from the center.

Deng Xiaoping had been able to learn from experience, including the bitter experience of failure and loss, and had been exposed to a genuine understanding of varieties of political development abroad. Thus he understood that China needed a new way forward after Mao's mistakes. He decided to launch a remarkable movement of reform, guided by two crucially important principles – liberation of the mind (*jiefang sixiang*) and seeking truth through facts (*shishi qiushi*).[33] What was most important, Li felt, was the recognition that Marxism should no longer be a dogma used for purposes of control, but a theoretical perspective which could be developed and applied to the identification and analysis of real problems.

It was this which led to evident improvement in people's lives and greater productivity in the economy. Rather than focusing on acrimonious distinctions between capitalism and socialism, scholars could look at genuine examples of development around the world, including examples of socialist principles in the welfare systems of many capitalist states. The very criteria of what constitutes socialism have been opened up for discussion and debate, Li felt.

Deng Xiaoping gave high importance to education, since he saw it as crucial to China's economic development, and this has proven

---

[33] See Chapter Two, p.45.

absolutely true. For Li, however, the reason for focusing on education must go beyond the economic rationale. It is the foundation for the quality of human persons, and encompasses intellectual, moral, aesthetic, emotional and spiritual aspects of life. Li introduced the concept of "quality education" (*suzhi jiaoyu*) into our discussion, something he believed would involve developing all dimensions of human potential to the full, in order to meet the challenges of the future in areas such as the environment, political culture, ethnic harmony and sustainable economic development. He remembered his teachers, such as Tai Shuangqiu, talking about "education to save the nation," and how this concept had been belittled by those who saw revolution as necessary. Now China's leaders had finally come to understand the fundamental importance of education.

China's traditional strength in moral education must remain the core of the concept of "quality education" but at the same time it must adapt to the changing needs of society. [34] Looking back on China's modern century, Li believes that one of the greatest problems was the fact of overdependence on ideas introduced from outside. Before 1949, Western ideas dominated the curriculum of colleges of education, and they remained largely on the surface; they did not penetrate deeply, nor have any lasting effect through educational experimentation. After 1949, Soviet ideas were introduced and emulated, but they likewise failed to take root, and the Great Leap Forward and Cultural Revolution left China in chaos. There was always a lack of balance, a tendency to lean too far towards external solutions and, as a result, an inability to absorb and adapt what was introduced from outside.

For Li, the Confucian morality, taught in his father's home, remains a kind of foundation for Chinese education. Its special feature lies in the fact that it rejects nothing, but is able to absorb all things into itself. It is open and accepting of others, and it is neither aggressive nor adversarial. Chinese intellectuals have also been greatly influenced by Buddhism and Daoism, Li believes. This can be seen in emphasis on the harmonization

---

[34] Li Bingde, "Hongyang Zhongguo zhishifenzi de youliang chuantong danfu qi jinri jiaoyu gongzuozhe de zeren," [Promote the excellent tradition of Chinese intellectuals and take up the responsibility of a contemporary educational worker] in *Xibei shida xuebao (shehui kexueban)* [The Journal of Northwest Normal University (Social Sciences Section)] Vol. 36, No. 2 (March, 1999). This article elaborates Li's views on "quality education" and its roots in China's intellectual traditions.

of the person with the natural environment, a feature that is evident in much traditional watercolor painting, where tiny figures are seen within a beautiful landscape. Buddhism emphasizes quiet reflection, while Daoism gives importance to the nurturing of the inner spirit. Many qualities of both have been adapted within Confucian thought, in Li's view.

Li made no direct reference to the neo-Confucian scholar, Wang Yangming, whose life story has been outlined in chapter one, yet one can see many parallels in Li's discourse. For Li, Confucianism remains central, and at its heart is the practice of self-examination – asking oneself three times each day, "whether in dealing with others I have not been honest, whether in intercourse with friends I have not been faithful, and whether I have not studied and practiced the precepts that have been handed down to me." These were, in fact, the questions used by Wang Yangming in the fourth stage of his study program.[35]

Li had published a number of books before 1949, including *People's Literacy Education* [Minzhong shizi jiaoyu] (1943) and *Research Methods in Educational Science* [Jiaoyu kexue yanjiufa] (1944), as well as numerous articles on aspects of educational research, and on social education. After 1947, he had introduced European educational ideas from his time in Switzerland and France. Once he had moved to Northwest Normal College in 1950, he threw himself again into educational research, as well as teaching and administration. He published numerous articles on language education at the primary level as well as a literacy primer for rural people called *Nongmin shizi keben* (1965). This was in spite of the political difficulties he experienced as a Rightist from 1957 to 1959, and the harrowing attacks he suffered during the Cultural Revolution.

However, it was only after 1978 that he was able to bring together a lifetime of educational research and experimentation into a number of important texts which are now widely used in normal universities: *Chinese Language Teaching Methods for Primary Schools* [Xiaoxue yuwen jiaoxuefa] (1980); *Research Methodology in Educational Science* [Jiaoyu kexue yanjiu fangfa] (1986); *The Theory of Teaching and Learning* [Jiaoxuelun] (1991). In 1987 he contributed an article on education to a prestigious book on the subject of problems in the study of socialist economic and scientific development. Other contributors to this work

---

[35] See Chapter One, p.34.

included the distinguished scientist Qian Weichang and the famous sociologist Fei Xiaotong.

In addition to his scholarly writing, Li's influence can be seen in the education of his children and their remarkable professional contribution to their country. His eldest daughter, Li Wan, graduated from Tianjin University in hydraulic engineering. His second daughter, Li Long, graduated from Lanzhou Medical College, and taught in a medical college in Lanzhou throughout her career. His third daughter, Li Yu, graduated from Lanzhou University in chemistry, and taught at Gansu Agricultural College and Lanzhou University, recently retiring as a full professor. His fourth daughter, Li Xuan, graduated from Gansu Agricultural College, and did graduate studies at Northwest Normal. She has taught at Northwest Normal, at Beijing Agricultural University and at the Central Minorities University in Beijing

His son, Li Chong'an, who was born in a tiny mountain hamlet in a remote part of Henan province in 1944, graduated from Peking University in mathematics and mechanics and served for many years at Lanzhou Railway Institute as professor and vice-president. He was subsequently appointed deputy director of Gansu province's education commission, in charge of higher education, and then vice-governor of the province. He now serves as vice-chairman of the Central Committee of the China Democratic League and a member of the Standing Committee of the National People's Congress. It is no wonder that Li Bingde's family has been honored as an "education family" by Gansu province, in recognition of their significant contributions to the province and to the nation.

An equally important aspect of Professor Li's legacy is the large number of graduate students whom he nurtured over the years. They are now making a significant contribution to the nation's educational development. In 1981, Li was among the first group of scholars to be recognized by the State Council's Academic Degrees Committee as a doctoral supervisor, and until fairly recently he was the only scholar having this status in education in the Northwest region. His doctoral graduates have taken up leading roles in universities and educational research institutes throughout the country.

One of them, Guo Ge, was a researcher at the National Research Center for Educational Development and subsequently a vice-director within the Research Institute of the Central Committee of the Communist Party. Most recently he has been appointed vice-mayor of the city of

Neijiang in Sichuan province. Another, Tian Huisheng, is deputy director general of the National Institute for Educational Research. Several have been inspired by Li's lifelong dedication to the Northwest and taken up leading roles in Lanzhou, including Wang Jiayi, vice-president of Northwest Normal University, Wan Mingang, dean of education, Xu Jieying, associate professor in education, and Zhang Tiedao, director of Gansu Province's Educational Research Institute from 1996 to 1999, and now vice-president of the Beijing Academy of Educational Sciences. Yet another, Baden Nima, the first Tibetan student to earn a doctoral degree in education, is now dean of education at the Sichuan Normal University in Chengdu.

In May of 2001 the final conference, which concluded our 12 years of collaboration in doctoral training, educational research and development, took place at Northwest Normal University in Lanzhou, with Professor Li Bingde presiding over the event. In his opening speech, he reviewed the many fruits of our collaborative work over the years, in moral education, in bilingualism and the education of minorities, and in women's education. The deep pride he took in the many young scholars from Northwest Normal University who were managing the conference beamed from his face. This time he had no need to take me aside and beg for help in gaining future projects for his beloved young scholars. They had now become highly successful in making their own applications to national funding bodies, and had recently been awarded a national center of excellence in the area of minority education.

They had also become sophisticated participants in a wide range of international projects, sponsored by agencies such as the World Bank, the Department for International Development (DFID) of the British government, the Ford Foundation, and the International Association for the Evaluation of Educational Achievement. What has been most remarkable about the contribution of this younger generation whom Li has nurtured is their ability to span the gap between academic research that wins international recognition and rural development projects at the local level, which have changed the lives of many children and teachers in the schools of Gansu province.

Conclusion: Educator of the Heart and Mind

Li Bingde's life and contributions in education draw us back to reflect on the Confucian tradition in a number of different ways. First, his passionate commitment to on-the-ground experimentation in education, in the two most basic subjects areas – mathematics and language – suggests knowledge based on action. For Li, this began with his studies under Li Lianfang in the 1930s and his first job as principal of a rural primary school where systematic experimentation to improve language learning was undertaken. His life-story shows how this commitment to educational experimentation at the most basic level has been a lifelong passion. During the dark days of the Cultural Revolution, it became a kind of solace when he was assigned to teach in a primary school as a way of demeaning his scholarly standing. He turned this work into a welcome opportunity for research on the learning of mathematics by young children.

The result of this lifelong commitment to educational experimentation in Chinese settings is an approach to teaching and learning which is firmly rooted in Chinese cultural soil, and which emphasizes the development of the whole person, mind, heart, and spirit, a concept he feels can be summed up in the idea of "quality education." The notion that facts or techniques of understanding could be learned effectively, without an accompanying development in moral understanding and moral agency would be simply unacceptable in Li's thinking. Thus his concern at Deng Xiaoping's rather instrumentalist approach to education for economic development, and his insistence on quality education as a good in itself, encompassing intellectual, moral, aesthetic, emotional and spiritual aspects of life.

Li Bingde discussing the concept of quality education with Ruth Hayhoe, May 1998, at Northwest Normal University in Lanzhou.

Li's approach to educational research has been flexible and many faceted. Guo Ge, one of Li's doctoral graduates, has written a thoughtful summary of his educational legacy, noting that his book on research methods in educational science introduces and illustrates 17 or 18 distinctive techniques and methodologies that can be adopted in educational research. The foundation, however, is in experimentation on learning processes at the basic level. The framework is a holistic one, with the following key elements seen as essential: the student, the educational aims, the educational content or curriculum, methods of teaching, the educational environment, educational feedback and the teacher.[36]

Just as his approach to teaching and research has been one that emphasizes understanding the whole and the parts in relation to the whole, Li's own life in education has been a life lived in community. Several levels of community can be seen in the evolving circles of his life. As a student and older brother, he supported three younger brothers through their study years and remains proud of their achievements in fields quite different from his own. As a father, he passed on a passion for education to his five children and has been blessed to see their professional contributions in biology, chemistry, medicine and engineering, also political leadership in the case of his son. As a teacher, his spirit and mantle has been passed on to generations of students, many of whom now do him honor through their educational leadership in different regions and spheres.

---

[36] Guo Ge, "Li Bingde xiansheng de jiaoyu sixiang" [Li Bingde's educational thought] in *Jiaoyu yanjiu* [Educational Research], No. 8, 1997.

Chapter Four

Zhu Jiusi –
A Visionary University Leader

Zhu Jiusi was born in 1916 in the city of Yangzhou in northern Jiangsu province, to a family of modest means. Like Wang Chengxu, he benefited from the progressive educational environment of the province in his early education, though his life choices and career were closely related to the tumultuous political developments of the time. His life-story is intertwined with the story of three distinctive universities, each representing different traditions and different aspects of China's modern development: Wuhan University, a comprehensive university of the Nationalist period where he spent three terms of undergraduate education; the Anti-Japanese Resistance University established by the Communist Party in Yan'an where he studied and then taught for a number of years during the revolutionary struggle; and finally the Huazhong [Central China] University of Science and Technology [HUST] in Wuhan, an institution which he led from 1953 to 1984, creating a nationally influential model of excellence. These institutions will be profiled in the first section of this chapter.

I first met Zhu Jiusi in May of 1992, when I was doing a regional study of higher education reforms in the Central South Region in cooperation with a colleague from the Institute for Higher Education Research of HUST. I was aware of the leading role this university had played in higher education reforms nationwide after the Cultural Revolution and the status of its influential *Journal of Higher Education Research* [Gaodeng jiaoyu yanjiu]. Thus I had asked for an opportunity to interview the retired president in order to learn how this had come about. President Zhu graciously agreed to meet with me for an afternoon interview, and I soon realized what an honor this was. About twelve members of the research institute asked if they could also sit in on the interview, as this was a rare opportunity for them to hear the president's story. As it turned out, three afternoon meetings and about seven hours of time were needed. All of us sat enthralled by the unfolding story of how Zhu had developed a vision for HUST in the darkest days of the Cultural Revolution, and the ways in which he had carried it forward step by step.

Zhu's record of this meeting was published in the *Journal of Higher Education Research*[1] and later given the place of honor as the first article in his book *Struggle and Transformation*.[2] My version appeared in an article on Chinese universities and the social sciences in *Minerva*,[3] and my subsequent research was greatly influenced by the deep insights I had gained from this seven-hour conversation with President Zhu. The decision I made in 1997 to find time to listen to and record the life experiences of the outstanding educators who appear in this volume was directly related to this experience.

In 1994, I had the privilege of teaching a graduate course in international academic relations in Chinese at HUST's Institute for Higher Education Research. I was deeply touched by the presence of the old president, along with the many graduate students and some faculty members, on each of the seven days I taught. Immediately afterwards President Zhu led a delegation of over 30 colleagues and students to an international conference, held in the Yuelu Academy at Hunan University, on Indigenous Knowledge and Cultural Interchange: Challenges to the Ideal of the University." [4] HUST's Institute for Higher Education Research and OISE/UT had jointly organized this event to continue the dialogue begun at the conference on "Knowledge Across Cultures" which has been described in chapter three.[5] In order to encourage as many students and colleagues as possible to join the event, HUST

---

[1] Zhu Jiusi, "Lishi de huigu" [A Retrospect on History] in *Gaodeng jiaoyu yanjiu* [Higher Education Research], No. 4, 1992, pp.1-13. The dates of the original meetings were May 23, 26 and 27, 1992.

[2] Zhu Jiusi, *Jingzheng yu zhuanhua* [Struggle and Transformation] (Wuhan: Huazhong keji daxue chubanshe, 2000), pp.1-25.

[3] Ruth Hayhoe, "Chinese Universities and the Social Sciences," in *Minerva*, Vol. XXXI, No.4, Winter, 1993, pp.500-503.

[4] Ruth Hayhoe, "Introduction: The Context of the Dialogue," in Ruth Hayhoe and Julia Pan (eds.) *East West Dialogue in Knowledge and Higher Education* (New York: M.E. Sharpe, 1996), pp.3-14.

[5] Chapter Three, p.87.

chartered a bus to make the long trip south over country roads from Hubei to Hunan, and President Zhu rode along with students and faculty!

There were many subsequent meetings, and my husband Walter developed a profound respect for President Zhu during several visits to HUST. Thus when we were preparing to leave the Hong Kong Institute of Education, where I had served for some years as director, in the early spring of 2002, one final trip to the Mainland had highest priority – a farewell to President Zhu. We spent the period between Christmas 2001 and New Year 2002 visiting him and other colleagues at the HUST's Institute for Higher Education Research. What a joy to find him in good health at the age of 85, and still active in teaching graduate courses and writing!

Zhu Jiusi between Ruth Hayhoe and her husband Walter Linde,
having lunch at HUST, December 2001

The Story of Three Universities: Wuda, Kangda and HUST

Wuhan University (Wuda), where Zhu Jiusi spent three terms as an undergraduate in the 1930s, is one of China's well known older comprehensive universities, with a history that has some parallels with that of Zhejiang University. The city of Wuhan is located in the middle reaches of the great Yangzi River and it has been an important industrial centre since the early part of the century.[6] It is also an important

---

[6] Wuhan is actually made up of three cities, Wuchang, Hankou and Hanyang, on the Yangzi River where it meets the Han River.

communications hub, with the main railway from Guangzhou in the south to Beijing in the north passing through it, and a key port for river traffic from East to West.

Wuda's institutional history devotes part of its first chapter to the Hubei Self-strengthening School (*Hubei ziqiang xuetang*).[7] This was one of the early modernizing institutions established in 1893 by the famous scholar-official Zhang Zhidong. It had four subject areas: foreign languages, mathematics, science and commerce.[8] Students were expected to be already well educated in Chinese classical subjects, and to learn Western subjects that would enable them to contribute to China's modernization or self-strengthening. During the first decade of the twentieth century, the school evolved into a language school, with classes in English, French, German, Russian and Japanese.[9] Many of its students were actively involved in various revolutionary activities, including the Wuchang uprising, which culminated in the collapse of the last imperial dynasty in 1911.[10]

The National Wuchang Higher Teachers School (*Guoli Wuchang gaodeng shifan xuetang*) was established in 1913, with a responsibility for training teachers for modern schools around the country. It was given the resources and library of the language school.[11] In 1923 it was upgraded to a university level institution, and between 1925 and 1927 it was briefly called the National Wuchang Zhong Shan University, after the birthplace of Sun Yat Sen, father of the 1911 Revolution, and in parallel with universities elsewhere such as Zhejiang University in Hangzhou and Henan University in Kaifeng.[12]

With the establishment of a national government in Nanjing by the Nationalist (Guomindang) Party in 1928, careful attention was given to higher education planning, and the new government decided that a major national university should be established in Wuhan on the basis of

---

[7] Wu Yigu (ed.) *Wuhan daxue xiaoshi 1893-1993* [An Institutional History of Wuhan University 1893-1993] (Wuhan: Wuhan daxue chubanshe, 1993), pp.1-17.

[8] William Ayers, *Chang Chih-tung and Educational Reform in China* (Cambridge, Mass.: Harvard University Press, 1971) pp.124-130.

[9] *Wuhan daxue xiaoshi*, pp.18-57.

[10] There is a historical dispute over whether Wuhan University can claim this institution as its forerunner, but there is no doubt that the National Wuchang Higher Teachers School was to develop into Wuda.

[11] *Ibid.* pp.58-71.

[12] *Ibid.* pp.91-96. See also Chapter Two, p.46 and Chapter Three, p.79.

this institution. A new campus was selected for national Wuhan University, in a beautiful location on the East Lake, and considerable investment was made for new buildings and infrastructure.[13] From 1928 to 1937 national Wuhan University developed as one of a small number of comprehensive universities with colleges of arts, social sciences, law, engineering and science.[14] Agriculture was added in 1933 and medicine in 1936. [15] By 1938, there was an enrolment of 2200 students, and 871 students had graduated since the move to the new campus.[16]

There were a number of outstanding scholars on the faculty, including such literary scholars as Wen Yiduo and Ye Shengtao, with a total faculty of 154 by 1937. [17] The President, Wang Shijie was a graduate of the London School of Economics and had a doctorate in law from the University of Paris. In the 1920s he had been Head of the Law Department at Peking University, and also served in senior legal positions in the Nationalist government. After being president of Wuda from 1929 to 1933, he was appointed Minister of Education in Nanjing.[18]

During the Sino-Japanese War, Wuda had to move inland to escape Japanese incursions, and in the summer of 1938, the faculty and student body moved to Le Shan in Sichuan province, taking as many books and other resources as possible for the war-time campus. Over the six years of war-time education new professors were appointed and the faculty numbers remained at over 100. Just under two thousand new students were enrolled, while 2,767 students graduated, quite a remarkable record for this difficult period.[19]

After the end of the war in 1945, the university moved back to its campus on the East Lake in Wuhan. The post-war president, Zhou Gengsheng, was a distinguished figure in legal scholarship, and emphasized raising academic quality as the main focus of his administration. In spite of the pressures he must have experienced from the Nationalist government, he resisted politicization of the campus, and supported progressive activities. After 1949 he remained in China, joining the

---

[13] *Ibid*. pp.102-106.
[14] *Ibid*. pp.108-111.
[15] *Ibid*. p.111.
[16] *Ibid*. p.112.
[17] *Ibid*. p.115.
[18] *Ibid*. p.123.
[19] *Ibid*. p.152.

Communist Party in 1956 and serving the Ministry of Foreign Affairs and legal circles in various advisory capacities.[20]

One final comment on the academic atmosphere at Wuhan University in the pre-1949 period will be left to Professor Liu Fonian, whose life story appears later in this volume,[21] and who wrote a preface for Wuda's institutional history. Like Zhu Jiusi, Liu Fonian had been a student at Wuda in the 1930s. In his preface he commented on his still vivid memories of the rather suffocating character of its traditional academic spirit and the highly didactic manner in which professors taught. Yet he also recollected how students had encouraged each other in progressive causes.[22] Zhu Jiusi's description of his years at Wuda, which is given later in this chapter, matches well with the atmosphere Liu depicted in his preface.

After 1949, Wuhan University was to have a happier fate than either Zhejiang University or Henan University, though both had a similar standing as national universities during the Nationalist period. We have seen how Zheda was required to re-shape itself as a university of engineering sciences along Soviet lines[23] while Henan University was demoted to a lowly teacher training college in the arts and education.[24] Wuhan University, by contrast, was assigned the role of the major comprehensive university for the Central South Region in the reorganization of higher education that took place in 1952. Under the Soviet model adopted at the time, this meant it maintained its programs in basic arts and sciences, while all other fields were moved elsewhere, including engineering, medicine and agriculture. The only other national comprehensive university in this region, encompassing the provinces of Henan, Hubei, Hunan, Guangdong and Guangxi, was Zhongshan University in the southern city Guangzhou.

For Zhu Jiusi, however, the new university of engineering sciences established on the basis of Wuhan University's college of engineering, and those of several other universities, was to be the focus his work. In between his experience as a student at Wuda and his leadership of this new institution were many years of revolutionary activism. They

---

[20] *Ibid.* pp.195-199.
[21] Chapter Eleven, pp.326-337.
[22] *Wuhan daxue xiaoshi.* p.1.
[23] Chapter Two, pp.48-49.
[24] Chapter Three, pp.81-82.

included a considerable period of time as both a student and a teacher at the Anti-Japanese Resistance University (Kangda) established by the Communist Party in Yan'an, and having branches on several other revolutionary bases. Its predecessor had been the Red Army University (*Hongjun daxue*) in Jiangxi, before the Long March.

Kangda might be viewed as a counter model to the traditional university. It was established for the purpose of short-term training of political and military leaders in strategy for the liberation struggle. Many of the revolutionary leaders, including Mao Zedong himself, offered lectures at Kangda, and it was administered by the Chinese Communist Party. Unlike Yan'an University, which had a three-year program, and a range of courses in the sciences, social sciences and humanities, Kangda focused on political and military subjects and students were enrolled for only six months.

The spirit of these revolutionary institutions owed much to Mao's educational ideas, which are well described in an article he wrote about the Hunan Self-Study University in the 1920s, where he felt the spirit of China's traditional academies or *shuyuan* could be seen. "In looking back at the *shuyuan*, although there were faults in their form of organization, there were not the faults of schools listed above (a mechanistic style of teaching that does harm to human personality, too many hours of class and too complex a curriculum so that students can't use their own ideas to initiate research). First, affectionate bonds between students and teachers were sincere. Second, there was no 'academic government by professors' (a Chinese term for university autonomy) but a free spirit and free research. Thirdly, the curriculum was simple and discussion ranged broadly, it was possible to work in a leisurely and carefree way and to play a little."[25] Kangda's motto was "Unity, Intensity, Liveliness and Seriousness" (*tuanjie, jinzhang, huopo, yansu*) and it had its own flag. These eight characters form a crescent over a single star, with a flying horse passing through the star on the flag.[26]

The other side of this informal, revolutionary style of higher education management was less attractive. It can be seen in the rectifi-

---

[25] Quoted in Zhang Liuquan, *Zhongguo shuyuan shihua* [The evolution of academies in China] (Beijing jiaoyu kexue chubanshe, 1982) p.135. Translation in R. Hayhoe, *China's Universities 1895-1995: A Century of Cultural Conflict* (New York: Garland Publishing, 1996) p.23.

[26] http://flagspot.net/flags/cn_runiv.html.

cation movements of the 1940s, where the free discussion encouraged in the early days was suppressed. Direct administration by Communist Party authorities and Mao's increasing tendency to claim absolute authority for himself as Party leader, showed the limits placed on learning in an institution such as Kangda. In some ways, by its integration into a newly emerging Communist bureaucracy, it began to take up a role similar to that of intellectual institutions in traditional China, which controlled classical knowledge for the purposes of ruling. When Kangda was held up as a model for revolutionizing higher education during China's Cultural Revolution, little was gained. Though this revolutionary idea of a university had served a valuable role in the liberation struggle, it had nothing to offer the kinds of human development and scientific research needed for China's modernization.

The third in the trio of universities, which provide the context for Zhu Jiusi's life as an educator, is the Huazhong University of Science and Technology (HUST). Neither a traditional comprehensive university, nor a revolutionary institution dedicated to the training of leaders, it was newly established as the Huazhong Institute of Technology in 1953, and given responsibility for educating engineering specialists for the Central South Region in four specific areas: mechanical engineering, diesel and auto engineering, electrical engineering and power engineering. It was created on the basis of engineering departments from four national universities, two of which had excellent reputations before 1949 – Wuhan University, whose history we have reviewed above, and Hunan University, a major national university in the province directly to the south. Engineering departments from Guangxi University, to the southwest and Nanchang University in Jiangxi province were also included in this merger.[27] One of the demanding initial tasks was to create an ethos for the new institution, which would bring together teaching faculty who had very disparate backgrounds.

This took a long time, and it is interesting to see the motto that was agreed on in the early 1980s, when the Party committee was making an effort to unite faculty and students after the chaotic period of the Cultural Revolution. Here is what they decided on: Unity, Truth, Rigor and Progress (*tuanjie, qiushi, yanjin, jinqu*). In style it has a ring similar to

---

[27] Yao Qihe (ed.) *Huazhong Ligong Daxue de Sishinian* [The forty years of the Central China University of Science and Technology] (Wuhan: Huazhong ligong daxue chubanshe, 1993), pp.5-7.

that of Kangda, but in substance it has taken quite a different tone, with an emphasis on making a practical contribution through applied science, on academic rigor, on progress and foresight.[28]

The new university was given a large campus in a pleasant suburb not far from the East Lake and backed by hills. Its front entry area is imposing, with a huge pillared entry gate and the name of the university in Chinese calligraphy written by Mao Zedong above the gate. Although in the early years, there was no wall around its large campus, one was built in the 1970s, to clarify its boundaries, and maintain possession of the land which had been given to it by the government – in the face of efforts by nearby farmers to re-take parts of the campus that had not yet been built up for agricultural development. This was also a necessary precaution during the chaotic times of the Cultural Revolution, when all kinds of vandalism took place under the name of revolutionary activism.[29]

Beyond the entry gate is a large open area, a kind of public square, with a statue of Mao Zedong, erected during the Cultural Revolution and kept in place up till now, even though such statues have been removed from many other universities. Two stainless steel frames with the university's eight-character motto stand in the front of this public square. Behind it is the main laboratory building, the largest building in the whole campus, with the university's emblem hung over the entry area – a pentagonal shaped figure, with an S inside it, and a Rutherford atomic model above it. The five sides of the pentagon represent the five institutions whose engineering faculties were merged to form HUST in 1952, while the S represents the university itself.[30]

The overall architectural gestalt of the university has features that root it in Chinese architectural tradition. It faces south, with a hill behind and from that hill one can look beyond the entry area to water and sky beyond. The overall pattern of building demonstrates a kind of axial symmetry, which is found in traditional Chinese palaces such as the Forbidden City. The main laboratory building stands in the centre, with major teaching buildings behind it towards the hill. Student dormitories,

---

[28] *Ibid.* pp.227-228. Zhao Junming, "The Making of a Chinese University: An Insider's View of an Educational *Danwei*," Ph.D. Thesis, McGill University, Montreal, October, 1998. p.41.

[29] Zhao, "The Making of a Chinese University," p.40.

[30] *Ibid.* p.42.

dining halls and related buildings are found in the two wings, but mainly towards the back. Across the centre of the campus is a major commercial street, which divides the buildings for teaching, research and administration in the front, from those for living quarters for staff and students at the back.[31]

The main point that might be made about the campus and buildings provided for this new college is that they were substantial, showing the great importance given by the state to the field of engineering. In many ways this reflected the Soviet model of higher education, with graduates of major polytechnical universities most likely to have successful careers within the Party and government. The phrase "socialist construction," more commonly used than modernization to express the hopes and plans for China's progress under the new regime, conveys the sense of an engineer's mind applied to the major tasks of nation building.

In spite of its firm standing as a major engineering college at the national level serving the Central South Region, HUST was subject to all of the same revolutionary challenges of the fifties and sixties as other universities. In the Great Leap Forward of 1958, HUST was transferred from the control of the national Ministry of Higher Education in Beijing to Hubei province. In the spirit of the time, there was a huge expansion in programs and student numbers, from four departments with nine programs to eight departments with 37 programs, with student numbers rising to about 10,000 at the peak in 1959.[32] New departments were set up in areas such as metallurgy, chemical engineering, engineering physics and shipbuilding. Programs in mathematics, physics and chemistry were also established.

Two themes seemed to inspire the changes of this period. One was a revolutionary theme, emphasizing opening up the university to young people of peasant and worker class, and connecting all learning to a revolutionary vision of rapid social progress. Thus students spent a great deal of time applying what they were learning in factory settings and helped the university in setting up and running factories in related areas. Some of these were successful, while many were not, and much study time was lost in the process.[33] A second theme of the reforms over this

---

[31] *Ibid.* pp.42-44.

[32] *Huazhong Ligong Daxue de xiaoshi*, p.68.

[33] *Ibid.* pp.77-78. Zhao, "The Making of A Chinese University," p.24.

period was an effort to strengthen links between applied and theoretical fields of the sciences, which had been institutionally separated under the Soviet model. Thus new programs in mathematics, physics and chemistry were added to the curriculum, only to be removed again in 1961 when a realistic reassessment was made of the reforms, and a subsequent retrenchment took place.

With the readjustments associated with a national decision to re-emphasize academic quality in higher education under the Sixty Articles of 1961, there were considerable reductions in programs and student numbers. Programs were cut from 37 to 18, and student numbers were cut back to about 6,000 undergraduates.[34] In 1960, HUST was given keypoint status at the national level, one of about 98, which were singled out as leading institutions. In 1980 its title was changed from institute to university, reflecting the changes that came with Deng Xiaoping's movement for reform and opening up.

If the Educational Revolution of 1958 had led to a dramatic yet unsustainable expansion in programs, research and student numbers, the Cultural Revolution of 1966 had the opposite effect. The years between 1961 and 1966 were called a period of "two-line" struggle in the radical rhetoric of the Cultural Revolution period. One of the movements to revive revolutionary activism after the retrenchment of 1961-62 was the Socialist Education Movement of 1964-65, which focused on eradicating feudal and capitalistic forms of thought and behavior through education. During that period Zhu Jiusi went to Peking University's department of radio electronics as the head of a workgroup.[35]

On his return to HUST in May of 1965, just as the Cultural Revolution was about to erupt, he took a stand against the radical trend of upholding Mao Zedong as a godlike figure, and hanging his portraits and quotations everywhere on campus.[36] This was to result in him being subject to particularly ferocious attacks by Red Guards and other radical revolutionary figures, when the Cultural Revolution began the following year. For several years the campus was more or less abandoned, as students were sent to the countryside or to factories, and faculty were

---

[34] Zhao, "The Making of a Chinese University," pp.23, 25.

[35] This is the department where Wang Yongquan was department head. See Chapter Eight, p.254.

[36] Yao Qihe, Xu Xiaodong, " Zhu Jiusi" in Xin Fuliang (ed), *Dangdai Zhongguo gaodeng jiaoyu jia* [Contemporary Chinese Higher Education Specialists] (Shanghai: Shanghai Jiaotong daxue chubanshe, 1995), pp.222-223.

given extensive re-education through living and working in rural areas. When the tide began to turn, however, in the early 1970s, HUST moved forward to become a nationally prominent model of reform.

The story of how HUST became one of the first 22 universities in China to establish a school of graduate studies, how it developed from a highly specialist engineering university into a comprehensive university with world-recognized standards in science and engineering, and how it became a leader in higher educational research, is also intimately connected with the life-story of Zhu Jiusi himself. This period in the university's development will thus be described later in the chapter, as a major aspect of Zhu's life-story.

In the mid 1990s, Chinese universities faced another set of changes, as the national government decided to encourage mergers that would make for a small number of world-class universities which could take the lead in China's development. The merger between Zhejiang University and Hangzhou University described in chapter two was a widely discussed example.[37] There was considerable pressure from Beijing for HUST to be merged with Wuhan University to create one leading university for the region. However, HUST managed to retain the unique identity which it had developed in the 1970s and 1980s, as a comprehensive university in a new mode. Two specialist institutions were merged with it which were able to complement and fill out this identity: the Tongji University of Medical sciences, originally established in Shanghai with support from Germany in 1908, and moved to Wuhan in 1952, and the Wuhan College of Urban Construction, originally under the Ministry of Construction in Beijing.

Wuhan University, for its part, absorbed the Wuhan University of Hydraulics and Electrical Engineering, the Wuhan University of Surveying and Mapping and the Hubei Medical College. Thus two major comprehensive universities take a leading role in the region, each having its own history and ethos. This outcome is a kind of tribute to the enduring nature of Zhu Jiusi's creative contribution to higher education thought.

It is now time to turn to his personal story, beginning with his family and early education, then his experiences of learning, teaching and leadership during the revolutionary struggle, and the development of his career under socialism. Unlike Wang Chengxu and Li Bingde, who

---

[37] Chapter Two, pp.50, 54.

were first and foremost scholars of education and then applied their research to action, Zhu Jiusi was primarily an activist, whose educational vision and higher education theories were built up through experience.

Growing up in Yangzhou 1916 to 1934

Zhu Jiusi was born in 1916, just five years after the 1911 Revolution, in the city of Yangzhou in southern Jiangsu province. Yangzhou had an important cultural history, due to its location on the Grand Canal. It had been well developed economically since the Tang dynasty, and in the early nationalist period it benefited from the province's interest in progressive education, which meant there were excellent teachers for the newly emerging modern schools. Yangzhou had a population of about 140,000 at this time, and so could be described as a middle level city.

Zhu was the youngest in a family of four, with two older brothers and an older sister. His father had started employment as an apprentice in a store, and later had been able to open his own small shop selling clothing. His mother could recognize a limited number of Chinese characters and was familiar with many traditional stories, but was unable to read Chinese texts for comprehension. His eldest brother died at the age of 18, and his other brother was educated for a few years in a *sishu* or traditional private school, then became an apprentice and helped his father in the clothing shop. While this brother only experienced minimal education himself, he was determined that his younger brother should be educated, and gave continual support and encouragement to Zhu Jiusi.

As was common in those years, Zhu studied first in a *sishu*, where he memorized the *Four Books* of the Confucian canon, without ever having any explanation of what they meant, or any discussion of their contents. He felt the effect of this experience of memorization was positive, in that this ancient wisdom was stored on his mind for future reference and reflection. Later the influence of Confucian thought in his development was considerable, due to this early study experience. "It teaches you how to be a good person," he commented. By contrast, he had little exposure to Buddhism, beyond finding Buddhist temples a pleasant location for play as a child, and even less exposure to Daoism.

When Zhu Jiusi reached the age of ten in 1926, his father decided to put him into a modern primary school. Every summer, one of his cousins, the son of his mother's sister, used to return to Yangzhou to visit the family. This young man was studying at the famous Tsinghua preparatory school in Beijing, and preparing to go to the United States for higher studies, which he did a year later. It was he who persuaded Zhu's father to take this step. Zhu's father then decided to give him a new name – Jiu Si, which can be simply translated as "nine things to think about." It was drawn from a phrase in the Analects of Confucius, one of the *Four Books*, where the Master encouraged his disciples to think about nine things, including acute observation and careful listening.[38] For Zhu, this new name signaled a new beginning in his life. In the *sishu* he had already learned some English and mathematics, which meant he was able to enter the first year of upper primary school and graduate in two years. He did not need the four years of lower primary.

On graduation from upper primary school in 1928, Zhu entered the Yangzhou secondary school. It was his own choice to study there. His family gave him complete freedom to choose the school he would like to attend, and the subjects he wanted to study. Now he feels that many young people in China do not have this freedom, as their parents make all such decisions for them. In fact there were only three secondary schools in the city to choose from at the time, and Zhu had his heart set on this one. It was funded by the provincial government, and so fees were low and the family could afford to support him. Also it had a nationwide reputation for academic excellence, and was regarded by some as the southern counterpart of the famous Nankai secondary school in Tianjin.

In retrospect, Zhu felt the school's success owed a great deal to a visionary principal, who had returned from the United States with a Masters degree from MIT, and who put his heart and soul into running the school. Mr. Zhao was a member of the Nationalist Party (the

---

[38] *The Four Books*, with Original Chinese Text, English translation and Notes by James Legge (New York: Paragon Book Reprint Corp., 1966) p.248: Confucius said: "The superior man has nine things which are subjects with him of thoughtful consideration. In regard to the use of his eyes, he is anxious to see clearly. In regard to the use of his ears, he is anxious to hear distinctly. In regard to his countenance, he is anxious that it should be benign. In regard to his demeanor, he is anxious that it should be respectful. In regard to his speech, he is anxious that it should be sincere. In regard to his doing of business, he is anxious that it should be reverently careful. In regard to what he doubts about, he is anxious to question others. When he is angry he thinks of the difficulties (his anger may involve him in). When he sees gain to be got, he thinks of righteousness."

Guomindang), but did not attempt to influence his students politically; rather he focused on fostering academic excellence. For this, he felt the quality of the teachers he hired was of the greatest importance and he managed to recruit excellent teachers from all over the province. When he was not satisfied with the teachers he could hire in Jiangsu, he would do a nationwide search, as was the case for teachers he recruited in physical education and art. He also made great efforts to ensure that the school had the best possible facilities, including well-equipped science laboratories in a building specially built for this purpose, and an excellent library. He was able to use his connections with the Nationalist Party to get financial support for these initiatives.

In the curriculum, there was equal importance given to the sciences and humanities. The learning of English was strongly emphasized, and he had managed to recruit a leading English teacher who had studied at Yenching University, the highly reputed American missionary institution in Beijing. In order to encourage students to read English, he had an English newspaper from Shanghai, the *Dalu Bao*, regularly posted on the school bulletin board. Zhu remembered many details about Zhao's visionary management of the school, and these were to remain with him as a source of inspiration in his later educational work. He noted that during the war Zhao moved to Chongqing and ran an excellent secondary school there, and then when he moved to Taiwan in 1947 he established a successful chemical engineering factory.

Learning through Revolutionary Practice 1935-1953

After six years at Yangzhou secondary school, Zhu graduated with honors. While most graduates went on to study at good universities in China at the time, Zhu was not able to continue his studies. His father could not provide the needed level of support. Rather he contacted a relative who was head of the department of chemistry in Zhejiang University and arranged a clerical position for Zhu at Zheda. There he earned 20 yuan a month, and gained some experience of life in a university environment.

While Zhu was disappointed not to be able to enroll in university studies, he felt the year he spent working in this modest position gave him much food for thought. The period that he worked on the Zheda campus, 1935 to 1936, was a momentous time in the university's development. Over that year, student activism led to the forced resignation of President Guo Renyuan and the appointment of a visionary new president in Zhu Kezheng. Zhu Jiusi was able to observe the methods used by students to oust a repressive president, the visit of the Nationalist leader, Chiang Kai-shek, to the campus, and the first months of leadership by the new president.[39] Zhu Kezheng had been persuaded to take up the position by Chiang Kai-shek on condition that he control all appoint-ments, and be given adequate funding for the university.

In 1936, Zhu's older brother persuaded his father to offer him support for university study. For this alone, Zhu feels he owes an immeasurable debt to his brother. Zhu's father advised him to apply to National Central University in Nanjing, then the national capital, and not far from Yangzhou, just a six-hour journey by river boat down the imperial canal and along the Yangzi River. Zhu, however, was determined to make a different choice. He could not tolerate the thought of living in the national capital under the rule of Chiang Kai-shek, and preferred to choose a university and a location in a different part of the country. As with his choice of secondary school, Zhu noted with gratitude his family's willingness to let him make the decision himself. He chose Wuhan University, and applied to study in a program where he would major in education and philosophy, with English as his minor.

The year was 1936, and Zhu was destined to spend only three terms of study at Wuhan University. During the first year, he took five courses, covering the areas of philosophical concepts, moral reasoning, educational psychology and educational principles, and English. Overall, he felt the content of most courses in his major area was poor, mainly a regurgitation of ideas drawn from Western textbooks in English. Teaching methods were also dull and lacking in interest. The one course which he enjoyed and still remembers was the course in philosophical concepts taught by Fan Xiujing, where dialectical materialism was introduced and used in a way that shed light on issues of national concern. Courses in the foreign languages department were generally of better quality, and this caused Zhu to change his major in the second year to English. He still remembers several excellent courses taken that year, including one in phonetics, which is helpful to him even now, more than sixty years later!

Overshadowing his first year of university was a profound sense of national destiny, as war with Japan loomed. Zhu's anxiety had begun

---

[39] See Chapter Two, p.47, for more of this story.

with the September 18th incident of 1931, when Japan began its incursions into Chinese territory. In his years as an upper secondary student he had read a great deal of progressive literature and social theory in translation and already had a high degree of awareness of the struggle that was unfolding for China's liberation. During his year in a clerical position at Zhejiang University he had observed the student movement and greatly regretted the fact that he could not participate, since he was not a student. Finally at Wuhan University he was able to join the student movement. This is how it came about.

In a basic course in Chinese literature taught by a highly conservative and traditional lecturer during his first year, he was criticized for progressive ideas expressed in an essay he submitted. The lecturer, Su Xuelin, was a novelist. She commented in a denigrating way that he had written a proletarian "eight legged essay," referring to traditional examination essays in the old style, which had come to represent form without content. Zhu was deeply discouraged by the comment from his lecturer and showed the essay to a fellow classmate. The classmate in turn introduced him to a group of progressive students who met secretly to discuss national affairs and consider what they could do to save their country from Japanese aggression. While this underground group had no connection to the Communist Party at the time, it did have links with other progressive groups throughout the country, and Zhu found himself more and more drawn into these circles.

Meanwhile, conditions in China were rapidly deteriorating. In November of 1937, the first term of the second year of Zhu's university program, he received the last letter he was ever to receive from his family. His brother wrote it, enclosing 70 yuan and letting him know that the Japanese had already entered Shanghai and were expected at any time in Yangzhou. While expressing his sense of impending disaster, his brother still urged him to continue his studies and follow the university inland, if it were forced to move. For Zhu, receiving this letter marked the end of his university studies. He simply could no longer concentrate on attending class, reading and studying. One month earlier, in October, he had become a member of the Communist Party, and he now decided to apply to go to the Party's base in Yan'an to continue his studies. Two fellow students who had also joined the Party made the same choice. Zhu was required to keep this plan secret and was not allowed to tell his family. He knew they would not approve, yet at the same time he felt a strong sense of their support and understanding. The Japanese invaded

Nanjing on December 13 of that year, and a few days later they entered Yangzhou. Zhu left Wuhan for Yan'an on December 12.

In reflecting on the years that followed, Zhu feels that he was extremely fortunate to have survived the difficult conditions of the Anti-Japanese War and the Civil War. So many of his close friends and comrades lost their lives, and they are always in his mind up to the present. He feels young people today simply cannot grasp what it was like to live under the shadow of the Japanese invasion, in a situation where China's very survival as a nation was in question. Of the other students in the progressive group Zhu had joined, some left the university, others followed it to Sichuan where it relocated during the War. Many did not survive the war years. He remembered particularly a close friend who led a battalion against the Japanese in 1942 and was killed.

Zhu reached Yan'an by late December, and spent a year there. For six months he studied at the Anti-Japanese Resistance University (Kangda), graduating in June of 1938. For the next three months he taught political education at the university, and subsequently worked as a counselor in another section of the university. In December of 1938, one year after he had left Wuhan, the Communist Party decided that the Anti-Japanese Resistance University should establish two branch campuses in other bases behind enemy lines. The first was in the southeastern part of the neighboring Shanxi province, and the second in a mountainous part of Hebei province, just a few hundred miles south of Beijing, a place called Jin Cha Ji. Several army routes passed through it, from Beijing south through Hebei, and from Tianjin West to Datong. Zhu remembers vividly the moment when Luo Ruiqing, vice-president of Kangda, read out the list of names of those assigned to go to each place. Zhu was assigned to Jin Cha Ji. One went where one was told, and there was no discussion of these assignments.

Zhu spent a whole month on the road to reach Jin Cha Ji, since travel was very difficult in this rugged mountain region. For the first three years he worked at Kangda's branch campus in Jin Cha Ji, a village with about 100 families. At first he was a counselor, responsible for giving guidance to one class of students, and later he taught political education. One of his courses was on the history of the Chinese revolution and another on the history of social development. Classes were typically quite large, with over a hundred students sitting on the ground in the village square. There was no building in the village large enough to accommodate them. No books were available and all teaching materials had to be prepared from memory and experience.

In 1942, Zhu was given a new assignment, to be the head of publicity for the third district of the Jin Cha Ji base, an area not far west of the famous Ding county, where James Yan Yangchu had done his literacy work. The cultural level of the peasants in this region was quite high, because of the legacy left by this famous literacy project.[40] It was only

Zhu Jiusi with his bride, Wang Jin, in 1947

at this time, more than four years after he had left Wuhan to go to Yan'an, that Zhu felt he could safely write a letter to his brother and ask for news of his family. He informed his brother that he was working as a rural primary school teacher in Hebei, and asked after his parents. Not long after he received a letter back informing him that both parents had died that year.

After the defeat of Japan in August of 1945, Zhu was released from the army for a new role as deputy editor of the *Qunzhong Ribao* [Masses' Daily] in the town of Rehe. The editor in chief Li Rui, had invited him to take up this post, but he hesitated feeling his first loyalty was to the army. Li Rui persuaded his army superiors that propaganda work was as important as military work and they released him. The following year Li Rui sent him to Harbin to purchase paper, which was not easy to get, and there he met his future wife, Wang Jin. She followed him back to Rehe in the spring of 1947 and they were married in January of the following year.

The People's Liberation Army reached Beijing in February of 1949, and from January to May of that year Zhu served as editor in chief of the *Tianjin Daily* (Tianjin ribao). On the road between Rehe and Tianjin their first daughter was born, and they were most grateful to a Party leader who arranged a place for the child's birth. Subsequently five more

---

[40] Charles Hayford, *To the People: James Yen and Village China* (New York: Columbia University Press, 1990), pp.117-142.

children were born, three daughters and two sons.

In August of 1949 Zhu and his family were posted to Changsha in Hunan province, where he worked first as deputy editor then as editor-in-chief of the Hunan provincial daily, which was managed by the Communist Party Committee of the province. He held this position for over three years until December of 1952. He felt that his role was to ensure the dissemination of accurate information, local news and political directives from the Party. There were only a few occasions when he wrote analytical articles himself. However, he felt these years in journalism opened his eyes to see and understand the world in new ways. The demands were very broad, encompassing political, economic, cultural, military and agricultural concerns, and included international as well as national perspectives. In January of 1953, Zhu was transferred to the Education Bureau of Hunan province, where he was the first deputy head of the bureau.

In May of 1953, Zhu was informed that he would be sent to the city of Wuhan, where the Education Bureau for the Central South Region wished him to take a leading role in the establishment of a new college of engineering sciences for the region. While he had no part in making this decision, it made him extremely happy, as he was greatly interested in higher education. He later learned the decision had been made by a Party leader in the bureau, who was familiar with his work in journalism and felt he would be suited to higher education leadership. The first president of the new institution, Zha Qian, was also appointed at the same time.

Thus began the work which was to absorb Zhu for the rest of his career, and lead to him becoming known as one of socialist China's most visionary university leaders. His revolutionary experience during the long years of the liberation struggle gave him uniquely important political qualifications for this role, but his educational experience in Yangzhou secondary school and Wuhan University were also important in his educational thought. A dedicated Party member and political educator, he was nevertheless open to experience of all kinds, and had the greatest respect for the academic excellence and visionary leadership he had observed in educators of the Nationalist period. Leadership of a newly established institution of higher education proved a demanding and absorbing task over a thirty-one year period. Zhu was delighted that this was to be his calling.[41]

A Visionary Leader in Higher Education Development

In June of 1953 Zhu moved from Changsha in Hunan to Wuhan, and took up his new role as vice-chairman of the preparatory committee for establishing the Huazhong Institute of Technology, which was formally opened in October of that year. In 1955, Zhu became vice-president and in 1956 he was made deputy party secretary. In 1961 he became party secretary, and from 1972 to his retirement in 1984 he was both president and party secretary.

As he focused all of his energy and effort in building up this new institution, Zhu naturally observed and reflected on the dramatic changes taking place in higher education across China. As we have noted earlier, this new institution was born from the reorganization of colleges and departments which took place in 1952 in a set of nationwide reforms that re-shaped Chinese higher education under Soviet influence. Zhu felt that it was inevitable the Soviet model should be chosen, given the political circumstances of the time, yet some aspects of the reform were more beneficial than others. The great expansion of institutions and programs, and their geographical distribution in all regions of the country, such that they could educate young people for the specific needs of socialist development, were positive and necessary.

The ways in which private universities were integrated into the new public system gave due recognition to their quality and past contribution, Zhu felt. The one outstanding secular private university, Nankai, was given public status and enabled to continue as a leading comprehensive university in the North China Region. The Christian missionary universities, some of which had high academic standards, did not fit ideologically with the needs of the new socialist system, yet their programs and campuses were respected and adapted into the new system. In some cases there was even continuity in leadership, as in the example of Chen Yuan, former president of the Catholic Furen University in Beijing, who was appointed president of Beijing Normal University when it took over the Furen campus.[42] Similarly, in Wuhan, Zhang Kaiyuan, a distinguished historian who had taught at the

---

[41] Most of the details described in this section were shared with the author in a lengthy interview with President Zhu on November 18, 1999 in Wuhan.

[42] Chapter Nine, pp.269-270.

Christian Zhonghua University later became president of Huazhong Normal University, which had taken over Zhonghua's campus. We have seen in chapter two how Hangchow Christian University was an important part of Hangzhou University, which was established on its campus after 1952.[43]

The greatest mistake of these reforms, Zhu felt, was the decision to dismantle the most outstanding comprehensive universities of the pre-1949 period, forcing them to adopt the exact contours of the Soviet model, and give up the breadth of programs that had characterized their original ethos. The greatest losses were suffered by universities such as Tsinghua in Beijing and Zhejiang in Hangzhou, which were required to give up their programs in basic sciences, humanities and a range of professional areas in order to focus entirely on specialist engineering fields narrowly conceived. Those institutions which were still allowed to be comprehensive universities along Soviet lines, such as Peking University, Nankai University, Wuhan University and about fifteen others, were required to give up all of their applied and professional program areas. Zhu had observed and reflected on the work of outstanding presidents of the Nationalist period, such as Zhu Kezheng at Zheda, Cai Yuanpei at Peking University, Mei Yiqi at Tsinghua University and Zhang Boling at Nankai University. He thus had a strong sense of the vision and effort over time that had been required to build these outstanding universities. It was deeply troubling to see the legacy they had left behind treated in such an arbitrary manner.

Only over time did he come to understand several other serious shortcomings of the model of higher education put in place in 1952. One was the institutional separation of research and teaching, with most important research tasks and funds allocated to newly established Institutes of the Chinese Academy of Sciences, while universities and colleges were expected to focus mainly on teaching. A second was the narrowly specialist character of university programs, which were planned in relation to national manpower needs in different sectors, rather than being shaped by the changing character of basic disciplines of knowledge. Thirdly, Zhu was aware of the top-down patterns of administrative control, especially for those institutions directly managed by the Ministry of Higher Education in Beijing. There was virtually no autonomy for leaders at the university level to take initiatives that might

---

[43] See Chapter Two, p.52.

be based on their vision or their awareness of what was needed. As Zhu reflected on these limitations of the Soviet model, a foundation was laid in his own thinking for the development of a unique vision that drew upon diverse aspects of his past experience. He also developed skills in leadership that enabled him to carry this vision into reality in the opportunities that opened up over the tumultuous period from 1956 to 1978.

The Great Leap Forward of 1958 provided the first opportunity for what Zhu describes as a kind of breakthrough (*tupuo*) from the constraints of the Soviet mould – with four new departments and a large number of new programs established, including some in basic science areas. In the years before the retrenchment of 1961, two new concepts were tried out. The first was the integration of research with teaching. Students and faculty members became intensely involved in research projects that had a practical application to local industrial needs. A great deal of learning and new thinking came out of this opportunity to engage in research. The second was the importance of the basic sciences as a foundation for the various specialist engineering programs. Zhu greatly regretted the fact that the new programs in mathematics, physics and chemistry initiated in 1958 were closed down again with the retrenchment of 1961. Without these, he felt the basis for innovation and the constant re-thinking of applied fields was lacking.

In reflecting on this first experience of action "outside of the mould" Zhu mentioned Mao Zedong's famous 1956 speech "On Ten Relationships." He noted that the last of the ten relationships was that between China and foreign countries. Mao made the point that mutually beneficial relationships with foreign countries were to be encouraged, in order to learn from their strengths, but it was important to make a critical analysis of what was learned and avoid blind copying or mechanistic borrowing of whole systems from abroad. In the re-publication of this speech in 1978, Zhu noted that Mao had made specific reference to the Soviet Union and other socialist countries in a part of the speech originally left out, emphasizing the principle that China should adapt critically any useful lessons, rather than simply copy others blindly. [44]

The first half of the 1960s was a time of adjustment and struggle for Chinese universities. In the retrenchment of 1961, HUST adjusted to a smaller number of programs and students, while focusing on raising

---

[44] Zhu Jiusi, "Lishi de huigu," pp.7-8.

academic quality. At the same time the ideological struggle, which was to culminate in the Cultural Revolution of 1966, began to affect campus life. In 1964, Zhu was sent to Peking University's department of radio electronics as head of a workgroup in the Socialist Education Movement, and he returned to Wuhan in May of 1965. This was a period which he did not wish to comment upon, but colleagues have written about his courageous actions. Having noted the trivialization of Mao Thought by revolutionary radicals in Beijing, he insisted that the display of Maoist quotations around the campus be halted. He also had the huge banner calling for the red flag of Mao Thought to be held high on the university's central administration building taken down. As a result, he was subject to public criticism at a major meeting of students and faculty in 1966, and also experienced the ransacking of his home by Red Guards.[45]

Zhu picked up his story a few years later, in 1970, when he was the first to return to a campus that had been largely abandoned. After several bitter years of revolutionary struggle on campus, all academic staff had been forced to move to the countryside in order to learn from the peasants in November of 1969. Zhu was the first to return to the campus, and it was another year before others began to return. As he wandered around a decimated campus, where there was little activity except for a few vegetable gardens and a factory that had moved onto the campus, he took time to think about the past and future. He was reassured by Mao's widely broadcast statement of 1968 that "universities would still be needed, especially colleges of science and engineering." His worst fear had been of a complete closing of the campus, or its appropriation for other purposes. This now seemed unlikely.

But how could he develop a new vision of a university to be created on the ruins of revolutionary excess? All of his books had been destroyed in the Red Guard attacks on his home, and he could only rely on memory and reflection. He recalled the years of teaching at the Anti-Japanese Resistance University when he had faced a similar situation. He also looked back to his educational experiences before 1949 at the Yangzhou secondary school and Zhejiang and Wuhan universities, and to the university leaders he had admired in the pre-1949 period. These recollections became germane to the new vision he was to develop.

---

[45] Yao Qihe, Xu Shaodong, "Zhu Jiusi," pp.222-223.

First of all, he had a deep sense that people were the most important and precious asset of a university. He remembered how the principal of Yangzhou secondary school had searched the province and indeed the nation to find the best possible teachers for his school. He also thought about the leadership of historic university presidents such as Cai Yuanpei at Peking University, Zhang Boling at Nankai University and Zhu Kezheng at Zhejiang University, all of whom had given highest priority to attracting and supporting excellent scholars. He noted how they had had to compete with Tsinghua University which had close links with the United States, and a source of funding in the Boxer Indemnity money that made possible high salaries.[46] Yet they had succeeded, in spite of funding constraints.

At a time when China was just beginning to recover from the excesses of the revolution and excellent academics from universities around the country were spending time in a forced exile from their normal academic work, Zhu got the idea of recruiting highly qualified people who would be willing to come and teach from wherever he could find them. He was determined to build up the fields of engineering where HUST had excelled before the Cultural Revolution, to re-develop strong programs in basic sciences and mathematics and to broaden the curriculum by gradually moving into new areas. He realized that an academically excellent teaching staff would be the essential element for the realization of this vision.

Between 1973 and the end of the decade, Zhu managed to attract about 600 academics who came from universities all over China. Many had spent long periods under re-education in the countryside, and welcomed this opportunity to return to teaching and research. A particular benefit of this visionary effort was the diversification of the teaching staff at HUST, with academics of many different backgrounds joining the staff. Since the early 1950s, it had been the practice for most universities to fill all new staff positions with their top graduates, and quite a serious problem of inbreeding had resulted. This was not to be the situation at HUST, however.

While Zhu focused on attracting mature scholars with excellent academic reputations, he also took every opportunity to develop promising younger scholars. When he encountered a group of young people performing revolutionary operas on the campus, and was

---

[46] See Chapter Eight, pp.238-239.

impressed by their talent and energy, he recruited quite a number to stay on as lecturers. He also created programs to develop those who were already part of the university's academic staff. He felt it was most important that all academic staff members should have good standards in English, no matter what field they were in, and launched a major program to enable all staff to upgrade their English standards. For those who were teachers of English, he provided a free copy of the *China Daily*, an English language newspaper. This was directly inspired by his memories of Principal Zhao at Yangzhou secondary school. The other area needing special attention, Zhu felt, was mathematics. All staff were encouraged to take courses in mathematics that would strengthen the foundations of their scholarship.

Particular attention was given to supporting young people who had come to the university during the Cultural Revolution as "worker-peasant-soldier" students, without the normal academic qualifications for higher education study. They were given special classes so that those who had been kept on as lecturers on graduation and were capable of academic work would be able to reach the needed standards. Another important measure in faculty development was the reinstatement of a system for classifying different levels of academic staff, from assistant teacher to professor. There had been no promotion exercises since 1965, and during the Cultural Revolution period no distinctions were made among different levels of faculty. Zhu initiated a process for promoting faculty on the basis of academic merit at an early period in the 1970s. This was an important incentive for serious academic work, and Zhu was proud of the fact that it had given encouragement to good scholars. He noted how one young scholar who had been promoted from lecturer to full professor entirely on the basis of academic merit at the time was now a member of the prestigious Chinese Academy of Sciences.

The second area on which he focused in this early period was the integration of research into the work of the university. Not only did he feel research should be connected to teaching, but he took the view that research should actually lead teaching. As new understanding unfolded with research, students would be drawn directly into the process of discovery, and teaching would be greatly enlivened. This was in striking contrast to the patterns of teaching established under Soviet influence, which emphasized high academic standards, but provided detailed outlines of the material to be covered in every area of specialization, leaving little room for innovation and new findings.

For research to be possible, of course there had to be well-provided laboratories and other equipment. Here Zhu again thought back to his secondary school, with its excellent science laboratories, and put great efforts into re-building a scientific infrastructure after the destruction that had taken place during the Cultural Revolution. In 1974, he was able to procure a huge shipbuilding laboratory for the university at the then astronomical cost of one million yuan. There had been a department of shipbuilding since 1959, yet it had been impossible to do research without this facility.

In 1975 he was determined to procure a computer for the computer science department. He had no foreign exchange, so could not consider importation, but spent the huge sum of 400,000 yuan to buy a large Chinese computer from Guizhou. He knew it would go out of date within a few years, but felt the computer science department needed it immediately. When this was replaced by a new generation of computers some years later, Zhu asked the department to consider keeping it as a museum piece. He felt faculty and students should know what an old-style computer looked like from inside, and how it filled a large room! Unfortunately, the department had no sense of history, and the old computer was dismantled and disposed of. As Zhu told this story, one could feel the intensity of the passion that had driven him to make these extraordinary efforts at a time when most other universities were still paralyzed by the political struggles of the Cultural Revolution.

Research money was also important, and here Zhu had to look outside of the university, since there was little provision for research funding in the Soviet oriented system where state-funded projects were mainly assigned to institutes of the Chinese Academy of Sciences or specialist research units affiliated with major ministries. In 1971 Zhu had the occasion to go to Beijing, along with nine other higher education leaders from Hubei province, for the first national education meeting in Beijing since the Cultural Revolution. The meeting was convened by an Education and Science group established by the State Council. Zhu stayed in Beijing for three months, participating in the meetings but also taking the opportunity to liaise with various national ministries, including the Ministry of Mechanical Industry [*Jijie gongye bu*] and the Ministry of Electronics Industry [*Dianzi gongye bu*].

Many of the cadres and research staff of these ministries had spent lengthy periods undergoing re-education in the countryside, and there was a dearth of intelligent and well-educated younger staff. Thus Zhu was offered funding to open new programs which would train people for the specific needs in education and research of these ministries. Nine new programs were set up, in areas related to lasers and electronics, and many research projects were initiated. In describing these encounters, Zhu noted how he himself had no specialist knowledge of these fields, but had confidence that his academic staff would be able to meet the challenge. The one area where he had some insights was that of laser technology, as he had observed its early development when at Peking University's department of radio electronics in 1964.

There was one more essential condition for good research to be done, Zhu felt, and it was probably more difficult than any of the others. That was up-to-date information on scientific research developments around the world. In 1976, Zhu launched a comprehensive project for scientific personnel to find out what was going on in their field abroad. He arranged for faculty members to go to Beijing and Shanghai and search out relevant materials in the best-provisioned libraries in the country. Then he had the university launch a scientific newsletter, entitled *International Scientific and Technological Trends* [Guoji keji dongtai] which had a total of 80 issues reporting on new developments abroad between 1977 and 1978. He also launched a sister publication with direct translations of important scientific papers from abroad.

In addition to these efforts to circulate up-to-date information on current scientific developments around the world, Zhu made a huge effort to develop the HUST library. He noted how from 1981 to his retirement in 1984, five percent of the budget provided by the government was put into the library every year. He made particular efforts to subscribe to large numbers of international journals and books, and all of these had to be ordered through Beijing, because foreign exchange was required. He noted that at the time the bureau in Beijing responsible for making these arrangements had told him there were only two universities in China that were ordering foreign books and journals on a large scale, Peking University and HUST. When Zhu visited the United States in 1979, one of the stories he heard was how Mrs. Stanford had sold her jewels in order to provide books for Stanford University in its early years – a piece of Stanford's lore which Zhu particularly appreciated.

Given the attention that Zhu gave to the development of research as a core part of the university's mission, it was not surprising that when Zhu went to Beijing in 1977, to help plan the agenda for the national meetings in Science and Education to be held in April of 1978, his major contribution was a paper entitled "Scientific research should be in the forefront of teaching and learning."[47] In this paper he was able to give concrete examples of research that had enlivened teaching. He was thus delighted when the formal policy was announced after these meetings that "universities should be centers of research and teaching," a completely new departure from the Soviet model that had dominated Chinese higher education since 1952. Zhu was also pleased that HUST was one of two universities, which were given special commendation for their research work at these meetings.

The third area of great concern for Zhu Jiusi as he developed a vision for HUST in the difficult years of the early 1970s was the curriculum. We have noted how he had been extremely disappointed by the retrenchment of 1961, which led to the dismantling of newly developed programs in basic sciences and mathematics. He was now determined to re-develop those programs, and to broaden the curriculum beyond the fields of science and technology, which had been the mandate given to HUST by the government. We have already noted how he managed to develop nine new programs in 1971, after his visit to Beijing, and in 1978 three more were added later, in systems engineering, biological engineering and management.

From 1981 he moved vigorously to develop a range of programs in humanities and social sciences, which he felt were needed to complement the work in engineering sciences. These included fields such as Chinese language and literature, scientific journalism, philosophy, history of science and higher education. Without the remarkable group of faculty he had recruited during the 1970s, it would have been impossible to open new programs in these areas. It was also an uphill task to gain the necessary approval of the Ministry of Education to recruit students. Zhu used his visit to Beijing for national higher education meetings in 1980 to persuade then Minister of Education, Jiang Nanxiang, to approve the program in Chinese, and many of the others were approved shortly after.

To the outside observer, Zhu's leadership initiatives in attracting top level faculty, giving vigorous support to research and broadening the curriculum, might not seem startlingly new. However, they must be

---

[47] Zhu Jiusi, "Kexue yanjiu yao zou zai jiaoxue de qianmian," [Scientific research should be in the forefront of teaching and learning] in Zhu Jiusi, *Gaodeng jiaoyu sanlun* [Essays on Higher Education] (Wuhan: Huazhong Ligong Daxue chubanshe, 1990), pp.1-5.

judged against a Chinese context where universities were emerging from a traumatic period of persecution during the Cultural Revolution. Most were thus simply struggling to revive the patterns that had been developed under Soviet influence in the early 1950s. Against this backdrop, Zhu's work could be seen as little short of revolutionary. His academic foresight was to be confirmed by two developments of the late 1970s and the early 1980s.

In 1979, Zhu went with four other senior university leaders from China on an extended visit to the United States, Canada and Japan under the sponsorship of UNESCO. He visited top universities in all three countries, and naturally had a particular interest in those with strong science and technology emphases, such as the Massachusetts Institute of Technology, and the California Institute of Technology. Several things that he observed left a strong impression. The first was the integration of research with teaching, and the fact that universities undertook large-scale national research projects on behalf of the government, such as those he saw at MIT and the Lawrence Centre at Berkeley. Secondly, he noted that virtually all universities were comprehensive in the wide range of programs they offered, even those that may have evolved from a specialist focus, such as the Texas University of Agriculture and Mechanics, which had begun its history as a Land Grant University. In Japan, he noted that Tokyo University of Technology had also evolved towards a more comprehensive institution after the Second World War, an opposite trajectory from that taken by Chinese universities under Soviet influence. Thirdly, he noted the great importance of strong academic secondary schools in preparing university entrants. These three observations confirmed the direction he had adopted in the early seventies, during those lonely days on the HUST campus after the Cultural Revolution.

The other important confirmation of the direction he had already taken came in 1982, when the first masters and doctoral programs in post-1949 China were in process of being approved. Because of the remarkable foundation for research, which Zhu had established from the early seventies, HUST was in a position to have 30 master degree programs and 13 doctoral programs go successfully through the strictly regulated assessment process of the newly established Committee for Academic Degrees under the State Council. Universities were required to have at least 10 doctoral programs in order to establish a school of graduate studies, and HUST became one of only 22 universities nationwide to have its graduate school approved that year. This was a remarkable achievement for a relatively new institution.

Conclusion: Setting a High Standard for University Leadership

In reflecting on Zhu Jiusi's contribution to higher education in China, and to the idea of the university more generally, one is struck by the remarkable degree of autonomy he was able to exercise. This was in spite of very real constraints coming from two different sources – the decision of China's political leaders to adopt a Soviet model of higher education in the 1950s and the revolutionary turmoil within China between 1957 and the early 1970s. These two factors constituted crucial aspects of the context for university development in China, yet we can see in Zhu's leadership an ability to find space within these constraints for visionary and effective action. Not one of the three initiatives which have been describe above – aggressive recruitment of excellent faculty from around the country, initiation of research as the leading factor in good teaching and moving towards a comprehensive curriculum – were either suggested or even understood by national higher education authorities at the time when Zhu acted on them. He was somehow able to find a space "between the cracks" for these visionary projects, and to gain the trust of those political and admini-strative leaders who pro-vided the needed appro-vals for action.

Zhu Jiusi, dynamic leader and thinker, expressing his views in an informal seminar session in the 1990s

Zhu himself explains the situation in a moving tribute to Liu Kunshan, the army leader who was head of the Mao Zedong Thought propaganda team in charge of the university during the late sixties and the early 1970s.[48] Liu had probably only completed secondary education,

---

[48] Zhu Jiusi, "Juan Shou Yu" [Preface], *Jingzheng yu Zhuanhua*, p.ii.

but he had great respect for knowledge and for professional judgment. He gave Zhu a completely free hand, approving all of the initiatives which he took to develop the university. During the three months which Zhu spent in Beijing in 1971, meeting with national authorities and discussing the development of new programs with various industrial ministries, he did not feel the need to telephone Liu and ask for approval. In the end, Liu agreed to nine of the ten new programs that were developed, questioning only the one in radar technology where Liu felt there was not adequate equipment for the university to take it on. Liu was familiar with the army's programs in this area, and Zhu felt this was wise advice.

In reflecting on Zhu's dynamic leadership and the tremendous influence of what might be called his "model" for university development throughout China in the 1970s, one might go a little deeper and consider whether or not the very concept of "autonomy" has a different meaning in the context of China's traditions of knowledge and scholarship than that of the West. Along with academic freedom, autonomy has been one of the core values of the European university tradition, and it is usually understood in terms of the need of the university to have control over its own destiny, and to be able to avoid the interference of external agencies in its decision-making, whether they be those of state or church. In an article which I wrote with a doctoral student from China on the concept of autonomy in the historical development of Chinese universities, we noted how there are several different ways of translating the English term autonomy into Chinese, and two may be of particular interest: One of these, *zizhiquan*, or independence, has a strongly political connotation, and is used to describe the autonomous regions, prefectures and counties in China where there is a predominantly minority population. The other, *zizhuquan*, became the preferred term used to describe the increasing degrees of freedom given to universities in the reform documents and legislation that has emerged since the early 1980s in China. It might be expressed as "self-mastery," with the emphasis being placed on "daring to think and daring to do things", in other words a liberated mentality (*jiefang sixiang*), within the broad framework of government policy.[49]

---

[49] Zhong Ningsha and Ruth Hayhoe, "University Autonomy in Twentieth Century China," in Glen Peterson, Ruth Hayhoe and Yongling Lu (eds.), *Education, Culture and Identity in Twentieth Century China* (Ann Arbor: University of Michigan Press, 2001), pp.265-267.

The European notion of university autonomy emphasizes the line between university leaders and the state, and the claim of the university to advance knowledge on a theoretical level, while abstaining from any practical involvement in political action. This is the kind of pact that has allowed for the persistence of a relatively high degree of university autonomy. In the Chinese epistemological context, where the line between theoretical and practical knowledge is less clearly drawn, and there has been a strong tradition of evaluating knowledge on the basis of its application to practice, this kind of pact is less possible. Chinese intellectuals have had a longstanding experience of sharing power with their political rulers, and consequently have an extremely high sense of responsibility for the governance of society and nation. Thus the concept of autonomy as self-mastery (*zizhuquan*) fits more closely their social role.

Zhu Jiusi's style of academic leadership provides us with a remarkable exemplar of how effective this kind of intellectual leadership can be. In one of the recent essays included in his book, *Struggle and Transformation*, Zhu comments on the movement encouraging mergers among major universities in the mid-1990s. The main point which he makes is that a successful merger must be based upon the free choice of each of the institutions involved, and cannot be imposed from above.[50] The different pathways chosen by HUST and Wuhan University in face of the opportunities and threats posed by recent reforms in Chinese higher education show how strongly held is this principle of self-mastery.

Since his retirement in 1984, Zhu has been actively involved in teaching and research on higher education at the Institute of Higher Education Research, which has had a doctoral program in the field since 1995. His years of active leadership and penetrating reflection on issues of higher education development have gradually been translated into a body of scholarship which is nationally recognized. Its validity and value have been demonstrated in the practice of reform, not merely through theoretical testing or elaboration. This reflects a profound aspect of the Chinese scholarly tradition, its insistence on knowledge being demonstrated in action.

---

[50] Zhu Jiusi, "Wo dui daxue hebing de yijian" [My views on university mergers] in Zhu Jiusi, *Jingzheng yu zhuanhua*, pp.177-180.

Zhu Jiusi with nine of his doctoral students in the late 1990s

When asked in 1999 what he saw as the most important issue for the future of Chinese higher education, Zhu mentioned the urgent message of progressive writer Lu Xun in his *Diary of a Madman* to "save the children" (*jiujiu haizi*) and suggested that the call now should be to "save education" (*jiujiu jiaoyu*). With the tide of market reform and commercialization sweeping China, Zhu was greatly concerned that the temptation for universities to join the fever to advance knowledge for commercial advantage could undermine the substantive achievements of the eighties and early nineties. Self-mastery thus remains a principle of urgent importance for Chinese university leaders in relation to the changing economic environment and the pressures of globalization.[51]

Where were the sources of inspiration for Zhu's remarkable life? Many answers could be given to this question: his exposure to influential educators during the Nationalist period, his study of progressive writings, the ways in which he was tempered through a dedicated period of revolutionary action, his openness to learning from a wide range of experiences. It is this latter point that takes us back to the name given to the young Zhu by his father in 1926 when he was sent to a modern

---

[51] Interview with President Zhu Jiusi, November 18, 1999 in Wuhan.

primary school – Jiusi, the Confucian admonition to "think about nine things." The first two of these nine, Zhu remembered clearly, were careful listening and penetrating observation. Probably what stands out most strongly in the life of this influential educator is his ability to listen to and observe at a penetrating level all that is going on around him, then to devise forms of action that could make a significant difference for the good. The beneficiaries were his beloved university, the Huazhong University of Science and Technology, and higher education throughout China, at a time of awakening, reform and new directions.

Chapter Five

Pan Maoyuan –
Founder of Higher Education Studies in China

Pan Maoyuan was born in 1920 in the city of Shantou, on the eastern coast of Guangdong province to a family who lived in extreme poverty. The fact that he was able to gain a basic education was remarkable, given the family's circumstances. His love of teaching led him to apply for studies at Xiamen University on its war-time campus in Changting on the border of Jiangxi province in 1939, and his subsequent educational career has been closely linked to the historical development of Xiamen University. The first part of this chapter will therefore tell the story of Xiamen University, which had its own unique development trajectory in the city of Xiamen, traditionally called Amoy, on the south-eastern coast of Fujian province, facing Taiwan.

As a student of Chinese higher education, I had become aware of Professor Pan Maoyuan's important work in the field at quite an early period, and first had the opportunity of hearing him lecture at a conference on higher education reform at Nanjing University in the autumn of 1988. The following year I moved to Beijing to work as cultural attaché in the Canadian embassy, and during my years in Beijing, I was delighted to be invited by Professor Pan to visit Xiamen University, and learn about its work in higher education research. I was stunned by the beauty of its ocean-side campus, and a style of architecture that combined Chinese and Western structural features in a harmonious way. Most of all, I was able to learn a great deal about the work of the Higher Education Research Institute which Professor Pan had founded in 1978, and whose roots went back to his work at Xiamen University in the 1950s.

It was to be some years before I had the opportunity of visiting the Higher Education Research Institute at Xiamen University again, and that was November of 1997. By this time I was living in Hong Kong, as director of the Hong Kong Institute of Education, and took the opportunity of visiting Professor Pan, in order to spend some time listening to the story of his life. The two lengthy talks we had provided the main source of information for this chapter.[1] I was also able to catch a glimpse of his teaching style through the opportunity to attend a salon he regularly held at his home for students on Saturday evenings.

Professor Pan lives in a two-story house on a hill in the main campus of the university. His spacious but rather spartan study on the second floor of the house was lined with book cases and furnished with a desk, sofa and extra chairs brought in for the occasion. About twelve graduate students from different regions of China had gathered, and I could sense an excitement and expectancy as the meeting was about to begin. Professor Pan led off with a few comments and introduced the topic that was to be the focus for the evening. This was an article written by one of the students criticizing the sociological perspective on education recently put forward by a leading scholar in Nanjing, because its premises totally excluded the function of higher education as a field. The Nanjing scholar had published a defence of his views, and this student was now preparing her response. All those present were invited to express their views and give her suggestions. Hours of passionate and lively argumentation followed with different students taking the side of one or other of the two protagonists, and exploring aspects of the sociological function of higher education in great depth. Professor Pan occasionally injected a few brief comments, if the argument began to lose

Pan Maoyuan surrounded by graduate students at his Saturday evening salon

---

[1] Interviews with Pan Maoyuan, December 6 & 8, 1997.

focus, but largely left it up to the students to carry it forward. I observed the whole evening's proceedings with fascination, seeing aspects of Professor Pan's teaching style and rapport with students that I had not seen in the more formal settings where I had encountered him on earlier occasions.

The portrait I attempt to draw in this chapter is based mainly on the personal account of his life, which he shared with me on that visit, as well as the perusal of some of his prolific writings in the field of higher education. I begin with an account of Xiamen University, the setting for his life as a student, lecturer, academic administrator and professor over the period from 1939 to the present.

The Story of Xiamen University

The story of Xiamen University (Xiada) is intimately connected with the special features of this region, which has close links with Southeast Asia, and a history of emigration there for several hundred years. In another sense the university's story begins with the life of one remarkable individual, Chen Jiagen, born to an emigrant family in the town of Jimei, near Xiamen, in 1874. His father lived in Singapore, running a number of businesses which included the marketing and distribution of rice, a pineapple canning factory and real estate. His mother came from a local fisherman's family, and his early years were spent close to his mother, and helping as a child with market gardening and fishing. [2]

At age ten, he joined his father in Singapore, and by the time he was thirty, his father's businesses had declined, but he had established his own successful business by this time. Chen Jiagen was 37 years old when the Qing dynasty was overthrown in the Revolution of 1911, and like many other overseas Chinese he was excited by these events, and eager to make a contribution to China's development as a republic. In returning to his home region, he was struck by its continuing poverty and isolation, and saw education as the key to its development. He started with his hometown of Jimei and established a whole system of schools, from kindergarten through primary school up to secondary schools, vocational schools and even teacher education. These schools were open to children of all backgrounds, and Chen was specially concerned that girls should have an equal opportunity for education.

---

[2] Liu Haifeng, Zhuang Mingshui, *Fujian Jiaoyushi* [The History of Education in Fujian] (Fuzhou: Fujian jiaoyu chubanshe, 1996), p.357.

Related community education projects included libraries, science centers and cultural centers.[3]

After nearly a decade of these efforts, Chen decided to found a university. In 1919 he called a public meeting and made the point that there was not one public or private university in the province of Fujian, and this meant it was extremely difficult to find teachers for the school system he had been creating. He made a public commitment of one million yuan for establishing the new university, and another three million for its ongoing running expenses. The new university opened its doors to students in March of 1921, recruiting 98 students in the two sections it first established, teacher education and commerce. In May of that year, Chen led students and faculty to the ocean-side site of the new campus, for a ceremony to lay the foundation stone. It was the 9th of May, known at the time as National Shame Day in commemoration of the indignities imposed by Japan's 21 Demands of 1915, which the Chinese government had reluctantly agreed to on May 8, 1916. Chen was determined to create an institution which would nurture young people committed to republicanism and able to serve China's economic development and self-strengthening.[4] It was China's first university to be established by an overseas Chinese, notes the institutional history.[5]

By February of 1922, the first buildings on the new campus were completed, and students and faculty moved in. A private institution, the university was managed by a Board of Governors, with Chen as the permanent chair. The board in turn appointed the president, Professor Lam Waiqing, and entrusted him with all aspects of academic management. Chen maintained a close interest in all aspects of the university's development, overseeing such major building projects as the large main teaching building, the administration building, the assembly hall and the student residences. He wanted to make sure the university was well equipped and spared nothing to get needed equipment from other parts of China and abroad.[6]

Over the subsequent years the university developed rapidly, having five colleges and 21 departments by 1930, including arts, sciences, law,

---

[3] *Ibid.* pp.349-352.

[4] *Ibid.* pp.353-355. Hong Yonghong, *Xiamendaxue xiaoshi diyizhuan* [The Institutional History of Xiamen University Volume 1] (Xiamen: Xiamen daxue chubanshe, 1990), pp.1-17

[5] Hong Yonghong, *Xiamendaxue xiaoshi*, p.15.

[6] *Ibid.* pp.19-27.

commerce and education. The college of education had departments of educational psychology, educational philosophy, administration and teaching methodologies, with well developed laboratories for experimentation. Entrance requirements were rigorous and the curriculum was well developed. In 1928, the university was registered with the newly established Nationalist government, under the regulations it promulgated for a university to be recognized. It was the only university in the province of Fujian, as the four other higher institutions, including two missionary colleges, qualified only for registration as colleges.[7]

In 1933, a team from the national ministry of education in Nanjing came to Fujian to advise on some adjustments in higher education provision, which would avoid the overlapping of programs. As a result, and due to severe funding constraints, Xiamen University decided to merge certain departments and colleges. The college of education became a department of education within the college of arts, while the colleges of law and commerce were merged. Altogether three colleges, with nine departments, remained by spring of 1937.[8]

With Japan's full-scale invasion of China in that year, it was an extremely difficult time for higher institutions. In the case of Xiamen University, an added difficulty arose from the fact that Chen Jiagen's business interests suffered greatly in the economic depression of the times, and he was no longer able to support the university financially. The Nationalist government agreed to take it over in the spring of 1937, and it became National (*Guoli*) Xiamen University, with a new President, Xue Bendong, appointed by the Nanjing government.[9] In November of that same year, President Xue had to oversee the university's move to Changting, near the border of Fujian and Jiangxi, to escape Japanese bombing. By the spring of 1938, there were 284 students, a staff of 83, including 22 professors, as well as other academic and administrative staff.[10]

The war-time university held classes on three campuses in different locations, with considerable difficulties of communication. Nevertheless, buildings were built, and a new library housed the large number of books that had been packed and brought from Xiamen. There were also

[7] Liu Haifeng, Zhuang Mingshui, *Fujian Jiaoyushi.* pp.407-408.
[8] *Ibid.* p.409; Hong Yonghong, *Xiamendaxue xiaoshi,* pp.121-122.
[9] *Ibid.* pp.411-412. Hong Yonghong, *Xiamendaxue xiaoshi,* pp.151-160.
[10] Hong Yonghong, *Xiamendaxue xiaoshi,* p.166.

science laboratories, as well as classrooms, dormitories and administrative offices.[11] Student numbers grew over the years, as displaced students from other parts of China came to study at Xiada, and new programs were developed. A college of law from Fujian University was merged with Xiamen University, and new programs were developed in accounting, banking, electrical engineering and aeronautics, reflecting some of the needs of the war-time period.[12]

Some scholars have noted that the scholarly atmosphere was richer and more serious than in the pre-war period, due to an intense concern for the nation's destiny. The institutional history notes proudly that this was the only national university that managed to remain open east of the major railway line connecting Canton to Wuhan and Beijing during the Japanese occupation.[13] All others had been forced to move inland.

At the end of the war in 1945, a new president was appointed to head Xiada, Wang Deyao, a biologist who had been dean of the college of science. He oversaw the university's move back to its campus in Xiamen.[14] His initial focus was on the strengthening of programs in science and engineering, including the establishment of a new department of marine science.[15] By 1948 there were five colleges, including science, engineering, arts, law and commerce, with 19 academic departments.[16] There was also a significant research program in areas such as marine sciences and economics. The student body had reached 1349 students by 1947, with 176 academic staff and 119 administrative staff, making it a fairly large university for its time.[17]

After 1949, under the new Communist regime, the university had to adapt to the Soviet-imposed model put in place in the reorganization of departments between 1952 and 1954. It was designated a comprehensive university with departments only of basic sciences and humanities. The college of engineering, which it had worked so hard to establish, was to see all of its departments dispersed and merged with other institutions. Aeronautics was moved to Beijing and became part of the newly established Beijing Aeronautics Institute. Mechanical engineering and a

---

[11] *Ibid.* p.177.

[12] Liu Haifeng, Zhuang Mingshui, *Fujian Jiaoyushi.* pp.531-532.

[13] Hong Yonghong, *Xiamendaxue xiaoshi.*

[14] *Ibid.* pp.229-237.

[15] *Ibid.* pp.243-244.

[16] *Ibid.* p.248.

[17] Liu Haifeng, Zhuang Mingshui, *Fujian Jiaoyushi.* p.567.

part of the civil engineering department were moved to Zhejiang University in Hangzhou. Another part of the civil engineering department was merged into the East China Institute of Hydraulic Engineering in Nanchang, Jiangxi province, while the department of electrical engineering was merged with the Nanjing Engineering Institute. The famed marine studies department was transferred to Shandong in Northeast China. Its college of agriculture was combined with that of Xiehe, a former missionary college in Fuzhou, to become an independent Institute of Agriculture. Its law department was made a part of the East China Institute of Law and Politics in Shanghai.

As for the department of education, where Pan Maoyuan had studied and taught, it was moved to Fuzhou, and became a part of Fuzhou Normal College. This was a newly established provincial institution for teacher education,[18] similar to the Nanjing Normal College in Nanjing[19] and the Zhejiang Teachers College in Hangzhou.[20] Like those two institutions, it was given the beautiful campus of one of the Christian institutions, the South China Women's College, which had been developed by American missionaries.[21]

Pan noted how this left Fujian province without a single program in engineering. In 1958, therefore, under the stimulus of the Great Leap Forward, the provincial government decided to establish Fuzhou University in the city of Fuzhou, as a provincial-level engineering institution.[22] Xiamen University assisted them by providing two years of basic science education for students before they entered the more specialist engineering education programs. This was a fairly unusual kind of cooperation for the period, illustrating the vision of the then president of Xiamen University.

This may also have been an expression of the sense of solidarity and cooperation that had been characteristic of efforts to build up higher education in Fujian province from the 1920s up to the 1940s. Due to its geographical location on the south-east sea coast, and the difficulties of

---

[18] Fu Xianqing (ed.), *Fujian gaodeng jiaoyu fazhan yanjiu* [Research into the Development of Higher Education in Fujian] (Fuzhou: Fujian jiaoyu chubanshe, 1997), pp.12-13.

[19] Chapter Ten, p.297.

[20] Chapter Two, p.52.

[21] William Purviance Fenn, *Christian Higher Education in Changing China 1880-1950* (Grand Rapids: William Be. Eerdmans Publishing Co., 1976), pp.97-98.

[22] Fu Xianqing (ed.), *Fujian gaodeng jiaoyu fazhan yanjiu*. p.14.

travel over land to major centers such as Shanghai and Nanjing, a train ride of over 20 hours, there was a strong spirit of local self-reliance. There was also a spirit of looking outwards, particularly to the southeast, where there were longstanding historical connections with overseas Chinese communities.

In face of the reorganization of departments and colleges, that took such a heavy toll on Xiamen University, the new president, Guang Yanen, was determined to maintain elements of Xiada's unique ethos. He insisted that Xiada's strong department of economics should remain at the university, rather than being combined with the economics departments of other universities to form an independent institute of finance and economics, as happened in most other regions of China at the time. Thus Xiamen University gained departments of economics and finance from the two former missionary institutions, Xiehe and South China Women's College.

President Guang was also reluctant to lose the department of education, which had had an important role in the university's history since its establishment in 1921. Unable to prevent its move to Fuzhou, he decided at least to keep Pan Maoyuan at Xiada, with the rationale that he was needed for the professional formation of secondary school teachers. In this he showed considerable foresight, since graduates of the university's departments of mathematics, physics and chemistry, also Chinese, history and geography, might well be assigned jobs as secondary school teachers. The university needed an educational program to prepare them for teaching careers. As far as I know, none of the other comprehensive universities had this kind of vision, being content to leave teacher education to the newly established normal universities. Only in the 1990s did they make efforts to establish programs in education. This decision of the president was to create unique conditions at Xiamen University for the birth of a new discipline, as we will see in the story of Pan Maoyuan later in this chapter

Over the years from the 1950s to the 1970s and 1980s, Xiamen University developed along similar lines to other major comprehensive universities. With the reforms of Deng Xiaoping after 1978, new economic opportunities opened up, and the city of Xiamen found itself in one of four special economic zones from 1984, with special advantages in terms of foreign investment and industrial development. For Xiamen University, the economic attractiveness of the region meant it was easier to recruit excellent faculty as teachers and researchers, in spite of the fact that it was still geographically rather remote from main centers of political and economic power. The university thus developed rapidly, with many new curricular initiatives.[23]

In 1986, Xiamen University gained approval to establish a school of graduate studies, and its masters and doctoral level programs burgeoned. Certain areas of the natural sciences were strongly developed, particularly fields such as marine biology and physical chemistry. By 1999, the university had one national laboratory leading a disciplinary field, and three nationally recognized keypoint laboratories, as well as several national key bases for humanities and social science research. These largely reflect the historical and geographical context, with research related to South East Asia, to the World Trade Organisation, and to special economic zones.[24] One, however, is in higher education, the only such base in China. While there are a number of other good centers of higher education research in Chinese universities, Xiamen's center was given the highest level of national recognition. This was the result of a vision which Pan Maoyuan has pursued with untiring dedication from the mid-1950s up to the present.

This brief sketch of the historical development of Xiamen University provides a context for understanding aspects of Pan Maoyuan's life-story, which is the focus of this chapter. By an interesting coincidence, Xie Xide, the first woman scholar in our group of ten and the subject of chapter six, was also a student at Xiada over this period. She was one year behind Pan. While he was a student of education, and her major field was physics, they shared the experience of being together in an elective class in psychology for one year.

Pan Maoyuan: Growing Up in Southeast China 1920-1949

Pan Maoyuan was born in 1920 in the city of Shantou, in the eastern part of Guangdong province, not far from its border with Fujian province, and fairly close to the city of Xiamen. His family was extremely poor, having neither land nor profession, and barely able to eke out a living.

---

[23] Liu Zhengkun, Yang Juqing, Zheng Wenjing (eds.), *Xiamen daxue yuanxi guansuo jianshi* [A brief history of Xiamen University's colleges, departments, centers and institutes] (Xiamen: Xiamen daxue chubanshe, 1990). This volume gives a detailed account of curricular developments over the whole period from 1921 to 1987.

[24] www.xmu.edu.cn.

Although his mother gave birth to ten children, six died in infancy and a seventh died as a young person. His family could not afford to send him to school, and so his early education was irregular and broken. He was taught to read by an older brother and by his father.

At the age of eight he was put into the third grade of a local primary school, and he remembers how the content of the curriculum was entirely traditional. The curriculum began with the *Trimetrical Classic* (Sanzi Jing), proceeding then to the Confucian classics and some ancient historical texts. Pan was educated entirely in classical Chinese in this school, first learning to write in the classical language (*wenyan*), and only later adopting modern Chinese. The use of a modern Chinese writing style (*baihua*), which is close to speech, began to be widespread after the May 4th movement of 1919, yet had not affected his school.

On completion of primary school, Pan had little hope of any further education, as his family was unable to support him. His father expected him to stay at home and help with grinding rice and preparing rice flour cakes for sale. Very fortunately, however, the principal of his primary school had noted his flair for writing Chinese when he read his examination script just before he graduated. Learning that he was at home and unable to continue his studies, Principal Yang helped him to get a study place in lower secondary education with fees reduced to half. He entered a rather traditional secondary school, called the Shizhong zhongxue, a name that reflected the view of Confucius as a master who could adapt to every age (*shizhong*). There he focused on studies in Chinese for three years. His teachers were holders of traditional degrees under the imperial examination system, and he later felt that this education in classical Chinese was a valuable foundation for his life. The most important aspect of it was learning how "to be a good person" (*zuo ren*), he commented in retrospect.

By this time Pan was fifteen years old, and he knew it would be impossible for his family to support him in any further education. However, a chance opportunity came his way to work as a primary school teacher, and he took it up with alacrity. He soon found that teaching young children was much more difficult than he had imagined. He would prepare his lessons for several hours, and then find after the first half-hour with the children, he had run out of things to say. Nor did he know how to keep order in the classroom or provide conditions for children to learn. Unwilling to accept failure, he decided that he must find a way to gain entry to a teacher education institution, and learn how to be a good teacher. He also searched for books on education, which would help him to get started.

His first important find was a book entitled *A General Theory of Education* (Jiaoyu tonglun) by Professor Zhuang Zexuan of Zhejiang University. [25] He found it theoretically complex and academically demanding. This confirmed his determination to find an opportunity to study at a teachers college. In 1936 he spent a year of study at the Haining Upper Secondary Normal School, as an auditor, following classes in educational psychology, primary education curriculum and teaching methods and educational administration. He managed to support himself by teaching evening classes and by writing. During his years of secondary school study he had written more than ten short stories, some of which were published.

From 1937 to 1939, Pan threw himself into teaching in a rural primary school. These were the first years of the Sino-Japanese War, which caused great deprivation and disruption to people's lives. Pan loved teaching, yet found himself more and more drawn into efforts to resist the Japanese, and his particular contribution was in helping with efforts to mobilize the population to resist Japan. He joined an association in Shantou organized by the Communist Party underground to distribute various kinds of information and stimulate resistance activities. When the Japanese attacked Shantou directly in June of 1939, Pan had to give up teaching and for some months he became absorbed full-time in various kinds of resistance activities.

In 1940, Pan decided to leave his home town for a number of reasons. One was that he felt the need for further education, if he was to meet the standards he set for himself as a teacher. By this time he was 19 years old, and the war-time conditions were worsening daily. He made the difficult trek through the mountains to Changting, where Xiamen University had moved in late 1937, spending a week on the way. He took the university's entry examinations, but failed to meet the necessary standards in foreign languages and mathematics, although his Chinese was excellent. He simply had not had time to prepare well. Greatly discouraged, he looked for other opportunities and was able to get into a normal school for training primary teachers, where he studied for a year. When he applied to the faculty of education at Xiamen University again the following year, he was finally accepted.

---

[25] See Chapter Two, p.60.

*Pan Maoyuan on his
graduation from Xiamen
University in 1945*

Pan found his years of study at Xiamen University from 1941 to 1945 enormously stimulating. Many of the professors were American-returned scholars and the chair of the department, Professor Li Peiyou, had translated a number of John Dewey's works into Chinese. Another influential professor on the faculty was Chen Jingpan, who had done his PhD at the University of Toronto in the 1930s, with a doctoral thesis on the significance of Confucius' life and writings as a teacher.[26]

Pan became a great admirer of Dewey's writings through these years of study. He also developed a special appreciation for the work of Tao Xingzhi, whose experimental efforts to adapt Dewey's ideas to the Chinese context had a nationwide influence. While Dewey had only visited Fujian briefly in 1921,[27] and Tao's work was mainly in the Nanjing and Shanghai area, Tao's ideas were particularly appreciated in Fujian.[28]

While a student at Xiamen University, Pan taught part-time in order to support himself, first in a primary school and later in a secondary school. During his fourth year of study at the university, he worked as head of the teaching affairs section of the local country middle school, and thus was in a position to try out many of the theories he was learning. On graduating in 1945, he taught briefly in primary schools in Jiangxi province. Then in 1946, he was asked by the president of Xiamen University and the head of the education department to become principal of the experimental primary school attached to the university, and a

---

[26] The thesis was successful defended in 1940 and finally published as a book fifty years later: Chen Jingpan, *Confucius as a Teacher – Philosophy of Confucius with Special Reference to Its Educational Implications* (Beijing: Foreign Languages Press, 1990). Like Pan, Chen was a Fujian native, although he spent the longest period of his career at Beijing Normal University.

[27] Barry Keenan, *The Dewey Experiment in China* (Cambridge, Mass.: Council on East Asian Studies, Harvard University, 1977), p.232.

[28] Liu Haifeng and Zhuang Minshui, *Fujian jiaoyu shi*, pp.422-438.

teaching assistant in the department. By this time the university had moved backed to its original campus in the city of Xiamen.

Pan noted how the books and ideas of Tao Xingzhi were particularly helpful to him in running the school. He regretted that he had never had the opportunity to meet Tao in person. It is interesting to note that Li Bingde also felt Tao's experimental work and the educational philosophy developed from it was most suited to the Chinese environment.[29]

New Directions and a New Career under Socialism

For Pan Maoyuan, the success of the 1949 Revolution opened up new vistas and new possibilities for his life and work as an educator. In the first year or two after 1949, he continued his work as a lecturer in the department of education. Then he was given the opportunity for further studies as a graduate student in education. In the autumn of 1951 he went to Beijing for studies in education at People's University, the year after Li Bingde had studied there. There was a large group of people studying education. Some were graduate students, like himself. Others were older professors who were expected to familarize themselves with Marxist-Leninist theories of education through this program. Yet others were cadres being prepared for leadership positions. Pan noted that he had the opportunity of getting to know quite a few well-known professors of education who were his fellows students at that time, including the psychologist Zhang Zhiguang, the philosopher Huang Ji, and education specialists Wang Cesan and Wang Tianyi, all of whom taught at Beijing Normal University thereafter. Early in 1952, the program was moved from People's University to Beijing Normal University, following the new patterns established in the reorganization of colleges and departments.

Pan has vivid memories of his studies over that year, with four Russian professors teaching courses in Marxism-Leninism, and various dimensions of educational theory from a Soviet perspective. He still remembers the names of the four professors, but can only recollect a few words of Russian, as his language studies were limited. The teaching was done with the assistance of interpreters. Pan was favorably impressed by what he learned, feeling that the method used to organize the curriculum

---

[29] Chapter Three, p.76.

and the teaching plans laid out for each subject were extremely rigorous and led to effective control over the teaching and learning process.

After a year in Beijing, Pan was called back to Xiamen in the summer of 1952 by Guang Yanen, the president of Xiamen University, who asked him to help with the reform of the curriculum and teaching across the university. He was appointed head of a section for teaching and learning reforms in the office of the provost, and given the task of facilitating the writing of new teaching plans for each of the university's specializations. It was a huge task, but it enabled him to think through Soviet educational ideas, and he found them both reasonable and applicable to the Chinese context. In the past he had greatly admired Deweyan educational philosophy and other aspects of American educational thought, for their liveliness and flexibility. Yet these American ideas had not been easy to implement within the rigid and controlled patterns of educational administration of the Nationalist period. By contrast, he felt Soviet educational ideas could enable students to acquire systematic knowledge and gain a solid foundation in their field. This was especially the case in fields such as engineering and natural sciences, which were crucial to the task of socialist construction.

Pan felt Soviet patterns of higher education were rooted in continental Europe, particularly France, and were quite distinctive from Anglo-American patterns. These patterns resonated with China's own knowledge traditions, which emphasized the importance of a strong foundation and a centralized and systematic approach to knowledge. Pan noted that Cai Yuanpei, the great chancellor of Peking University who was the most respected university leader of the Nationalist period, had combined elements of German, French and Chinese ideas in his thinking on higher education. He had embraced a German approach to scholarship, particularly the integration of research and teaching, based on his years at the Universities of Berlin and Leipzig.

In terms of the higher education system, Cai had tried to emulate French patterns, because of their rational administrative structure and their even geographical distribution throughout the country. In terms of a teaching philosophy, Cai drew deeply on his knowledge of traditional Chinese approaches to self-study, particularly those of the *shuyuan,* where students were expected to manage their own learning process. Cai had promoted the notion of separating comprehensive universities dedicated to theoretical fields of knowledge and specialist professional and technological institutions, tasked with the training of high level manpower for all sectors of the economy. Pan felt that the reforms of the early 1950s, which created a large number of specialized institutions while maintaining a smaller number of comprehensive universities, were well-suited to the Chinese context of the time, and served China's development needs well.[30]

Pan did have some reservations, however, about the fact that excellent comprehensive universities of the Nationalist period had been required to reduce the breadth of their programs to fit the Soviet model of a comprehensive university. This could have been avoided, he felt. He also had some comments to make on the regional distribution of higher education that took place with the reorganization of colleges and departments. With reference to his own field of education, he noted that the geographical distribution of key centers had been based more on political considerations than educational ones, and this had resulted in some anomalies. In the case of the Central South Region, there had been real strength in the educational department of Zhongshan University in the southern city of Guangzhou, which was combined with other education departments to form the South China Normal College in 1953. However, given its rather lowly status of a provincial institution, with limits on its funding and faculty development, the field of education was not as well-developed as it should have been.

Overall, however, Pan felt the reorganization of colleges and departments under Soviet influence was beneficial, leading to the training of professionals who contributed greatly to China's economic development in the 1950s. At the Eighth Party Congress of 1956, Zhou Enlai had stressed the importance of respecting intellectuals.[31] If only this policy had been followed, Pan believed that China would have been able

---

[30] These comments about Cai Yuanpei were made during my interview with Professor Pan in 1997. Pan published a lengthy scholarly article analyzing Cai's educational philosophy and contribution to higher education thought in the Xiamen University social science journal *Xiamen daxue xuebao (she)*, No. 4, 1955. A revised version was published in *Liaoning Gaodeng jiaoyu yanjiu* [Liaoning Higher Education Research], No. 1, 1982, and republished in *Pan Maoyuan lun gaodeng jiaoyu* [Pan Maoyuan's Higher Education Writings] (Fuzhou: Fujian jiaoyu chubanshe, 2000), pp.521-560.

[31] Zhou Enlai, "On the Question of Intellectuals," *New China News Agency*, January 29, 1956, in Robert Bowie and John Fairbank (eds.) *Communist China 1955-1959: Policy Documents with Analysis* (Cambridge, Mass: Harvard University Press, 1962), pp.128-144.

to keep up with the kinds of economic development going on in Japan and other parts of East Asia. Instead, twenty years were lost as a result of political movements, such as the Anti-Rightist Movement of 1957, the Great Leap Forward of 1958 and the Cultural Revolution of 1966.

Such weaknesses as there were in the Soviet higher education model could have been addressed in a balanced and reasonable way, and did not call for the extreme rhetoric that characterized these revolutionary movements, he felt. One problem was an inadequate emphasis on understanding and fostering students' ability in different areas. Students were expected to meet the high academic standards set out in their programs through hard work and concentrated study, but not much attention was given to research on the learning process. Another problem was an over-reliance on translated materials from the Soviet Union, not all of which were relevant to the Chinese context. These were genuine concerns that could have been dealt with through a gradual process of reform.

For Pan himself, 1954 was an important year. He knew Xiamen University's department of education was slated to move up the coast to Fuzhou, the provincial capital, and become integrated into the newly established Fuzhou Normal University. He was keen to go along, and excited about taking the history of education as his main area of research interest. However, the president had decided that Xiamen University could not do without him. He was asked to stay in his position in the provost's office, and continue to guide the teaching and learning process at Xiamen University. His acceptance of this decision was to set the stage for the emergence of a new discipline, and change the direction of his life and work.

In all of his years of educational study, school teaching and school leadership, little of what he had learned was relevant to the field of higher education. A completely different approach to educational theory was needed for dealing with university-level students, and forms of curricular development, teaching and learning in tertiary institutions. Higher education was a field of research that seemed to have been totally neglected by educational theorists; as far as he could see this was not only the case in China, but also in the Soviet Union and Western countries at the time. He had been struck by reading a speech given by a Czech professor at a conference on educational science, which noted that educational theory tended to focus only on problems related to schools, and had little relevance for higher professional institutions. This stimulated him to write an article entitled "The important status of teaching and learning problems in higher professional education."

This article was published in Xiamen University's *Scholarly Forum* (Xueshu Luntan) in 1956. In the following year, he organized several colleagues to work with him in producing an edited book entitled *Teaching Notes for Higher Education as a Field of Study* (Gaodengxuexiao jiaoyuxue jiangyi). This was widely distributed among comprehensive and normal universities in China in the years that followed, as a resource for those responsible for curricular reform and the development of teaching plans.[32] Although never formally published, it was China's very first scholarly book in the field of higher education.

Pan was energized to develop this as a new field of study, and excited about its importance for providing a scholarly basis for higher education planning, curriculum development and teaching methods. However, 1957 was the beginning of a series of political movements, which made it nearly impossible for him to build up the kinds of research and development which he had hoped for. The Anti-Rightist Movement of 1957 did not affect him personally, given his own family background, but he was distressed to see some older professors at Xiamen University, who had made significant scholarly contributions, labeled as rightists and cut off from their academic work.

What followed in 1958, with the launching of the Great Leap Forward, was equally disturbing to Pan. He could see the need for greater emphasis on Chinese content in teaching material, given the number of textbooks that had been translated from Soviet sources. He also felt the decision to establish colleges of traditional Chinese medicine was helpful in balancing the development of the field of medicine. Since Chinese traditional medicine looked at the whole body as a system, and promoted a different approach to health than that of Western medicine, it was a valuable heritage that should not be lost. In most other ways, however, Pan felt that the educational reforms of 1958 were misguided.

He was closely involved in all the curricular changes, since he was working in the provost's office. He felt many of the ideas were not well thought through, but were forms of political rhetoric with little genuine educational understanding. For students to write the teaching outlines

---

[32] Zhang Xiangyun, "Pan Maoyuan," in Xin Fuliang (Ed.) *Dangdai Zhongguo ogaodeng jiaoyu jia* [Contemporary Chinese Higher Education Specialists] (Shanghai: Shanghai Jiaotong daxue chubanshe, 1995), p.199.

and textbooks was clearly beyond their capacity, since they did not have an adequate knowledge in their disciplines for such a task. Great emphasis was placed on giving students the opportunity for practical involvement in production activities, but this was largely to expose them to labor for political reasons, and had little pedagogical value. Generally, the emphasis on political rhetoric and involvement in labor was so disruptive that in one year he remembers students having only 70 days to listen to academic lectures. The idea of open door learning (*kaimen banxue*), one of the slogans of the time, was appealing. But it could not replace the systematic teaching of scientific knowledge necessary to educate professionals in all the areas China needed, Pan felt.

Given his burgeoning interest in higher education as a field of study, Pan also paid close attention to the wider changes going on in China's higher education system. There was a huge expansion in the provision of learning opportunities with a large number of so-called "red and expert colleges" opening up learning opportunities to young people from disadvantaged backgrounds. However they did not have the resources to do serious higher education work and most closed down within a few years. Several new Communist labor universities were opened, including a famous one in Jiangxi, but they did not have qualified teachers, and could not survive. The new institutions that did survive, such as Fuzhou University, were recognized as crucial to the province's economic development needs, and given adequate support from provincial authorities. It offered the only programs in engineering available in the province,

After the retrenchment of 1961, when the more academic patterns of the early 1950s were restored, and greater emphasis was put on academic quality, Pan again hoped for the opportunity to develop higher education as a field of study. Once again, however, this was to be interrupted by a political movement, the Cultural Revolution, which broke out in 1966. As early as 1964, Pan was asked to move to Beijing and work in the Central Institute for Educational Research under the Ministry of Education on a project in educational theory. Basically the group was asked to organize a series of essays that would criticize the Soviet educational model as revisionist, and demonstrate its inappropriateness for China. Other members of this group were Liu Fonian from East China Normal University, Li Fang from Shenyang Normal College, and other well known educational specialists. They had little heart for the work they were asked to do, and were thankful when the group was dissolved in 1965.

Pan was in Beijing when the Cultural Revolution broke out in May of 1966, and he commented that he was fortunate not to be a target of criticism, since he was from outside of Beijing. Before long, however, he was called to return to Xiamen University by the Rebel Group of Red Guards that had taken charge of the Xiada campus. By the time he got there from Beijing, they were too busy with other things to give much attention to him, and he was grateful to have some time to spend with his family. Before long, the Xiada revolutionary group went traveling to different parts of China, and he was simply asked to write a report on what he was thinking and doing each day, and to re-educate himself through labor.

How did Pan Maoyuan feel during this difficult period? He replied that he was deeply upset and unable to understand the movement. It seemed to be a complete reversal of all that had been achieved in the hard work of the early fifties. If the Soviet model was to be criticized, there should be a discussion of both positive and negative elements in its patterns, rather than an all-out rejection of them. The notion of attacking the "four olds" (old ideas, old customs, old culture and old habits), one of the slogans of the Cultural Revolution, was hard to comprehend. After all, Mao himself had read many classical texts, and been a great admirer of certain traditional ideas. Overall, Pan felt, the Great Leap Forward and the Cultural Revolution had been accompanied by genuine emotional fervor in their initial stages, with young people believing in the need for reform. However, they had soon been taken over by a small number of people seeking power. The educational reforms that were initiated by Deng Xiaoping in 1978 were of an entirely different character.

Establishing a New Discipline

When Deng Xiaoping came to power in 1977, Pan Maoyuan was ready for a new phase of his career. He had held positions of administrative leadership in the past, including a period of time as provost of Xiamen University, but now his focus was on the establishment of higher education as a new discipline, first in his own university, and then nationwide. We have seen how he had made a beginning in the mid-1950s, with the publication of his 1956 article on the important status of teaching and learning questions in higher education. The turbulent years of political movements which followed gave him an even deeper sense of the importance of theoretical research into higher education as a field of knowledge, which could provide a deep-level understanding of its relation to social, economic, political and cultural development. One of the most serious problems of higher education development, from the 1950s up to the late seventies, was the lack of any systematic theoretical research, which could provide a sound basis for higher education policy. With the new freedoms of the Deng era, and the nationwide embrace of Deng's famous call for education to "face modernization, the world and the future," Pan finally found the space and time to pursue his dream.

Pan began at Xiamen University, where he established a higher education research room in 1978, which became a higher education research center a few years later. In 1983, higher education became recognized by the Ministry of Education as a sub-discipline of education, which qualified for the establishment of masters and doctoral programs. Pan's centre at Xiamen University was the first to recruit students at both masters and doctoral level in higher education, and by the time the 20th anniversary of the centre was celebrated in 1998, 20 doctoral students had already graduated and over 80 masters students.[33] They are now working in universities all over China, and contributing to the further development of the field. Major research programs on many aspects of higher education have been undertaken by the centre, and at least ten conferences at the national and international level have been held.

While several other universities have also developed strong graduate programs in higher education, including HUST, Peking University, and the East China Normal University in Shanghai, Xiamen University was recognized in September of 2000 as the one and only national center for research in the field to be named a key base for research and gain substantial funding for its ongoing development. This was part of a Chinese government program across the humanities and social sciences to enable a certain number of centers to achieve world-class standards, and be able to participate actively in international

---

[33] Liu Haifeng, *Xiamen daxue gaodeng jiaoyu kexue yanjiusuo jiansuo ershi zhounian gongzuo baogao* [A work report on the 20th Anniversary of the establishment of Xiamen University's Research Institute in Higher Education Science] in *Jiansuo ershi zhounian jinian huodong zhuanji* [A Festschrift for the 20th Anniversary of the Institute's Establishment], October, 1998, p.33-35.

research networks.[34] The fact that Xiamen University gained this recognition, in spite of its relative disadvantage in terms of geographical location, was remarkable. It was a highly significant affirmation of Pan Maoyuan's lifelong leadership in establishing higher education as a discipline, showing the difference one dedicated educator could make, in spite of the constraints of the Chinese political and social context.

Pan Maoyuan speaking on the occasion of his 80ᵗʰ birthday and the 65ᵗʰ anniversary of his first year as a teacher in 1935.

After 1978 Pan focused his energies on intensive academic work, teaching and research at Xiamen University. The glimpse we have seen into his Saturday evening salon shows how deeply personal have been his relationships with students. Yet, he also had a vision for the discipline on a national level, and for the contribution which Chinese higher education as a discipline might make to the world of international scholarship. In 1979 he worked with a group of representatives from seven other universities and the Shanghai Higher Education Bureau to hold the first ever national meeting on higher education research. In 1981, he organized a meeting to bring together a group of researchers on different aspects of higher education, and edited the first book in China on higher education as a discipline, *Gaodeng jiaoyu xue*, which was

---

[34] Yang Rui, and King Hau Au Yeung, "China's Plan to Promote Research in the Humanities and Social Sciences," *International Higher Education*, No. 27, Spring, 2002.

published in 1984.[35] This made it available as a course reader for the first formal programs in higher education, after the establishment of the discipline by the Ministry of Education in 1983. Over the subsequent years Pan has continued as a visionary leader in the field, stimulating new ideas and new approaches to research, encouraging others to do research, write and publish, as well as publishing a large number of articles and books in the field himself.

At the heart of his work has been a desire to ensure that this newly recognized discipline would have a solid theoretical basis, clear conceptual definitions and well-established research methodologies. When the Chinese Higher Education Society was established in 1983, he felt it was oriented more towards broad developments in the field, rather than toward higher education as a discipline. Thus in 1992 he organized an academic conference at Xiamen University to put forward the view that higher education should be regarded as a discipline needing research. At a follow-up meeting the next year in Shanghai, a new organization called the Society for Research into Higher Education as a Discipline was established under the umbrella of the Chinese Higher Education Society, and regular meetings have been held since then. In an article reflecting the progress made in its first three meetings, Pan laid out the objectives of this new society, the scope of its work, and the main theoretical debates that it should encourage.

The main objective was to establish a systematic theoretical basis for understanding Chinese socialist higher education, and the scope of this work was organized around five thematic areas: theory, history, contemporary practice in higher education, future developments, and research methods.[36] Pan's overview of some of the theoretical debates and controversies that made these meetings lively and full of interest gives insight into core concerns of the field in China. One of the key theoretical questions is around the function of higher education, and its

---

[35] Pan Maoyuan, "Gaodeng jiaoyu yanjiu zai Zhongguo fazhan de guiji" [The trajectory of higher education research development in China] in Pan Maoyuan, *Pan Maoyuan lun gaodeng jiaoyu* [Pan Maoyuan's theoretical discourses in higher education] Fuzhou: Fujian jiaoyu chubanshe, 2000), p.96.

[36] Pan Maoyuan, "Gaodeng jiaoyuxue xueke jianshe de huigu yu qianzhan" [A Retrospective and Prospective View of the establishment of higher education as a discipline] in Pan Maoyuan, *Pan Maoyuan lun gaodeng jiaoyu* [Pan Maoyuan's theoretical discourses in higher education] Fuzhou: Fujian jiaoyu chubanshe, 2000), p.86.

relation to society, the economy and the political system. Related to this are the aims of higher education. Chinese researchers have agreed on three aims, which are probably universally accepted – nurturing talent through teaching, advancing knowledge through research, and service to society. The third, however, has come under vigorous scrutiny in recent years, due to the practice in many Chinese universities of "creating an income" [*chuangshou*] through various forms of consulting and direct relationships with economic enterprises. Some believe these activities have drawn universities too far from core scholarly pursuits and concerns.

Thus a new formulation has been developed, suggesting six aims of higher education: teaching, preserving knowledge, disseminating knowledge, advancing knowledge, criticizing society and exercising supervision over society.[37] This is an interesting attempt to highlight the special responsibility of higher education to have critical and pro-active forms of interaction with economic, social and political forces, rather than being purely responsive to those forces.

Another lively area of debate, which Pan outlines in a second article on the development of the discipline, relates to the relative importance of the individual and society in the functioning of higher education. One group of scholars has recently been putting great emphasis on the development of the self (*ziwo*), and the importance of higher education enabling individuals to realize their full potential and to experience a satisfying sense of subjective (*zhuti*) participation in that process. Opposite to this approach is the more traditional socialist approach, which emphasizes education as a social function, shaping people in ways that will ensure that they contribute to society's progress as the overarching principle.[38] It is interesting to see an open recognition of the importance of individual development and the pursuit of individual fulfillment. This may take us back to the discussion in chapter one of neo-Confucian education as "learning for the sake of the self," and the importance within Confucian philosophy of the development of a sense of individual worth. In spite of the restrictions on individual freedom of choice in the macro-planning patterns of the early1950s, and the immense suffering caused by the political movements of the fifties and sixties, this value of the Chinese educational tradition has remained resilient.

---

[37] *Ibid.* p.87.
[38] Pan Maoyuan, "Gaodeng jiaoyu yanjiu zai Zhongguo fazhan de guiji" p.101.

In his comprehensive and broad-brushed approach to the development of higher education as a discipline, Pan sees two broad sets of theoretical challenges. The first is to define the relationship between higher education and the political, social, economic and cultural systems, and to find a systematic way of exploring the inter-relation between these systems and higher education. The second is to develop a coherent understanding of the inter-relationships within higher education itself, among such differing aspects as scholarship and professionalism, general education and specialist professional formation, teaching and research.

One of the reasons Pan has found this process of developing the discipline both demanding and exciting is the pioneering aspect of the work. While educational theories relating to the school system and the learning process have had a history of over one hundred years, higher education is a relatively new discipline, not only in China but also in the rest of the world. Theory building for basic education and school education in China was strongly influenced by Western ideas – European, American and Soviet – as Pan had been aware from the earliest years of his educational studies. The same has not been the case, however, for higher education as a discipline. In looking back over the years of building the discipline in China, Pan has a strong sense of the unique contributions which China can make, and is proud of the fact that the ideas and perspectives developed in China are not derivative, but firmly rooted in China's own intellectual, social and cultural soil. Only in recent years, have theories of higher education developed elsewhere been introduced.

In challenging his colleagues to take seriously the responsibility to contribute to higher education scholarship in the global community, Pan lays out four reasons why Chinese scholars have an important role to play in developing the field. First, China has an ancient scholarly culture, which has had a considerable historical influence in Asia. Secondly, China now has one of the largest higher education systems in the world, approaching the size of that of the United States and larger than that of Russia. Not only is it a very large system, but one that has experienced rapid and dramatic changes in recent years with the successful development of a socialist market economy, and many interesting problems and challenges arising in the process. Thirdly, China has a huge group of higher education researchers, probably more scholars engaged in studies in the field than any other country. Fourthly, Chinese higher education has developed as a field through the initiatives and energy of individual scholars and local institutions, so that its infra-structure is flexible and self-reliant. This marks it out from most other disciplines in the Chinese context, which have been established by administrative decision from above. Finally, Chinese higher education theories might be described as "grounded theories" since they have arisen from research into practical problems emerging in the dramatic change process of recent years, as scholars have sought to understand the regularities or sociological laws that become evident through this research.[39]

Pan accords considerable importance to China's cultural traditions. One of his articles goes into some depth on its special characteristics and its contribution to China's modernization process. Pan notes that modernization cannot be equated with either industrialization or Westernization, but is a process that affects all aspects of social deve-lopment and that must be shaped by the different cultural contexts in which it takes place. Given that the transmission and transformation of the cultural heritage are important functions of higher education, it is intimately involved in shaping the distinctive form which modernization takes in different societies. Pan rejects the notion that Western society has already entered a postmodern phase, leaving a set of standards as to what constitutes a fully modern society. Rather, he suggests, the concept of modernization itself cannot be fully understood until unique aspects of China's modernization trajectory are taken into account in the sociological literature. He would apply the same argument to other non-Western societies going through the modernization process.[40]

Pan's very definition of modernization puts cultural values in the centre. He suggests it should be seen as a value which all humanity seeks in common. Its ultimate purpose is to enable human beings to realize their full humanity, at the level of the individual, the group and society as a whole. This common pursuit should lead to the emergence of a common cultural heritage for all of human kind, which draws upon the

---

[39] *Ibid.* pp.107-110.

[40] Pan Maoyuan and Zhang Yingqiang, "Chuantong wenhua yu Zhongguo gaodeng jiaoyu xiandaihua" [Traditional culture and the modernization of Chinese higher education] in Pan Maoyuan *Pan Maoyuan lun gaodeng jiaoyu* [Pan Maoyuan's theoretical discourses in higher education] (Fuzhou: Fujian jiaoyu chubanshe, 2000), pp.229-241.

diverse heritages of different civilizations.[41] Many positive aspects of China's educational traditions, which have contributed to China's rapid development, are an important part of this shared cultural heritage. These ideas bring us close to the views expressed in the United Nations' commitment to a dialogue among civilizations, as noted in chapter one:

"a focus on human cultural, spiritual dimensions and on the inter-dependence of mankind and its rich diversity."[42]

Pan Maoyuan visiting a cultural site in China

Conclusion: The Integration of Several Heritages

When asked what had been the most important influences shaping his educational career, Pan replied jokingly that he had benefited greatly from all three of the ideologies criticized during the Cultural Revolution: feudalism (*feng*), capitalism (*zi*) and Soviet revisionism (*xiu*). From his early studies in Chinese classical literature, he had gained a sound moral foundation for his life. His lifelong experience in education gave him the sense that Confucianism was indeed a philosophy that could adapt to every age or time period. From all he had learned of American educational thought in his university studies, particularly the theories of John Dewey, he had gained many useful ideas for school improvement, for lively methods of teaching and learning and for curricular development. From his extensive experience of Soviet educational theories and patterns in the 1950s, he had come to appreciate the value of unified academic standards across the country, of well-structured teaching materials, and of thoroughness in the preparation of teaching work. In reflecting on the two external heritages which had influenced him most, he felt Soviet teaching materials and approaches to education, which were rooted in European rationalism, had been historically more suited to the Chinese context than American ones, due to China's tradition of

---

[41] *Ibid*. p.231.
[42] Chapter One, p.2.

centralized patterns of knowledge, and to the realities of its development needs.

When asked his views on the future of higher education in China, Pan commented that the greatest challenge was for reforms in teaching and learning that genuinely took into account students' diverse abilities, and stimulated the fullest development of their potential. This in turn highlighted the need for an excellent teaching force in higher education. Overall, Pan was pleased at the progress that had been made in graduate education over the past fifteen years, and the quality of the younger university teachers coming into the system, but he emphasized the importance of their being given adequate support. He felt higher education reform should focus more on teaching and research quality than on changes in the management structure, since these are linked to wider issues of political reform.

For China's system of higher education, Pan felt that it would be likely to follow world trends of development more and more in future. There will be an emphasis on breadth of knowledge and adaptability, and on the overall intellectual and moral quality of graduates. Lifelong learning will be a rising trend, since people in China will realize the need to constantly upgrade their own knowledge, in order to keep abreast of rapid changes in society. As China moved rapidly towards mass higher education Pan believes that private higher institutions will play an increasingly important role, if the rising social demand is to be met.

In the year 2000, Pan Maoyuan celebrated his eightieth birthday, and his colleagues and students at Xiamen University organized a special series of celebratory activities. One of them was the publication of a major collection of his most important theoretical contributions to the discipline of higher education.[43] This was by no means a retirement party, however, as Pan continues active as a scholar, and teacher. In 2002, he published a new volume, entitled *Multi-disciplinary Perspectives on Higher Education Research* [Duoxueke shejiao de gaodeng jiaoyu yanjiu]. It attempts new theoretical methods to advance higher education as a discipline.

What has enabled this modest individual, who came from the most impoverished of family backgrounds, to be so passionate about contributing to knowledge, and so effective in developing a new discipline

---

[43] Pan Maoyuan, *Pan Maoyuan lun gaodeng jiaoyu* [Pan Maoyuan's theoretical discourses in higher education] (Fuzhou: Fujian jiaoyu chubanshe, 2000), 727pp.

over a period of nearly fifty years? Professor Pan has probably given us the key to answering this question in the comments he made on his early exposure to a classical Chinese education. He may never have mastered a foreign language, or gained high level qualifications in mathematics or the natural sciences, but he learned, first of all, "how to be a good person" (*zuoren*) in his early education. Secondly, he learned how to express himself articulately in the Chinese language, turning his love of literary expression into a critical asset for educational work. Thirdly, he learned how to integrate useful knowledge from diverse sources into the solid intellectual and cultural framework he had developed in his schooling and university years.

Chapter Six

Xie Xide –
An Outstanding Scientist and Educator

Xie Xide was born in Quanzhou, Fujian province, in 1921, into a family that prized education. Although she spent much of her youth in Beijing, and her career as a scientist and university leader in Shanghai, she did her undergraduate studies at Xiamen University, and thus was a fellow student of Pan Maoyuan, whose story has been told in chapter five. The daughter of a physicist, Xie Xide chose physics as her main subject in university, and pursued a distinguished career as a scientist, making important contributions to the field of solid-state physics in China. She was also an outstanding educational leader, the first woman president of a major comprehensive university in socialist China, and a key figure in the development of China's educational relations with the international community.

Two universities provide the main context for Xie Xide's life. Xiamen University, where she did her undergraduate studies, has already been profiled in chapter five, while Fudan University in Shanghai was her academic home from 1952 until her death in February of 2000. She began working there as a lecturer in 1952, and went through the turbulent years of educational and cultural revolution there, finally being appointed vice-president in 1978, the year of China's opening up to the outside world under Deng Xiaoping's policies. From 1983 to 1988 she served as president. She also founded and led Fudan's center for American studies, playing a nationally prominent role in Sino-American relations. Among the photographs in the book of her selected works, published as a memorial in 2001, are pictures with US President Ronald Regan, when he visited Fudan University in 1984, and with President Bill

Clinton and his wife Hilary, on their visit to Shanghai in June of 1998.[1]

My relationship with Xie Xide goes back to February of 1980, when I moved to Shanghai from London to take up a position as foreign expert in Fudan University's department of foreign languages and literatures. Xie Xide was vice-president, responsible for the university's international affairs at that time She hosted a welcome banquet for me and another newly arrived foreign expert, at the Jin Jiang Hotel where we were given accommodation. Towards the end of my two-year teaching assignment, during the Chinese New Year holiday of February, 1982, I stayed in Shanghai over the festive period, and attended some of the university's celebrations. Most of the other foreign experts had taken the opportunity for travel to different parts of the country. When Xie Xide learned I would be in town, she invited me for dinner at her home, and this was the one occasion where I met her husband, also a renowned scientist. This personal gesture of warmth and hospitality in the life of a busy scientist and university vice-president is something I have never forgotten.

In subsequent years, I had a number of opportunities to meet Xie Xide again, through her frequent trips to England and North America for international meetings, to represent Fudan University, and in her leadership work on World Bank projects. In the autumn of 1991, as we were planning the conference on "Knowledge Across Cultures" which has been described in some detail in chapter three,[2] we wanted to have participation from some outstanding scientists and historians, as well as scholars of education, and we invited Xie Xide to be one of the keynote speakers. She agreed to come many months ahead, but after all detailed arrangements had been made she let us know there was a time conflict. The 14th Congress of the Chinese Communist Party would be meeting in Beijing close to the same time, and as a member of the Central Committee and a representative from Shanghai she had to be there.

---

[1] Xie Xide, *Xie Xide Wenxuan* [Selected Works of Xie Xide] (Shanghai: Shanghai Scientific and Technical Publishers, 1988) p.10.
[2] Chapter Three, p.87.

In the end, she managed to nego-
tiate an arrangement to miss several
preparatory sessions in order to keep her
promise to give our keynote lecture.
Then she flew from Toronto to Beijing
immediately after her lecture, and just in
time to play her role in the Congress
itself. We were honored and touched by
the special effort she made to keep her
commitment to our conference in these
circumstances. It somehow typified the
consideration and dedication she brought
to a life of commitment to science, international cooperation and service to her
beloved China. Two years later in June of
1994 she came to Canada again to receive
an honorary doctorate from McMaster
University in Hamilton, where her outstanding achievements as a leading
scientific figure were recognized. It gave
me the greatest pleasure to celebrate that
event with her.

*Xie Xide with Ruth Hayhoe
and Julia Pan at the
Knowledge Across Cultures
Conference in Toronto,
October, 1992.*

The Story of Fudan University

In 1985, Fudan University celebrated its 80th anniversary. Xie Xiede had
become president just two years earlier and gave a speech at the
anniversary celebration. She emphasized its history as a patriotic and
revolutionary institution, and mentioned some of the outstanding
Chinese literary figures who had been associated with it in the pre-1949
period, such as the literary critic Chen Wangdao, the dramatist, Hong
Shen and others. Her main focus was, of course, on its contributions to
science and to the nation in the period after 1949.[3]

It is difficult for me to provide a sketch of Fudan's history that is
suitably brief, as was done for the other university histories in earlier

---

[3] Xie Xide, "Zai Fudan daxue jianxiao bashi zhounian qingzhu dahui shang de
jianghua" [Speech at the meeting to celebrate Fudan University's 80th anniversary]
in *Xie Xide Wenxuan*, pp.87-90.

chapters, since Fudan University's history was a focal point of my doctoral studies. A great deal of time was spent looking at archival materials about its early years in the library during my two years teaching there from 1980 to 1982. My interest in Fudan's history had been peaked when I was beginning a doctoral thesis on the development of modern Chinese universities over the 20th century, and the different ways in which European, American and Soviet patterns of scholarship had interacted with Chinese values in their development.

Fudan was a fascinating example of an institution founded as a result of a clash of scholarly values between Ma Xiangbo, an outstanding Chinese Catholic scholar and leader, and French Jesuits, who were seeking to impose French patterns of administration and curricular organization on a newly established private and patriotic institution of higher learning. Zhendan University, or L'Aurore, had been founded by Ma Xiangbo in 1903, to fulfill his dream of a "new-style Chinese university that would keep pace with Western universities."[4] He had given a part of his family property in Shanghai to the Jesuits to make this possible, believing that their educational expertise was needed for the new institution. In the end, Zhendan went on to develop as a French Catholic University, while Ma and his students created a second Aurore in 1905, giving it the name Fudan, and seeking land and financial support from local government and patriotic gentry sources.

Ma's ideals for Fudan were an interesting combination of Chinese and European values. The curriculum was divided into four parts including language and literature, philosophy, mathematics and natural sciences. For language and literature, Ma wanted the students to have a thorough knowledge of Chinese classical literature, and to balance that with a knowledge of European languages, including Latin, such that they could integrate Western learning into a Chinese frame of reference. The focus was on basic disciplines of knowledge, and the guiding principles were to place a priority on science, to emphasize both Chinese and Western culture and to avoid religious disputes.[5]

The clash with the French Jesuits whom Ma had invited to assist him arose from three differences in emphasis. On curriculum, they felt Ma's categories were too broad, and wished to "impose order on the

---

[4] Ruth Hayhoe, "Towards the Forging of a Chinese University Ethos: Zhendan and Fudan 1903-1919," in *China Quarterly*, No. 94, (June, 1983), p.328.

[5] *Ibid.* p.329.

chaos" by adopting the curricular patterns used in Jesuit colleges in France. They also wished to see the French language given a predominant place. On student recruitment, they wished to recruit young students who could be easily molded, while Ma had accepted a number of older students, heavily involved in constitutional reform or revolutionary activities and often seeking support and protection as well as a higher education. On governance, the Jesuits wished to have a strong top-down administration, while Ma had encouraged student self-government, along the lines of China's *shuyuan* tradition.[6]

The new institution established in 1905, Fudan, was thus from the beginning a Chinese and patriotic institution, which had been born out of a determination on the part of its Chinese leaders to create a university which was modern yet not Western. After its establishment, Ma Xiangbo maintained an interest in Fudan, but effectively had little time to nurture it, due to other political responsibilities. Its day-to-day running was put in the hands of Li Denghui, who was recruited by Ma to be dean of Studies in 1905. Li was an overseas Chinese, born in Indonesia, and educated at the secondary level in an English medium school in Singapore, then at Yale University in the United States, where he had graduated in 1899. [7]

Between 1905 and 1911, Fudan was a public institution, with a location in Wusong provided by local officials and some public support. The famous translator, Yan Fu, was president for a couple of years, supporting Ma Xiangbo when he was away, and the teaching staff took their responsibilities very seriously. Over the years from 1905 to 1911, a total of 57 students graduated from Fudan.[8] It was considered a higher institution (*gaodeng xuetang*) between secondary school and university in the educational system of the time. The curriculum was broad, with a strong basis in Chinese language, literature and history, and the teaching of most Western subjects, including the sciences, geography and history in English or other foreign languages. This was to ensure the new knowledge was understood on its own terms, at a time when the development of a modern scientific terminology in Chinese was contested.

---

[6] *Ibid.* pp.331-333.

[7] Fudan daxue xiaoshi bianxiezu (ed.), *Fudan daxue zhi* 1905-1949 [Fudan University History] Vol. 1, (Shanghai: Fudan daxue chubanshe, 1985). See pp.247-259 for a short biography of Li Denghui.

[8] *Ibid.* p.60.

Most of all, there was a strong emphasis on nurturing students who could take active part in social and political reform. Thus public speaking was strongly emphasized, as well as lively debates over contemporary political, economic and social issues. [9] Fudan's institutional history contains many original documents of interest, including a short article by Ma Xiangbo, written in 1913, which describes how he organized a salon in his home every Sunday, where students were encouraged to practice public speaking and debating.[10]

In the Revolution of 1911, Fudan lost its campus, and lost its status as a public (*gongli*) institution. It had to make a new start in 1912 as a private higher school, with a board of governors chaired by the prominent legal scholar Wang Chonghui, and funds raised from various sources. Ma Xiangbo took up the role of president again for two years, and was able to raise some financial support, and get permission from the new political authorities in Nanjing to use the Memorial Garden of Li Hongzhang in Xu Jia Hui in suburban Shanghai, as a campus for the institution. In 1913 Li Denghui was appointed president by the Board of Governors, and he continued in this position up to 1936, making its development into a private university of some stature his life-work.

Between 1912 and 1916, it continued as a specialist higher institute conforming to government regulations for higher schools below the university level. Its charter, drafted in 1913, set the aims of the institution as "to research scholarship and train specialized personnel." [11] The detailed curriculum laid out in this document covered three years of secondary education and another three of university preparatory studies.[12] Subjects ranged from mathematics and sciences to languages, literature, rhetoric, anthropology, geography, philosophy etc. While Chinese and English were the main languages, a choice between German and French was also encouraged, and Latin was provided for in the last year of the preparatory course. There were electives in the final year of the university preparatory studies, to prepare for entry into specific fields, but it was otherwise a common curriculum. Li may well have been influenced by his years at Yale University in some aspects of this

---

[9] *Ibid.*
[10] *Ibid.* p.46.
[11] *Ibid.* p.93.
[12] *Ibid.* pp.93-97.

curriculum.[13]

Between 1912 and 1916, Fudan had educated about 15 students in the university preparatory studies, and about 150 at the secondary level. Li himself lectured in English, French, philosophy, ethics and psychology. Among the other early teachers at Fudan, were the economist Xue Xianzhou, a specialist in cooperative banking, who also taught German, the famous journalist, Shao Lizi, who taught Chinese, Li Songquan, who taught physics and chemistry and Zhu Baofeng, who taught mathematics.[14]

In 1917, Fudan changed its name to a university, and added a program in commerce to the two programs it had been developing in arts and sciences. Li was aware that it would need a new campus, and set off to raise funds in Southeast Asia, successfully raising enough money for the purchase of a spacious site in Jiang Wan, a northern suburb of Shanghai. Further fundraising undertaken by Li and Xue Xianzhou, in Southeast Asia and the US made it possible to build the first buildings in 1920, and the new campus was occupied in 1922.[15] Subsequent development of the campus depended on significant donations from various large companies and banks in Shanghai, whose leaders were involved in the university's management board. Many of the early buildings still grace Fudan's campus now, an interesting architectural blend of Chinese and Western influences. Once Fudan had gained the title of university, and a new campus, student numbers rose dramatically. By 1921 there were 432 university-level students, with these numbers growing to 790 in 1925, 1215 in 1930 and 1550 in 1935.[16]

Fudan's leadership of the May 4th Movement in Shanghai in 1919 was a defining moment in the development of this private university. In some ways, one can see in the leadership of Li Denghui some of the vision and remarkable ability that we have noted in Zhu Jiusi's leadership of HUST in the dark days just after the Cultural Revolution, [17] although the circumstances were very different. When the May 4th Movement broke out in 1919, Fudan was still in its campus in Xu Jia Hui.

---

[13] Ruth Hayhoe, "Sino-American Educational Interaction from the Microcosm of Fudan's Early Years," in Cheng Li (ed.), *Bridges Across the Pacific: Sino-American Educational Relations.* (Lanham, Maryland: Lexington Press, 2005), pp.28-30.

[14] *Fudan daxue zhi*, p.63.

[15] *Ibid*. p.107.

[16] *Ibid*. p.108.

[17] See Chapter Four, pp.132-137.

Shao Lizi, a well known journalist, who also taught Chinese at Fudan, received news of the movement from Beijing in the early morning of May 6th. Normally he went to the campus to teach in the afternoons, doing newspaper work in the morning, but on this day he rushed to the Fudan campus in the early morning. He rang the bell to arouse students, and held a meeting in the student canteen, one of the traditional buildings of the memorial complex.

Once students had learned the news, and held preliminary discussions, they fanned out throughout the city of Shanghai, spreading the news to students on other campuses, and organizing a Shanghai-wide student organization. It in turn animated the different dimensions of the movement – including liaison with national student organizations, cooperation with labor organizations in Shanghai and related work. Fudan student He Baoren was the first head of the Shanghai Student Association, and many other Fudan students assisted in the intense period of activism that followed the outbreak of the movement.[18]

There were many different responses to the May 4th Movement on the part of university authorities of the time. Cai Yuanpei was then chancellor of Peking University and in many ways the architect of the movement, due to the remarkable group of faculty and students he had attracted to Peking University. Many of them were in the forefront of the movement. Cai's view, however, was that students should be encouraged to enter into lively debates over political and social issues, but refrain from political activism. He used his own resignation as chancellor as a way of showing how important this principle was to him.[19]

Many government-supported universities and higher institutions used what means they could to suppress the movement, in some cases dismissing politically-active faculty members. Missionary colleges and universities also tended to do what they could to repress student activism, in some cases expelling student leaders. In this situation, Li Denghui saw a window of opportunity for Fudan University. He made it known that Fudan would consider accepting students expelled from other tertiary institutions due to their activism, and managed to recruit a considerable number of students with strong academic backgrounds. He

---

[18] Joseph Cheng, *The May Fourth Movement in Shanghai*, (London: E.J. Brill, 1971), pp.74ff.

[19] Cai Yuanpei, *Cai Yuanpei xuanji* [Selected Writings of Cai Yuanpei] (Beijing: Zhongguo shuju, 1959), p.98. See also Chapter Eight, p.235.

also actively sought out faculty members who had been dismissed from government institutions and invited them to come and teach at Fudan, where they would be given freedom to teach and research as they wished, and also to participate in activist causes. Li's education at Yale University, and exposure to an American academic ethos, gave him a rather different outlook than that of Cai Yuanpei, who had done higher studies in the Univeristy of Leipzig, and been deeply influenced by a German academic ethos.[20]

Two of the most famous literary figures who came to Fudan from just after the May 4th Movement were Liu Dabai and Chen Wangdao. Both had been dismissed from the government-managed Zhejiang Teachers College. Chen was a specialist in Chinese literature and rhetoric, also in journalism, and was famous as the translator of the Communist Manifesto into Chinese. Liu Dabai was a well-known literary figure, who was committed to progressive causes.

One of the best-known students who came to Fudan at this time was Zhang Yi. Originally a student at the secondary school attached to the highly respected St. John's University, an American missionary institution associated with the Episcopal Church, Zhang Yi had been planning for a career in medicine. However, he was expelled from St. John's secondary school as a result of his active participation in the May 4th Movement, without being given a graduation certificate. This meant it would be extremely difficult for him to find acceptance in any university program, let alone the medical faculty of St. John's University where he had hoped to study. In a moving interview with Zhang Yi in 1980, he told me how Li Denghui had accepted him as a student at Fudan, in spite of his lack of a secondary school graduation certificate. He noted that many other students in similar straits were welcomed by Li.[21] For his part, he decided on education as a more important focus for his life work than medicine, and a 1920 picture of the student executive in Fudan's journal shows Zhang as president.[22]

After graduation from Fudan in 1924, he pursued graduate studies in education at Washington State University in the United States and

---

[20] Ruth Hayhoe, *China's Universities 1895-1995: A Century of Cultural Conflict* (Hong Kong: Comparative Education Research Centre, The University of Hong Kong, 1999) pp.46-47.
[21] Interview with Zhang Yi, Shandong Normal University, March, 1982. The story is also told in Zhang Yi's autobiography, included in *Fudan daxue zhi*, pp.276-283.
[22] *The Fuhtan Banner*, Vol. II, 1920, p.x.

returned to teach in Fudan's education department, later becoming dean of education and ultimately president of Fudan in the 1940s. A patriot who put love of country before political affiliations, Zhang Yi told me how he was twice expelled, from St John's in 1919, due to his political activism, and from the Guomindang party in 1949, due to his decision to remain in China rather than moving Fudan University to Taiwan. His years after the 1949 Revolution were spent at Shandong Normal University, where he was a professor of education engaged in teaching and research up to his death in 1986.

Fudan gained national fame as a result of the May 4th movement, and its faculty and students continued to be active in political and social reform throughout the 1920s and 1930s. In 1928 it was registered with the newly established Nationalist government in Nanjing, as a private university having colleges of arts, sciences, commerce and law. Its college of arts had departments of Chinese literature, foreign literature, journalism, education, history and sociology. Its college of sciences had departments of biology, chemistry and civil engineering. Its college of commerce had departments of banking, accounting, foreign trade, and management. Its college of law had departments of law, politics, city government and economics. [23] The breadth of curricular offerings reflected the traditional strengths it had developed since the time of Ma Xiangbo, its openness to newly developing fields of knowledge such as journalism, banking and trade, and its responsiveness to the employment needs of the city of Shanghai at the time.

Fudan never had an academic reputation that could come close to that of famous national universities of the time such as Peking University, Tsinghua University, and Zhejiang University, nor the better missionary universities, such as St John's and Yenching. In fact it was described as a "wild chicken university" (*yeji daxue*) by some of the old professors of history and literature at Fudan whom I interviewed in the early 1980s. It nevertheless carved out an important place for itself in the turbulent conditions of the time. Well known for its activism, and openness to political debate and social causes, it was probably most respected for its patriotic spirit, the point which President Xie Xide chose to emphasize in her speech made on its 80th anniversary in 1985.

In 1936, the tension between political activists on the left, and the increasingly rightwing members of the ruling Nationalist party on

---

[23] *Fudan daxue zhi*, Appendix I, p.533.

campus reached a crisis point, and Li Denghui found himself forced to step down from the presidency. Unwilling to accept an honorary position in the Nationalist government and move to Nanjing, he remained in Shanghai and during the difficult years of the Sino-Japanese War he continued to lead a branch campus of Fudan there. In 1937-38, Fudan began its move inland, finally settling down in Beipei, a small town on the Jialing river south of the war-time capital of Chongqing. In 1941, after lengthy debates and in face of the opposition of retired president Li Denghui, Fudan became a national public university, a necessary measure for survival in the war-time years. In February of 1943, Zhang Yi was appointed president by the Nationalist government. [24]

During the war years, Fudan was able to attract even more well-known professors, and its curriculum was broadened to meet war-time needs, with new departments of historical geography, mathematics and statistics, also a college of agriculture, with departments of tea, horticulture, agricultural technology and an experimental farm. Student numbers are difficult to ascertain, but over the war years, from 1939 to 1945, a total of 2,570 students graduated, a considerable achievement under the difficult conditions of the times.[25]

Much could be said about different aspects of the university's contribution over these years, but perhaps the best depiction is that it was "a bastion of democracy."[26] This was mainly due to the remarkable activities of some of the progressive faculty members. One of the most outstanding, Sun Hanbing, had a Masters degree in economics from Washington State University and had pursued graduate studies at Harvard before returning to China in 1927. Successively head of the department of politics, dean of the law faculty and provost, Sun was best known for having launched a progressive journal called *Wenzhai*, which was widely read and provided a wealth of information and independent analysis relating to national and international issues. Sun was killed in a Japanese bombing attack on Fudan's Beipei campus in 1940,[27] but the magazine continued throughout the war years. It was a kind of beacon of the progressive role Fudan played over those difficult years.

---

[24] *Ibid.* pp.151-158.
[25] *Ibid.* Appendix II, p.534.
[26] *Ibid.* p.158.
[27] *Ibid.* pp.498-506.

With the end of the war, Fudan moved back to Shanghai in 1945 and gradually re-established itself on its former campus in Jiang Wan. Its reputation by now was such that 11,512 students applied for entry in 1946, with about 400 being selected. In 1947, 12,318 students applied and 512 were selected.[28] Now a national university, it had a considerable number of well known progressive scholars in areas such as political science, history, literature, law and journalism, It was thus actively involved in various radical movements, and known for the stand many of its professors took against the corrupt Nationalist government.

After 1949, Shanghai was given a special status as an independent municipality, on the same level as a province. It was center of the East China Region, which was made up of one municipality and six provinces, from Shandong in the north, through Jiangsu, Zhejiang, Jiangxi, Anhui, down to Fujian in the south. Just as Wuhan was made the most important higher education centre for the Central South Region, Shanghai had the highest concentration of national universities, intended to serve the region and the nation as a whole. Fudan University was chosen as the most prominent comprehensive university for the region in the reorganization of colleges and departments that took place as part of a macro planning exercise in 1952.

Fudan had never had a high standing in the natural sciences, but this was remedied by having many renowned scientists and mathematicians move there from Zhejiang University in 1952. Fudan also absorbed excellent faculty members from Christian universities such as St John's and Hu Jiang in the sciences and in some areas of the humanities. Its college of agriculture, and its programs in engineering were moved out. Much of its college of law was integrated into the newly established East China Institute of Law and Politics, while most departments of its college of commerce became part of the Shanghai Institute of Economics and Finance.

In a sense, the areas for which it had won greatest renown were now removed, with two important exceptions – the fields of Chinese literature and journalism. Fudan's department of journalism had been famous in the pre-Liberation period, fulfilling a key role in the support of progressive causes. The continuation of this department in the new Fudan gave it a profile a little bit different from that of other major comprehensive universities. Fudan also managed to keep its department

28 *Ibid.* p.181.

of economics, and in 1955 a small department of law was added, then a department of philosophy in 1956.[29]

Overall its gains were much greater than its losses in the re-organization, the opposite experience to that of Zhejiang University and Henan University, as we have seen in chapters two and three. It now became a highly respected comprehensive university with 11 departments: physics, chemistry, mathematics and biology on the science side; Chinese literature, foreign literature, history, journalism, economics, law and philosophy on the humanities side.

The factors that lay behind this decision to make Fudan the most prominent university in the region were mainly those of macro planning. Shanghai was the natural location for a major comprehensive university and Fudan's history as a patriotic and progressive institution enabled it to fit this role well. In 1952, Chen Wangdao, the famous leader of Fudan's journalism and literature programs, was appointed president, a position he held until his death in 1977. The symbolic importance of having as president the scholar who had first translated the Communist manifesto into Chinese enhanced Fudan's status in the atmosphere of the time. Chen had actually been an early member of the Communist Party, present at the Party's first congress in 1921.He had left the party a few years later, due to differences of opinion with Chen Duxiu. He had nevertheless always supported progressive causes, though not a party member. In 1957, he was again accepted back into the Party, though this was kept quiet at the time. In addition to the presidency of Fudan, Chen held many other important positions, including director of the East China Higher Education Bureau in charge all of higher education in the region, vice-chairman of the Shanghai People's Political Consultative Committee, and a representative in the National People's Congress.[30]

The second president was to be Su Buqing, a world-renowned scholar of mathematics, who had served as provost of Zhejiang University before 1949, and moved to Fudan with the reorganization of colleges and departments of 1952. The third president, as we have already seen, was Xie Xide, who served in this role from 1983 to 1988.

Throughout the 1950s, Fudan was able to recruit top students from around the country through unified national entrance examinations, due

---

[29] *Zhongguo gaodeng xuexiao jianjie* [A Short Introduction to Chinese Higher Iinstitutions] (Beijing: Jiaoyu kexue chubanshe, 1981), p.224.
[30] *Fudan daxue zhi*, pp.284-298.

to its status as one of a small number of national comprehensive universities. The early fifties were thus a golden period of growth and development. With the Anti-Rightist Movement of 1957, however, a number of famous older professors were attacked and sent into exile. In the Great Leap Forward that followed in 1958, Fudan took a leading role, with the establishment of factories on campus where students could apply what they were learning to productive practice, and efforts to re-write curricular materials in ways more directly applicable to the Chinese context.

In May of 1959, President Chen Wangdao made a major speech at the Shanghai People's Congress on the subject of "letting a hundred flowers bloom, a hundred schools of thought contend." He began with comments on how lively scholarly debates had raised the quality of scientific research in the past. However, he noted that many scholars were hesitant to speak out and take an antithetical position on scientific issues, in case they should be attacked on political grounds. Chen made the point that errors were essential to scholarly progress. They should not be simplistically explained in terms of the scholar's political stand-point, and condemned as remnants of a bourgeois scholarly mentality, as had happened. Rather a distinction should be made between problems of scholarly standpoint and those of political standpoint, which might involve opposition to the Communist Party or to socialism.[31] In this speech Chen tried valiantly to revive the principle of respect for intellectuals which Zhou Enlai had made the center of his important speech in 1956,[32] and to create space for free scholarly debates in an increasingly radicalized environment.

With the outbreak of the Cultural Revolution in 1966, Fudan found itself in the maelstrom of struggle and revolutionary activism. It is difficult to estimate how far this was linked to its own history of political activism, or to the fact that three of the radical leaders who came to be known as the Gang of Four, including Mao's wife, Jiang Qing, were Shanghai people with close links to Fudan. A number of Fudan faculty, especially in the departments of journalism, Chinese literature and history, became drawn into the political struggle, in some cases as the

---

[31] Chen Wangdao, "Guanyu guanche zhixing dang de baihua qifang baijia zhengming fangzhen de jidian yijian" in *Chen Wangdao Wenji* [Selected writings of Chen Wangdao], Vol. I (Shanghai: Renmin Chubanshe, 1979), pp.273-279.
[32] See Chapter Five, pp.158-159.

anonymous "pens" of radical political leaders. Fudan's academic journal was renamed "Struggle and Criticism" (*Xuexi yu pipan*) and was an important mouthpiece for radical rhetoric.[33] As a result, Fudan was at the centre of some of the most bitter struggles of the Cultural Revolution, with academic staff and students greatly affected.

Only with the restoration of national entry examinations in 1977, and the recruitment of two remarkable classes of students from a ten-year cohort in January and September of 1978, was a degree of academic normalcy restored on the Fudan campus. Efforts were made to provide upgrading opportunities for the remaining "worker-peasant-soldier" students and for the young lecturers who had been recruited during the radical years. With scientific development in the forefront of Deng Xiaoping's modernization drive, Fudan's new president, the mathematician Su Buqing, naturally focused on teaching and research in the hard sciences. As vice-president from 1978, Xie Xide was a key figure in these efforts, Her story over that period was thus in many ways Fudan's story, and we will return to that in a later part of this chapter.

Growing up in War-time Conditions

Xie Xide was born in Southeast China in the ancient port city of Quanzhou, a short distance up the coast from Xiamen. Her grandfather was a merchant, involved in import and export between China and Taiwan, and family circumstances were comfortable until he passed away in 1900, leaving his wife and a five-year old son, Xie Yuming. Xie Xide's grandmother strongly believed in modern education and was able to get her son into Peiyuan Secondary School, a Presbyterian mission school in Quanzhou, where he supported himself by working part-time. On graduation, Xie Yuming was able to gain a scholarship for university studies in the United Christian University (later merged into Yenching University) in Beijing.[34]

---

[33] Ting Wang, "Propaganda and political Struggle: a Preliminary Case Study of Hsueh-hsi yu P'i-p'an", in *Issues and Studies*, Vol. XIII, No.6, June 1977, pp.1-14; Gardner, John, "Study and Criticism: The Voice of Shanghai Radicalism," in Christopher Howe (ed.), *Shanghai: Revolution and Development in an Asian Metropolis* (Cambridge: Cambridge University Press, 1981), pp.326-347.

[34] Jessie Lutz, *China and the Christian Colleges* (Ithaca, New York: Cornell University Press, 1971), pp.121-123. See also Chapter Eight, p.246.

After graduating, Xie Yuming returned to teach at Peiyuan Secondary School in Quanzhou, and married one of the Peiyuan students. In the year Xie Xide was born, 1921, he went back to Beijing to teach at Yenching University, then in 1923 gained a Rockefeller scholarship to go to USA for higher studies. Over these years, Xie Yuming's young wife was a student at Xiamen University, from 1921 till her death in 1925, a rather unusual situation for a young woman of her time. Xie Xide was clearly born into an education family!

After her mother's death, Xie Xide was cared for by her grandmother, until her father returned with a Ph.D. in Physics from the University of Chicago in 1926, and took his young daughter with him to Beijing. There he took back his teaching position at Yenching University. His second wife was a Yenching graduate, and three sons were born to the couple, giving Xie Xide three younger half-brothers.

Xie Xide, aged 14, with her father, stepmother and two of her stepbrothers on the campus of Yenching University where her father was teaching.

Growing up on the beautiful campus of Yenching University was certainly a privileged educational environment. Xie Xide had her primary education in the attached primary school, with some of the lessons being given in English. Once she reached secondary education, she studied in the famous Bridgeman Academy, an American Methodist missionary school with excellent academic standards. In 1937, just before her last year of secondary school, the Japanese invaded Beijing in the Marco Polo Bridge Incident, and her father decided to move the whole family south to Changsha, where he taught for a time at Hunan University. During that year she experienced periods of study in two other Christian missionary girls schools, St Hilda's in Wuhan and Fuxing in Changsha. She also took the national university entrance examinations, being accepted at Hunan University. Unfortunately, however, she took ill with tuberculosis, and was hospitalized for several years, before finally enrolling at Xiamen University in 1942, where her father was teaching by then.

In talking about her education during these years, Xie Xide noted how important her years of secondary education in these three secondary schools were. She felt the environment of girls' schools was important in giving her confidence in her own abilities, and preparation for future leadership. Her father's education and example were also very important in her years of growing up. As a scientist, he was open-minded and curious. Yet as a father, he was a rather traditional Confucian gentleman, she felt. He took a strong interest in his children's studies, and did not want to see them waste any time on other activities while they were young. He was very proud of her decision to study physics, and encouraged her from an early age to consider studying abroad. He also held her up as an example to her younger half-brothers. At the same time, he was politically very cautious and conservative, and was anxious that his children should not become involved in political activism in any way.

In 1942, she began her studies in the department of physics and mathematics of Xiamen University. Due to the Japanese invasion, the university had re-located temporarily to Changting, near the border between Fujian and Jiangxi provinces. There were only about six students majoring in physics and they all shared the same textbook, borrowed from the professor. Conditions were extremely primitive in this remote location in the mountains, but there was an excellent academic spirit, and she worked hard. Many talented students from universities in Zhejiang, Hubei and Jiangsu had come there when it was not possible for them to follow their universities to locations further inland. It was thus a stimulating academic environment, and also one of lively student activism. Her father's admonitions kept her from joining the active student movement, which was linked to the Communist underground, but she became more and more concerned about the country's destiny.

In 1946 Xie Xide graduated from Xiamen University, just before it moved back to Xiamen. She went to Shanghai and taught at Hu Jiang University, an American Baptist institution, for one year, then was able to get a scholarship to Smith College in the United States to do a Masters degree in physics. From there she went on to the Massachusetts Institute of Technology for a Ph.D. degree in semi-conductor physics. She felt her experience of American education had been ideal, and well suited to her needs. As a women's college with a strong liberal arts focus, Smith had provided her with a nurturing environment, which enabled her to adapt to life in the United States, and gain a strong foundation in physics through a Master of Science Program. She particularly appreciated the close relations between student and professor, which she experienced there. As for her years at MIT, she greatly admired the teaching system, with research integrated into teaching and virtually leading teaching. After completing her Ph.D. in two and a half years, she stayed on for six months to participate in research with a group working in the area of solid-state physics.

By this time it was 1951. The Communist Revolution had taken place successfully in 1949, and her father had been working in the Philippines for some years. He had kept in close touch with her, and strongly advised her not to return to the Mainland. She, however, had different views, and felt a strong calling to make a contribution to China as well as to science. The other important factor in her decision was her friendship with Cao Tianqin.

While a secondary school student in Beijing, she had got to know Cao well, as his father was also a professor at Yenching University and the two families were close. During her difficult years of struggle with tuberculosis in war-time conditions, Cao wrote to her regularly from Beijing, and subsequently kept in touch when he followed Yenching University to its war-time campus in Chengdu. When the young couple wished to get engaged in 1946, Xie's father at first objected, only giving in when he learned the young man had been offered a scholarship to study chemistry at Cambridge University.

So it was the two young people followed their graduate studies at the two Cambridges, in England and USA, and kept up a lively correspondence. When Xie Xide had difficulty in making arrangements to return to China in 1952, under conditions of an American prohibition, Dr. Joseph Needham, a family friend and professor at Cambridge, helped her to get temporary admission to England. There she was re-united with her fiancé and they were married in an Anglican church in the countryside near Cambridge by a sympathetic Anglican priest, whom she described as being known for his "red leanings." A month later they traveled back to China on the ship *Guangzhou Hao*, arriving in Shanghai around the time of the reorganization of colleges and departments.

Xie was never to see her father again. In the 1960s he moved to Taiwan, and lived there until his death in 1986. She sent him photos of their wedding, of their only son, who was born in 1956, and on subsequent occasions, but she never received any reply from him. Much later, a friend visited Taiwan shortly after his death, and brought back his ashes to her, as well as a few personal effects. Among them she found all of the photos she had sent over the years. It was comforting to know he had opened her letters, and had wanted to keep the photos, in spite of the fact that he had never replied.

Xie characterized her father, Xie Yuming, as a determined, even stubborn person, a Christian, but most of all, a scholar. He had been ambitious for his children, and encouraged them to excel in their studies. He had claimed to believe in freedom of choice in matters of marriage and career, yet in fact he very much wanted them to conform to his thinking. Thus he had been reluctant to approve Xie's engagement to Cao, and had firmly opposed the young couple's decision to return to China. For her part, she treasured the education he had given her and the example set by his devotion to science. She saw that he had somehow kept one foot in the world of the Confucian gentleman, while the other was firmly planted in the soil of modern science.

A Career devoted to Science and to Socialist China

For Xie Xide and her husband Cao Tianqin, a new life began, as they established themselves in the city of Shanghai in 1952. They had chosen Shanghai since it was a major intellectual centre, and Xie had had some teaching experience there before going to the US in 1946. As a specialist in chemistry, Cao was attracted to the Institute of Biochemistry and Physiology of the Chinese Academy of Sciences, which immediately offered him a position. They took up residence in Yueyang Road in a pleasant southwestern corner of Shanghai, near to the Institute. It was also not far from the famous Jiaotong University, one of China's oldest modern universities, which had been founded in 1896. Although this was now socialist China, where Mao had declared that "women hold up half the sky," Xie's job assignment was arranged for her by her husband's employer.

The Institute where Cao Tianqin worked arranged a position for Xie Xide under a professor of physics at Jiaotong University. Before she could take up her position, this professor was transferred to Fudan University, under the reorganization of colleges and departments. That meant a very lengthy daily commute for Xie Xide to a northeastern suburb of Shanghai. Nevertheless, she was pleased with this opportunity, since Fudan was about to become one of the leading universities in the basic sciences, under the new identity given to it in the reorganization. She remembered how Su Buqing, who had recently moved to Fudan from Zhejiang University[35] and was vice-president and provost, told her she still had a great deal to learn. She had little teaching or research experience, he reminded her, in spite of her Ph.D. degree from MIT. She was thus offered the humble position of lecturer.

Over the years from 1952 to 1956, Xie Xide worked hard in teaching and research, and made a great effort to adapt to an academic environment where Russian scientists exercised enormous influence, and there were strong anti-American feelings. She was fully aware that work in her area of specialty, semi-conductors, was more advanced in the United States than in the Soviet Union but she simply kept quiet on this point, given the political atmosphere of the time. She was concerned also about the political interference into Soviet science under Stalin, the standing of scholars such as Lysenko, and the tendency for Soviet scientists to make claims about being the first in certain scientific discoveries, which she knew to be false. What she found most worrying in the Soviet higher education model then being adopted in China was the separation of teaching and research, with most research funding being awarded to institutes of the Chinese Academy of Sciences or specialist research units attached to major national ministries. There was little expectation or provision for research to be done in universities, and it was up to individual scholars to find opportunities for research in this difficult environment.

In spite of these qualms, Xie Xide threw herself into academic work enthusiastically. She and her husband enjoyed the sense of building their scientific careers in tandem. They also made efforts to educate themselves politically, and to adapt to the political opportunities and demands of socialist China. One of the delightful surprises for both of them was to find they had been independently accepted as members of the Chinese Communist Party on the very same day in 1956. They had each applied separately, without discussing it, and their applications had been processed in different work units, thus the surprise. Twenty-four years later, both were honored with appointments to the prestigious Chinese Academy of Sciences as academicians, again on the same day.

---

[35] Chapter Two, p.49.

Their oneness of purpose in their devotion to science and to serving their country had somehow bound them together in special ways on their life's pathway.

In 1956, their one and only son, Weizheng, was born. When he was only five months old, Xie was asked to move to Beijing for two years, in order to learn Russian, and work under Russian scientists at Peking University. She was also invited to work on the first textbook for semi-conductor physics in China. Her husband Tianqin agreed to take care of their child in Shanghai, in order to give her the freedom to go. She thus lived on the campus of Peking University for two years, keeping touch with her family through letters and pictures, and devoting herself to scientific work. Since Peking University had moved to the beautiful campus of Yenching University in 1952, she was now back in the place where her father had taught physics for so many years, and she had experienced a happy and privileged childhood and education. What a sense of dramatic change and underlying continuity she must have felt over those two years.

Her major achievement was co-authorship of an authoritative work on "Semi-conductor Physics" with Professor Huang Kun, a leading scientist in the field, who had returned to China from the University of Liverpool in 1951. She also worked with a team developing new teaching outlines and teaching materials for semi-conductor physics, solid state physics, transistors and related areas. In addition, she learned enough Russian to be able to collaborate in the translation of two books from Russian to Chinese in the area of atomic physics. She had mixed impressions of the Russian scientists. Some were good, others mediocre, others quite chauvinistic. On the whole, she felt the scientists who had been sent to help in China were mainly second-level scholars, not leaders in the various scientific fields they were trying to develop. There were very few women among them but she was pleased to meet one woman professor of physics who was teaching at Peking University from the Soviet Union. A very pleasant personality, not condescending in her attitude to Chinese colleagues, but not of the highest caliber, was Xie's judgement.

The Anti-Rightist Movement of 1957 came as a shock to her, although she was not personally affected. She did feel compelled to take some part in criticizing the older professors who were targeted, and she regretted the suffering caused to them. As for the Great Leap Forward of 1958, she felt it was totally unrealistic, as there simply was not the economic base needed to support the rapid expansion of higher education that was attempted. For herself personally, the timing was unfortunate. She had just returned to Shanghai from Beijing after making heroic efforts over two years to learn Russian and work with Russian scientists in positive ways, when suddenly the Russians were criticized and forced to leave China. The rhetoric about involving students in research and teaching was little more than rhetoric in the areas of physics where she was working, since students were simply unable to make meaningful contributions. As for research, little changed in the allocation of research funding, in spite of all the talk about animating new research projects in universities. Most state funding was still allocated to institutes of the Academy of Sciences.

The first half of the 1960s was a period of retrenchment and a return to the patterns that had been put in place in 1952. Xie Xide found this period the most rewarding in her career up till then. For the first time, she felt she was able to make considerable progress in the teaching of physics, and she was also able to initiate her own research program. In 1956 she had been promoted from lecturer to assistant professor, and in 1962 she was made a full professor, at the age of 41. In 1962 and 1963 she published two parts of a major work on "Solid State Physics," co-authored with Professor Fang Junjin. She also made her first trips abroad, since her return to China in 1952. In 1960 she was part of an academic delegation visiting the Soviet Union, Romania and Bulgaria. In January of 1966, she went to England to participate in an international conference in physics at the University of Manchester. This was a period when Zhou Enlai had taken the initiative to open up educational and cultural relations with European countries, in spite of the continued freeze in relations with the United States.

A political storm was brewing, however, and Xie Xide was aware of that as she returned to China from England early in 1966. At the same time her health was threatened with the discovery of breast cancer and the need for major surgery towards the end of that year. The combination of fragile health (with two more recurrences of the cancer) and political turmoil made the following years the most difficult of her life. For two and a half years her husband was held in detention and was unable to have any contact with his family. For part of that time she herself was also held by Red Guards on campus, first in a women students' dormitory, later in one of the low temperature physics laboratories she had established. There was also a period in which she was forced to join a re-education through labor program on a farm.

The fact that Xie Xide and her husband Cao Tianqin had returned from the capitalist West to China put them under suspicion as possible spies. To compound this, the political struggle at Fudan University and in Shanghai intellectual circles generally was particularly fierce, resulting in extremely difficult circumstances for both of them. Meanwhile their young son, who was ten years old at the outbreak of the Cultural Revolution, was left to care for himself for lengthy periods of time. It was truly a trial by fire, and it was to be six years before Xie Xide was able to begin teaching again. In 1972 she started some classes for undergraduates and in 1973 for the first graduate students. In 1976, she began work in writing and editing a new book in semi-conductor physics, under difficult circumstances, and in 1977 she initiated new research in surface physics. By this time her husband had returned from detention and the family was finally reunited.

In a moving tribute to his parents, written at the time of his mother's death in 2000, Xie's son, Cao Weizheng, describes the way in which his parents passed these difficult days. They read as widely as they could, and spent many hours at the Foreign Language Bookstore, looking out as much new material in their respective fields as they could find. Weizheng usually accompanied them on these trips to the bookstore

Xie Xide with her husband Cao Tianqin and her son, Cao Weizheng, in 1971, during the dark days of the Cultural Revolution.

and greatly enjoyed the atmosphere and the conversations with service people in the store. He too became a lover of books, as he associated the happiest moments of family life with these visits.[36]

A Vision for Science and Internationalism

The fall of the Shanghai-based Gang of Four in 1976, and Deng Xiaoping's return to power in 1977 opened up a whole new era for China, a period when Xie Xide's remarkable scientific background and talents were finally valued and given scope for development. In 1977 she established the Modern Physics Research Institute at Fudan University, gaining support from the Ministry of Education and the State Commission of Science and Technology to purchase equipment for surface studies. Over time eight university laboratories were associated with the Institute.

In late autumn of 1977, Xie participated in the preparatory meetings to set the agenda for the National Science Conference in Beijing in March of 1978. Finally, the vital importance of modern scientific development for China's modernization was recognized, and Xie took up leadership in a range of areas, nationally and internationally. In her own field of surface physics, she was active in the organization of a series of international congresses, and also served as vice-president of the Chinese Physics Society for many years, and as President of the Shanghai Association of Science and Technology.

Xie Xide discussing a scientific problem at Fudan University in 1984

---

[36] Cao Weizheng, "Zhuisi – Huiyi Muqin Xie Xide" [Memories of my mother, Xie Xide] in *Selected Writings of Xie Xide*, pp.17-21.

As vice-president and subsequently president of Fudan University, Xie's leadership gained wide attention. She was the first woman to head a major Chinese university, and her qualifications and international network were second to none. She also achieved a political standing that was unusual among Chinese university presidents. She was thus able to give Fudan a high profile over the crucial first decade of China's modernization and opening up to the world.

In chapter four, we have noted how Chinese universities were given a dual mandate as centers of teaching and research in the reform documents coming from the 1978 national conference on education. Thus Xie was finally in the position to provide conditions for the vigorous combination of research and teaching which she had experienced herself as a graduate student at MIT, and which she had advocated ever since the 1950s. A series of World Bank loans in support of higher education was negotiated by the Chinese government in the early 1980s, and Xie was a key figure both at Fudan and in the national context in overseeing their development.

Her vision was not limited to the natural sciences, and she told me proudly in 1998 how she had overseen the development of a new school of management studies, as well as new schools of economics and life sciences during her tenure as president. Fudan had never had a medical school, but she mentioned talks she had had with the president of the Shanghai No. Two Medical University, the successor to Aurora University after 1949. They wished to cooperate, yet at the time, Xie remarked, they agreed that the two universities were simply too poor to "get married." "So we decided – let's just be lovers," Xie remarked jokingly. Fudan thus began to take students for their first two years in the basic sciences, who would then continue their medical studies at Shanghai No. Two Medical University. A decade later, Fudan did finally gain a medical school through a merger with Shanghai No. One Medical University, which took place in April of 2000.

It would be impossible to provided a detailed account of Xie's wide-ranging accomplishments as president of Fudan, but I will try to give some insight into her leadership in relation to the World Bank higher education projects in China. The first project involved a loan of 200 million US dollars for 28 leading Chinese universities, with Fudan being one of the eleven national comprehensive universities included in the project. It was one of nine institutions given priority status for funding so that they could be leaders in curriculum development and the strengthening of research. The overall aims of the project were to increase enrollments in the natural sciences and engineering, to improve the quality of teaching and research and enhance the management effectiveness of major universities.[37]

The project ran from about 1982 to the later 1980s and provided a remarkable opportunity for upgrading and opening up to the world. While a considerable proportion of the budget was devoted to purchasing scientific equipment, there was also provision for international experts in the major science areas to visit and give advice on research and curriculum development, also for younger faculty members to pursue higher studies abroad, as well as research visits for more established faculty. It was a fantastic opportunity for vigorous engagement with the international community of universities after years of isolation and Xie was in a position to encourage, advise and lead on many aspects of these developments for Fudan.

She also took on a major responsibility for the second World Bank university development project, which focused on specialized universities in engineering, finance and economics managed by national ministries other than the ministry of education. A unique feature of these World Bank projects was the fact that important dimensions of each project were led by an international advisory committee and a Chinese advisory committee, whose members were leading scientists and scholars. Xie Xide accepted the responsibility of chairing the Chinese advisory committee for the second university development project, which involved supervising the development of new laboratories in about 40 project universities,[38] as well as overseeing aspects of the selection of international experts, and the sending of Chinese scholars abroad.

In an article written in June of 1998, recollecting those busy years, Xie described how she took the opportunity of her trips abroad to attend meetings with the international advisory committee for the project to visit as many university laboratories as possible, in order to gather ideas and advice for the development of laboratories in the Chinese project universities. She also describes how her footprints could be found in many of the project universities in different Chinese cities, as she felt responsible to see as much as possible of what was going on on the

---

[37] Ruth Hayhoe, *China's Universities and the Open Door* (Toronto: OISE Press, New York: M.E. Sharpe, 1989), p.170.

[38] See *Ibid*. pp.176-178 for details on this project.

ground, before submitting her yearly report as chairman of the Chinese advisory committee.[39]

The second area where Xie was able to play a very special role arose from her close links to the United States, which went back to her father's doctoral studies in Chicago, her own secondary education in American missionary schools and her years at Smith College and MIT. This was the area of Sino-American relations. In 1985, while she was president of Fudan, and just six years after the normalization of Sino-American relations, she established a center for American studies, and took on the position of director. The center's objectives were to initiate research, teaching, exchange and consultancy related to American studies. The four areas of priority for research were Sino-American relations, security and defense, the American economy, and culture and religion in America.[40] After her retirement from the presidency in 1988, Xie continued as an active and dynamic leader of the center for American studies, untiring in promoting exchanges and research, also in fundraising.

In 1995 a new building was completed on the Fudan campus with funds which Xie had raised in the United States. About 45 international conferences have been sponsored by the center and a stream of research publications have come forth, making it the most prominent center for research on the US in China. In November of 2003, I was honored to present a paper at a conference sponsored by the Center and entitled "Building Bridges Across the Pacific" in commemoration of 25 years of Sino-American educational exchanges. I was touched to see an impressive bronze bust of Xie Xide inside the entrance to their beautiful new building. The artist had somehow managed to capture her humor, her humanity and the spirit of dedication that had marked all aspects of her career.

Much more could be said about her remarkable contributions. I will end this section by saying something about her national political leadership. I will also try to depict the way in which she exercised leadership at Fudan University. The motto which Xie Xide chose for her

---

[39] Xie Xide, "Wei guojjia yonghao daikuan" [Making good use of loans for the country] in *Selected Works of Xie Xide*, pp.96-98.

[40] Center for American Studies, Fudan University, "Meiyan zhongxin de chuangshi, Zhongmei guanxi de tuidongzhe – Huainian Xie Xide Jiaoshou" [Founder of the Center for American Studies and Promoter of Sino-American Relations – In memory of Professor Xie Xide] in *Selected Works of Xie Xide*, pp.33-34.

life appears on the cover of her biography, which was published in 1993: "A person should do as much as possible for their country, and give minimal attention to whether or not they gain personal fame."[41] We have noted how Xie Xide joined the Chinese Communist Party at the same time as her husband in 1956. In spite of the bitter experiences of the Cultural Revolution she remained an active and committed Party member, taking up considerable responsibility after 1977.

Interwoven among her many professional and scientific meetings, honors and obligations, listed year by year in an appendix to her *Selected Works*, is a record of participation in important plenums of the Communist Party's Central Committee, from the time she was elected to this prestigious Committee at the Party's 12th Congress in September of 1982, right up to its 14th Congress in October of 1992. On that occasion she attended as a representative of the Shanghai People's Political Consultative committee, which she had chaired from 1988 to 1992. Altogether she participated in eight plenums over this ten-year period, as well as being responsible for the Chinese People's Political Consultative Committee in Shanghai.[42] While most Chinese university presidents are members of the Communist Party of China, this record of leadership within the Party is quite rare. It demonstrated the respect within which Xie was held in top political circles, and her determination to make a contribution on this level, as well as through academic and scientific activities.

Another angle of her political leadership can be seen in a story told to me by Dr. David Vikner, president of the New York-based United Board for Christian Higher Education in Asia for many years. David had many meetings with Xie Xide over the years, seeking her advice on projects of support for Chinese universities. Usually they were one-on-one affairs, over a quiet evening meal. On the last occasion in which he met her, however, the circumstances were different. She invited him to a lunch in central Shanghai, not telling him ahead why she was making this arrangement. When he reached the restaurant, he found she had about 12 young Shanghai leaders around the table, individuals who held senior positions in the different offices and bureaus of the Shanghai government. Beaming with pride, she introduced them one by one,

---

[41] Wang Zengfan, *Xie Xide* [A Biography of Xie Xide] (Fuzhou: Fujian kexue jishu chubanshe, 1993).

[42] *Selected Works of Xie Xide*, pp.282-290.

noting how most of them had Ph.D. degrees from top American universities. "Here is the reason why Shanghai will outdo Beijing in its development and contribution to the nation," she commented proudly to David.[43]

While Xie was a widely respected political leader, this made her no less accessible to students and faculty members at Fudan University. If anything, it strengthened her determination to remain close to faculty and students. Her son comments how he and his father often tried to protect her from too many visitors coming to her door to ask for help, during the times when her health was not good. When she found this out, she would berate them for chasing away her guests.[44] Even in the last months of her life in hospital, she had a constant stream of visitors, including students seeking advice from her on their research projects and their careers.

While still president of Fudan, one of the projects she gave special attention to was a scheme for providing a faculty mentor to each new student entering Fudan. This academic staff member was expected to give personal guidance to the student, meet with them to discuss their study goals, assist them in developing self-study habits and generally provide all-round support.[45] Xie had particularly appreciated the close faculty-student relations she experienced at Smith College, and hoped to provide a similar atmosphere for students at Fudan during her presidency.

One personal vignette gives a picture of this aspect of her presidential style. A friend and colleague of mine from the University of Southern California was staying at Dong Yuan, Fudan's hotel on campus for international visitors, while pursuing a research project related to his interests in political science. While he was eating dinner alone in the dining room one evening, a modest looking elderly woman approached him, and asked about his research work. "How is it progressing? Are you getting the help you need at Fudan?" After some minutes of conversation,

---

[43] This story has been included with permission from Dr. David Vikner, who is now president of the Japan International Christian University Foundation Inc. in New York.

[44] Cao Weizheng, "Zhuisi – Huiyi Muqin Xie Xide" [Memories of my mother, Xie Xide] in *Selected Writings of Xie Xide*, p.19.

[45] Xie Xide, "Zongjie jingyan, gaijin gongzuo, zhubu wanshan daoshizhi" [Summarize experience, improve our work and gradually enhance the tutorial system] in *Selected Works of Xie Xide*, pp.23-25.

in which he told her about his research, he said, "Could I ask your name?" "Oh, I am Xie Xide, president of Fudan," she replied. He was stunned to find he was talking with Fudan's president![46]

Conclusion: An Open yet Committed Heart and Mind

Throughout her life, Xie Xide experienced intense periods of exposure to very different ideological and cultural influences. She somehow managed to create her own balance and nurture a remarkable tolerance of spirit, which enabled her to adapt the best features of these influences in pursuit of her lifelong commitment to her country and to science.

As a child and young person, she was exposed to the liberalism and humanitarianism of an American missionary campus, that of Yenching University, and three different missionary schools for girls. The importance she attached to this single sex education in terms of developing her self-confidence as a young woman has already been noted. Overall, she commented that American missionary education had made a positive contribution to China's development, although the scope of this influence was limited to relatively elite circles.

She had a particular admiration for John Leighton Stuart, the longstanding president of Yenching University where her father had both studied and taught. She felt he had made a great contribution to China, which needed to be more fully recognized.

Several Yenching graduates had become senior leaders in China after 1949, and she noted that Huang Hua, famous as China's Foreign Minister from 1976 to 1982, had invited Stuart to Beijing at the end of the war of liberation in 1949, just before he returned to the United States. (He had served as US Ambassador to China from 1946-49). History might have developed differently, she remarked, if the US government had let him accept the invitation. Stuart had died in 1962, leaving a wish that his ashes be buried on the campus of Yenching University, now Peking University. Xie remarked that almost all of the approvals necessary for this had been given by the late 1980s, and it was unfortunate that the events of June 4, 1989, had delayed this final reconciliation.

For Xie, the second great influence in her life came with her decision to join the Communist Party of China and give wholehearted

---

[46] Personal communication with Professor Stanley Rosen of the University of Southern California, autumn of 1999.

support to its leadership, in the face of strong opposition from her father and an estrangement that lasted until his death in 1986. This was not a blind or uncritical decision, but a careful judgment arising from her determination to devote her professional life to China's development. The price had been very high, including the painful experiences of the Great Leap Forward and the decade spent under political oppression during the Cultural Revolution. It was a dedication she shared with a beloved husband. The devotion of this scientific couple to their country and to one another was an inspiration to many. Two moving personal essays, written in English and appearing in Xie's *Selected Works*, express her feelings for her beloved Tianqin.[47]

The third influence, that of the Soviet Union, was one she accepted as a part of her dedication to China's development. She sought to learn what she could from visiting Soviet scientists in the 1950s, and adapted this to the Chinese context. At the same time she remained critically aware of some of its shortcomings, which others were only to recognize much later.

As a physicist rather than a specialist in education, Xie had little to say about Confucianism or Chinese cultural and educational traditions. However, her gentle pragmatism, tolerance and ability to balance the several major influences that have shaped her professional development reflect the best of Confucian humanism. In many ways she moved far beyond the world of her father, with his unresolved tensions between Confucian traditionalism and Western science. A Chinese feminist scholar looking at the lives of contemporary women in China, made the following comments on Xie Xide: "She preserved the kindheartedness of the traditional Chinese woman, while absorbing the progressive spirit of contemporary Western women. There was a beautiful melding of enlightenment and tolerance in her spirit."[48]

A senior scholar, who worked under Xie Xide in the Center for American Studies, made the following comment after reading the first draft of this chapter. "Madam Xie seems to me a fine product of both Chinese and Western culture. She was like a shining ball – Westerners

---

[47] Xie Xide, "My Personal Impressions About My Husband – Tianqin", in *Selected Works of Xie Xide*, pp.269-272; Xie Xide, "Memorable Reflections of my Late Husband," in *Ibid.*, pp.272-276.

[48] Zhu Li, "Xie Xide" in Ji Quansheng (ed) *Fudan yishi* [Fudan Anecdotes], (Shenyang: Liaoning chubanshe, 1998), p.178.

tended to see its Chinese side, while Chinese saw its Western side. She was actually a perfect combination or integration of these two. Her time and her background made it possible for her to become an educator so memorable that later generations will never match her qualities."[49]

---

[49] Personal communication with Professor Zhou Dunren, Center for American Studies, Fudan University, February 16, 2004.

Chapter Seven

Wang Fengxian –
A Leading Philosopher of Education

Wang Fengxian was born on the Changshan islands, to the northeast of the city of Dalian in 1928. His early life and history was greatly affected by the turbulent developments in this part of China over the first half of the 20ᵗʰ century. For Japan, Dalian was a crucial entry point for its incursions into Northeastern China, which it dominated and effectively colonized from 1931 to 1945, as it had done Korea from much earlier. Russia's need for an ice-free port on its Eastern coast meant that rivalry between the two powers was an important part of the history of the region up to 1949.

Wang was growing up over these turbulent years, and he managed to find his way out of poverty into an opportunity for teacher education in remarkable ways. His university education spanned the 1949 Revolution, so that the last two years were spent at Northeast Normal University in the city of Changchun, Jilin province, the middle one of China's three northeastern provinces. After graduation and some graduate study in Beijing, he returned to Changchun, and was to spend his whole career at Northeast Normal University. The first part of the chapter will therefore give an overview of this university.

My relationship with Professor Wang goes back to 1989, when we were planning a joint doctoral program in education with Chinese universities and Northeast Normal University joined the group of universities under the leadership of Beijing Normal University as our partner in the project. Professor Wang sent two of his doctoral students to Canada under the project. When we held our conference on "Knowledge Across Cultures" in 1992,[1] he came and gave a paper. On

---

[1] See Chapter Three, p.87.

that occasion, and at the project's closing conference in Lanzhou in 2001, Professor Wang showed a delightful sense of humor which brought warmth to his passion for moral education and broader issues of education and social development. While he was visiting Hong Kong in March of 2000, I found the opportunity to talk with him, and was privileged to learn the details of his life and thought which are shared later in this chapter.[2]

Wang Fengxian and Xie Xide at the Toronto conference, 1992.

The Story of Northeast Normal University

The story of Northeast Normal University is very closely linked to the story of the Chinese revolution. The Japanese occupation of the whole of Northeast China, from 1931 to the end of the Second World War in 1945, was one of the focal points for student protest and patriotism over this period. When the occupation of the Northeast was extended into a full-blown war of invasion in 1937, the whole of China was threatened. We have noted already the heroic stories of universities that made the long trek from major cities such as Shanghai, Beijing, Hangzhou, Kaifeng and Xiamen into the hinterland, to continue higher education on temporary wartime campuses.

The Japanese were finally defeated in August of 1945 and departed from China. The Nationalist government moved its capital from Chongqing back to Nanjing, and attempted to re-assert its authority over all of the areas it had controlled up to 1937. It had never had full control of the Northeast, however, having had an uneasy truce with Japanese occupiers and earlier with the war-lord, Zhang Zuolin. Re-taking the Northeast was thus a strategic concern.

---

[2] Interview with Professor Wang Fengxian, Hong Kong Institute of Education, March 17, 2000.

Leaders of the Communist movement, who had gained considerable support and sympathy due to their effective resistance to Japan, were also determined to gain control of the Northeast at this important juncture. Behind the struggle between Communist and Nationalist forces lay the larger global struggle of the emerging Cold War, with the Americans assisting Chiang Kai-shek and the Nationalist Party, while the Soviets were positioning themselves for the possibility of a Chinese Communist victory, although supporting the Nationalist government on the surface.[3]

It was in these circumstances that Northeast University, later to be called Northeast Normal University, came into being in 1946. The university's institutional history begins with the story of how Mao Zedong went to the leaders of Yan'an University in September of 1945 and asked them to send some leading academics to the Northeast to establish Northeast University. Mao noted that the Northeast had been under Japanese imperialist occupation already for 14 years, and young people in the region needed an opportunity to learn about recent and contemporary Chinese history, and also to understand the goals of the Communist movement. Mao made the point that it is easier to set up an army than to establish a university, but it must be done!

In January of 1946 the new university was established in the town of Benxi, in the central part of Liaoning province, the southernmost of the three provinces known as Fengtian at the time. Its goals were to educate specialist personnel in politics, economics, culture, education, industry and medicine who would serve the people.[4] Over its first year of existence, it had to move several times, due to the conflict between Nationalist and Communist forces, and the temporary success of the Nationalists in taking back major urban centers of the Northeast. In Benxi it had just recruited 70 regular students, and another 200 in short-term training courses, when it had to move north under attack from Nationalist forces, taking the 70 regular students along.

The first stop was Tonghua in southern Jilin province; then it moved on to the city of Jilin, and finally to Changchun, the former

---

[3] Steven I. Levine, *Anvil of Victory: The Communist Revolution in Manchuria 1945-1948* (New York: Columbia University Press, 1987) gives an insightful analysis of these complex circumstances.

[4] Dongbei daxue xiaoshi bianji weiyuanhui, *Dongbei shifan daxue xiaoshi 1946-1986* [An Institutional History of Northeast Normal University 1946-1986] (Changchun: Dongbei shifan daxue chubanshe, 1986), p.6.

Japanese capital of Manchuria. There it was able to absorb some scientific personnel from a former Japanese higher institution, and increase its enrolment to 300 students.[5] By May of 1946, however, conditions were such that the Communist Bureau for the Northeast had to leave the city of Changchun and move further north. Northeast University thus packed up all its books and equipment and moved up to Harbin by train, then on to Jiamusi in the far northeast of the province of Heilongjiang.

This beautiful northern city was called by some "the Yan'an of the North," and the university took over hospital buildings there for its campus. With the help of the revolutionary government, it was able to expand its facilities and establish four colleges – arts, social sciences, natural sciences, and medicine. In September of 1946, its second class of students was recruited, a total of 600, and student numbers swelled to 1100 by October. Some of the students had taken entry examinations and entered through an academic channel, while others had been sent for short-term training by various Party organs. There were two main groups of professors, those who had come over from Yan'an University or the Huabei Public Institute and some renowned intellectuals from the Northeast who wanted to support the revolution. The lifestyle on campus was simple, with everyone sharing and making do with what was available.

The curriculum was a practical one, emphasizing understanding of the struggle for liberation, and many students took part in land reform, which gave them personal experience of the revolution. The textbook was Mao Zedong's famous report on the rural people's movement in his home province of Hunan. Students were also involved in protests against American intervention in the Northeast. Overall the university carried forward the educational traditions of the Anti-Japanese Resistance University (Kangda)[6] and Yan'an University.

In December of 1946, the Northeastern Bureau of the Communist Party asked Northeastern University to take on the task of training secondary school teachers for the whole region. This was felt to be a very important task, as it was urgent to bring up a new generation of intellectuals in this complex region, that had undergone so many years of Japanese colonization and was now caught up in the struggle between

---

[5] *Ibid.* p.8.

[6] *Ibid.* pp.12-31. The institutional history gives quite a lyrical account of the spirit and style of this revolutionary institution. See also Chapter Four, pp.115-116.

Soviet and American forces on opposite sides of the Civil War. This task was taken very seriously, and 200 teaching staff went to work in various secondary schools in the region to train teachers in their schools.

In April of 1947, the Northeastern Bureau established a college of education at Northeastern University, which took responsibility for developing many new courses relating to current issues of importance, such as problems of the Chinese Revolution, international issues, Chinese-Soviet relations, Chinese geography and Chinese recent history. The new college sent its staff members to head up eight secondary schools, which were to be leading institutions in strategic locations. By the summer of 1947, when the third class of students was recruited, the education college was particularly attractive, with its mandate to train educational administrators, as well as teachers in the areas of politics, history and Chinese. A total of 324 new students were recruited in the autumn of 1947, and another 150 by the end of the year.[7]

Northeast University stayed a full two years in the remote city of Jiamusi, and during that time two classes of students in short-term training courses had graduated, and the rest had progressed through their courses. A large number of the graduates became primary or secondary school teachers, and others played other roles in the revolution. A survey done in 1984 of 84 students who had studied at Northeast University, while it was at Jiamusi, found that 69 of them were then holding important positions in government, Communist Party and higher education settings.[8]

In March of 1948, the city of Jilin, in Jilin province, was liberated from the Nationalist forces, and came under Communist control. In August of that year, Northeast University made the long trek south from Jiamusi and settled in Jilin, absorbing the former Jilin University, and several other tertiary institutions that had been under Nationalist control. Student numbers now reached 2,200.

A few months later, in October of 1948, the city of Changchun was liberated from the Nationalists, and the university prepared to move back there, where it had spent a brief period of time in 1946. A huge merger was to follow, with a number of other institutions being combined into Northeast University, including the Changbai Teachers College, a well-known Nationalist institution, which had been esta-

---

[7] *Ibid*. p.38.
[8] *Ibid*. p.42.

blished as Jilin University in 1929, then had moved to Beijing for a number of years during the Civil War. Also included in this merger was a part of Northeast University, which had been established in Shenyang in 1923, and had a considerable history as a reputed academic institution.[9]

In August of 1949, just two months before the revolutionary leaders entered Beijing and established the People's Republic, Northeast University moved from Jilin to its present location on People's Street in Changchun. It was completely reorganized under the leadership of the Northeast revolutionary bureau, and began a new phase of life as a "regular" university with a strong academic emphasis. At this time it had three colleges, in humanities, social sciences and natural sciences, with 2,200 regular undergraduate students. It also established a political college to continue its work of short-term training for cadres in the region, with 2,670 students in these programs.[10]

In March of 1950 the authorities of the Northeast regional bureau decided that its name should be changed from Northeast University to Northeast Normal University, reflecting the importance placed on the education of teachers for the new regime. This decision also anticipated the changes that would come about in the reorganization of colleges and departments in 1952, when each of China's six major regions were given a normal university. Some of the hopes and aspirations around this decision are explained as follows in the institutional history: "Education is as important as heavy industry for a new socialist country. It is necessary to train people for all the different professions to develop the country after the revolution. There is a need for new thought, new culture, new knowledge, and a need to have teachers who will serve the country throughout their lives."[11]

New programs that were added to the curriculum were in music, educational psychology and educational theory – with a focus on training lecturers for the normal schools that trained primary school teachers. In 1950, the university adopted a secondary school and a primary school to serve as sites for educational research. More than twenty teaching and research groups were established to work on

---

[9] Gavin McCormack, *Chang Tso-lin in Northeast China 1911-1928: China, Japan and the Manchurian Idea* (Stanford: Stanford University Press, 1977), pp.96-97.

[10] *Dongbei shifan daxue xiaoshi*, p.56.

[11] *Ibid*. p.64.

curricular planning and by the autumn of 1951 these groups had written over one hundred new sets of teaching material, as well as a great deal of reference material.[12] In many ways Northeast Normal University was at the forefront of the educational changes across the country because of its geographical location in the region of China where Communist liberation came about earliest.

The history of the university over the 1950s and 1960s followed a similar pathway to that of most other institutions. Early in 1953, the renowned leftwing literary scholar, Cheng Fangwu, came up from Beijing, where he had helped in the establishment of People's University, to serve as president up to 1958. His reputation raised the university's profile. With the reorganization of colleges and departments in 1952, the college level was removed, and NENU had eleven departments: education, politics, Chinese literature, history, Russian literature, geography, music, mathematics, physics, chemistry and biology.[13] In 1953 it was given responsibility within a national plan to recruit graduate students in the areas of contemporary Chinese language, history of the ancient world and modern world history.

Over the three years from 1953 to 1957 a total of 239 graduate students followed two-to-three year programs.[14] The undergraduate student enrolment was a little over 3000 students.[15] In the field of education, I. Kairov's *Pedagogy* [Jiaoyu xue] was the main text, and provision was made for all academic staff to attend study classes on it, so they could take it as the framework of their teaching. The other major text, which everyone studied, was a book on teaching instruction in normal universities by another Russian scholar, Popov.[16]

The institutional history gives considerable profile to the January 1956 meeting of the Communist Party's Central Committee in which Premier Zhou Enlai gave his famous speech on respecting intellectuals and supporting their work for China's development.[17] It elaborates on

---

[12] *Ibid*. p.79.

[13] *Ibid*. p.70.

[14] *Ibid*. p.77.

[15] *Ibid*. p.73.

[16] *Ibid*. p.77.

[17] Zhou Enlai, "On the Question of Intellectuals," *New China News Agency*, January 29, 1956, in Robert Bowie and John Fairbank (eds.) *Communist China 1955-1959: Policy Documents with Analysis* (Cambridge, Mass: Harvard University Press, 1962), pp.128-144.

how this policy influenced Northeast Normal University's policies and development.[18] By contrast, only one short paragraph is devoted to the Anti-Rightist Movement of 1957, noting how many innocent scholars and students had suffered unfairly in the movement.[19] Chapter three is entitled "Searching for our own approach to education in the turns and twists of political movements" (1958-66).

Under the Great Leap Forward of 1958, Northeast Normal University was given to the province of Jilin, and became Jilin Normal University, only taking back its national standing in 1981, after Deng Xiaoping had come to power. Over the period from 1958 to the early sixties, the idea was to link its work more closely to its own locality, and move away from the unified patterns imposed under Soviet influence. There are details on efforts to create branch campuses in the countryside, on the integration of labor into the curriculum, and the rapid increase in enrolment, as well as the retrenchment and effort to restore academic standards that came with the Sixty Articles for Higher Education in 1961.

Chapter four is called "Ten years of serious destruction under the pounding of wind and rain" (1966-76). It depicts the trials of the Cultural Revolution decade. Given the fact that education was at the heart of the storm over these years, and Northeast Normal had a particularly strong revolutionary tradition, it is clear that the struggle was intense. It began with criticism of the Soviet heritage of educational theory, which was followed by violent class struggle, and an ultimately empty and even cynical set of revolutionary educational slogans.

Chapter six, covering the period from 1978 to 1986 is entitled "Overcoming the Chaos and returning to Normalcy: Vital Reforms in the Creation of Northeast Normal's New Profile." It details the rapid developments that followed Deng Xiaoping's call for education to "serve modernization, the world and the future," including the establishment of graduate programs in the early 1980s, and the development of a range of research centers and programs in the new space opened up by the national policy that universities should be centers of research as well as teaching.[20]

Considerable detail is given on the various fields of research that developed over these years, as well as the many sets of new teaching

---

[18] *Dongbei shifan daxue xiaoshi*, pp.91-94.
[19] *Ibid*. p.102.
[20] *Ibid*. pp.187ff.

material developed by NENU's academic staff. In addition to its noted strengths in Chinese history, world history, Chinese literature and education, Northeast Normal became a centre for studies in the Japanese language and literature, with the establishment of a language training center there by Japan's Ministry of Education, where the majority of scholars from all parts of China who were preparing for study or scholarly visits to Japan were given language training. It was a natural recognition of its long history of closeness to Japan, which had some positive memories associated with it, in addition to the painful ones of occupation and exploitation. This becomes clear in Wang Fengxian's story below.

In 1981, the first professor to be appointed a doctoral supervisor was in the field of ancient Chinese history. In 1986, another seven professors in various fields were approved as doctoral supervisors. Professor Wang Fengxian was the only educational scholar among these seven.[21]

In the 1990s, Northeast Normal University moved forward rapidly, developing a new campus for undergraduate students in a suburb of Changchun, and adding a considerable number of programs in areas outside of teacher education, though that remained the core of its identity. In 1997, it was the first of the national normal universities to be accepted into the national government's 21/1 project, and gained priority funding to further develop its areas of strength. In December of 2000 it was awarded sustained funding for a national center in rural education research under the government's program for national key bases in humanities and social sciences research.[22]

Northeast Normal University retains a primary focus on education, while having strong programs in the arts and sciences. It has also kept the unique historical identity established in the revolutionary struggle of the 1940s. It will be interesting to see how this carries it forward in the new era of mass higher education in China. By 2002, Northeast Normal University had nearly 12,000 undergraduate students and close to 2000 graduate students, as well as many students in correspondence or adult education programs. Among its staff of 1,107, are 210 full professors, 383

---

[21] *Ibid.* p.197.

[22] www.moe.edu.cn/wreports. See also Yang Rui and King Hau Au Yeung, "China's Plan to Promote Research in the Humanities and Social Sciences," in *International Higher Education*, No. 27, Spring, 2002.

associate professors and 70 scholars who have been appointed doctoral supervisors. It has six attached primary and secondary schools, and a well-established academic press.[23]

National policy has encouraged large-scale university mergers in recent years, as we have seen in the case of Zhejiang University.[24] However, normal universities have been largely kept out of these mergers, as the government has wanted them to maintain their focus on education. Thus Northeast Normal University has retained its historical identity, in contrast to Jilin University, also in Changchun and the only national comprehensive university in the Northeast region. Jilin has recently been the lead institution in a merger, which has brought in the Normal Bethune University of Medical Sciences and three specialist engineering institutions that had previously belonged to various national ministries.[25]

We turn now to the story of Wang Fengxian, a scholar and thinker who has spent most of his life at Northeast Normal University, first as a student in the early 1950s, and subsequently as a scholar and thinker in the fields of philosophy of education and moral education.

Growing up in Northeast China

Wang Fengxian was born in 1928 on a small island off the coast of China northeast of Dalian, which is part of the Chang Shan group of islands. His father was a fisherman, and had had no opportunity for education. He had one older brother, and the family was extremely poor. The Chang Shan islands were administered by the Japanese, with Japanese currency in use, from the time when the Japanese had defeated the Russians in 1904. The Japanese had colonized the islands, just as they colonized Korea from 1910 to 1945.

Wang was sent to primary school at the age of ten, and studied there for four years. There was only one school on the island, a four-year primary school. The language of instruction was Japanese, and the subjects included Japanese, mathematics, physical education and painting, also some Chinese language. No history or geography was taught in the curriculum, as this might have aroused nationalist feelings

---

[23] www.nenu.edu.cn.

[24] See Chapter Two, pp.50, 54.

[25] www.jlu.edu.cn.

among the children.[26]

One of his Chinese teachers took a special interest in him, feeling that he was talented and hoping that he might continue in upper primary school. This would mean going over to the Mainland. His teacher took him up to the top of a hill on the island one day, and told him to look out over the ocean. "There is a huge mainland over there," he said, "where there are houses, lamps and cars. Here on the island there are only pigs and dogs." This was an entirely new idea to the young Wang – he had always believed there was only sea and sky beyond the island where he lived, which was only five kilometers long.

This teacher then went to his father, and begged him to allow the young Wang to go to Dalian for two years of upper primary school study. His father explained that there simply was no money to pay for that. The teacher then went to the Japanese officials in the local government, and asked them for support for this talented student. They replied that they had no money for this purpose and were unwilling to help. Finally he went to the most prosperous man on the island, who owned a fishing boat, and begged him to do a good turn for a talented young boy who needed an opportunity to study. He was an opium smoker, and refused to offer any help. Still refusing to give up, the teacher went back to his father, and again made a plea that the boy be given support to continue his studies. At this point the family had a discussion and his father said he would try to support him.

He traveled by sailboat to Pikou, the nearest town on the mainland in what was then Fengtian province (now Liaoning) and took an examination for entry to an upper primary school. He was successful in entering this school, and started his two-year program there. All of the teachers were young Japanese men, with the exception of one Chinese who was teaching "the Manzhou language" (i.e. Chinese). The first semester he found very difficult. Being from the islands, he was poor, alone and looked down upon. However, one of the Japanese teachers found him to be very diligent and accepting of discipline. This teacher loved painting, and so he encouraged Wang to paint. Wang found he greatly enjoyed painting, and it aroused his interest in other subjects as well. This teacher was kind and supportive in other ways.

---

[26] This was an intriguing point made by Wang Fengxian in the interview, March 17, 2000.

In his second year he found he loved his studies and came first in every course. One of the reasons for this, he mused on recollection, was that all of the other students went home on weekends and holidays, but he had nowhere to stay except at the school. He remembered how kind the Japanese teachers were, helping him out with food and clothing beyond what his parents could provide for him, and giving him important emotional support. Tuition, however, was still a problem. Living and study conditions were extremely primitive, with no electricity, but oil lamps for study. After a time he had had to live in a fellow villager's house.

One of the Japanese teachers who was particularly close to him was drafted into the Japanese army that year, and had to leave his teaching position. Before leaving, he had a long talk with young Wang, asking him not to go back to the island and life as a fisherman, but to continue his studies. When Wang said he had no money for this, the teacher found him a place in the Lushun normal school near Dalian, which had a four-year program. This was a school set up by the Japanese and providing a free education for young people willing to be primary school teachers. He studied there for one year, but then classes were constantly suspended due to American bombing of nearby Anshan. In the summer of 1942, students of this school helped in building an airport for the Japanese military.

At the time of the spring festival, February of 1943, he decided it was time to return to his family on the island. He was unable to get a ticket for the ferry-boat going across, as there were too many people. When the boat sunk due to the mistaken attack of an American submarine, with all aboard lost, his family believed he had gone down with it. Shortly after, however, he managed to reach his home and family by sailboat. It was a joyful reunion.

On return to his home, with little expectation of being able to go back to school, he found a temporary position as a teacher in the local primary school, and taught there for six months. In August of 1945, the Japanese were defeated and withdrew, leaving a desperate situation behind them. There was no food, the school closed down, and there were no police to maintain basic security on the island. Neither Nationalist nor Communist authorities came to fill the vacuum. He was the most educated person on the whole island. At eighteen years old, all he could think of doing was returning to the Mainland to find a future for himself.

On return to the Mainland he went to a small place near Pikou. He found a job in a store selling fish, and every evening after work he would read and study till late. One of the customers at the store, who was a businessman from Dalian, noted that he served customers well and also studied late at night. He invited him to go with him to Dalian. Wang arrived in Dalian, only to find it occupied by Soviet soldiers, with Russian money being used, but most stores closed. From there he managed to get to Shenyang, where there were many Nationalist and American soldiers. Since he was no longer a student, and had left his job, he had to seek help from a UN refugee station.

Then he went on to Changchun and studied in a secondary school which accepted wandering students like himself. In 1947, when the city was taken over by the People's Liberation Army, he went back to Shenyang. He found a place in a training school for primary teachers, which charged no fees. Many of its teachers were invited over from Northeast University and had good standards. This was a period of great freedom of thought and expression, he felt, with many ideas circulating from American, Russian and Chinese sources. He has a particularly vivid memory of reading Gorky's *My University*, and of how enlightening he found it.

Once Shenyang fell to the People's Liberation Army in 1948 he went to Beijing, along with other students in the same situation. There he entered national Changbai Normal College, and studied history and geography. At this time he found himself among many student activists, and became involved in the underground youth organization of the Chinese Communist Party. He was in Beijing in February of 1949, when the city was peacefully liberated.

An Educational Career in Socialist China

In March of 1949, Wang chose to leave Beijing and return to Changchun, at the time the Changbai Normal College was merged with Northeast University, which has been described earlier in this chapter.[27] He was grateful to the Communist Party that he was able to continue his studies. His field was geography. In the autumn 1951, he was one of twenty students chosen to undertake graduate studies at the newly established People's University. At the time Wu Yuzhang was president of People's

---

[27] See p.208.

University and Cheng Fangwu was vice-president. He was excited to be studying under their leadership.

After six months there, however, the program moved to Beijing Normal University, with the nationwide reorganization of colleges and departments. He was enrolled in the same graduate program for higher education administrators as Pan Maoyuan, whose experience has been described in chapter five.[28] Huang Ji was the class instructor, while Qu Baokui was a fellow student. Both were later to become renowned educators at Beijing Normal University and East China Normal University respectively. In addition, lectures were given by Soviet experts, and Wang attended these, along with a group of 100 teachers majoring in education and psychology who had been recruited by the Ministry of Education. All of the lecturers teaching in the program were from the Soviet Union, and each was provided with a Chinese interpreter.

Wang has vivid memories of the Russian lecturers who taught these education courses. Most of them came from the Lenin Normal College in Moscow as far as he knew, and most were at the lecturer level. Each was given a Chinese interpreter. Although Wang tried to learn Russian, both at Northeast University in Changchun and in Beijing, he was never able to master it. As for the Russian lecturers, their task was to disseminate the educational theories of I. Kairov, who was then minister of education in the Soviet Union.

Wang was a successful student and vice-monitor of his class that year, yet he confessed to having a lot of doubts at the time as to whether this approach to education was as "scientific" as it was said to be. The three courses he took were in educational psychology, educational theory and the history of education. In 1953 he graduated with a certificate, as no higher degrees were offered at that time. He returned to Changchun to teach in the department of education at Northeast University. In that same year Cheng Fangwu was appointed president of Northeast Normal University, as we have seen above.

Wang had a number of comments to make on his experience of study under the lecturers from Russia. He noted that there were many lively and interesting Chinese scholars sharing the classes he was in, and lots of discussion took place among them, and there were many disagreements. When the Russian lecturers presented their standard criticisms of capitalism, for the way in which theory was separated from

---

[28] See p.156.

practice in school education, one of the students, who had a doctorate from Germany, remarked that he had observed cars and airplanes functioning well in Germany. This was clearly related to the education system, he suggested, so what did it mean to say theory and practice were separated in the capitalist world? The Russian lecturer became angry at this question, and replied curtly that he had not been to Germany, and could not comment. However, he was sure that Lenin could not be wrong. For the first time, Wang felt how undemocratic this attitude was.

Wang himself kept quiet in this situation, however. He took the advice of the dean of studies at Beijing Normal University, Ding Haochuan, who asked students not to raise questions with the Russian lecturers which might affect friendly relations between the two countries. A leading education scholar, Ding later moved to Northeast Normal University to become deputy president in 1958.

After his return from Beijing to Changchun in 1953, Wang began his career as an assistant lecturer in the department of education at Northeast Normal University. By this time both of his parents had died, but his older brother was still living, and had a job in a watch factory in Dalian. Wang was the only member of the family privileged to have an education.

Wang met his wife after he had returned from Beijing. She had enrolled in the department of education in 1952, and graduated in 1956. She was an outstanding student, and in May of 1956 went to Bandung, Indonesia, as a member of the Chinese student delegation to an Asia-Africa student conference. She was from Shanghai, and had graduated from a girls' secondary school there. She had also been involved in activities of the student movement led by the Communist underground at Jiaotong University. Wang got to know her during her years as a student at Northeast Normal, and they married in 1957. Their one and only child, a daughter, was born in 1958. His wife taught in the department of psychology for some years after her graduation in 1956, but later worked as a translator in the university's library.

Wang had little to say about his years of teaching, from 1953 to the Cultural Revolution. He felt he did not have as strong a foundation as many others, due to his years as a "wandering scholar," moving from one school to another, before 1949. However, he read widely and was very diligent in teaching. As a result, he was given high appraisals by students and fellow teachers. He also loved to work in cooperation with primary and secondary schools, and with educational officials at all levels, doing research and teaching that would improve education on the ground. He never had the ambition of "being an official" but was content with his life and his teaching work.

During the Cultural Revolution, Wang was labeled as a second-rank capitalist reactionary academic authority. Several factors may have contributed to this. He had worked as a primary school teacher in a Nationalist school. Also one of his cousins had gone to Taiwan, which meant he might have overseas connections. More importantly, he had spoken out in the Hundred Flowers movement of 1956 and criticized some members of the Communist Party. Basically he felt both Lenin and Mao had made some mistakes in implementing Marxism. Nevertheless, Wang was allowed to stay on campus during the Cultural Revolution, and was not as severely treated as many others. This was probably due to his teaching work, and to his impoverished family background. The Red Guards could not find anything against him. For him, however, it became very clear, during the Cultural Revolution, why he could not be easily be accepted into the Communist Party or become an official.

Wang Fengxian and his family in the 1970s.

Recovering the Sense of the Self – Independent Thinker and Educator

Like each of the other educators introduced in this volume, Wang Fengxian came into his own in the period after Deng Xiaoping came to power, bringing to an end the chaotic decade of the Cultural Revolution. Wang's brief curriculum vitae gives a summary of his accomplishments over the recent two decades. They include directing 21 doctoral students,

16 of whom had completed their theses and graduated by 2000, writing about one hundred scholarly articles and numerous books, contributing to the review of research projects and articles, teaching, scholarly exchange, collaborative research and the joint training of doctoral students with other institutions (including the Ontario Institute for Studies in Education in Canada). Wang was director of the institute for basic education at Northeast Normal University for many years, and served as vice-chair of the university's academic committee.

When the University gained funding for a prestigious key research base in rural education in December of 2000, Wang was put in charge of it. He has also held many important memberships in national and provincial committees. These include academician of the Central Institute for Educational Research, member of the educational branch of the Academic Degrees Committee of the State Council, member of the National Education Science for Moral Education Group, and chairman of the Jilin Province Institute for Educational Research.[29]

In our conversation, Wang noted that he has always been an independent and critical thinker and this has got him into difficulty at times. After many misunderstandings, he was finally accepted into the Communist Party in 1985, but he has never sought the opportunity to be an official. Rather he has chosen the pathway of a scholar and thinker.

In the early 1980s, Wang took advantage of a new freedom of expression to develop his thinking about the importance of the individual and the value of the individual's subjective awareness. He noted that China has long tended to be closed to individual initiatives, and education has been viewed in a highly instrumental way. During the Cultural Revolution, education was an instrument of political struggle or class struggle. Then after Deng launched his reforms in 1978, it became an instrument of economic development.

Part of the problem, Wang feels, is a long tradition in China of education as the route to officialdom through the civil service examination system. This has led to a situation where all cadres in the Chinese system tend to be overly deferential to those in authority over them, not daring to speak out or be original in their ideas. He noted how when he began to develop his thesis on human alienation and education in the mid-1980s, he was subject to a lot of criticism from leaders and organiza-

[29] www.nenu.edu.cn/webE/faculty/stte/wangfx.htm.

tions within the government and the Communist Party. Similar criticisms were directed towards the well-known sociologist of education, Li Yixian.

When asked his views on the Confucian education tradition, Wang said he considered humanism to be the fundamental bedrock of education. He quoted the phrase which Tu Wei-ming has suggested as the "new golden rule" of Confucianism – "Do not do unto others what you would not want others to do unto you."[30] Wang also used the phrase "taking human beings as the foundation" (*yi ren wei ben*). At the heart of his thinking is a global humanism, that is rooted in Greek philosophy as well as Confucian thought, with links to the market economy and industrial development. It is thus something universal.

From another perspective, Wang feels that Confucianism has tended to be restrictive of human development, emphasizing conformity to societal patterns and expectations. He particularly takes issue with the famous Confucian phrase, "suppressing the self and upholding ritual" (*keji fuli*), seeing it as a negative aspect of the tradition. Rather, it is most important to awaken the self. Insofar as Confucianism does that, and promotes love and care for others, it is a valuable heritage.

Wang went on to explain why he feels the nurturing of the self, of individualism and of a strong subjective awareness, is important. The future cannot be predicted, and no social theorist can discover laws that will tell us where humankind is going. Rather it is up to human beings to create their own future. If human beings are nurtured in a way that brings out their essential goodness, this is what they will project into the future of human kind, and we can expect a positive future on that basis. Education should not be seen as an instrument of the state, a tool to control and mould people in the hands of government. Rather it should be a way of encouraging children to explore and go beyond the boundaries set around them.

Failing or making mistakes is an important part of learning. The child should be made to feel there is no absolute guide, it is for them to create new frontiers. Education should be seen as leading social development, rather than a service to social development. It must include moral, cultural and political dimensions, as well as economic ones. Wang did not hesitate to express his criticism of much that goes under the name of moral education in contemporary China, noting that there is a great deal of hypocrisy, as efforts are made to mold student thinking to

---

[30] See Chapter One, p.4.

conform to prevalent political trends in a passive way, and prevent them from pondering questions for themselves. "Students see through this immediately, and will not accept this kind of preaching," he noted.

Different dimensions of Wang's approach to education come across in three recent articles. The first is an essay under the title "A reconsideration of the strategy of giving priority to education in development." [31] Here Wang outlines three approaches to the relationship between education and development – the first sees education as following the development of the economy, the second sees education and the economy as moving forward in tandem, while the third puts the development of education ahead of that of the economy. In arguing for the third position, Wang explores the notion of the "quality" of human life, and argues for nurturing a high level of subjective rationalism in each individual as the most crucial motor of social and economic development.[32] While discussing arguments about the shape of the future, and the information revolution, Wang affirms the important role of information technology in social change, yet warns against the "mystification" of the computer. How much greater is the richness and potential of the human mind, he asserts.[33]

The second article is entitled "Continue to liberate our thinking and nurture one generation after another of new creative individuals in order to fashion a future society where human beings are the foundation."[34] This is a densely argued philosophical piece, which critiques a lot of futurology for its tendency to be constrained by frameworks such as the Cold War, and postmodern obsessions with a range of social ills. It puts forward the idea of almost unlimited possibilities for the future, if human

---

[31] Wang Fengxian, "Dui jiaoyu youxian fazhan zhanlue de zai renshi" [A Reconsideration of the strategy of giving priority to education in development] in *Zhongguo jiaoyu xuekan* [Scholarly Journal on Chinese Education] No. 1, 1998, pp.8-11.

[32] *Ibid.* p.10.

[33] *Ibid.* p.9.

[34] Wang Fengxian, "Jixu jiefang sixiang, wei chuangzao yiren weiben de weilai shijie peiyang yi daidai chuangzaoxing xinren" [Continue to liberate our thinking and nurture one generation after another of new creative individuals in order to fashion a future society where human beings are the foundation] in Zhongguo jiaoyu xue, Zhongguo gaodeng jiaoyu xue hui (eds.), *Zhongguo jiaoyu gaige fazhan ershinian* [Twenty Years of Chinese Education Reform and Development] (Beijing: Beijing shifan daxue chubanshe, 1999), pp.434-447.

beings can understand and develop their true potential, particularly in the arena of personal values and the creative self. From the individual, Wang moves to consider the concept of sustainable development from an environmental perspective, which has been put forward by the United Nations, and shows the close consonance between China's goals and those of the global community.

In this article, Wang comments on the human person as a subjective participant in societal production and societal relations, and thereby the creator of history and of the future.[35] He continues with an analysis of essential elements of human existence, drawing upon Chinese traditional thought. He develops concepts of self-mastery, independent agency, and a creative energy that rises above the constraints of reality. Genuine quality education would focus on nurturing human potential along these lines, Wang argues.

The third article was presented by Professor Wang at our 1992 conference on Knowledge Across Cultures in Toronto, and later won an important national prize in China. There Wang explores "meeting points of trans-cultural exchange" from a Chinese historical perspective. He starts from the position that "educational modernization in China has been faced with the challenge of preserving Chinese culture, rooted in Confucian moral values, and integrating new Western knowledge with the existing wealth of cultural knowledge." [36] His premise is that "Chinese and foreign cultures have to be harmonized with each other to form a new integrated cultural system."

Wang then examines four periods of recent Chinese history. The first was the period from 1840 to 1895, in which the transfer of military and technological knowledge from the West was encouraged, after many years of isolation. China's defeat in the Sino-Japanese War in 1895 brought about a shift to the next period, when there was a realization of the complex inter-relations between educational and political change, and of the need to change the Chinese political system. The third period Wang identified as beginning with the May 4th movement of 1919 and being characterized by a rejection of Chinese traditional culture and a call

---

[35] *Ibid.* pp.436-437.
[36] Wang Fengxian, "Meeting Points of Trans-cultural Exchange – A Chinese View," in Ruth Hayhoe and Julia Pan, *Knowledge Across Cultures: A Contribution to Dialogue Among Civilizations* (Hong Kong: Comparative Education Research Centre, The University of Hong Kong, 2001), p.295.

for all-out Westernization. Wang saw this as a movement of intellectuals, which did not reach the masses of ordinary people, who were not prepared for such a radical departure from their own cultural foundations. The fourth shift Wang identified with the spread of Marxist thought. He noted that "the transfer of educational knowledge between Western Marxist and socialist regimes and China was facilitated by the fact that the societal conditions in these countries were similar to those experienced by China. The new ideas about Chinese education were welcomed by the national psyche of the people and found tacit approval."[37]

From this overview of China's historical experience, Wang pointed out the importance of trans-cultural exchange. He also highlighted the difficulties in trans-cultural exchange, which were not only problems of political system, but of the various understandings of the formation of different cultures, their characteristics and values. "There is a need to emphasize the value of the diversity of human cultures. In fact, human cultures have never evolved into a single unified whole, marked by the sameness of traditions, values and learning. Human cultures will always exist in different formations, places, times and strata in independence of one another. Human cultures will develop their own permeability to new ideas, inertia in creating change, unique patterns of transmitting values to the young, all in an effort to strive towards perfection and rejuvenation."[38]

In the conclusion to this article, Wang calls for cross-cultural exchanges that are not limited to scientific and technological areas of knowledge, but also lead to a dialogue about ethical and spiritual values of the great civilizations in the East and West. He suggests that universities are in a unique position to function as the bridge between cultures, as they have the necessary human and material infrastructure needed for the communication, transmission, preservation and storage of knowledge.[39]

How did the child of a fishing family, growing up on a small island totally unaware of the larger world of his own nation, let alone of the global community, become a philosopher of vision, with a passionate commitment to the development of the individual's potential? How did

---

[37] *Ibid.* p.298.
[38] *Ibid.* p.299.
[39] *Ibid.* p.300.

he survive the vagaries of a war that involved not only China and Japan, but also the Soviet Union and the United States? How did his painful experiences as a "wandering student" during those difficult years shape his later thought and development? In many ways, Professor Wang is himself the embodiment and example of the power of the subjective self to rise above the harshest of circumstances and to plumb its own depths in the search for spiritual and mental resources to create a future. Given the ways in which the concern of caring teachers changed his life, one can understand the extravagant hopes he places in education for China's children and young people, and indeed for the future of the global community.

Wang Fengxian celebrating his 70th birthday with his former students.

Chapter Eight

Wang Yongquan –
Higher Education Thinker and Leader

Wang Yongquan was born in 1929 to a father who had grown up in an impoverished rural family, similar to that of Pan Maoyuan and Wang Fengxian. His father had managed to study abroad, however, and returned to Shanghai as a professor in the mid-1920s, later moving to Beijing. Wang grew up in Beijing during the dark days of the looming Japanese invasion. After 1937, when the Japanese occupied Beijing, he followed his father to hinterland cities such as Kunming and Chongqing, thus receiving his education in different places along the way. At the time of the successful Chinese Revolution of 1949, Wang was 20 years old and an undergraduate student of physics at China's famous Tsinghua University. On graduation in 1950, he was assigned to the physics department of Tsinghua, then in 1952 moved to Peking University (Beida)[1] at the time of the reorganization of departments and colleges, when all of Tsinghua's basic science departments were transferred to Beida. Wang has spent his subsequent career at Beida. From leadership at the department level, he rose to become provost in 1986, while he was also the founding director of Peking University's Institute of Higher Education, which became a faculty of education in 2000. He has thus had a lifetime of association with China's most famous comprehensive university.[2]

---

[1] Beida is the commonly used nickname of Peking University. In this chapter, I will use Beida and Tsinghua as convenient short designations for the two universities.

[2] All of the details about Wang's life in this chapter were communicated in an interview with the author in Beijing, May 3, 1998.

This chapter will begin with an overview of the two universities which have framed Wang's life – Tsinghua University, where he studied, and Peking University, where he taught and exercised wide-ranging academic leadership. No one would question the pre-eminence of these two institutions in modern China's history, and in some ways they have been mirror opposites in the roles they have played, especially in the period since 1949. Chinese people love puns, and a favorite one going around among higher education leaders in the present time compares graduates of China's top universities. In a recent interview with one of the vice-presidents of Zhejiang University (Zheda), he made the following joking comparison among the top institutions: Tsinghua is famous for graduates who "zuoguan" (become officials), while Beida is known for graduates who "zuolao" (sit in prison). Zheda's graduates, by contrast, are known as able to "ganhuo" (get things done).[3] "Zuoguan" and "zuolao" are a play on words – the first "zuo" meaning to do or be (an official) and the second "zuo" meaning to sit (in prison).

Under Soviet influence in the 1950s, Tsinghua's star rose, as it was re-shaped into a polytechnical university, and graduated engineers and technologists who were assigned leading positions in China's three decades of socialist construction. By contrast Peking University was made into a pure comprehensive university on the Soviet/German model, with departments only of arts and sciences, and a loss of its schools of medicine, engineering and education. In addition, its tradition of academic freedom and democratic struggle, going back to the May 4th Movement of 1919 and earlier, gave it a more contested and difficult role in socialist China.

Wang's personal career in some ways reflects the nation's move from an emphasis on the science and engineering needed for massive projects of socialist construction to an understanding of the complex human and social dimensions of modernization, and the need for critical thinkers with a strong foundation in the humanities and social sciences. My first encounter with him was in October of 1992, when he presented a thoughtful comparative paper on concepts of general education in American and Chinese universities at our conference in Toronto on "Knowledge Across Cultures." His paper gave compelling insights into the reasons why China's traditional cultural orientation towards breadth

---

[3] Interview with Professor Ni Mingjiang, vice president of Zhejiang University, Hangzhou, July 20, 2004.

and integration of knowledge had been submerged by external pressures for rapid industrialization and national self-strengthening, that resulted in extreme specialization of the curriculum.[4] The following year I visited Peking University's Institute of Higher Education on his invitation and became aware of the burgeoning research on the economics and management of higher education taking place at this important center, which had been established in 1979.

Five years later, in 1998, I was honored by an invitation to the celebration of Beida's 100th anniversary, held in the Great Hall of the People, and presided over by Communist Party Chairman Jiang Zemin himself, and the whole politbureau. The presidents of 100 top universities from around the world were there to congratulate Beida on this august occasion. Much of the preparatory work had been done by Min Weifang, an economist of education who had returned to China with a doctoral degree from Stanford in 1988, and succeeded Wang as director of the Higher Education Institute in 1992. He was concurrently Beida's executive vice-president at the time.

Wang Yongquan presided over a celebratory higher education seminar and dinner on campus which followed the official ceremony,

Wang Yongquan (center) hosting a seminar for visitors at the 100th anniversary of Peking University.

[4] Wang Yongquan and Li Manli, "The Concept of General Education in Chinese Higher Education," in Ruth Hayhoe and Julia Pan (eds.) *Knowledge Across Cultures: A Contribution to Dialogue Among Civilizations* (Hong Kong: Comparative Education Research Centre, The University of Hong Kong, 2001), pp.311-322.

and attracted a number of scholars and researchers in the field, who recognized Beida's important contribution to the field of higher education. There was a serenity and poise in his manner which made one feel that he had finally achieved a degree of inner satisfaction in the balance among the differing demands of his academic life, as a scientist, a university leader and a scholar in the sociological and economic dimensions of higher education. Before telling the story of Wang's life and giving some insights into his educational ideas, we will turn to the stories of the universities with which he was so closely associated.

The Story of Three Universities – Beida, Tsinghua and Yenching

Only a high degree of hubris could allow one to attempt telling the story of three outstanding universities, whose destinies have been closely intertwined with that of modern China, in a few pages. That is what I plan to do, however, since all three were an important part of the context of Wang Yongquan's life. His father had come to study at Beida in 1917, a young village boy whose family had given their all to enable him to be educated. This was also the university where his father had taught in the 1950s. Wang himself served Beida throughout most of his academic career, and he remains active there in retirement. Tsinghua was also important in Wang's life, as he studied there from 1946 to 1950, and became one of the many proud Tsinghua graduates who took up leadership positions in socialist China. But what has Yenching to do with Wang's story? This was the crown jewel of American missionary universities, whose beautiful campus was given to Beida in the reorganization of Chinese higher education in 1952, leaving also some of the imprint of its spirit.

The story will be structured in three parts – first an overview of Beida's history between its founding in 1898, and the outbreak of the Sino-Japanese War in 1937, followed by a parallel look at the evolution of Tsinghua from its founding in 1911 to 1937. Next is a brief depiction of the experience of these two institutions during the Sino-Japanese War when they moved to Kunming and formed the Southwest Associated University, affectionately known as Lianda, in cooperation with Nankai University of Tianjin. Then the very different roles and contributions of these two leading Chinese universities after the Revolution of 1949 will be sketched out. Yenching's story is told at the beginning of this section, as this was the time when all missionary and private universities were closed, and their staff and facilities were re-assigned to other institutions.

Chapter four has noted Zhu Jiusi's comments on the reasons for the abolition of missionary institutions in the early years of socialist China. He pointed out that the new government paid respect to their contributions by ensuring that the facilities they had developed and the people they had nurtured were well integrated into the new system.[5] The fact that Yenching's campus was given to Beida was certainly a recognition of its standing and the spirit of scholarship it had fostered – not only in terms of physical facilities, buildings and library, but also in terms of people. An interesting comment by Xie Xide, who grew up on the Yenching campus where her father was a professor,[6] gives some insight into its relationship with the new socialist government. Xie commented that there had been a plan to rebuild Yenching University in Taiwan, after the Nationalists moved there in 1949, but in the end the new Christian university established in collaboration with the New York-based United Board for Christian Higher Education in Asia in Taiwan was called Tunghai. The reason for this, Xie recollected, was that Chiang Kai-shek's finance minister, H.H. Kung, had objected to a new Yenching in Taiwan. Too many Yenching graduates had become dedicated Communists and were serving in the new Chinese leadership![7] Perhaps the most famous was Huang Hua, Foreign Minister of China from 1976 to 1982.

This story of these three universities is also a comparative story, since one can see in their development aspects of China's classical traditions, both those of the imperial examination system and those of the more informal *shuyuan*, interacting with the competing Western models that influenced China's higher education over the century: the German research university, the American college and university, the Soviet polytechnical university and the Soviet comprehensive university. Aspects of these different models were interwoven with the evolving experience of Beida, Tsinghua and Yenching.

Beida was founded in the Hundred Day Reform Movement of 1898, as the Metropolitan University or the Imperial University. It was one of the few institutions to survive this brief period of reform. It was a time of strong influence from Japan's modern educational system, and the

---

[5] See Chapter Four, p.129.
[6] See Chapter Six, p.187.
[7] Interview with Xie Xide, Shanghai, October 17, 1998.

university was first designed to stand at the apex of a modern educational system, with a dual role as university and supervisor of the modern education system under the legislation passed in 1902.[8] With subsequent legislation passed in 1904, a Minister of Education was appointed, but the Imperial University and its president remained the leading modern academic institution of the late Qing imperial government. In 1905 the traditional civil service examinations were abolished, and the university took over the task of educating those destined to become officials.

The new university had a preparatory section with programs in the arts (including classics, politics, law, commerce and economics) and in the applied sciences (including sound, light, electricity, chemistry, agriculture, engineering, medicine and mathematics). After three years, students who passed the examinations could qualify to enter one of two schools, the school for officials (*shixue guan*) or the school for teachers (*shifan guan*), and those holding official posts at certain levels within the bureaucracy could also be accepted for entry.[9] In these early years, the Imperial University was thus somewhat of a transitional institution, between the traditional civil service system and the modern university.

In 1908, the school for teachers became independent of the imperial university,[10] and its historical development has been sketched out in chapters three and nine, which give the history of Northwest Normal University and Beijing Normal University. The school for officials continued to recruit students in eight major subject areas – classics, humanities, political science and law, science, agriculture, engineering, commerce and medicine. By the time of the 1911 Revolution, there were about 400 students enrolled.[11]

After the Revolution of 1911 the Imperial University became Peking University, and higher education legislation passed by the fledgling republican government in 1912 specified a clear distinction between universities and specialist higher schools, with universities mandated to focus on arts and sciences, with some related applied fields, and to be

---

[8] Hiroshi Abe, "Borrowing from Japan: China's First Modern Education System," in Ruth Hayhoe and Marianne Bastid (eds.), *China's Education and the Industrialized World: Studies in Cultural Transfer* (New York: M.E.Sharpe, 1987), p.60.

[9] Xiao Chaoran et al, *Beijing daxue xiaoshi 1898-1949* (Beijing: Beijing daxue chubanshe, 1988), p.16.

[10] *Ibid*. p.26.

[11] *Ibid*.

responsible both for teaching and the advancement of theoretical knowledge.[12] In 1912, Yan Fu, the famous scholar and translator of European classics such as Huxley's *Evolution and Ethics,* and Mill's *On Liberty,*[13] was appointed president of Peking University. He almost immediately faced a crisis in funding and the threat of closure for the university. With the support of students he borrowed funds several times to keep the university open. In spite of his success, he was forced to resign that same year in face of government pressure.[14]

In the following year two others were appointed to the university's leadership, first Zhang Shizhao, who never took up the post, and then Ma Xiangbo, who was living in Beijing at the time and seeking to establish an independent Academy of Science.[15] Ma used the university's property as collateral to borrow money to keep the university going, but in so doing lost the support of students.[16] He thus resigned at the end of one year and was succeeded by He Yushi, a well-known scholar of geology who had returned from study in Japan. Under his leadership, Peking University doubled its student body to over 800 students, but continued to struggle for government funding and for its very existence. By 1914, he too felt compelled to resign.[17]

Next to be appointed to the presidency was Hu Renyuan, an official in charge of applied sciences in the ministry of education.[18] Between 1914 and the end of 1916, he led the university through several crises, the most notable being the efforts of President Yuan Shikai to gain support and legitimacy from the university in his campaign to re-instate the imperial system, and have himself crowned as emperor. Hu and the faculty resolutely refused to cooperate in this scheme, and one of the professors

---

[12] Ruth Hayhoe, *China's Universities 1895-1995: A Century of Cultural Conflict* (Hong Kong: Comparative Education Research Centre, The University of Hong Kong, 1999), p.43.

[13] Benjamin Schwartz, *In Search of Wealth and Power: Yen Fu and the West* (Cambridge, Mass.: The Belknap Press of Harvard University Press, 1964).

[14] Xiao et al, *Beijing daxue xiaoshi*, pp.37-40.

[15] Lu Yongling, "Standing Between Two Worlds: Ma Xiangbo's Educational Thought and Practice" in Ruth Hayhoe and Yongling Lu, *Ma Xiangbo and the Mind of Modern China* (New York: M.E. Sharpe, 1996), pp.177-188. See also Chapter Six, pp.175-177.

[16] Xiao et al, *Beijing daxue xiaoshi*, p.40.

[17] *Ibid.* p.41.

[18] *Ibid.* p.42.

of philosophy, Ma Xulun, resigned in protest against the president's actions. Ma was an outstanding philosopher, later to be Minister of Education in the early 1950s.[19]

Meanwhile student numbers grew rapidly over this period, reaching a total of 1,503 in 1916.[20] There were enormous pressures for space, and the sum of 200,000 yuan was borrowed in 1916 to build a student residence with 300 rooms, to accommodate this growing student body. It was completed in 1918, and has been known ever since as the "Red Building," a famous and representative symbol of the Beida spirit, close to the original Beida campus in central Beijing.[21]

Over these years the curriculum had undergone some changes, with agriculture being separated out as a specialist college in 1914, leaving programs in arts, sciences, law and engineering. Under Hu's leadership, between 1914 and 1916, efforts were made to regularize teaching, develop new textbooks, and appoint new faculty in each of the major fields. Science laboratories were constructed, and the library was improved.[22]

In the period from the Revolution of 1911 to 1916, the institutional history concludes, the university did not manage to separate itself from the semi-colonial semi-feudal governmental system of the time, in spite of considerable development in student numbers, curricular organization and faculty appointments. The turning point came with the appointment of Cai Yuanpei as its new chancellor in December of 1916. Although Beida was to have many famous presidents in the years to follow, Cai Yuanpei has undoubtedly been the president most closely associated with the Beida spirit, as well as the scholar having the greatest influence on the development of China's modern universities during the Nationalist period.

Born in 1868, Cai had gained a thorough grounding in Chinese classical scholarship through study in a traditional *shuyuan*, then had taken the civil service examinations and passed with the highest honors, becoming a Hanlin Academician in 1892. His first mentor in the Western academic tradition was Ma Xiangbo, with whom he studied Latin and philosophy while he was a teacher at the Nanyang Public Institute in

---

[19] *Ibid*. pp.43-44.
[20] *Ibid*. pp.47-48.
[21] *Ibid*. p.43.
[22] *Ibid*. pp.45-46.

Shanghai of the late 1890s.[23] Cai subsequently had two extended periods of study in France and Germany, from 1906 to 1911, and again from 1912 to 1916. He helped to establish a Sino-French university in Lyons, Shanghai and Beijing, as well as doing higher studies at the universities of Leipzig and Berlin. On his return to China in 1911, he was appointed Minister of Education for the new republican government.[24] When Yuan Shikai took over the new government and moved the capital to Beijing, Cai had returned to Europe, unwilling to work under Yuan.

After the death of Yuan, he accepted a call back to China to take up the chancellorship of Beida in December of 1916. Greatly influenced by the German model of the university, he was determined to put an emphasis on academic freedom and university autonomy. In the higher education legislation he had drafted for the new republic in 1912, it was specified that universities should be governed by a senate, made up of the academic deans and representatives of professors, and the institutional history describes how this pattern of governance had been put in place in 1915.[25] Once Cai became Chancellor, he stressed the university's autonomy from government, and tried to attract scholars of the highest caliber to teach. He insisted that they should not hold concurrent positions with the government, and sought to foster a spirit of critical scholarship that would contribute to China's long-term development. He felt one of Beida's greatest weaknesses was its tendency to maintain the old tradition of education for the civil service examinations and for official careers. Cai also strongly emphasized academic freedom, and tried to recruit scholars from many different scholarly backgrounds, encouraging them to engage in lively debates.

His personal statement on academic freedom has become one of the classics of modern Chinese higher education: "I am open to all schools of thought; according to the general standards of the universities of all nations and the principle of freedom of thought, I believe we should be inclusive of diverse viewpoints. Regardless of which school of thought, if their words are logical, those who maintain them have reason, and they have not yet met the fate of being eliminated by natural selection, indeed even if they are mutually contradictory, I will allow them to develop

---

[23] For more on Ma Xiangbo, see Chapter Six, pp.175-177.
[24] William Duiker, *Ts'ai Yuan-p'ei: Educator of Modern China* (University Park and London: University of Pennsylvania Press, 1977).
[25] Xiao et al, *Beijing daxue xiaoshi*, p.48.

freely."[26]

With these words, Cai revealed an interesting combination of European and Chinese views. On the Chinese side, he had no difficulty with tolerating views that were mutually contradictory, while on the European side, he favored theoretical over applied scholarship. Academic freedom was thus associated with theoretical debates in basic scholarship, as in the German tradition. It was premised on the assumption that professors and students would refrain from direct social or political activism, in favor of contribution to knowledge over the long term. Implicit in this was the continental European view that knowledge is advanced more through critical debate and experimentation, than through application to practice.

There can be little doubt that Cai Yuanpei created the conditions for the outbreak of the May 4th movement in 1919. The high quality and diverse views of the professors he had appointed, combined with the intelligence and passion of the students attracted to Beida, also the determination to maintain independence from the warlord government, resulted in a movement that transformed China's intellectual life, culture, literature, and politics. The institutional history naturally highlights the role of famous Communist thinkers, such as Chen Duxiu and Li Dazhao, and the activities of the fledgling Communist movement, with nearly one hundred pages given to this subject. [27] Its authors also noted Cai Yuanpei's hesitation over the direct involvement of professors and students in political activism.[28] Cai resigned his presidency in protest against governmental suppression of students and faculty, yet also in a plea to students to give their attention to the longer term, rather than immediate political protest: "You have the opportunity of receiving education and the chance to take part in pure scientific research, so that you can lay the foundation for a new national culture for China and participate in world scholarly activities."[29]

In the end he was persuaded to stay at Beida until 1923, when he took extended leave for a period of further study in Europe, and Jiang Menglin was appointed acting chancellor and subsequently served as

---

[26] *Ibid.* p.65 (author's translation)

[27] *Ibid.* pp.80-169.

[28] *Ibid.* pp.89-90.

[29] Cai Yuanpei, *Cai Yuanpei xuanji* [Selections from Cai Yuanpei] (Beijing: Zhonghua shuju, 1959), p.98.

Beida's longest lasting chancellor, from 1930 to 1945. In the years following Beida's leadership of the May 4th movement, with its remarkable intellectual, cultural and political consequences, the university continued to develop, in spite of the chaotic political conditions in Beijing, with new programs in education, psychology and biology being established in 1924 and 1925.[30]

So many intellectual luminaries served on the Beida faculty, that it would be impossible to mention all of them in this brief overview.[31] One of Cai's important appointments, however, was that of the famous American-returned philosopher, Hu Shi, to be Beida's dean of arts. Hu's commitment to philosophical pragmatism and a problem-solving approach to social change complemented that of Cai's European-based rationalism, creating a kind of three way dialogue which included the leading Communist thinkers whose influences have been noted above. These three external influences in turn interacted with the two poles of China's own tradition – the civil service examination system and the traditional *shuyuan*.

In a thought-provoking essay on the influence of China's *shuyuan* tradition on modern Chinese universities, Ding Gang has shown how Cai's personal experience of the Hanlin Academy, and of teaching at Beida in its early years, formed a strong resolution in his mind to ensure that the tradition of education for officialdom was replaced by the progressive scholarly tradition of the *shuyuan* in developing modern Chinese universities.[32] Ding Gang shows how he supported the creation of research institutes in each basic discipline and emphasized the integration of teaching and research along lines inspired as much by the *shuyuan* as by the German universities he so greatly admired.

Perhaps the most interesting and influential of the research institutes established over these years was the research institute for Chinese studies, headed by Hu Shi, and emphasizing systematic and critical research in China's rich tradition of classical, literary and historical texts. Hu Shi was so successful in the leadership of this institute

---

[30] Xiao et al, *Beijing daxue xiaoshi*, pp.190-191.

[31] For an in-depth account, see Timothy B. Weston, *The Power of Position: Beijing University, Intellectuals and Chinese Political Culture 1898-1929* (Berkeley: University of California Press, 2004).

[32] Ding Gang, "The Shuyuan and the Development of Chinese Universities in the Early Twentieth Century,"in Ruth Hayhoe and Julia Pan (eds.), *East-West Dialogue in Knowledge and Higher Education* (New York: M.E. Sharpe, 1996), pp.226-229.

that he was invited to assist the neighboring Tsinghua to found a parallel institute. Tsinghua's institute for national studies (*guoxue yanjiuyuan*) became even more famous because of the caliber of the scholars teaching there and the greater resources available at for their support.[33]

With the establishment of the Republican government in 1928 under the Nationalist Party, Beida had a brief setback in face of pressures for merger, but these were successfully resisted. New legislation required that a university should have at least three colleges, with one of them being in the basic or applied sciences. Beida fit this profile well with its basic arts and sciences program re-organized into colleges of arts, sciences and law. Lively debates among the different schools of thought continued, and there was considerable student participation in the escalating movements against Japanese imperialism and governmental corruption. With the Japanese invasion of Beijing in 1937, a new phase in its life began, as professors and students made the long trek to the far southwest of China to continue its academic work through the war years.

There can be little doubt that Beida remained pre-eminent as the leading national university of China in the period between 1919 and 1937. Over these years, however, a rival institution was taking shape, which was to become an outstanding center of scholarship under somewhat different conditions. It was American rather than European influences that played a core role, alongside of China's own scholarly traditions. These two institutions shared a campus in Kunming from 1937 to 1945, and ever since that time they have stood for academic excellence in the minds of most Chinese. Indeed the phrase Beida Tsinghua has a similar ring in the Chinese context to that of Oxbridge in the United Kingdom.

We turn now to the story of Tsinghua, which was founded in 1911 as a preparatory school for young Chinese intending to do their university studies in the United States. Its early curricular emphasis was on the teaching of English, as well as practical subjects of importance to China's economic development. The story of its founding and the development of its unique ethos has been recounted in a recent doctoral thesis by Dr. Pan Suyan, who has explored the fascinating question of Tsinghua's changing relationship to the government over a 90-year period, identifing patterns of semi-independence as a persisting

---

[33] *Ibid*. pp.232-233.

characteristic of its standing.[34]

Tsinghua was actually the brainchild of forward-looking Americans who persuaded their government that the best use for the Indemnity funds, which the Qing government was forced to pay to the United States in recompense for the lives lost in the Boxer Rebellion of 1900, was the education of young Chinese in the United States. The US government therefore negotiated an agreement with the Chinese government in 1908, whereby a preparatory school would be established under official government auspices for Chinese students interested in studying in America. While some patriotic Chinese objected to the clause that gave the US government shared supervisory powers, seeing this as cultural imperialism, the Qing government accepted this US condition.

The school was to recruit Chinese students preparing to study in the United States, and educate them in fields relevant to economic development, including subjects such as industry, agriculture, railway, mining, architecture, trade, banking and management. Successful candidates were required to pass examinations in both English and Chinese as well as history and geography. The Qing government provided a historic imperial garden as a site for the new college, and its first day of school was in April of 1911. Two months later the dynasty was overthrown, and the new institution, now called Tsinghua College, was given over to the Ministry of Foreign Affairs of the new republican government to manage.[35]

Tsinghua thus experienced strong American influence in its early development, and had a unique identity in its relation to the Ministry of Foreign Affairs, and the American Ambassador to China. This was in striking contrast to Beida, with the European influences on its curriculum and style of governance which had come first through the Japanese patterns emulated in the late Qing, and then more directly through the ideas of Cai Yuanpei.

Tsinghua's early curriculum had many subjects relating to the cultural and social conditions of American life, as well as practically oriented fields. Many of its teachers were recruited from the United States, others among American-returned Chinese. English was the

---

[34] Pan Suyan, "How Higher Educational Institutions Cope with Social Change: The Case of Tsinghua University, China," Unpublished Ph.D. thesis, The University of Hong Kong, 2004.
[35] *Ibid.* p.93.

medium of instruction for all courses, except those on Chinese literature, language and history. Student numbers grew from around 500 in 1911 to 665 by 1918 and reached 1,223 in 1937, not including graduate students.[36] Over this period, Chinese teaching staff engaged in a struggle to ensure more Chinese teachers were recruited, and foreign staff included Europeans as well as Americans, also to bring more Chinese studies into the curriculum.

Tsinghua's funding was dramatically higher than what was available at other public or private institutions, a per student allocation of 1,300 yuan per year in 1916, contrasting with 299 per year at Beida and 738 at Fudan.[37] In subsequent years the gap was to grow. This munificent funding had its own costs, in terms of the direct involvement of the American Embassy in Tsinghua's management. The American Ambassador was always consulted by China's Ministry of Foreign Affairs in the appointment of successive presidents. Pan notes how all of them had studied in the United States and also had had experience as officials in the ministry, showing how this American influence was combined with a continuance of China's own traditions of direct governmental control over higher education.[38]

The buildings on the Tsinghua campus also expressed a strong and unapologetic Western influence. The beautiful auditorium was in traditional Greek and Roman style, while the main academic block was in classical German style, and other buildings, such as the science laboratories and the sports hall, were in modern American style. When British philosopher Bertrand Russell saw it in 1920, he was said to have described it as "a school transplanted from the United States to China."[39] This was in striking contrast with the buildings in classical Chinese style constructed under American missionary influence on the nearby Yenching campus.

At the same time Pan charts the movement of Tsinghua professors and students over the 1920s to assert greater and greater control over their institution in the face of governmental bureaucratism and American influence. Students organized themselves to express strong opposition to

---

[36] Tsinghua daxue xiaoshi bianxie zu (ed.) *Tsinghua daxue xiaoshi gao* [Draft History of Tsinghua University] (Beijing: Zhonghua shuju, 1981), pp.66, 147.
[37] *Ibid.* p.56.
[38] Pan, "How Higher Educational Institutions Cope with Social Change," p.105.
[39] *Ibid.* p.98.

several of those appointed president, with the result that three were forced to resign. Students were determined their college should be headed by a scholar of the caliber of Cai Yuanpei at Beida. Faculty, for their part, insisted on participating in college government, and set up a professors' association composed of all full professors and administrative heads, which was chaired by the president and had the right to nominate members of the senate as well as faculty deans.

While Tsinghua was called a college up to 1928, when the Nationalist government came to power, in fact one can see the influence of the American research university, rather than the college on its development. Given its substantial funding and high profile, it is not surprising to see a strong orientation towards research emerging during the 1920s, with much of the initiative coming from senior professors who were members of the professors' association.

Ding Gang explains how Hu Shi developed a blueprint for a research institute in national studies (*guoxue yanjiusuo*) at Tsinghua in the mid 1920s, [40] and Pan explains how generous funding by the Tsinghua College president enabled it to build a valuable research library in the Chinese classics, linguistics, philosophy and foreign scholarship on the Chinese classics.[41] Most importantly, Tsinghua was able to appoint four outstanding Chinese scholars to the Institute, whose renown has reverberated through the 20th century: historians Wang Guowei and Chen Yinke, linguist Zhao Yuanren, and philosopher Liang Qichao, who was to spend the last few years of his life at Tsinghua. One of the ideas which Hu Shi used in designing the institute was the tutorial model of British universities, which melded well with China's *shuyuan* tradition, and provided conditions for the mentoring of graduate students by these outstanding scholars.[42]

In its curricular developments after it achieved university status in 1929, one can see again the patterns of the American research university, with four colleges or faculties established, arts, sciences, law and engineering, the latter being added in 1932. New research institutes reflected the Nationalist government's determination to strengthen the applied sciences, and the fact that Tsinghua had a large number of faculty who had returned from the US with degrees from MIT, the

---

[40] Ding, "The Shuyuan and the Development of Chinese Universities," p.233.
[41] Pan, "How Higher Educational Institutions Cope with Social Change," p.103.
[42] *Ibid*. p.232.

University of Michigan and Cornell in applied science areas. These institutes included ones in agriculture, radio communication, and metal materials, as well as an institute of aeronautics.[43]

Of all the details on the Tsinghua history recounted in Pan's thesis, the issue of autonomy with reference to the appointment of the president is most notable. We have seen the American involvement in this decision in the early years. Once Tsinghua became a national university under the Nationalist government, the appointment of the president was a key decision in shaping the university to serve government goals. At the same time the tradition of the professors' association, and the college's success in ousting presidents during the twenties made this a contested issue. Luo Jialun, the president who was successful in negotiating Tsinghua's change of status from a college to a leading national university, was a close associate of Chiang Kai-shek, and thus able to gain governmental support at a high level. He succeeded in having Tsinghua transferred from the jurisdiction of the Ministry of Foreign Affairs to the Ministry of Education, and also in having its ties to the American Embassy cut. While faculty and students were pleased with this new status, they were highly resistant to President Luo's subsequent efforts to bring the university in line with the Nationalist government's political goals, which included a strong emphasis on political education, the creation of party organs on campus and military training. Students and faculty saw this as antithetical to academic freedom and put such strong pressure on Luo that he resigned.[44]

In the subsequent period, the Nationalist government temporarily lost control of Northern China, and the Northern warlord, Yan Xishan tried to appoint a president who would link the university to his leadership, giving it greater legitimacy. His appointed candidate, Qiao Wanxuan, came to the campus to take up the presidency with the support of troops, yet met such strong resistance from students and faculty that he failed to enter. Tsinghua remained without a president for 11 months. When the Nationalist government regained control, it appointed Wu Nanxuan, again a political figure, who soon lost the faculty and students' support because of his refusal to involve the professors' association in major academic decisions. The association therefore wrote to the Ministry of Education demanding his dismissal,

---

[43] Tsinghua daxue xiaoshi bianxiezu, *Tsinghua daxue xiaoshi gao*, p.113.
[44] Pan, "How Higher Institutions Cope with Social Change," pp.119-124.

and threatening that all of the senior Tsinghua professors would resign, if he was not dismissed. Wu responded by moving his office to the foreign embassy district in Beijing, thus subjecting himself to further criticism from students, and to Chiang Kai-shek's judgment that "he had badly damaged the authority and prestige of the Nationalist government." At this Wu had no choice but to resign.[45]

Meanwhile the professors' association wrote a letter to the Ministry of Education laying down their criteria for a new president – a scholar who was "knowledgeable, noble-minded, capable of pursuing Tsinghua University's development," and who had no official governmental position, nor affiliation with any political party." [46] The Ministry of Education then selected Mei Yiqi as Tsinghua's next president, thus putting into a position of leadership a scholar who was able to gain the support of faculty and students and to lead the university with distinction from 1931 to 1948. In Zhu Jiusi's judgment, Mei Yiqi was next to Cai Yuanpei in terms of the visionary leadership he brought to Chinese higher education during the Nationalist period.[47]

Mei had been among the first group of students associated with Tsinghua that were sent to the United States for study in 1909. He had done a degree in electrical engineering at the Worcester Polytechnic and returned to China in 1914, beginning his career at Tsinghua College as a teacher of physics, then taking on more and more administrative work until he had become provost. Although he was not a member of the Nationalist Party, he did have close links with Northern party members such as Li Shizeng and Li Shuhua, and was nominated for president by Fan Yuanlian, an early republican minister of education.[48] He proved a visionary leader, developing Tsinghua into an outstanding comprehensive university, and taking overall leadership for the Southwest Associated University during its years in Kunming.

Much more could be said about the development of both Beida and Tsinghua over the first few decades of their history, but I have tried to focus on highlights relating to their leadership, their relationship with government and the ethos that one can see emerging from their teaching programs and research. The activism of students and faculty in face of

---

[45] *Ibid*. p.126.

[46] *Ibid*. pp.126-127.

[47] Interview with Zhu Jiusi, May 23, 1992.

[48] See Chapter Three, p.83.

the increasing dangers of the Japanese incursion, and the corruption and ineffectiveness of the Nationalist government is another part of the story. Beida students were the undisputed leaders in the early years, with the May 4th Movement starting there, but students of Tsinghua and other universities around the nation were equally involved in the later movements. Cai Yuanpei's hope of separating university education from politics was simply not possible in these tumultuous times, when university students had a high degree of concern for the nation's very survival.

The next phase of this story will move to the war years, when the Japanese occupation of Beijing, and gradually of the whole Eastern part of China, caused most universities to move to the hinterland. One of the bright spots in Nationalist education policy was the decision to give as much support as possible to their universities under war-time conditions, and encourage students and professors to continue with their academic work, on the understanding that the country would need their professional contributions once the war was over. University research was naturally greatly affected by the moves, with tremendous loss of equipment and libraries. Nevertheless great efforts were made to do kinds of research that would contribute to war-time needs, in fields such as aeronautics and other war-time industries.[49]

Beida, Tsinghua and Nankai all moved to the city of Kunming in the distance southwestern province of Yunnan, and shared a campus and a life. While they maintained their separate identities in certain ways, they worked in close cooperation and Tsinghua's President, Mei Yiqi, chaired the senior administration committee, proving a visionary leader for Lianda, the Southwest Associated University. The fact that each of the three institutions brought particular areas of strength to this union meant the institution was truly comprehensive, combining Beida' strengths in basic sciences and humanities, with Tsinghua's greater emphasis on engineering and applied fields and Nankai's fame in economics and social theory.

John Israel's recent volume, *Lianda: A Chinese University in War and Revolution*, provides copious information on the richness of its intellectual life, as Chinese traditional literature, history and philosophy were rethought in relation to the dilemmas of modernization and war, and Western style social sciences were adapted to Chinese realities in ways

---

[49] Ruth Hayhoe, *China's Universities 1895-1995*, pp.56-58.

that had not happened earlier.[50] China's greatest sociologist, Fei Xiaotong, produced path-breaking work based on social surveys done during this period, while literary theorists such as Wen Yiduo did some of their most creative work. In spite of the severe limitations on laboratory equipment and supplies under war-time conditions, teaching and research in areas of basic science and mathematics continued at a high level, as did work in the applied sciences and engineering. The first two Chinese physicists to receive the Nobel prize, T.D. Lee and C.N. Yang were undergraduate students at Lianda during these years, later developing their careers in the United States.

One of the most important aspects of Lianda's context was the fact that it was geographically distant from the war-time capital of Chongqing, and thus there was less possibility of interference in its work from the Nationalist government, than in the nearby universities. Lianda thus enjoyed a relatively high degree of autonomy and one could see an ethos emerge which represented a blending of the progressive spirit of the *shuyuan* with elements of both American and German academic values. John Israel captures the spirit of Lianda rather well in the following quotation:

"In sharing poverty for the sake of education, faculty members and students felt drawn to each other and a sense of community emerged. It was more akin to that of the traditional *shuyuan* than to that of the status-conscious universities of pre-war days. The existence of a 'vital, upbeat, creative spiritual life' was a matter of pride and satisfaction for those who survived the mid-war Lianda years."[51]

With the end of the war in 1945, the three universities moved back to their original campuses, Beida and Tsinghua to Beijing, Nankai to Tianjin. Mei Yiqi continued as president of Tsinghua up to the autumn of 1948, not long before Beijing came under the control of the victorious Communist Party. The new president of Beida, after it moved back to Beijing was Hu Shi, who had been dean of arts at Beida in the 1920s, then Chinese ambassador to the United States during the war years. This gave him a high status in the Nationalist government.

The re-established Beida had a student body of over 3,500 by 1947, and three new faculties were added to the original faculties of arts,

---

[50] John Israel, *Lianda: A Chinese University in War and Revolution* (Stanford: Stanford University Press, 1996).

[51] *Ibid.* pp.331-332.

sciences and law – medicine, engineering and agriculture. [52] It thus became fully comprehensive in its curricular offerings, perhaps reflecting the influence of its American-educated president. Tsinghua had a similar profile, with faculties of arts, sciences and law, and a new faculty of agriculture set up after its return to Beijing and based on the successful work of its agriculture research institute during the war. [53] Tsinghua's student numbers were 2,300 in 1946. [54]

The years from 1946 to 1948 were extremely troubled, with an ongoing Civil War between the Nationalist and Communist parties. It was a time of intense student activism, and of increasing economic chaos, as the Nationalist regime lost control of the economy and finally had to retreat to Taiwan. The majority of students and intellectuals had become disillusioned with the regime and welcomed the success of the liberation struggle, even though only a minority had joined the Communist Party during the war years.

When the new Communist regime established itself with Beijing as its capital, there was a sense of excitement and expectation. Creating a socialist education system was a priority, and particular attention was given to higher education, with a strong sense of the need for professionals to serve the rapid development of industry and agriculture after the years of war. In spite of the significant achievements and scholarly profile of the top national universities, it was decided to create an entirely new system of higher education modeled on that of the Soviet Union, and to make a thorough reorganization of all the departments and faculties of the existing institutions to fit in with this new plan. The purpose was to achieve greater geographical rationalization than in the past, and to organize knowledge specializations that would prepare experts in very specific ways for each of the sectors of the planned economy.

While Beida and Tsinghua had become more similar in the character of their curriculum as comprehensive universities before 1949, they now were to be assigned very different roles in the new socialist system. Beida would become a Soviet-style comprehensive university with departments only in the basic disciplines of knowledge – the arts and sciences. Tsinghua was to become a polytechnical university, with a

---

[52] Xiao et al, *Beijing daxue xiaoshi*, pp.406-407.
[53] Tsinghua daxue xiaoshi bianxiezu, *Tsinghua daxue xiaoshi gao,* p.433.
[54] *Ibid.* p.433.

wide range of engineering disciplines, but no basic science departments and no humanities or social sciences. Since Tsinghua already had a campus of adequate size and facilities it stayed on its original site, while Beida was given the beautiful suburban campus of Yenching University, which was fairly close to Tsinghua.

At this point a paragraph or two on Yenching may be helpful. It was founded in 1916 on the basis of several Christian missionary colleges, which were merged to ensure consolidation and coordination of Christian higher education efforts. Its name, Yenching, was decided on the suggestion of Cai Yuanpei and Hu Shi, after much debate among missionary educators.[55] Yenching was the literary name for the city of Peking. In 1920 it acquired its beautiful campus, one of the summer gardens of a Manchu prince in the northwest superb of Beijing, not far from Tsinghua's campus.[56] The subsequent decision to create buildings in a style that melded Chinese traditional architectural features with Western building standards,[57] reflected the cultural sensitivity of the American missionaries and their appreciation of the Chinese philosophical heritage. These buildings gave the campus a strikingly different appearance from that of Tsinghua.

Yenching University was an interesting exemplar of the American tradition of the liberal arts college on Chinese soil, with wide ranging undergraduate programs in the humanities, social sciences and natural sciences, as well as small graduate programs in areas of strength. While English was used for much of the teaching, Yenching also developed a strong program in Chinese literature and history, in many ways having greater influence in this area than in its small theological program.[58] It was also involved in various kinds of social responsibility. Chapter three described how Li Bingde won a scholarship for graduate study at Yenching on rural education development, which would have provided for one year of further study in the United States, on condition that he returned to work in rural education projects. As it turned out, the

---

[55] Philip West, *Yenching University and Sino-Western Relations, 1916-1952* (Cambridge, Mass.: Harvard University Press, 1976), p.36.

[56] *Ibid.* p.37.

[57] See Jeffrey W. Cody, *Building in China: Henry K .Murphy's Adaptive Architecture* (Hong Kong and Seattle: Chinese University Press and University of Washington Press, 2001).

[58] Peter Ng, *Changing Paradigms of Christian Higher Education in China (1888-1950)* (Lewiston: The Edwin Mellen Press, 2002), Chapters One and Three.

opportunity was lost to him because of the Japanese invasion of Beijing in 1937.[59]

The one further comment on Yenching which needs to be made relates to its famous president, John Leighton Stuart, who took up this post in 1919, and served until the end of the Sino-Japanese War in 1945. In 1946 he was appointed American Ambassador to China, indicating the high regard in which his intellectual and cultural leadership was held. Stuart had been himself the son of a China missionary, and began his missionary career in China in 1905, becoming a professor of theology at the Nanking theological seminary in 1908. From there he was recruited to lead Yenching. Stuart was a dedicated Christian leader, fluent in Chinese and a greater admirer of Chinese thought and philosophy. He also had a genuine social conscience and was deeply sympathetic to student activism. He was known to have kept his personal door open to Communist youth,[60] even while the university struggled with accusations of cultural imperialism in an increasingly radicalized environment. Chapter six noted Xie Xide's comment that Huang Hua and other Yenching graduates in the new Communist administration had invited Stuart to Beijing in 1949, before he returned to the United States. Stuart would have liked to go, she felt sure, but he did not get permission from his government. History might have developed differently, Xie reflected, if he had gone.[61]

As we move to a brief overview of the development of Beida and Tsinghua under China's new socialist regime, one general point of comparison is worth noting. Behind the Soviet patterns, which were implemented with a remarkable degree of thoroughness and consistency, were European views of knowledge and traditions of academic organization quite at variance with Chinese tradition. They included the German tendency to make a strict demarcation between theory and practice, and the French penchant for a high degree of specialization of knowledge for the service of national development goals. By contrast the more integrative characteristics of American pragmatist epistemology had demonstrated their capacity for creative synthesis with progressive aspects of China's *shuyuan* tradition, and we have noted the curricular

---

[59] Chapter Three, pp.94-95.
[60] West, *Yenching University and Sino-Western Relations*, p.31.
[61] See Chapter Six, p.201.

breadth of both Beida and Tsinghua under American influence in the post war period, as well as that of Yenching.

Under the Soviet patterns adopted in the reorganization of faculties and departments in 1952, there was first a strict separation between theoretical and applied fields of knowledge. Basic humanities and sciences were to be nurtured in new-style comprehensive universities, while broad applied sciences were to be located in polytechnical universities. All other subject areas were placed in narrowly specialist institutions – for agriculture, medicine, foreign languages, specific fields of engineering, finance and economics, political science and law, all reporting to the respective sectoral ministry which would deploy the graduates. There can be little doubt that Tsinghua suffered greater losses than Beida under this new regime.[62] At the same time, it was to be rewarded with greater influence and power in a setting where engineers held the highest standing in the context of socialist macro-planning.

Tsinghua was to lose its faculties of law, science and agriculture, keeping only the basic science teaching necessary to support its focus on engineering. Beida lost its department of education to Beijing Normal University, its college of engineering to Tsinghua, and its college of medicine to a newly founded medical university. It was, however, greatly enriched by the gift of basic science, social sciences and humanities departments from Tsinghua, Furen and Yenching universities, which enhanced its critical mass of leading scholars in these areas.[63] It was also allowed to maintain the only department of philosophy in the whole country, absorbing the departments of philosophy of Nanjing, Wuhan and Zhongshan universities.[64]

In the years between 1952 and 1978, when Deng Xiaoping came to power there was little fundamental change in the curricular orientation of these two top institutions. Beida graduated students who typically became scientists researching in basic fields of knowledge or higher

---

[62] In my first interview with Zhu Jiusi, May 23, 1992, he remarked that the then Head of Tsinghua's Higher Education Research Centre, Madam Li Zuobao, had told him they simply could not bring themselves to write Tsinghua's institutional history for the period after 1952, since too much had been lost.

[63] Du Qin & Sui Xingyan, *Beijing daxue xuezhi yangai* [The Evolution of Peking University's Academic System] (Beijing: Beijing daxue chubanshe, 1998), p.12-13.

[64] *Ibid.*

education teachers, writers, journalists and thinkers.[65] Tsinghua graduated top quality engineers, many of whom climbed the ladder to senior positions in government and industry. Both preserved a sense of pride and connection to their pre-Liberation past, but were given very little leeway to take new initiatives on their own, or plan their own futures.

Pan has described Tsinghua's development between 1949 and 1976, showing the close links it had to the Communist Party and new socialist administration, with its president Jiang Nanxiang being a Tsinghua graduate of 1932, who had been active in the Chinese Communist Party before the Revolution. While president of Tsinghua he concurrently held very senior positions in the Party and was Vice-minister of Education and subsequently Minister of Higher Education. He thus ensured that Tsinghua exercised leadership in political education, and adhered closely to the educational policies of the new regime.[66] This in turn gained the government's trust in the political reliability of Tsinghua graduates and guaranteed their career opportunities.

At the same time, as Pan has shown, this very closeness to the Party and government made it possible for Tsinghua professors to develop a range of new scientific specializations inspired by their pursuit of excellence and desire to maintain the high standards of the past. They further gained permission to develop graduate programs in a number of key areas, and also to develop academic ties with leading universities in Britain and the United States, at a time when there were no diplomatic relations with the United States, and only low levels of representation with Britain.[67] After 1978 there was a remarkable new openness and much greater autonomy for universities. Tsinghua has thus been able to rebuild many of its areas of excellence of the past, including basic

---

[65] Two of the books published in celebration of Beida's 100th anniversary reflect this profile. The first is a collection of essays by well known writers who were Beida graduates, and the second is a collection of essays on Liberalism and Beida's tradition: Chuan Mu, Min Zi, Gao Wei (eds.), *Wo Guan Beida* [My View of Beida] (Beijing: Wenhua yishu chubanshe, 1998); Liu Junning (ed.) *Ziyou zhuyi de xiansheng: Beida chuantong yu jindai Zhongguo* [The first voice of Liberalism: The Beida tradition and recent Chinese history] (Beijing: Zhongguo renshi chubanshe, 1998).

[66] Pan, "How Higher Institutions Cope with Social Change," pp.141-142.

[67] *Ibid.* pp.148-153.

sciences, humanities, management, education and a range of social science areas.

Beida's story was somewhat different, given the very different character of its knowledge-base. Although it had the one and only department of philosophy in all of China, the traditional approaches to philosophical study had been overtaken by a pre-dominant emphasis on Marxism-Leninism. In the basic sciences its scholars were able to do important work. We have seen, for example, how Xie Xide spent two years in Beida's physics department from 1956 to 1958 working on a new textbook in semi-conductor physics with Professor Huang Kun.[68] Nevertheless, the majority of the research funding was given to institutes of the Chinese Academy of Sciences under the new macro planning system. In fields such as literature and history Beida professors continued to play a leading role, writing new texts and carrying out such research as they could manage, but their graduates did not have as promising career prospects as those of Tsinghua.

With Deng Xiaoping's reforms, Beida also moved into a new era of development, with so many new initiatives it is not possible to recount them all here. It has once again become a fully comprehensive university, with the former Beijing Medical University now merged with it, and a wide range of new programs in applied science areas as well as humanities and social sciences. The area of greatest interest for this chapter was the establishment of an Institute of Higher Education in 1979. Its mandate and role has recently been further broadened, as a new faculty of education was established in 2000, giving Beida a role in educational thought that it has not had for half a century, in spite of its pre-eminence as a comprehensive university.

We turn now to Wang Yongquan's personal story. Professor Wang has expressed some reserve about his inclusion in this volume of portraits of influential Chinese educators. This can be understood in light of the history of Beida, described above, especially the fact that it has been cut off from educational thought and theory for so long. Nevertheless, his close affiliation with China's two top universities, and his well-respected achievements in higher education research, will enable us to understand aspects of the Chinese educational heritage that we might not encounter in other chapters of this book.

---

[68] Chapter Six, p.192.

Growing up in War-Time China

Wang Yongquan was born in Shanghai in 1929, but the family moved to Beijing when he was eight months old, and he lived there until the Japanese occupation drove the family into exile. Wang's father story bears some attention, as his values and ideals had a profound influence on Wang's life. He had been born into rural poverty in Hubei province, and all of his brothers were peasant farmers. They saved enough money to send him to an excellent secondary school near the city of Wuhan, and from there he was successful in passing entrance examinations to Beida in 1917, the year after Cai Yuanpei took up the chancellorship. From Beida, his father went to France with the renowned Work Study Movement, which enabled so many working class young people to go abroad in that period. He studied philosophy and logic at the University of Lyons. In 1925 he returned to China, first teaching in Shanghai, then moving to Beijing where he taught at the Université Franco-chinoise and National Beiping University.

Wang has happy memories of his first seven years of life in a courtyard house in Beijing, with his professor father fully occupied with teaching and research. His mother was an illiterate peasant woman, as his father had honored the marriage arranged by his family, and settled

Wang Yongquan with his mother in their courtyard house in Beijing around 1932

down with her on return from France. Wang noted how this was an unusual marriage, given the intellectual gap between these two, yet his mother was a true Confucian woman, gentle and kind, yet strict about politeness and good manners. She particularly emphasized the importance of sincerity in friendship, and honesty in all dimensions of life.

This idyllic childhood was shattered by the Japanese invasion of Beijing, and his father's decision to leave the city in order to avoid any compromise with the occupiers. His father first returned to Wuhan, near his family home, then went on to Guilin, and finally to Kunming.

Wang stayed in Peking until 1939, with strict orders from his father that he should study at home with his older sister, in order to avoid any contact with the Japanese controlled education system. Wang noted how his father had instilled in him a strong sense of patriotism from this early period, as well as a democratic consciousness.

From 1938 to 1939, Wang and his mother and sister moved to Wuhan, then Guilin and finally Kunming, to join his father. His sister, who was ten years older, enrolled at Lianda, while he begin his formal schooling at the middle school attached to the Université Franco-chinoise. Between 1939 and 1941, his father moved to several places in Sichuan and Shaanxi, and began to teach at Sichuan University. Naturally he followed and enrolled in the secondary school attached to Sichuan University. He noted how most of the teachers at both of these schools were associate professors in the university who gave some of their time to secondary teaching, and their academic quality was thus very high. He particularly remembers the excellence in the teaching of English, Chinese and mathematics, with some math and science textbooks being in English. One teacher with remarkable fluency in English has a special place in his memory – for introducing Beethoven's Moonlight Sonata to the class and singing while teaching. This made him realize how language can encompass a whole culture.

If his schooling was important over these years, Wang explained that the "school of life" taught him even more. When he was just twelve years old, his mother took seriously ill with cancer, dying after six months at home in bed. While his father went to work each day, he stayed at home to do the shopping, cooking, carrying of water and washing for his sick mother. He felt over this six-month period he had learned to be totally independent and self-reliant, a lesson that influenced him later to feel there was nothing he could not do.

Wang noted that his father was greatly influenced by both European and Chinese philosophy. While he had studied mathematical logic in France, his interests and publications in the end were largely related to Chinese philosophy and the history of logic in China. In his teaching, Wang's father focused on Confucian philosophy, seeing Daoism and Buddhism as secondary strands that should be taught, but not adopted. He was particularly critical of the monastic tradition and the Daoist notion of escape to the countryside, since he felt it was incumbent on each person to accept their responsibility to society. He also strongly emphasized the importance of the social order, and of each person nurturing appropriate relationships with parents, siblings and friends, and being loyal to the country. Confucianism meant being strict with oneself, but generous and forgiving of others.

Wang is deeply aware of the imprint of his father's value system in his own life. From childhood he was taught to keep a diary, in which he would examine his own attitudes and conduct every day, to see if it measured up to Confucian standards, then show the diary to his parents once a week, for their feedback. He learned that it was important to be true to one's principles, whether or not anyone else was observing him. Also obedience to his parents and elders was deeply ingrained.

In 1943, Wang's father married a professor of mathematics from Sichuan University and Wang found her to be a wonderful stepmother. Her advice was to shape his most important decision at the end of his secondary education, which coincided with the end of the Sino-Japanese War. He wanted to study language and literature, and hoped to be able to enroll in a classical academy or *shuyuan*, but she advised him to learn something practical that would enable him to earn a living. There would always be time for literature as a hobby, she suggested. On her advice he took the examinations for Tsinghua, and was accepted into the department of physics in 1946. He lived on campus for four years, until his graduation in 1950, while his parents had also returned to Beijing, and his father first taught in the education department of Beijing Normal University, and subsequently in the philosophy department of Beida.

Wang Yongquan with his father and stepmother in Southwest China in 1944

These were tumultuous times for students in Beijing, with Tsinghua students being involved in a series of protest movements against the Nationalist government and the American forces supporting them in the Civil War against the Communists. Wang notes how he refrained from joining the Communist Party over these years out of respect for his father, who was strongly opposed to him becoming involved in politics. While he did attend some of the major demonstrations, he was not directly involved in the planning or organizational work. He does have a vivid memory of the lively debates that went on in December of 1948, just two months before the Communist Party entered Beijing. The question being debated was whether the Soviet Union should be viewed as a socialist or an imperialist country. The surprising conclusion of this student debate was that the Soviet Union should be seen as an imperialist power! This was clearly at variance with the views of the new leadership. Wang's point in recalling this incident was how open were the debates of the time, with complete freedom for students to take whichever side they found most persuasive.

Career under Socialism

Wang was 20 years old when Beijing was liberated by the Chinese Communist Party, and the following year he graduated and was assigned a position as assistant teacher in Tsinghua's Physics Department. Two years later, he moved to Beida, with the reorganization of colleges and departments which has been described earlier. Wang joined the Communist Youth League immediately on graduation, later qualifying for membership in the Communist Party. He commented how at this time he transferred all that he had learned from his father about traditional virtues of loyalty and filial piety to his relationship with the Communist Party. He felt there was a kind of absolutism in his thinking at the time, which called for respect and unquestioning obedience.

In 1958 the physics department at Beida was divided into four, with three new departments emerging in radio electronics, nuclear physics and geophysics. Thus at the young age of 28 he found himself chair of the department of radio electronics. This reflected the emphasis on electronic engineering in his study of physics at Tsinghua. In addition to department chair, he also served as party secretary for the department, giving him even wider responsibilities. He felt well able to take up this challenge, given all he had learned about independence and responsibility while growing up in war-time. He made the highest possible demands on academic staff and students, both in terms of professional knowledge and moral-political behavior. In retrospect, he felt his emphasis was on ensuring conformity to Party standards and unity, while little attention could be given to the individual talents and capabilities of the staff and students he was responsible for. This was a reflection of the dominant spirit of the time.

When the Hundred Flowers Movement was launched in 1956-1957, Wang felt fortunate that he was at Beida and not Tsinghua. Several of his former fellow students, who had stayed on to teach at Tsinghua after graduation, used this opportunity to express some criticism of the new regime. A number of them were subsequently labeled Rightists and suffered serious consequences. At Beida, Wang recollected, they were fortunate to have Jiang Longji as party secretary, a thoughtful and experienced leader who was concerned about protecting the staff. He advised them not to go out and demonstrate, thus saving quite a few from the consequences that might have followed. The situation was more serious for students according to some accounts.[69]

The most high profile casualty of this movement, however, was Beida's distinguished president, the economist Ma Yinchu. He had taken the opportunity of the Hundred Flowers Movement to put forward his new population theory and was criticized by Mao Zedong as a Malthusian. He published his own defence in a moving essay, "My Philosophical Thought and Economic Theories," and refused to retract it, even at the persuasion of Zhou Enlai. His parting words, before resigning and going into a long period of exile, were as follows: "After writing articles, one should be brave enough to correct mistakes, but one must adhere to the truth and bear all consequences, even if they are disadvantageous to his private interests or his life. I do not teach and have no direct contact with students, but I always want to educate them by means of action."[70]

Wang noted that Ma Yinchu had been more of a figurehead in his presidency of Beida, than an active presence on campus. Much of his time had been taken up with important meetings and commitments elsewhere. Nevertheless, Wang was disturbed by this incident, and by the radical activism and anti-Soviet rhetoric of the Great Leap Forward period, and the subsequent Cultural Revolution. While Wang had prepared for the possibility of study in the Soviet Union through studies of Russian, he had not been sent in the end. However, he had worked closely with a number of Russian professors who had come to assist at

---

[69] Rene Goldman, "The Rectification Campaign at Peking University May-June, 1957," in *China Quarterly*, No. 12, October-December, 1964, p.150.

[70] Howard Boorman, *Biographical Dictionary of Republican China*, Vol. 2, (New York: Columbia University Press, 1968), p.478. See also Ronald Hsia, "The Intellectual and Public Life of Ma Yin-ch'u" in *China Quarterly*, No. 6, April-June, 1961, pp.53-63.

Beida. He noted how they quickly gained respect from Chinese colleagues, as the teaching material they prepared was systematic, their
presentation style was clear and the content was substantial. His contact
with these academics served to dispel some of the negative feelings he
had had earlier towards the Soviet Union, caused by the rapacious
behavior of some Russian soldiers in China's northeast after the defeat of
the Japanese in 1945.

For the first time Wang began to have doubts and criticism with
regard to the judgments of the Party, and to realize that directions given
to him from above were not necessarily always correct. In all the rhetoric
about educational revolution, Wang felt a sense of nihilism. He could not
see anything to replace the Soviet patterns that were being repudiated,
nor could he find firm educational principles on which to build. As head
of the department of radio electronics from 1958 to 1976, he discovered
how impossible it was to solve educational problems without clearly
established educational principles.

The Cultural Revolution was, of course, even more devastating than
the Great Leap Forward, and Wang was locked up for three years on the
Beida campus between 1966 and 1969. Then in 1969 he moved to
Hanzhong, in Southwestern Shaanxi provinces. Beida had a branch
campus there, and he lived there for nine years, from 1969 to 1978.
During these years he did a great deal of reading, not only Marxist
classics, but also classical works on education from both China and the
West. It was over this period that his interest in educational thought and
theory was stimulated. He could see how destructive were the political
battles taking place on university campuses. Every faction wanted to be
able to control Beida, because of the prestige and legitimacy it could
confer, but this politicization of education could only be harmful to true
learning. He also noted how Beida in the end could not be controlled or
made to serve a particular political faction – its tradition of academic
freedom going back Cai Yuanpei, and still evident in the stand taken by
Ma Yinchu, meant that there would always be lively debates and diverse
viewpoints.

In 1978, Wang was appointed to head a new centre for audiovisual
education at Beida, and from this period onward he devoted himself
wholeheartedly to educational research. Four years later, in 1982, he was
appointed vice-provost, responsible for teaching and learning programs
across the whole campus. In 1986 be became provost and served in this
role until 1988. From 1979, he had been concurrently director of Beida's

Institute for Higher Education, where he served up to his retirement in 2000. Over the years since retirement he has continued to guide doctoral students, and contribute to teaching and research.

Higher Education Thinker and Leader

Wang Yongquan's life at Beida over half a century has given him cause to reflect on deep questions of education and national development, of the need for unity of purpose and firmness of direction on the one hand, and the value of open debate and the encouragement of diverse voices on the other. In comparing Tsinghua and Beida, he noted how it was somehow easier for Tsinghua to have a unified sense of purpose and a high degree of productivity, because of its focus on the applied sciences, which were so urgently needed for China's modernization. By contrast, Beida was extremely difficult to lead, given its long tradition of academic freedom and the wide range of subject areas being taught, from philosophy to law to theoretical physics.

In building up a graduate program in higher education economics and management Wang has felt a great responsibility for the quality of teaching and research. He himself has contributed to research in areas ranging from the economics and macro-structure of higher education to curriculum issues and comparative higher education. His excellent grounding in English, going back to secondary and university studies during the war, and his familiarity with the international literature, has enabled him to connect the work of the institute to that literature.

An example of this can be seen in his essay on the concept of general education,[71] which draws on a wide range of American literature, both historical and contemporary, from Thomas' historical overview of the 19th century and early 20th centuries,[72] to Hutchins' famous synthesis of the Chicago experience,[73] to successive Harvard Redbooks (1945 and

---

[71] Wang Yongquan and Li Manli, "The Concept of General Education in Chinese Higher Education," in Ruth Hayhoe and Julia Pan, *Knowledge Across Cultures*, pp.311-321.

[72] Russell Brown Thomas, *The Search for Common Learning: General Education 1800-1960* (New York: McGraw Hill, 1962).

[73] R.M. Hutchins, *The Higher Learning in America* (New Haven: Yale University Press, 1967).

1992), and recent theorists such as Ernest Boyer and Alan Bloom.[74] In this essay Wang explicates the importance of general education for Chinese higher education and its resonance with China's own knowledge tradition. The barrier to its implementation in the modern period has to be understood in relation to economic and political history, he suggests. Throughout the twentieth century, China had been under extreme pressure to industrialize and modernize as quickly as possible, with external threats and a series of political revolutions and upheavals. Thus even though scholars and theorists such as Mei Yiqi strongly advocated a broad and integrated higher curriculum, the political leadership chose to institute extremely specialized forms of higher education which would serve immediate development goals.

Only after 1978, in the period of reform and opening up, was it possible for scholars to reflect on optimal approaches to the undergraduate curriculum based on educational principles. Then a range of curricular reforms emerged, which gave students exposure to interdisciplinary fields of knowledge and elective courses in areas of special interest. The main burden of Wang's paper was to encourage China in learning from other countries, while emphasizing the importance of developing an approach suited to China's specific conditions. It was essential for Chinese thinkers to have a historical understanding of the barriers to greater curricular breadth in China's modern history, as well as a critical awareness of the characteristics of China's own traditional knowledge system.

A second impressive comparative paper takes up the topic of comparative higher education structure, and the question of an optimal structure for higher education systems. The essay deals with the United States, Japan, France, Germany and the Soviet Union, and draws upon UNESCO statistics to provide comparative profiles of indicators such as the percentage of students in different fields of knowledge, the percentage of students at different stages of higher education, from short-cycle to graduate education, and the relation between these ratios and economic indicators such as GNP per capita. This paper also charts changes over time in many of the tables presented, covering the decades

---

[74] Alan Bloom, *The Closing of the American Mind* (New York: Simon and Schuster, 1987; Ernest Boyer, *College: The Undergraduate Experience in America* (Cambridge, Mass.: Harper and Row, 1987).

from 1940 to 1980.[75]

In his concluding section to this richly empirical paper, Wang makes the point that there is no exact science of higher education, nor is there any one country whose scholars believe that the structure of their system of higher education is optimal. In fact, he reported, in an informal survey of higher education specialists in USA, England, Germany, Japan and several other countries, not one was satisfied with the structure of his or her own system. Given the complexity of the relation between the structure and various other contextual factors in each country, it would not be wise to copy any particular case, no matter how attractive it might seem. It was possible, however, to discern certain trends of change across a number of countries, such as the increasing importance given to short-cycle higher education, and the changing ratios of enrolments in the applied natural and social sciences, over against the basic sciences and humanities. These trends needed to be understood in relation to broader economic and political changes, and could be a useful reference point for China as its modernization moved forward.

Wang has written on a wide range of other topics, including faculty development, higher education strategy, relations between higher education and local economic development, yet his real interests are in higher education thought and philosophy. Why has he not published more in this area? Wang explained that he would rather think about new problems and raise related questions on appropriate occasions, rather than publishing articles or books on past problems. He greatly values freedom of expression and lively academic debate, yet feels once one's ideas are committed to print, there is always the possibility of mis-understanding. He gave the example of his thoughts on the widely discussed issue of quality education (*suzhi jiaoyu*) in the mid 1990s.[76] He found his views were quite different from those of others, and some educational leaders took offence, although he had only intended to stimulate debate. Thus his long intended book on the philosophy of higher education has never come to fruition.

---

[75] Wang Yongquan, "Waiguo gaodeng jiaoyu jiegou de bijiao" [A Comparison of the Structure of Foreign Higher Education] in *Jiaoyu yanjiu* [Educational research] No. 2, 1988, pp.3-13.

[76] See Chapter Three, pp.103, 107, for a discussion of Li Bingde's views on "quality education."

Wang Yongquan, the thinker in his study, in 1993.

Half a century spent at Beida gave Wang a unique perspective and set of experiences. What he values most about the Beida spirit is its openness and the way in which lively debates on all kinds of topics are always taking place. *Avant-garde* in embracing new ideas, Beida has often set in motion influences that cascaded into the wider society. For this reason, it has been brought to heel by the political leadership on a number of occasions. Yet its spirit has never been subjugated. Beida teachers and students have always had an elusive quality in their intellectual life. Less unified and less productive than those of Tsinghua, in terms of teaching and research for nation building, they have by the same token acted as a conscience to the nation.

Chapter Nine

Gu Mingyuan –
Comparative Educator and
Modernization Theorist

Gu Mingyuan was born in 1929 in the small town of Jiangyin, about halfway between Shanghai and Nanjiing in southern Jiangsu province. His father was a secondary school teacher and his grandfather was a shop assistant in a tea store. The rest of the family lived by subsistence farming, as they did not own any land. However, the location of Jiangyin in proximity to these major cities meant that it benefited from a highly developed progressive education movement in the early 20th century, as well as regional traditions of scholarship going back many centuries. Thus Gu was able to benefit from the excellent primary and secondary education, which his family arranged for him in spite of their modest means. This laid a foundation for him to become one of China's outstanding educators and leading specialists in comparative education in the period after Deng Xiaoping set China on a course of education for modernization in the late 1970s.

I was privileged to work quite closely with Professor Gu over a six year period, from 1989 to 1995, since he was the Chinese coordinator of a major project in joint doctoral training in education, which brought together Beijing Normal University, Northeast Normal University, Northwest Normal University, East China Normal University, Southwest Normal University, Nanjing Normal University and the Ontario Institute for Studies in Education (OISE), University of Toronto. In the spring of 1986, Huang Xinbai, then Vice-minister of Education in China, visited OISE in Toronto bringing a special request – that we undertake joint doctoral training in collaboration with Chinese normal universities. He understood that OISE was the major centre in Canada for doctoral work in education, and hoped that it could support China in the development of strong doctoral programs in education. The response of OISE's Director, Walter Pitman, was positive, and I was asked to contact the Canadian International Development Agency (CIDA) for financial assistance in developing the project.

Later that year Professor Gu Mingyuan visited us, and we began the complex process of preparing a proposal for funding from CIDA. Two and a half years later, in April of 1989, the Canada-China Joint Doctoral Program in Education was approved by CIDA and the Chinese Ministry of Foreign Economic Relations and Trade, with a budget of close to $500,000. It was, however, a difficult time to start a major collaborative program. The 70th anniversary of May 4th had stimulated a student movement in Beijing that year, as students mourned the sudden passing of former Party leader, Hu Yaobang, and criticized the government for its lack of openness to democratic change. The movement was to culminate in the well-known tragedy of June 4th, 1989.

When Gu Mingyuan and I met that June at the 7th World Congress of Comparative Education Societies in Montreal, it was a somber time in China's relations with western countries. I feared the project might be put on hold indefinitely, but Professor Gu was positive about going forward with implementation. His leadership over the following several years was instrumental in making it possible for 22 Chinese doctoral students and visiting scholars from all seven partner institutions to study in Canada, and for 11 Canadian students to carry out doctoral research in China. It was particularly rewarding to note how he encouraged the active participation of institutions in the hinterland, which had few opportunities for this kind of exchange. By the time we held our major conference on "Knowledge Across Cultures" in Toronto in October of 1992, the educational relationship between China and Canada had been normalized and a large number of Chinese scholars, including seven doctoral supervisors in education, participated.

As we worked together on this project, I got to know Gu Mingyuan well, and became aware of his high standing in educational circles in China, and the tremendous influence of his writings on educational policy after the opening up of China under Deng Xiaoping. While he held such senior positions as vice-president of Beijing Normal University and dean of its school of graduate studies for many years, Gu always remained close to students and young teachers, offering support and encouragement to countless young people over the complex years of transition from a planned socialist system to a socialist market economy. This reflected the passion for education he had discovered as a young secondary school graduate, when he took up a primary school teaching post in Shanghai in 1948 while waiting for an opportunity for university entrance.

While Gu grew up and attended primary and secondary schools in the southeastern province of Jiangsu, his university studies were taken at Beijing Normal University and he has been associated with that university throughout his life. The next section of this chapter will therefore give an overview of the history of Beijing Normal University, where Gu's remarkable career has unfolded.

The Story of Beijing Normal University

Beijing Normal University traces its history back to 1902, when a teacher education school was added to the Imperial University, founded in 1898.[1] A brief overview of the early history of Beijing Normal has been given in chapter three of this volume, as Northwest Normal University in Lanzhou shared its early history.[2] Up till 1922, it was known as the Beijing Higher Teachers School, and its leaders were educators who had studied in Japan and were closely associated with national efforts to establish a modern education system.

A part of the story of Beijing Normal University which was not told in chapter three is that of its sister institution, the women's normal school (*shifan xuetang*) established by the Qing government to train teachers for the newly developing primary schools for girls in 1908. After the Revolution of 1911, it was renamed the Beijing Women's Normal School (*shifan xuexiao*) and in 1919 became the Beijing Women's Higher Normal School.[3] A number of famous scholars taught there, including the well known Confucian scholar, Liu Shipei, and one of the early Communist leaders, Li Dazhao, who taught a course on the history of the women's movement.[4]

---

[1] See Chapter Eight, p.231.

[2] See Chapter Three, pp.82-83.

[3] Beijing shifan daxue xiaoshi xiezu (ed.), *Beijing shifan daxue xiaoshi* [An Institutional History of Beijing Normal University] (Beijing: Beijing shifan daxue chubanshe, 1982), pp.51-52.

[4] *Ibid.* p.52.

After the May 4th Movement, the Beijing Women's Higher Normal School became well known for its activism, and some of the progressive scholars associated with it, including the famous writer, Lu Xun, who lectured there on Chinese fiction and literary theory from 1920 to 1926, on a part-time basis. Its journal, the *Beijing nuzi gaodeng shifan wenyi huikan,* published articles by scholars such as Cai Yuanpei, Li Shizeng, Huang Yanpei and Hu Shi. It was upgraded to normal university status in 1924,[5] two years after Beijing Normal attained university status. In 1925, it gained nationwide attention with the struggle of students and faculty against a conservative president who was closely allied with the warlord government. In 1927, it was one of nine Beijing universities which were linked together under a university district system reform plan, and was renamed the Number Two Normal College, with Beijing Normal University being the Number One Normal College.[6] In fact, the two institutions continued to operate as independent universities, since the Nationalist government was not able to implement this reform in face of strong opposition from all of the Beijing universities.

Professor Xu Bingchang was appointed president of the Number Two (Women's) Normal College in 1929, and immediately established a research institute and a scholarly journal in order to nurture new research initiatives in a wide range of areas, including language, history, geography, philosophy, and education. More than 58 articles were published in six issues of the journal between March of 1930 and July of 1931, and an ambitious project of collaboration was initiated with the Shanxi provincial library and a museum in the United States. In July of 1931, the Nationalist government mandated a merger between the women's and the men's normal universities, and appointed Xu Bingchang as president of the newly merged institution.[7]

In 1932, a new president was appointed, Li Zheng, and the Minister of Education, Zhu Jiahua, ordered the university to cease recruiting new students for one year in order to carry out a reorganization. This was strongly opposed by the council of professors and the students' self-governing association, who saw it as a ploy to repress student activism. The reasons given by government were to prevent social chaos, and to clarify the special characteristics and responsibilities of a normal univer-

---

[5] *Ibid.* p.74.
[6] *Ibid.* pp.79-80.
[7] *Ibid.* p.83.

sity. While there had been higher normal colleges in other regions of China, most had been integrated within comprehensive universities in the early 1920s. The experience of the Nanjing Higher Normal School, which became part of Dongnan University in 1922, is described in chapter ten of this volume.[8]

In December of 1932, a paper was submitted to the national convention of the Nationalist Party, suggesting that Beijing Normal University be closed, since there were now too many universities in Beiping. Better support could be given to Peking University and Beiping University (the former Sino French University), if Beijing Normal were closed, it was argued. Once the news of this planned closure leaked out, there was a strong reaction from the scholarly community and the wider society, forcing the government to go back on the plan, and allow the university to survive.

Beijing Normal University's new aims focused on the training of secondary school teachers and lecturers for normal schools, also scholarly research in the field of education.[9] It had three colleges, arts, sciences and education, as well as a research centre and attached primary and secondary schools. Even though its aims formally limited research to the field of education, in reality scholars in the arts and sciences also carried out research, and made great efforts to retain legitimacy and status among universities of the time. In a sense this was a struggle between the American model of the comprehensive university, which had considerable influence in China at the time, and the more sectorally oriented higher education patterns of Europe, and particularly France, whose Ecole Normale Supérieure had been an influential model for normal universities in the Soviet Union.

During the Japanese occupation of Beijing, Beijing Normal University moved first to Xi'an, to become a part of Northwest United University, then to Lanzhou, where it operated from 1939, laying the basis for the later development of Northwest Normal University.[10] With the end of the war in 1945, students and faculty wanted to move back to Beijing, as other universities were doing, but again they faced opposition from the Nationalist government. Once again it tried to close them down, or lower their status to that of a normal college and send them to the

[8] Chapter Ten, pp.299-300.
[9] *Beijing shifan daxue xiaoshi*, p.95.
[10] See Chapter Three, pp.83-84.

smaller city of Shijiazhuang.[11] In the end they were able to recover their original campus in Beijing and re-establish themselves there, but they got no support or assistance from the Nationalist government in the move.[12] They had nevertheless managed to survive the difficult war years, and now had a student body of 1,050, and 12 departments, including Chinese, English, history, geography, mathematics, physics, chemistry, museum studies, education, physical education, music and home economics.[13]

The Revolution of 1949 was particularly beneficial to Beijing Normal University, as finally its struggle for legitimacy as an institution with parallel status to a comprehensive university yet special responsibility for teacher education and educational research was recognized. In the Soviet model of higher education, which Chinese leaders implemented in the reorganization of colleges and departments of 1952, a national level normal university was established in each of the six regions of the country, alongside one or more national comprehensive universities, one national polytechnical university and a range of other specialized institutions devoted to training personnel for particular sectors of society and economy. The status which Beijing Normal University's professors and students had struggled for under the Nationalist government was now assured, and Beijing Normal became a national model in the field.

It is interesting to note that when a large number of normal universities were established in 1952, including six at the national level and a much larger number at the provincial level, the campuses of a number of Christian missionary universities, together with some of their staff, their library resources and their program experience, were given to these institutions. The Christian Zhonghua University in Wuhan was given to the newly established Central China Normal University in 1952, while Jinling Women's College in Nanjing was given to the newly established Nanjing Normal University[14] and South China (Huanan) Women's College in Fujian was given to Fuzhou Normal College.[15] In his comments on the reorganization of higher education in 1952, Zhu Jiusi noted that the closure of private and missionary institutions was to be

---

[11] See Chapter Three, p.84.
[12] *Beijing shifan daxue xiaoshi*, p.121.
[13] *Ibid.* pp.121-122.
[14] See Chapter Ten, pp.296-297.
[15] See Chapter Five, p.150.

expected under the new socialist system, but the way in which their resources were used showed respect for the heritage they represented.[16]

The prize that was to be given to Beijing Normal University with the implementation of the Soviet model in 1952 was the beautiful campus of one of China's most distinguished Catholic Universities, Furen, which had a history going back to 1927. Professor Chen Yuan, Furen's president since 1929 and a highly respected historian, was appointed president of Beijing Normal University in 1952 and held this position up to his death in 1971. We have noted how Professor Li Bingde, after his return to Beijing from France and Switzerland in 1949, had been offered a professorship at Furen by the provost, a possibility which he considered quite attractive.[17] Just as he was deliberating over the offer, he was informed by the Ministry of Education that he was to be sent to the Northwest, and so he missed the opportunity of taking part in the merger of Furen and Beijing Normal University two years later.

Given the prestige which the Furen campus, some of its academic staff and its well known president brought to Beijing Normal, it may be useful to give a brief overview of Furen's history here, before we continue with the history of Beijing Normal University under the socialist system. Furen's history is linked in interesting ways to the history of Fudan University, which has been outlined in chapter six.[18] The noted Chinese Catholic scholar and statesman, Ma Xiangbo had founded both Zhendan (L'Aurore) and Fudan shortly after the turn of the century. While Zhendan had developed as a French Catholic institution under Jesuit leadership, Fudan had become a secular private institution, which made its own distinctive contribution to progressive and patriotic causes. Neither, however, had fulfilled Ma's passionate wish for a modern Catholic institution of higher learning which would integrate the patterns of European and Chinese classical scholarship at a profound level[19] and carry forward the traditions of scholarship represented by the work of 16th and 17th century Jesuits and Chinese Catholic converts such as Xu Guangqi. In 1911, Ma thus collaborated with Ying Lianzhi, founding

---

[16] See Chapter Four, p.129.

[17] See Chapter Three, p.99.

[18] See Chapter Six, p.172.

[19] Lu Yongling, "Standing Between Two Worlds: Ma Xiangbo's Educational Thought and Practice" in Ruth Hayhoe and Yongling Lu, *Ma Xiangbo and the Mind of Modern China* (New York: M.E. Sharpe, 1996) pp.143-203.

editor of the *Da Gongbao*, to send a petition to the Pope in Rome for the founding of a Chinese Catholic University in Beijing.

While waiting for a reply to this petition, Ying established the Furen Society (*Furen She*) and drew together about 40 young scholars from all parts of China who were interested in Christian and classical scholarship. They were given access to his remarkable library, and many of the works of the 16th and 17th century Jesuits and their Chinese collaborators were re-published, as a way of stimulating an interest in serious scholarship within the Chinese Catholic Community. Chen Yuan, a promising young historian interested in the history of religion, joined this group and published a series of articles in the *Dongfang zazhi* [Eastern Miscellany] on Christianity in China during the Mongol (Yuan) dynasty, which was to launch his career as a social historian.[20]

Although he never became a Catholic, Chen supported the idea of a Chinese Catholic University, and when it was finally established in Beijing in 1927, under the guidance of American Benedictines entrusted by Rome to oversee its early years, Chen was appointed vice-president. Two years later, in 1929, he became president. In that year Furen established colleges of arts, sciences and education to meet the requirements of Nationalist legislation for the registration of a private university. When the American Benedictines had to withdraw in 1933, due to economic problems resulting from the Great Depression, the German Society of the Divine Word took up responsibility for leading the institution. This enabled it to remain open in Japanese-occupied Beijing during the Sino-Japanese War, from 1937 to 1945.[21]

The institutional history of Beijing Normal University devotes close to fifty pages to the history of Furen University, indicating the pride they attach to this heritage. While Furen University moved to Taiwan in the early 1950s, some aspects of the Furen spirit of scholarship and heritage of research survived in the work of Beijing Normal University after 1952. Beijing Normal also benefited from Furen's beautiful campus, with several buildings in classical European style architecture.

Furen's spirit of patriotism was particularly appreciated, and details are given of how it functioned in Beijing during the eight years of Japanese occupation, with President Chen Yuan taking a firm stand

---

[20] Ruth Hayhoe, "A Chinese Catholic Philosophy of Higher Education in Republican China," in *Tripod*, No. 48, 1988, p.54.

[21] *Ibid*. p.58.

against any form of collaboration with Japanese authorities, and sheltering students and faculty from external interference. Over the years from 1937 to 1945, a total of 2,247 undergraduate students completed their studies, and 38 graduate students, showing the important contribution the university made to occupied China over those years. From 1946 to 1952, when the merger took place, another 2,068 under-graduate students and 34 graduate students completed their studies.[22]

The other aspect of the Furen contribution to Chinese higher education was its commitment to high levels of scholarship which blended both Chinese and European standards of excellence. Its valuable publication series was sustained right through the difficult years of the Sino-Japanese War, keeping alive a sense of hope and value during those dark days. Three important titles were maintained over time. The *Huayi xuezhi* [Journal of Chinese heritage] was published in English, French and German, and contained articles on history, literature, and archaeology. The *Furen xuezhi* [Furen journal of scholarship] was published in Chinese with two editions each year right up to 1948, and contained scholarly articles by members of the Furen faculty, including Chen Yuan, as well as many other famous scholars, on a wide range of historical, philosophical and literary topics. The *Minsu zazhi* [Journal of folk cultures] contained articles about issues relating to different minority cultures in China, one of the areas of special research interest at Furen. There was also a series of scholarly books published under the Furen imprint, and overseen by President Chen Yuan, whose own historical works were among the offerings.[23]

In the spring of 1952, Furen University was merged with Beijing Normal University and its campus became Beijing Normal's north campus. Departments and programs from several other universities were also moved to Beijing Normal as part of the reorganization of colleges and departments. The high profile education training class at People's University, where scholars such as Li Bingde, Pan Maoyuan and Wang Fengxian were given classes in Marxist-Leninist theories of education,[24] was also moved to Beijing Normal University that year. The departments of education of both Peking University and the American missionary university, Yenching, were also moved to Beijing Normal University.

---

[22] *Beijing shifan daxue xiaoshi*, p.265.

[23] *Ibid.* p.243.

[24] Chapter Three, p.98, Chapter Five, p.156 and Chapter Seven, pp.216-217.

Under the Soviet model, comprehensive universities no longer had faculties of education, but all educational work was concentrated in normal universities.

The presidency of Professor Chen Yuan brought enormous prestige to Beijing Normal University, enhancing its status in the new socialist higher education system. The institutional history, however, suggests that his presence was largely symbolic, and there are very few references to his leadership over the years from 1952 to 1971. It appears that successive party secretaries and vice-presidents were the de facto leaders. One mention of him notes how he joined the Chinese Communist Party at the advanced age of 80 in 1959.[25] A second reference mentions how he chaired an important committee charged with raising academic standards in 1964, shortly after the promulgation of the Sixty Articles for the restoration of an academic approach to higher education management and two years before the outbreak of the Cultural Revolution.[26] Otherwise he is virtually absent from the story of the university's development as outlined in the institutional history.

Beijing Normal University's new aims, under the Soviet model, were to train secondary school teachers and educational administrators, and to be a model setting standards for educational theory and practice throughout the country.[27] While research was not a significant responsibility of universities under the Soviet model, given the fact that most research laid out in the nation's five year plans was entrusted to institutes of the academy of sciences and the major ministries, there was certainly an expectation of applied research relating to the improvement of schooling. Beijing Normal had a number of attached primary and secondary schools for this purpose. After the merger and reorganization of 1952, student numbers rose from 1,300 to 2,367[28] and teaching and learning was organized within 12 academic departments: Chinese language and literature, Russian language, history, geography, mathematics, physics, chemistry, biology, education, physical education and hygiene, music and drama and fine arts. In 1953, physical education was moved

---

[25] *Beijing shifan daxue xiaoshi*, p.163.
[26] *Ibid.*
[27] *Ibid.* p.137.
[28] *Ibid.* p.139.

out to become the Central Institute of Physical Education, and a new department of political education was established.[29]

As a national model for teacher education, with a particular responsibility for the political reliability of all teachers as well as their educational effectiveness, Beijing Normal University was the natural location for a large number of educational experts from the Soviet Union who were sent to assist in the massive efforts to establish a new socialist system. A total of 18 Soviet experts worked together with faculty members of Beijing Normal to create 137 new course outlines. Of the 137, 18 were direct translations from Russian, 94 were closely modeled on Soviet courses, and 25 were developed especially for the Chinese context. These courses were used in normal universities throughout the country and thus had a nation-wide impact on the education of teachers.

Intensive studies in Russian were required for students and faculty at Beijing Normal, and the institutional history notes how the cancellation of the teaching of English was later regretted.[30] Another facet of Soviet expertise was leadership in the development of teaching practice activities at the universities' attached secondary schools and in a group of 26 secondary schools in Beijing.[31]

In retrospect, the writers of Beijing Normal's institutional history saw this period as one of both positive learning and serious mistakes. The formalism and dogmatism of some aspects of the Soviet model of teaching and learning were criticized on the grounds that this model was not adapted to the realities of the Chinese context.[32] Nevertheless, a great deal was learned and achieved. Over 880 teachers from all parts of China, as well as 335 graduate students, were given training by the 18 Soviet experts.[33] Many members of Beijing Normal's academic staff, who had benefited from working with them, were sent out to all parts of the country to assist in the establishment of normal colleges at the provincial level in 1956.[34] Beijing Normal itself prospered as well, with student numbers growing to over 4,000 by 1957.[35]

---

[29] *Ibid.* p.140.
[30] *Ibid.* p.146.
[31] *Ibid.* p.144.
[32] *Ibid.* pp.146-147.
[33] *Ibid.* p.147.
[34] *Ibid.* p.153.
[35] *Ibid.* p.156.

In that year, the Soviet experts departed, amid recrimination and lack of trust at the national level, with Chinese leaders intent on creating their own pathway towards revolutionary transformation, and launching the ambitious but ill-judged Great Leap Forward in 1958. Beijing Normal University participated actively in the new emphasis on labor in learning which involved sending over three thousand of their students and faculty to work on the creation of a major water reservoir in a suburb of Beijing near the Ming tombs, and other such projects.[36] With the restoration of a more normal academic emphasis in the early 1960s, there was some relief among faculty, and efforts were made to raise academic standards, and adapt all that had been learned from the Soviet experts to Chinese conditions. It was to be but a lull before the storm, however, with the Cultural Revolution breaking out in 1966.

Given its important position as the leading institution for socialist education, as well as its leading role in political education, it is not surprising that Beijing Normal University was caught up in radical activities during the Cultural Revolution decade. While the institutional history says very little about the radical excesses of the Anti-Rightist Movement of 1957, and other political campaigns, a whole chapter is devoted to the Cultural Revolution. It notes that over four hundred teaching and administrative staff were subjected to various forms of investigation, struggle and humiliation, while four famous professors in the fields of education, politics, Chinese literature and physics were persecuted to death. Rampaging students led by radical staff members traveled as far as Qufu, the hometown of Confucius in Shandong province, to destroy national cultural relics which were seen as continuing trammels of a feudal past, and a Song dynasty edition of the thirteen classics, belonging to one of the old professors was burned. Some students and staff even took part in the attack on the British diplomatic mission.

Not long after this radical activism subsided, parts of the nearby People's University were merged with Beijing Normal University in 1973, including its departments of philosophy, political economy and history of the Chinese Communist Party. People's University had been set up on the model of the Moscow Planning institute in 1951 and had been an even more important centre of Soviet expertise in the 1950s. If the Cultural Revolution is seen, even partially, as a reaction against "Soviet

---

[36] *Ibid.* p.159.

social imperialism" one can understand why People's remained closed throughout this period, and why the political struggles at Beijing Normal University were particularly intense.

Once the Cultural Revolution decade ended, however, and Deng Xiaoping gave support for educational reform as a key element in China's new orientation towards modernization, Beijing Normal was in a position to move forward very quickly. It was over the period of the early 1980s, that Gu Mingyuan found his knowledge of comparative education and his first-hand experience of Soviet education had prepared him to fulfill a crucial role in developing educational theory that would give this new course a firmly professional rationale and justification. We will leave discussion of Gu's significant role to a later part of the chapter, and just note here some of the milestone's of Beijing Normal University's development after China's opening up to the world in 1978.

By 1980, Beijing Normal University had 15 academic departments, with departments in astronomy and electrical engineering that had been added during the late 1950s. In subsequent years, it was to add many more "non-education related programs," as well as a large number of research institutes and centers. It maintained and enhanced its leading role in teacher education, while also developing excellent programs of teaching and scholarship in many newly emerging fields of study. By the early 21st century, it had over 1,300 academic faculty members, including 9 academicians and 300 full professors, a student body of 2,661 graduate students, 6,483 undergraduates, 813 international students and over 10,000 students in various forms of adult education.

In the late 1990s, it was one of the first group of universities to be accepted within the 21/1 project, whereby the Ministry of Education supported up to 100 universities to move towards worldclass quality and status, and several of its departments and research institutes had been recognized as national key bases in the humanities and social sciences, including the areas of history, Chinese language and literature, psychology and comparative education. Several of its departments or institutes in pure and applied sciences also achieved this status. Of particular note for this chapter is the fact that its comparative education research center, led by Professor Gu Mingyuan since the 1960s, was one of eight programs in education nation-wide to be recognized as a national key base in the field of education.

In October of 2002, Beijing Normal University marked its 100th anniversary with a high profile international conference on education and globalization and many other celebratory events. Following on the pace-setting celebration of Peking University's 100th birthday in the Great Hall of the People in 1998, which has been described in chapter eight, Beijing Normal held a similar event, which was also presided over by Party Chairman Jiang Zemin, and recognized the particularly important contribution which education and the formation of teachers has made to China's economic and social progress over the last two decades of the 20th century. Just two years earlier in 2000, Professor Gu Mingyuan, who had contributed so much to his beloved institution, was elected chairman of the Chinese Education Society, the highest honor and recognition that can be given to a Chinese educator by his peers.

How did Gu manage to make such an enormous contribution to his university and his nation, given his humble birth in a small town in Jiangsu province, and the periods of war, revolution and political struggle which framed the successive phases of his life? In the rest of this chapter we will first give attention to his life-story, then consider some of his major contributions to the fields of educational modernization and comparative education.

Growing Up in Southern Jiangsu

Gu was born in 1929 in the small town of Jiangyin in southern Jiangsu province. None of his relatives owned any land, and most were employed in farm labor. When he was just one year old, in 1930, his father went to Japan for a short period of study. On return, he stayed in Shanghai and started a new family, abandoning his wife and young son. Gu's mother had no choice but to accept this situation. She did not agree to a divorce, however, and stayed close to Gu's grandparents. The whole family thus focused on ensuring that this fatherless child could get as good an education as was possible.[37]

From 1935 to 1937 Gu studied in a modern primary school in Jiangyin. With the Japanese invasion in 1937, the family fled to the countryside and many of the modern schools were closed. From 1937 to 1938, Gu was placed in a traditional private school [*sishu*] in the village, where he was taught passages from the *Four Books* and *Five Classics* under

---

[37] All of the details of Gu's life experience, as well as his educational views, are derived from two lengthy interviews with him, the first on October 21, 1998, in Beijing, and the second on December 11, 1998, in Hong Kong.

a traditional teacher. On return to Jiangyin in 1938, Gu was able to re-enter a modern primary school and he completed his primary education at several different schools between 1938 and 1942.

In 1942, while the Sino-Japanese War and the Second World War were wreaking devastation in China and around the world, Gu enrolled in the Nanqing Secondary School in Jiangyin, one of only two secondary schools there at the time. Nanqing had been established on the foundations of a classical academy [*shuyuan*], and had excellent academic standards. Gu's mother had managed to complete four years of primary education, which was unusual for a woman of her time, and she was determined to support her son's education, difficult as this was. His grandfather had only one son who had survived childhood, so he too was devoted to the education of his grandson, and did everything possible to support him. Friends and relatives were also helpful.

Gu felt his six years in the lower and upper secondary programs of this excellent school laid an important foundation for his life. He remembered how lively were the learning experiences, and how many of the activities were organized by students themselves. He remembers a student who had returned from Shanghai and taught them all football, another who taught them calligraphy, and yet another who was a good at seal making. Generally southern Jiangsu was an area with a rich cultural atmosphere and highly developed traditions of learning.

During his lower secondary years from 1942 to 1945, Gu was greatly influenced by older classmates in the upper secondary program, many of whom were to enter excellent universities. During the summer they returned to Jiangyin and ran drama groups, set up rural libraries, circulated good literature and organized other activities in support of progressive causes. Gu was able to join many of these activities and felt he learned a great deal. Though he was too young to become directly involved in the revolution, he was aware that some of these older classmates had joined the Communist underground; some had gone to Yan'an, while others had become members of the New Fourth Army (*Xinsijun*).

During his upper secondary years, after the end of the Sino-Japanese War, Gu ran a small culture and arts salon in his school, using the name "Daybreak" (*Shuguang wenyi shi*). He felt the academic program was excellent, and he noted how the school attracted teachers of a particularly high standard after the war was over. On graduation in 1948, Gu took the entrance examinations for university, ar.d applied to three different programs in top universities which he thought would open up promising career opportunities – civil engineering in Tsinghua University, railway management in Jiaotong University and water conservancy in Nanjing University. To his chagrin, he was unsuccessful in gaining entry to any one of the three programs. He then went to Shanghai and found a position as a primary school teacher. His family members were still so poor that they had not been able to afford the uniform he had needed for the football team in secondary school, so he felt this was the one way open to him of earning some money to support them.

*Gu Mingyuan (far right) with the group of students in his
Daybreak Culture and Arts Salon in 1947*

To his surprise and delight, he found teaching in the primary school exciting. It gave him great pleasure to see children learn, and he was very happy as a teacher. This one year of teaching experience shaped his career from then on – he had somehow discovered his destiny! In the new opportunities that opened up with the revolution, he applied to the education departments of Fudan University in Shanghai and Beijing Normal University. He was accepted by both, but the Beijing Normal acceptance had arrived first. Therefore he set off for Beijing in August of 1949, sad to move so far away from his mother, but excited at the opportunities that lay ahead. In October of 1949, he stood on Tiananmen Square, taking part in the formal celebration of China's liberation, with

Mao Zedong making the declaration that was so important to all Chinese patriots: "China has stood up!"

Study in the Soviet Union

After two years of study in the education department of Beijing Normal University, Gu was selected for study in the Soviet Union – a unique and important opportunity for a young educator in those times of collaboration between China and the USSR. Altogether he was to spend five years in Moscow, first having a year of Russian language study, then four years of study in education. He lived in a residence with foreign students from countries such as East Germany, Hungary, and North Korea. Since most Chinese students were studying in the sciences and engineering, few in education, he was under great pressure to learn Russian well enough for basic communication, and within a year he found himself fairly comfortable with the language.

It was the high tide of Soviet socialist society, and he was deeply impressed by the richness of the cultural life, including the opportunity to see many films. He was also able to make many friends. Overall he found the Russians he met very open and welcoming to the Chinese. It was here also, at the Lenin Normal College, that he was destined to meet his future wife, Zhou Qu. She was the daughter of Zhou Jianren, brother of the famous progressive writer, Lu Xun (Zhou Shuren). She had been accepted for study at Tsinghua University in 1951, and the university authorities had decided to send her immediately to the Soviet Union to pursue studies related to socialist publishing. After a year of study in this area, she applied for a transfer to the Lenin Normal College to study early childhood education and educational theory and history.

Gu's studies at the Lenin Normal College focused on educational theory, including pedagogy and psychology. The program he was enrolled in actually trained students to become primary school teachers, and he had the opportunity of two lengthy periods of observation and teaching practice in a Russian primary school during his second and fourth years of educational studies. He valued this practical experience tremendously, but was less impressed with his intensive studies in pedagogy and psychology in the education department of the Lenin Normal College. Whereas at Beijing Normal he had majored in education yet also had a minor in geography, in the Lenin Normal College, there was no minor and no elective courses. His studies in pedagogy and psychology were guided by the leading theorist at the Lenin Normal College, Professor Odronikov, and he noted how his theories were very similar to those of Ivan Kairov, whose text on pedagogy had such a wide influence in China in the 1950s.

*Gu Mingyuan with his classmates in the
Lenin Normal College in Moscow in 1953*

He was struck over these years at the tendency to narrowness in Soviet educational theory, with a high degree of centralization evident and little tolerance of divergent theories or approaches. This was in contrast to the greater breadth of the curriculum he had been exposed to in Beijing Normal University. It was only in the history of education that alternative theories were given some consideration, largely from a critical perspective. For example, the theories of child-centered education and the relation between education and experience associated with John Dewey's work were criticized as chaotic and lacking in rigor.

Systematic academic knowledge was considered most important, and it was believed that discipline-based knowledge could be introduced to children at an early age, basically from the fifth year of primary education. Under the influence of Soviet theorist Zankov, the Russians had become convinced that all the basic skills in literacy and mathematics could be inculcated in the first four years of formal education, and from the fifth year, children could begin to master the main disciplines of knowledge. Gu noted how this tendency to a formal, discipline-based curriculum at an early stage of schooling has influenced Chinese approaches to school curriculum right up to the present time.

Where Gu found his studies in Russia exhilarating and mind-expanding was in the areas of philosophy, history and economics. About 25-30% of the curriculum was devoted to the Marxist-Leninist classics and he immersed himself in the dozens of volumes of Karl Marx's original writings, as well as other socialist classics. He felt this gave him a strong foundation in understanding economics and historical processes of social change. Indeed it was this which enabled him to advise the Chinese leadership about the importance of human capital and investment in education after two decades of destructive ideological movements between 1957 and 1977. He could see clearly that the same basic economic principles applied to both capitalist and socialist societies, and he could understand why it was China had fallen so disastrously behind other parts of the world.

Career under Socialism

Gu Mingyuan with his wife Zhou Qu in Beijing in the early sixties

Gu returned to Beijing with Zhou Qu in 1956, and they were married shortly after their return. Originally he was to be assigned a post in the East China Normal University in Shanghai, and she in the Beijing Normal University, but in the end they were both allowed to stay in Beijing and assigned positions at Beijing Normal University. She took up teaching in early childhood education, while he began his career as an assistant lecturer, teaching pedagogical principles to students in the geography department who were being trained as future secondary school teachers. One year later, the Anti-Rightist Movement broke out, and he was dismayed by the criticisms of older professors. It was the beginning of a series of ideological movements, which were to take China away from the Soviet patterns that had been implemented since 1952. With his years of exposure to Soviet education, Gu was impressed by its academic rigor, its systematic approach to education and manpower planning and its capacity to support rapid and focused economic development. However, he was in no position, as a young lecturer, to affect the tumultuous directions of change that were to unfold under the radical political vision of Mao Zedong.

In 1957, after one year at the university, he was given a post as a teacher in a primary school in Beijing's Xicheng district, and he had the opportunity of classroom teaching as well as continuing to lecture at the university. A year later, in 1958, he was invited by Wang Huanxun, a senior educational scholar who had spent some years in Yan'an during the revolutionary struggle, to go to Beijing Normal's affiliated secondary school in an old neighborhood in the center of the city, Liu Li Chang. Professor Wang took on the principalship of the school for four years, and invited Gu to work there as his assistant. Gu reveled in this opportunity to observe the lessons of many older, experienced teachers and to work with Professor Wang and the teachers to develop a Chinese approach to the curriculum and to pedagogy at the secondary level, after the intense experience of Russian educational influences in the early 1950s. He also taught Russian to students in the lower secondary section of the school. Four years were spent at the school, and during this time Gu also observed the changes coming about at Beijing Normal University.

He saw both positive and negative effects of the Great Leap Forward of 1958. On the positive side, there was an intense debate about the status and standing of normal universities, emphasizing their importance to socialist transformation and the idea that the professional and applied knowledge at the heart of their work should have equal standing with the theoretical knowledge fostered by the more traditionally academic comprehensive universities. A new emphasis on research was introduced, and the importance of research to the development of educational theories and models suited to Chinese realities was recognized. Beijing Normal University also had the opportunity of developing several new academic fields at this time, the most notable being astronomy, which emerged from the physics department and has become one of three leading programs in China.

The negative side of the movement was the over-emphasis on kinds of labor that made little contribution to learning, and the neglect of systematic academic studies. Many academic problems were construed as political problems, causing enormous suffering and loss to a generation of older professors, many of whom were labeled as Rightists and subjected to persecution or sent into exile. In the plethora of new institutions founded around the country over the years between 1957 and 1960, there were positive elements of development. Beijing Normal University's loss became the gain of hinterland regions, where some of the exiled professors as well as younger lecturers and graduating students were sent to "help the revolution." At the same time the quality of teaching and research was of a relatively low standard, and there was a great deal of waste. The reorganization of higher education under the Sixty Articles of 1961 was a necessary adjustment, in Gu's view. Of course he himself was a young lecturer over these years, in a position to observe and learn, but not to lead or advise.

In 1963 Gu left the secondary school where he had spent four years and returned to work full-time in the Department of Education at Beijing Normal University. In 1965 he was appointed vice-dean of the department, and in this role he established China's first center for foreign educational research, and its first journal about foreign education. These years before the outbreak of the Cultural Revolution were a time of radical activism, with movements such as the Four Clean-ups [*Siqing*], but also of new efforts at the national level to restore ties with the West, especially with Europe. A number of students were sent to study in European countries and research institutes for the study of European and North American economies were established in several universities, under the stimulus of Zhou Enlai's efforts to develop a diversified set of foreign relations.[38] Gu had the foresight to see the importance of studies in comparative and international education as a way of considering a range of models and possibilities for educational reform in China's future development. Now that the Soviet model had been tried out, critiqued and adjusted to Chinese cultural and social realities with the new directions adopted in the early 1960s, it was time to learn about the educational experience of other countries as well.

As it turned out, however, his timing was unfortunate. With the outbreak of the Cultural Revolution in 1966, students criticized him for this journal on foreign education, even though it had been approved by the Ministry of Propaganda. Before long all classes stopped and he was assigned backbreaking labor in several factories, one doing stone cutting,

---

[38] Huang Shiqi, "Contemporary Educational Relations with the Industrialized World: A Chinese View," in Ruth Hayhoe and Marianne Bastid (eds.), *China's Education and the Industrialized World: Studies in Cultural Transfer* (New York: M.E. Sharpe, 1976) pp.225-226.

another cement making. His wife was assigned labor in a chemical engineering factory. Then in 1970 he went to Linfen in southern Shanxi province, where he had helped to establish a branch campus of Beijing Normal in 1965, so that students could gain experience of life in a remote and poor rural region. In 1970 he went to live there for two years, growing vegetables and raising pigs. While some students were there as well, this was not a time for educational experimentation, or learning through labor – it was a matter of bare survival in an extremely difficult period.

In 1972, Gu returned to Beijing and became principal of Beijing Normal's second attached secondary school for three years. It was a chaotic period, and all he could manage to do was impose some order and ensure that students could learn. It was a striking contrast to the period of exciting experimentation and curricular innovation he had experienced between 1958 and 1960, when he had worked under Professor Wang Huanxin in the first attached secondary school.

In 1974, Gu was suddenly given the opportunity to go abroad, for the second time in his life. After years of isolation, China's Ministry of Education decided to send a high-level delegation to the 18th General Conference of UNESCO in Paris. Gu was invited to go along with the group, since they wanted to have at least one scholar with a solid professional knowledge of the field. Most of the other members of the delegation were radical cadres accustomed to mouthing revolutionary rhetoric about opposition to Western imperialism and Soviet revisionism. The meeting itself was brief, but Gu took the opportunity of staying in Paris for over a month, looking around and doing a lot of sightseeing. He had much to reflect on, since the UNESCO meeting had opened his eyes to all that was going on around the world in education. One of the themes was lifelong education, a concept that was unknown and unthought of in China at the time.

In an article reflecting on the dramatic changes that were to come in the 20 years that followed, Gu described how foolish he had felt, when asked by an Australian delegate how China was dealing with its youth unemployment. He had replied at the time that there were no unemployed youth in China, since all had been given the opportunity to work in the countryside and in mountainous areas. In his heart of hearts, of course, he knew this was simply a technique of avoidance, and China's youth had enormous needs which were being unmet by the leadership.[39]

On his return to Beijing, he was assigned to the provost's office in Beijing Normal and given responsibility to oversee all of the courses being taught in the area of humanities and social sciences, including the courses in economics, philosophy and Party history being offered to students from People's University, before it re-opened in 1978. In 1979, he went back to the department of education as its head, and re-established the center for foreign education research and the journal on foreign education. From this time onward, he exercised vigorous leadership in teaching and research related to the reform of education, and to the field of comparative education. From 1979 to 1984, he was head of the department of education, and director of the foreign education research center. Then from 1984 to 1991 he was vice-president of the University, and concurrently dean the school of graduate studies from 1987 to 1997. His writings have been widely read, and have undergirded many aspects of the lively reforms that carried the country forward since 1978. In 2000, he was elected president of the Chinese Education Society, the highest honor for an educator in China.

Cultural Tradition and Chinese Educational Thought

Nineteen significant and representative essays written by Gu over the period between 1980 and 1998 have been translated into English and published in a recent volume.[40] Through reading these essays, one can trace the main contours of Gu's contribution to educational thought in China. One can also see a progression from educational ideas rooted in the European and Soviet experience, in the early 1980s, to an increasing awareness of the importance of China's cultural traditions, and the need for them to be understood as a foundation for Chinese educational development, and a resource to be shared with the global community.

---

[39] Gu Mingyuan, "The Complete Shift in Educational Ideas: Twenty Years of Ideological Liberation," in Gu Mingyuan, *Education in China and Abroad: Perspectives from a Lifetime in Comparative Education* (Hong Kong: Comparative Education Research Centre, The University of Hong Kong, 2001), p.114.

[40] Gu Mingyuan, *Education in China and Abroad: Perspectives from a Lifetime in Comparative Education* (Hong Kong: Comparative Education Research Centre, The University of Hong Kong, 2001).

The first of these essays, "Modern Education and Modern Production" sparked a national debate when it was published in 1980.[41] Gu was subsequently invited to present it on more than 40 occasions all over China. It was a classic analysis of the relation between education and economic development in Europe, rooted in Gu's careful reading of the complete works of Karl Marx while in Moscow, and tracing the historic changes in education which had accompanied and in turn stimulated economic development in capitalist Europe. Gu emphasized the constant and increasingly rapid changes taking place in modern production, and the resultant need for the all-round development that would enable people to understand the scientific foundation of the entire process of modern production. He made the point that this was a law applying to both capitalist and socialist societies.

He then gave a historical overview of modern educational development in six countries – the United States, the United Kingdom, France, West Germany, Japan and the Soviet Union, focusing on their development between 1960 and 1976, the very period when China had been convulsed by the Cultural Revolution. He outlined the many different dimensions of modern education systems, from compulsory education at the basic level to lifelong learning that enabled people to be prepared for the increasingly rapid pace of change in modern production and the changing demands of the employment market. In the concluding section, he highlighted the lessons that China should learn as it embarked on educational reforms to support the ambitious program for economic modernization laid out by Deng Xiaoping.

The first and most important lesson was the need for investment in education that would prepare the labor force needed 20 years into the future. This would require rapid growth in the rate of educational investment. Gu provided figures for educational expenditure as a percentage of GNP and of public expenditure between 1965 and 1976 for the six nations he held up as examples. He thus forced the Chinese leadership to look carefully at their commitment to education, which had never come close to these levels of funding. He also made a wide ranging set of suggestions for reform, including strengthening science education

---

[41] Gu Mingyuan, "Modern Production and Modern Education," in *Ibid*, pp.27-51. This article appeared originally in Chinese in *Hong Qi* [Red Flag], Vol. 19, 1980; it was also published in *Waiguo jiaoyu dongtai* [Foreign Educational Conditions] No. 1, 1981, and *Baike zhishi* [Encyclopedic Knowledge], No. 5, 1981.

and foreign language teaching at the basic level, greater emphasis on technical education, a broadening of the higher education curriculum and the importance of enabling students to gain self-study skills that would enable them to learn independently throughout their lives.

With this influential essay, Gu stimulated the Chinese leadership to launch a series of reforms in education that focused on the human development needed for the achievement of modernization in agriculture, industry, science and technology, and national defence. This was a dramatic change from the education for class struggle that had dominated the Cultural Revolution. Suggesting that China was a "late modernizer," Gu emphasized the possibilities of learning from the modernization experience of other nations, including the Soviet Union, which had influenced China so much in the 1950s, Japan, a close neighbor with a shared cultural heritage, the United States and Europe. The wide-ranging comparative essays that followed on this first influential piece expounded a series of lessons for Chinese educational development from these countries and regions.

Gu had a particularly close knowledge of Soviet education, due to his years of study in Moscow, and after the end of the Cultural Revolution, the fundamental patterns to which China returned were those put into place under Soviet influence in the 1950s. In two major essays, he pointed out some lessons that could be learned from Soviet experience. The first was the crucial importance of getting a balance in secondary education between general academic education and forms of vocational education suited to a changing labor market. Gu here emphasized the importance of diversity in secondary education, with different degrees of emphasis on basic academic knowledge and vocationally oriented studies, so that students would be prepared for a changing employment market as well as for higher education opportunities. He drew particular attention to the quality of Soviet teachers and to reforms in the secondary school curriculum.[42]

The second lesson related to the importance of striking a balance between tradition and change, heritage and development. In a situation where China's cultural and educational traditions had been submerged through conscious efforts to follow the Soviet socialist model in the 1950s, then ferociously attacked by young rebels during the Cultural Revolution decade, Gu noted that the Soviet Union had maintained and built upon

---

[42] Gu Mingyuan, "Basic Education Reforms in the USSR," in *Ibid.* pp.119-141.

some of their own worthy traditions from pre-revolutionary times, and suggested that China needed to do the same.[43]

In his comments on Japanese education, he noted how China and Japan share some common roots in the Confucian tradition, and one of these is a shared emphasis on moral development, with values such as devotion to the nation, strict self-discipline combined with a forgiving spirit towards others, and the golden rule of not giving to others what one does not want for oneself. A subtle difference he identified is that between an emphasis on education in courtesy in Japan, and ideological education in China. The Chinese could learn from Japan's emphasis on "observable behavior," he suggested.[44]

In a comparative essay on teachers and students in China and the United States, Gu noted the *laissez-faire* attitude of American teachers, giving students a great deal of freedom and encouraging them to take part actively in various learning experiences. He noted that this was beneficial to students' intellectual power, creativity and dexterity. At the same time, American students often missed the kind of rigorous training needed to have a sound foundation in the basic disciplines of knowledge. This was where China's more teacher-centered and examination-driven education system had an advantage. In suggesting how Chinese education might integrate more child-centered approaches to pedagogy from the American experience, Gu developed a comparative historical argument.

He first introduced the German educator, Johannes Herbart and showed how his emphasis on the teacher's authority and strict discipline in managing students reflected the historical situation of Germany in the late 18th and early 19th centuries, when the capitalist class was ambivalent about the revolutionary changes being introduced by industrial development, and wanted to maintain the social order. Gu then compared Herbart's view of the teacher with the ideas of John Dewey one hundred years later, suggesting they indicated a wholehearted embrace of modernity. He noted Dewey's strong emphasis on the equality of students and teachers, and teachers' responsibility to understand children's abilities and interests and create opportunities for them to

---

[43] Gu Mingyuan, "Educational Development in the USSR 1917-1987," in *Ibid.* pp.142-149.

[44] Gu Mingyuan, "Learning from Each Other: A Comparative Study of Education in China and Japan," in *Ibid.* pp.199-204.

learn through activity and the understanding of experience. Gu saw Dewey's pragmatic philosophy as arising naturally out of the industrial revolution and the situation of a world characterized by increasingly fierce competition

He then went on to note how these opposing sets of ideas about the teacher's role in learning had enormous influence around the world, with Herbartian ideas being particularly influential in the Soviet Union, where Deweyan child-centered education had been strongly criticized. Given the Soviet influence on Chinese education in the 1950s, it was not surprising that this rather traditional view of the role of the teacher had become the dominant one. It also combined with aspects of China's own cultural traditions, which stress the authority of the teacher and the importance of the teacher's role in maintaining the traditional social order.

The interesting twist which Gu brings into this comparative essay is to show that the historical Confucius had an informal and warm relationship with his disciples and encouraged them to question his teaching, to explore alternative ideas and to develop their own visions for the future. It was only later, beginning with the teaching of Xunzi in the 3rd century BCE, that the role of the teacher became integrated into the traditional social order. The teacher came to have an authority that paralleled that of the emperor, and was expected to convey one orthodox set of teachings which would ensure the subordination of all to the ruling authority.

In his conclusion to this essay, Gu noted that the transformation of ideas is relatively slow and it will take time for China to move out of its long lasting historical situation as a closed society with an agricultural economy to a truly open and modernized society. He also noted that it would be important for China to maintain some of the strengths of its own traditions while learning from the independence, creativity and dexterity fostered by teachers in the American context. Chinese teachers should maintain the rigorous demands on students and the attention to systematic knowledge and the cumulative development of understanding associated with Chinese tradition, while worrying less about the preservation of their authority and moving towards more interactive and open-ended forms of pedagogy.[45]

Gu's first important contribution to China's educational and economic transformation was his analysis of the links between education and

---

[45] Gu Mingyuan, "Cultural Differences and Perspectives on the Roles of Teachers and Students in China and the United States," in *Ibid.* pp.182-198.

modernization in Western experience, and the relevance of these lessons to China at the time of its opening up. His second equally significant contribution was to highlight elements in China's own cultural and social heritage that would support the new openness in education, and stimulate the kinds of competitiveness and creativity necessary to effective modernization. Between 1991 and 2000, the period of China's 8th and 9th five-year plans, Gu led a major research project on cultural tradition and educational development, including many graduate students in its wide-ranging explorations. In the process of this research, Gu identified aspects of Confucian culture which were supportive of China's modernization efforts, and could provide a foundation for effective and well-rooted educational reform.

The first was the remarkable capacity of Confucian culture to accommodate other cultures, and absorb some of their best elements into itself. The best example of this over a long historical period was the introduction of Buddhism from India, and the ways in which it was embraced and transformed, as it became a widely influential religion of China. The second aspect of Chinese culture, which Gu identified, was a high degree of integration in Chinese epistemology – with diverse streams of thought blended into an organic whole. This he felt had potential to contribute to the next phase of human development. As China moved towards a knowledge society, its philosophical heritage was especially suited to emerging problems and needs.[46]

This idea comes across imaginatively in a paper on the future university presented by Wang Yingjie, a well-established scholar of comparative education who was one of Gu's early doctoral students. Wang suggests that the American research university, which has been the dominant model of the latter part of the 20th century is like a house with rooms that are not connected to each other. This is due to its close historical links to the industrialization process, which led to the segregation of specialist disciplines, of research and teaching, of knowledge transmission and the cultivation of character, of university and society. Wang sees the possibly of increasing integration in the next phase of the university's development, with the support of several Confucian philosophical principles: the integration of humanity with the universe, balancing individuals, society and the natural environment; the integration of

---

[46] Gu Mingyuan, "Modernization and Education in China's Cultural Traditions," in *Ibid.* pp.101-110.

learning with life, balancing individual goals with national and global ones; the integration of morality with knowledge; the integration of knowing and doing; and finally, the integration of teaching and learning through a dialogic approach.[47]

Gu's reconsideration of China's traditional culture also created an awareness of the possibilities for individual development within Confucianism. This is evident in the sympathetic description of the teaching style and teacher-student relationships of the historical Confucius alluded to above. It was an aspect of Confucianism that had been most notably developed by the 16th century Ming neo-Confucian scholar, Wang Yangming, who explored with his disciples the power of the subjective mind, and pointed to knowledge as arising out of action, not only out of the systematic study of accumulated scholarly texts.[48]

Through his ten-year collaborative study of China's cultural traditions and educational modernization, Gu raised the awareness of China's educational community about the possibilities of a selected reinvigoration of Confucian cultural traditions in support of China's modernization goals. Other leading educational scholars moved into the space thus created. The last two chapters of this book present two women among them: Lu Jie of Nanjing Normal University and Ye Lan of East China Normal University in Shanghai. Each called attention in different ways to students' individual needs, to the dignity of students as individuals, and the cultivation of the subjective self. This constituted a significant move beyond the instrumentalist obsession with economic and social goals, which had characterized the early years of reform.

Conclusion: Comparative Educator in a Changing China

Gu is probably best known in China as an inspiring teacher, with a large number of graduate students and many voluntary commitments to helping schools and teachers learn to adapt to the increasing pace of modernization. He has chaired numerous national level committees for curricular reform, for audiovisual education, for evaluation of tertiary

---

[47] Wang Yingjie, "A New University Model for the New Century: from Perspectives of Chinese Philosophy," Paper prepared for the Learning Conference 2003 organized by the Institute of Education, University of London, held on July 15 – 18, 2003, in London, U.K.

[48] See Chapter One, pp.34-35.

institutions and in other areas. He travels constantly both in China and abroad, giving keynote addresses at conferences, doing advisory and liaison work and supporting new educational initiatives. His wide-ranging publications on education in China and abroad have had an enormous impact on educational theory and policy in China, and he has received numerous national awards as well as significant international recognition.

A brief overview of the books he published between 1981 and 1996 gives an idea of the wide reach of his interests, and his remarkable contribution to the contemporary Chinese literature in comparative education. The earliest book is on the educational thought and practice of the progressive writer Lu Xun. Next is the first comparative education textbook in socialist China, published in 1982 and co-written with Zhu Bo and Wang Chengxu, whose leadership in the field has been described in chapter two. This was followed in the same year by a textbook in comparative education translated from the Russian.

Gu Mingyuan being conferred the first Honorary Doctorate of Education given by the Hong Kong Institute of Education, with Ruth Hayhoe, and colleagues of the HKIEd in November of 2001

Subsequently Gu was coauthor and editor of a major book on education theory (1983), and chief editor of a book on secondary education (1987). In 1989 he authored a study of world educational trends, which had considerable influence in Chinese educational policy circles.[49] It enabled the Chinese leadership to gain a critical under-standing of educational reforms around the world and relate them to broader socio-economic changes. In 1990 he edited a book on prag-matism in education. Then over the period between 1990 and 1992 he was chief editor of a 12 volume educational dictionary, which became an essential reference work for those involved in educational reform policy. This was followed by an edited book on the major achievements of Soviet education after the Second World War, published in 1991, the year of its sudden collapse. In 1993 Gu published a guidebook to education around the world, and in 1994 he edited a book on the Chinese education system. In 1996 he co-authored a second book on Comparative Education.[50] In addition he published more than 200 articles in academic journals and in other media over these years.[51]

Gu was responsible for founding the China Comparative Education Society (CCES) in 1979 and served as its president from 1983 to 2002. He also had a leadership role in the foundation of the Comparative Education Society of Asia (CESA) in 1995. As China moves more and more onto the global stage, with its continuing economic achievements and increasing demands for it to exercise concomitant political and diplo-matic leadership, its educational and cultural ideas need to be better understood. Gu Mingyuan has probably done more than any other Chinese educator to lay a foundation that will enable Chinese thinkers to articulate a global vision for education and culture.

---

[49] Gu Mingyuan, *Shijie jiaoyu fazhan de qushi* [What can be learned from World Educational Trends] (Chengdu: Sichuan jiaoyu chubanshe, 1989).
[50] Gu Mingyuan et al, *Bijiao jiaoyu daolun* [A Guide to Comparative Education] (Beijing: Renmin jiaoyu chubanshe, 1996).
[51] Gu Mingyuan, *Wo de jiaoyu tansuo* [My educational explorations] (Beijing: Education Science Press, 1998), pp.674-683.

Chapter Ten

Lu Jie –
A Woman Educator of Standing

Lu Jie was born in 1930 into the family of a professor in Shanghai, China's most open and international city at the time. She grew up in the turbulent period of the Sino-Japanese War, and the Civil War. In 1949 she made a crucial decision, which she has never regretted – to refuse her father's help to go the United States for higher studies and join the Communist underground in its struggle for China's liberation. Her older brother Lu Ping made the same decision, and became known internationally many years later. He was the official in charge of Beijing's Hong Kong-Macao office over the crucial period of Hong Kong's return to China, from the late 1980s to 1997.

Lu Jie graduated from Nanjing Normal University in 1953, and has spent her entire academic career there, beginning as a political education instructor and rising to professor of education, head of the department of education and later head of the institute of educational research. Her undergraduate studies spanned the revolutionary period, with the early years of her college study being spent at Ginling Women's College in Nanjing. This campus was to be given to Nanjing Normal University in 1952. The first part of this chapter will therefore give a historical overview of these two academic institutions.

As the main supervisor of doctoral students in education at Nanjing Normal University in the late 1980s, Lu Jie became a key member of our Canada-China collaborative project for joint doctoral education and was active in sending her doctoral students to Canada and receiving Canadian students doing doctoral research in China. She was the only woman member of the delegation of seven Chinese professors of education who gave papers at our conference on "Knowledge Across Cultures" and subsequently traveled across Canada to visit universities with doctoral programs in education in Montreal, Edmonton and Vancouver.

Much later, during the years in which I was director of the Hong Kong Institute of Education, it was a pleasure to develop close relationships of cooperation with Nanjing Normal University, especially in the field of early childhood education where we developed a collaborative degree program. I was able to meet with Lu Jie on a number of occasions over those years, and learn about her life experience and educational ideas.[1] Before recounting her life-story, however, I will give an overview of two institutions, which have provided the context of her life.

Ginling Women's College

Ginling Women's College was one of only two tertiary institutions developed by Christian missionaries for women in China, with the remaining fourteen all being co-educational. Christian missionaries had also pioneered primary and secondary schools for girls, and we have already noted Xie Xide's comments on the value of her experiences in three different Christian secondary schools for girls, the Bridgeman Academy in Beijing, St Hilda's in Wuhan and Fuxing in Changsha.[2] There were many debates within the mission over the value of higher institutions open only to women. In the end two initiatives strongly supported by the principals and teachers of girls' secondary schools and women missionaries did succeed. Hwa Nan Women's College in Fuzhou was to serve the southern part of China, while Ginling Women's College in Nanjing would be open to graduates of mission secondary schools in the central and eastern part of China, and indeed nationwide. At a meeting of the China Christian Educational Association in Shanghai in 1911, a resolution was passed that a college for women in the Yangzi River valley area be established. In 1913 the Council responsible for this task appointed Mrs. Lawrence Thurston as President. The college opened its doors in 1915 with 13 students. By 1920 there were 70 students and a staff of 16.[3]

---

[1] The dates of my interviews with Lu Jie were October 14, 1998 in Nanjing, and March 14, 2000, in Hong Kong.

[2] Chapter Six, pp.187-188.

[3] William Purviance Fenn, *Christian Higher Education in Changing China 1880-1950* (Grand Rapids: William B. Eerdmans Publishing Co., 1976), pp.69-70.

Five women students graduated from Ginling in 1919, the first Chinese women to receive a fully accredited university degree in modern China. While quite a few women had studied abroad before this, China's own national universities only opened their doors to women in 1919, at around the time of the May 4th Movement, and private universities such as Fudan were also not yet open to women students.[4] By 1924, enrolment at Ginling had reached 133 students, and a beautiful new campus with a Chinese style quadrangle had been developed.[5] Its buildings were of great elegance, integrating western construction standards into a Chinese gestalt. Most of the students who enrolled in these early years were either graduates of Christian secondary schools for girls, many on scholarship, or children of wealthy Chinese who could afford the relatively high fees.[6] Of the first 43 Ginling graduates, fully half went abroad for graduate studies, indicating the ability of their families to support this kind of expense, and their openness to new ideas.[7]

One of the five students to graduate in the first class in 1919, Wu Yifang, was to play an important role in the history of Ginling and of Nanjing Normal University. She obtained a doctoral degree in entomology from the University of Michigan in 1928, and returned to China to take up the Ginling presidency that year. It was a crucial time in the college's history. The Northern expedition of 1927 had spawned strong feelings of nationalism, and considerable anti-Christian sentiment, particularly with regard to the dominating position of western educators in Christian schools and colleges. In 1928, the new Nationalist government required that all Christian institutions be led by a Chinese president, and have a predominant number of Chinese members on their governing boards, also that all religious studies be made optional. This required considerable adjustments on the part of the missionaries and their boards in the United States, Canada and Britain.[8]

The situation in Nanjing was particularly difficult. In 1927 the American vice-president of the University of Nanking, the other main

---

[4] Ruth Hayhoe, *China's Universities 1895-1995: A Century of Cultural Conflict* (Hong Kong: Comparative Education Research Centre, The University of Hong Kong, 1999) p.48.

[5] Fenn, *Christian Higher Education in Changing China*, pp.93-94.

[6] Jessie Lutz, *China and the Christian Colleges* (Ithaca and London: Cornell University Press, 1971), p.169.

[7] *Ibid*. p.143.

[8] *Ibid*. pp.255-264.

missionary institution, had been killed by the stray bullet of a rampaging solder. Many of the missionaries had returned to their home countries as a result. The University of Nanking was thus the first to become registered with the new government.[9] The nearby Ginling Women's College was taken over by an administrative committee of alumnae in 1927, and the committee immediately appointed Wu Yifang as the next president. Enrolment had dropped to 95 in the autumn of 1927, in face of this crisis, but numbers soon rose to 200.[10]

On taking up the presidency in 1928, Dr. Wu Yifang's first task was to have the college registered with the Nationalist government. In face of the government's demand for religious neutrality, it maintained its Christian identity through a commitment to "conforming to the highest educational standards, promoting social welfare and higher ideals of citizenship, and developing the highest type of character 'in accordance with the original purpose of the five Christian Mission Boards which were its founders.'"[11]

By the early 1930s Ginling was offering degree programs in 12 different majors, including biology, chemistry, physics, mathematics, economics, Chinese, English, history, music, philosophy, sociology and political science. It also had a program in nursing, and pre-medical education. President Wu Yifang took up important leadership roles nationally and internationally. She was vice-president of the World Council of Churches at one time, and chairman of the Chinese National Committee of the Young Women's Christian Association,[12] which played an active national role in supporting women's causes over this period.

[13] Ginling also became particularly well known for its work in physical education, as it had taken over the YWCA's Shanghai physical training school for women.[14] One of its important contributions was the training of teachers for physical education and public health for mission secondary schools and the YWCA network. Although it did not have a department of education in the early years, all students were required to

---

[9] Fenn, *Christian Higher Education in Changing China*, p.92.

[10] *Ibid.* p.94.

[11] *Ibid.* p.117.

[12] *Ibid.* p.155.

[13] Karen Garner, *Precious Fire: Maud Russell and the Chinese Revolution* (Amherst and Boston: University of Massachusetts Press, 2003), Chapter Seven.

[14] Lutz, *China and the Christian Colleges*, p.135.

take common courses in education and psychology,[15] and about 30-40% of its graduates became teachers.[16] Its attached senior middle school was used for teaching practice.

Ginling Women's College developed rapidly over the years up to the Japanese invasion in 1937, when it had to face the disruptions of war. It moved to Chengdu and joined three other refugee mission institutions, Yenching from Beijing, Cheeloo from Shandong and the University of Nanking, on the campus of the West China Union University. The journey from Nanjing to Chengdu was an arduous one – by steamer to Hong Kong, then by train to Hankou, then by river boat to Chongqing, and finally by bus to Chengdu. When President Wu arrived with her faculty and students, there were only 35 persons, but by the end of the war student enrolment had grown to over 300.[17] One of the interesting aspects of Ginling's international involvement was a longstanding partnership with Smith College in the USA, whose gifts provided one quarter of its budget over the war years.[18]

With the end of the war Ginling moved back to its campus in Nanjing in 1946. By that autumn it had an enrolment of 332 students, and 68 graduated in June 1947. By 1948, its enrolment reached nearly 500 students, but these numbers were to drop in face of the Communist victory.[19] The People's Liberation Army entered Nanjing in April of 1949, and Ginling Women's college was combined with the University of Nanking to become National Ginling University. With the reorganization of colleges and departments under Soviet influence in 1952, its campus was given to the newly established Nanjing Normal University, and most of its staff and students were integrated within this institution.

Lu Jie graduated from secondary school in 1947, and chose to study at Ginling Women's College in the autumn of 1947, deliberately making a different choice from that of her older brother and sister who were studying at St John's and Daxia in Shanghai. She wanted the opportunity to leave home and be independent of her family. The idea of studying in a women's college in the not-too-distant city of Nanjing

---

[15] Feng Shichang (ed.) *Nanjin shifan daxue zhi 1902-1992* [History of Nanjing Normal University 1902-1992] (Nanjing: Nanjing shifan daxue chubanshe, 2002), p.31.

[16] Fenn, *Christian Higher Education in Changing China*, p.156.

[17] *Ibid.* p.204.

[18] Lutz, *China and the Christian Colleges*, p.388.

[19] *Ibid.* p.219.

appealed to her. Since Ginling was merged with Nanjing Normal, Lu Jie graduated from Nanjing Normal in the early fifties. Subsequently she was to dedicate a whole career to teaching there. Its history thus became the context of her evolving life-story.

Nanjing Normal University

Nanjing Normal University celebrated its 100th anniversary in 2002. This was an occasion for republishing its institutional history, covering the period from 1902 to 1992, with a second volume for the period from 1993 to 2002. Although still a provincial level university, it has become a leading institution in the field of education. In the late 1990s it was selected to become one of the 100 institutions given support by the national 21/1 project.[20] This can be attributed to excellent leadership and strong support from the important and economically developed province of Jiangsu, also to its illustrious heritage as the cradle of progressive education in China.

The first hundred pages of volume one tell the complex story of the development of teacher education and of those institutions which became a part of Nanjing Normal College's heritage when it was established in 1952 on the former campus of the Ginling Women's College. It was in fact the inheritor of several heritages, as is clear in the story of its founding in 1952. Grouped together in this new college were the college of education of Nanjing University (which had been called National Central University under the Nationalist regime), as well as the departments of education, child and social welfare, and some arts and sciences, of Ginling University, itself a merger of Ginling Women's College and the Christian University of Nanking. The child development program of the former French Catholic Aurora College for Women in Shanghai and the child welfare program of the former Lingnan University in Guangzhou were also given to Nanjing Normal.[21] It thus inherited programs from several missionary institutions, both Protestant and Catholic, as well as the traditions of progressive education that had developed at Nanjing University since its founding in 1902.

---

[20] Da Zuoling (ed.) *Nanjing shifan daxue zhi 1993-2002* [History of Nanjing Normal University 1993-2002] (Nanjing: Nanjing shifan daxue chubanshe, 2002), pp.19-27.
[21] Feng Shichang, *Nanjing shifan daxue zhi 1902-1992*, p.33.

The first president of Nanjing Normal College was the well-known early childhood educator, Chen Heqin. He had studied with John Dewey at Columbia University in 1917 and 1918, and returned to China to develop this field with distinction. One of the two vice-presidents of the newly established college was Wu Yifang, former president of Ginling Women's College.[22]

Nanjing Normal has chosen to regard the teacher education program of Nanjing University as its main predecessor. In May of 1902, the governor of "Liangjiang" (now Jiangsu province) made a petition to the emperor for the founding of a teachers college in the city of Nanjing. He argued that higher schools for teachers should be the first priority in the move to transform *shuyuan* into modern higher schools. He was succeeded by the famous modernizer Zhang Zhidong, who had put forward the concept of 'Chinese learning as the essence, western techniques for their usefulness.'[23]

In 1903 Zhang established the Sanjiang Normal School (*shifan xuetang*), later called the Liangjiang Normal School. His intention was to make the teaching of the Confucian classics the basis of the curriculum, and introduce some western cultural and scientific knowledge. The objective was to prepare teachers for primary and secondary schools. The teaching staff included teachers of the Chinese classics, Japanese teachers and Chinese teachers who had returned from Japan and were able to teach such modern subjects as history, geography, literature, mathematics and physical education. At its height, this institution had 50 Chinese teachers and 30 Japanese teachers. Among the Chinese were scholars who later became nationally famous. By 1904 there were about 300 students studying there, and students numbers rose to 1000 by 1911.[24]

The 1911 Revolution brought about dramatic changes in education, with the end of the Qing dynasty and efforts to establish a modern republic. Education was now to instill republican values rather than Confucian ones, and a new set of legislation was passed during the short period when Cai Yuanpei served as Minister of Education. In 1914, the Nanjing Higher Normal School was established on the basis of the

---

[22] *Ibid.*

[23] William Ayers, *Chang Chih-tung and Educational Reform in China* (Cambridge, Mass.: Harvard University Press, 1971).

[24] Feng Shichang, *Nanjing shifan daxue zhi.* pp.5-6.

former Liangjiang Normal School, and in 1915 it was able to attract an influential American-returned scholar of education, Guo Bingwen. Guo became president in 1919 and recruited Tao Xingzhi as dean of studies.

In 1919, the Nanjing Higher Normal School had two main divisions and six program areas: Chinese literature and history, and mathematics and sciences were the two divisions. The programs included education, English, agriculture, industry, commerce and physical education, and the purpose was to prepare teachers across a range of fields including teachers for newly developing vocational education institutions.

One of its important innovations was the recruitment of women students at an early period, with eight women being formally enrolled in 1920, and another 50 allowed to audit classes.[25] The school was also very active in community education and regularly held summer schools for teachers and educational administrators from all over the country. Nanjing Higher Normal School was one of the institutions that hosted John Dewey and his wife Alice during their two years in China from 1919 to 1921,[26] and a number of Dewey's students were on the staff, including Tao Xingzhi. The school had a reputation for both openness and an intense nationalism, and great efforts were made to integrate progressive ideas from abroad onto a foundation in Chinese progressive traditions of education.

When the first class of students was enrolled in 1915, 126 students had been selected from 534 applicants from several provinces. When the last group of students completed their studies, the total number of graduates added up to 779, out of 966 who had been enrolled. There were 102 teaching staff, with 55 of them holding the title of professor, and thirty having returned from abroad. This early center of teacher education had clearly played a significant role in bridging the Chinese and western worlds.[27]

In 1920 a group of 10 well known intellectuals, including Guo Bingwen, decided it was time to establish a university in Nanjing, and submitted a proposal to the Ministry of Education for the creation of Dongnan (Southeastern) University. In 1922, it was decided that Nanjing Higher Normal School should be merged into Dongnan University, and

---

[25] *Ibid.* p.11
[26] Barry Keenan, *The Dewey Experiment in China* (Cambridge, Mass.: Harvard University Press), pp.31, 56-57.
[27] Feng Shichang, *Nanjing shifan daxue zhi*, p.8.

become its faculty of education. It continued to play a leading role in education, with departments of education, psychology and physical education and a staff of 34, 13 of whom had graduate degrees from abroad. Among the professors were such well known names as Tao Xingzhi, Chen Heqin, Meng Xiancheng, Lu Zhiwei and Zheng Zonghai.[28]

With the establishment of the Nationalist government in Nanjing in 1928, Dongnan University was given the new name of National Central University, as the leading intellectual center of the new regime, and the faculty of education continued to play an influential role, though it was under considerable pressure to support the Nationalist government's political agenda. By this time Tao Xingzhi was no longer on the staff, but had become active in developing alternative educational ideas and models for rural educational development, such as his model educational community, Xiao Zhuang.

With the outbreak of the Sino-Japanese War, National Central University moved to Chongqing, the war-time capital, and the faculty of education was asked by the government to become a teacher training college, operating first in Anhui province, then moving to the more remote Guiyang province and finally to Chongqing in 1941. In addition to its departments of education and psychology, it established programs in Chinese literature, English, history, mathematics, sciences, education and moral instruction over this period. Over the war years, the teachers college graduated four classes of students, sending more than 500 new teachers out to the secondary schools.[29]

With the end of the war in 1945, the teachers college moved back to Nanjing and was reunited with National Central University. Before long, it found itself caught up in the maelstrom of the Civil War, culminating in the Communist liberation of Nanjing in April of 1949. In spite of the political pressures of the Nationalist regime, it had clearly been a leading center for educational research and teacher education over the modern period in China. No wonder Nanjing Normal University looks upon it as an important predecessor. All of its renowned scholars of education became part of the faculty of Nanjing Normal College in 1952. Since Nanjing University, the national comprehensive university, did not have a faculty of education under the Soviet model adopted in 1952, this new

---

[28] *Ibid*. p.16.
[29] *Ibid*. p.23.

normal college had a significant leadership responsibility for education in the region.

Between 1952 and 1956 Nanjing Normal College developed smoothly as the main center for the training of educators for the normal schools and teachers for top tier secondary schools in the province of Jiangsu. It had departments of Chinese, education, early childhood education, arts, music, and sciences, as well as short-cycle training programs in mathematics, biology, geography, early childhood education, arts and music.[30] The main focus over these years was on learning from Soviet models of pedagogy and educational administration, a considerable adjustment for faculty who had had long exposure to American progressive ideas in education. Soviet Minister of Education I. Kairov's theories and texts were translated into Chinese and widely used as the core teaching material in the field. The organization of faculty, and curricular planning also followed Soviet models, with teaching and research groups established for each specialization.

With the Anti-Rightist Movement of 1957, however, many of the older educators were attacked and sent into exile. Given the history of the education department, it was not surprising that it should become a target. Even the president, Professor Chen Heqin, was forced to step down in face of criticism. The institutional history gives only a brief mention to this movement, noting that it was mistaken in confusing academic with political errors, and that it greatly dampened the enthusiasm of many staff members.[31] In fact the devastation in the lives of older educators could never fully be remedied.

Meanwhile Nanjing Normal grew in size over these years, from just over 2,000 students in 1956, to a total of 4,396 by 1960, as well as 3000 students in correspondence programs and another 842 in short-cycle training programs for rural teachers.[32] The outbreak of the Cultural Revolution in 1966 brought radical tendencies to a head, and the institutional history provides a factual overview of the struggles, noting the suffering and indignity imposed on professors and administrative staff, and the death of some. No new students were enrolled until 1972, with the first group of 589 "worker-peasant-soldier" students that year. Between 1972 and 1976, a total of 3,755 secondary school teachers were

---

[30] *Ibid.* p.34.
[31] *Ibid.* p.36.
[32] *Ibid.* p.38.

trained in programs that had been shortened to two or three years.[33]

The period from 1977 to 1982 is defined in the institutional history as one of "restoration and reordering" after the chaotic period of the Cultural Revolution. In 1980, it is noted, 133 staff members were rehabilitated, many of whom had been labeled as Rightists in 1957.[34] By 1982, Nanjing Normal's curriculum had developed from the original 6 departments to 13 departments, including education, political education, Chinese language and literature, foreign languages and literature, mathematics, physics, biology, chemistry, geography, music, arts, physical education and history.[35] Four-year academic programs were once again the norm, and a small number of graduate programs were begun.

In 1984, Nanjing Normal College was raised to the status of a normal university, and began to engage in vigorous programs of graduate education, in addition to its undergraduate work. It also added new departments in areas of demand outside of the field of teacher education, such as law, economics and management. In 1987, Ginling Women's College was established as a new entity with a special program for women. The intention was to restore the spirit of the original Ginling Women's College. Its role, however, was quite different. It offered short-cycle programs in areas like culture, tourism and foreign trade that would provide opportunities to young women who could not get into the academic mainstream of the university.[36]

In the 1990s, a major new development was the acquisition of a large new campus in a suburban area, where most undergraduate education is being moved, leaving the core campus in the city for graduate programs.[37] This has facilitated the huge expansion of undergraduate education that has taken place as China has moved towards a mass higher education system reflecting and contributing towards its remarkable economic growth. In 1998, Nanjing Normal University was accepted into the 21/1 project as one of the top 100 universities in the country, after five years of competitive strategic planning, with the support of Jiangsu province, to pass scrutiny of rigorous academic committees at the national level.[38] In September of 2000, it was granted

---

[33] *Ibid.* p.43.

[34] *Ibid.* p.46.

[35] *Ibid.* p.47.

[36] Da Zuoling, *Nanjing shifan daxue zhi 1993-2002*, pp.117-119.

[37] *Ibid.* pp.9-12.

[38] *Ibid.* p.26.

funding for a core base in moral education by the Ministry of Education, one of only eight such bases in the field of education throughout the country.[39]

Many different factors have contributed to this provincial normal college developing into a major university with a national reputation in the field of education and related areas: its rich heritage in progressive educational ideas going back to the traditions of the Nanjing Higher Normal School, National Central University and the several Christian universities and colleges which were merged with it in 1952, its location in the capital of Jiangsu province, one of China's most economically dynamic and socially progressive regions, and its good fortune in having sound leadership through the many twists and turns of its development. This university has been Lu Jie's home throughout her career as an educator, and she has contributed to its educational leadership in several arenas, including moral education, rural education and educational sociology.

Growing up in Shanghai during War and Revolution

Lu Jie was born in 1930 to the family of a professor. Like Xie Xide and Wang Yongquan, she grew up in relatively privileged circles, until the Japanese invasion of 1937 turned the family's life upside down. Her father had in fact come from a very poor family, and was born in a small town far north of Chengdu in the Western province of Sichuan. Left an orphan at an early age, he had been fortunate to find his way into a Christian mission primary and secondary school, then to go to France with the Work-study Movement organized by enterprising young leftists during the First World War to take advantage of opportunities for factory labor in France. This was another parallel with the family of Wang Yongquan.[40]

Her father returned to China from France with some savings, and was subsequently able to go to the United States and study under John Dewey at Columbia University. At the age of 30, he returned again to China, and taught briefly at Zhejiang University in Hangzhou. Then he took a long-term position as a professor of education and subsequently provost at the private Daxia (Utopia) University on the outskirts of

---

[39] www.moe.edu.cn/wreports.
[40] Chapter Eight, p.251.

Shanghai. From her father, Lu Jie felt that she inherited a profound love of books that has stayed with her till this day, and an unquenchable thirst for knowledge. She also felt he had passed on to her certain fundamental Confucian values of integrity and reliability.

Lu Jie's mother came from a very different background from that of her father. She grew up in a well-established Shanghai family, which owned land and was prosperous. She was educated at St Mary's Girls School, a school attached to St. John's University. She refused to allow her parents to choose a husband for her, and remained single until her late twenties, which was very unusual at the time. She was the only one of her sisters to go to school and wanted to be a teacher. However, it was only possible for her to teach in a family school for some years, given the social constraints of the period. When she made her own decision to marry in 1922, she chose a non-Shanghainese, who was without land or money. Her parents were strongly opposed at first but finally agreed, since he was a professor and had some social standing.

Three children were born to the couple: a daughter in 1923, a son, Lu Ping in 1927, and Lu Jie in 1930. Her father bought a piece of land near to the campus of Daxia University and built a house for the family. He was able to secure a mortgage since his professorial income was substantial. Lu Jie noted in passing that the 1920s and early 1930s was one of the best times to be a professor in China. In chapter eight, we have seen how Wang Yongquan's father was in a similar situation, with the courtyard house he purchased for his family in Beijing.

Her parents brought up their children in a way that was strict yet loving. They made it clear that they had the highest expectations for their education, and that they should study hard. While they held to traditional Confucian values in terms of respect for elders and family discipline, they were unusual in giving them considerable freedom over their study choices and career decisions. Her father's theories of education were strongly influenced by his study under John Dewey, and this, combined with her mother's independence of spirit, resulted in a remarkably liberal household for the times.

Lu Jie remembers a great deal of laughter and joking in this happy household of her early childhood. The room she remembers with greatest poignancy in their large family home was her father's library, full of the many books, which he had collected over the years. In an article about her love of reading, written many years later, she describes how she used to creep in quietly, sit on the floor and gaze up at all the books with light reflecting from the glass doors of the cabinets, and ask herself what might be written in there, and would she ever be able to write a book?[41] She also remembers learning to write characters with her mother's help at the age of three, and attending a progressive kindergarten on the university campus. At age five she was sent to a primary school in Shanghai's international concession, which was run by Chen Heqin, the famous professor of early childhood education mentioned earlier in this chapter. He was a close friend of her father. She would go daily by bus from her home near the university campus into the center of the city where the school was, along with other children of professors living on or near the campus.

When Lu Jie was only seven years old, in 1937, the Japanese invaded Shanghai, destroying her family home and shattering the idyllic world of her childhood. The family had to move to a small apartment in the international concession, and most of their belongings were lost. Her father was able to save only his books, and never again did he have a personal study or library to keep them in. They were stored with various relatives and friends whom he felt he could trust. Lu Jie commented how her brother, Lu Ping, never accumulated a personal collection of books because of the trauma associated with his father's loss in these early years.

During the Japanese occupation of Shanghai, her father elected to stay there and take responsibility for a local branch of the university, while the main institution was re-located to Guiyang. He was entrusted with this task by the president, she noted, because he was known as being politically neutral but strongly committed to the profession. It was a difficult responsibility, and she remembers vividly the day in which he received a threatening letter from the Japanese occupation authorities, demanding that he join in cooperation with those working under Wang Jingwei, the famous Chinese puppet governor. He immediately fled to Guiyang and stayed there for a while, only returning to Shanghai when he was sure Japanese attention had been deflected away from the Daxia branch school.

The family remained in Shanghai during the war years, and after graduating from a progressive primary school, Lu Jie was sent to a

---

[41] Lu Jie, "Wo he shuben" [I and Books] in Dai Liquan and Yang Huaining (eds), *Jiangsu xueren suibi* [Essays by Jiangsu Scholars] (Nanjing: Nanjing daxue chubanshe, 1997), p.181.

Catholic girls school attached to the Aurora College for Women. The strict discipline of the nuns was quite different from the more permissive environment of her primary school but her parents felt this would be beneficial to her. The principal of the school, Yu Chingtang, was a well-known woman educator, and there were a number of Chinese teachers on the staff as well as the European nuns. She thus had a sound academic education at the secondary level, as well as being exposed to both English and French. As for the nuns, Lu Jie felt they had real love for the students, were patient with them and never got angry. She benefited greatly from both the discipline and the sense of loving care that she experienced in this school.

During these years in secondary school she observed the brutality of the Japanese close at hand, as well as the many efforts to protest, which she was too young to participate in. She remembers seeing Japanese soldiers on horseback attacking civilians in the streets. She also remembers how her school became a kind of internment camp for nuns from all different parts of the city, after the Japanese attack on Pearl Harbor and the American entry into the war. At one point, a Japanese male teacher was sent to ensure that the students learned Japanese, but they all refused to learn. He gave up after a week.

These years were important for her in developing a strong sense of national identity and patriotism. She remembers vividly the celebrations in Shanghai after the victory of August 1945. She took part in one of the victory parades at age 15, and saw President Chiang Kai-shek, from a distance. She also remembers how soon it became evident that little had really changed. China was still weak and vulnerable. Supposedly one of the five powers that had won the war, along with Britain, France, the United States and Russia, China actually faced worsening conditions of poverty and economic collapse. She remembers how much she hated seeing the American solders in Shanghai after the war, and how bitter were the feelings aroused by the infamous case of a Chinese student being raped by an American soldier. It was somehow an empty victory.

Lu Jie completed secondary school in 1947, two years after the end of the war. There had never been any question in her mind that she would pursue higher education, but at which university? Her brother, Lu Ping, had chosen to study agriculture at St. John's University in Shanghai, while her older sister had studied chemistry at Daxia University, where her father was teaching. After some reflection, she decided she would like to leave Shanghai and be independent from the family. She chose

Ginling Women's College in nearby Nanjing, and decided to study chemistry, a field she felt would be useful to the country. Her father was pleased by her decision, since he had the greatest respect for President Wu Yifang of Ginling. Lu Jie thus enrolled in the second entering class after Ginling returned from Chengdu to Nanjing, at time when student numbers had reached a peak of over 500.

She began her studies in chemistry, but soon came to find the subject bitter and dry. After one year in the sciences, she chose to transfer to the department of sociology and the child welfare program. With all the suffering she had seen during the war she felt drawn to work with children, and hoped some day she might be able to run an orphanage.

Only after making this decision to transfer, did she write to her parents, and let them know. She will never forget the four-page letter she got back from her father, expressing his delight at having one of his children freely choose to enter the field to which he had devoted his life and career. He explained in the letter how important it was to him that his children have complete freedom of choice, yet at the same time how much it meant to him to learn of her choice. The rest of the letter expounded on the meaning and value of education, an outpouring of his own devotion to the field.

Lu Jie greatly enjoyed her second year of study in the child welfare program at Ginling, in spite of the dramatic changes going on around her, with the Civil War culminating in a successful Communist Revolution in 1949. That year she took ill with tuberculosis and had to rest for two years, only returning to university studies in the autumn of 1952, when Nanjing Normal College had been established on the Ginling campus. She graduated in 1953.

For her parents, this was a time of extreme testing. Her father had always taken a firmly apolitical stance, and in face of the revolution he decided to move to Hong Kong, and briefly to Taiwan. He tried very hard to persuade his two younger children to make applications for study in the United States, and was able to obtain a scholarship for Lu Ping at Stanford. For Lu Jie, he obtained application forms for study in several American institutions. She firmly refused to fill out any application and her brother turned down the Stanford scholarship. She noted how friends and colleagues asked her many years later whether she regretted her choice at this time, given all she was to suffer later. Her reply was a firm "no." It was a rational decision, not an emotional one, and it was the decision she had to take, given China's desperate circumstances at the time.

Lu Jie explained that she felt there were three major influences in her life – her family, her schooling experiences and the political circumstances in which she grew up. Due to these turbulent conditions, she and her brother reached political maturity very early, and felt a deep need to offer themselves in service of their country. They both joined the Communist underground, seeing this as the only way forward for China.

For her parents, this was a great disappointment. They spent a few years in Hong Kong, and were able to buy their own apartment there, but they missed their children so deeply that they decided to return to China in 1958. Only after they had returned, did Lu Jie and Lu Ping tell them of the oldest sister's death, knowing how painful it would be for them. With the onslaught of the Cultural Revolution in 1966, they were forced to go down to a remote rural area in Henan provinces with their son Lu Ping, where living conditions were terrible. Lu Jie's father died in 1977 and her mother spent the last years of her life with Lu Jie in Nanjing, passing away in 1978. In the forty years since they had lost their home in the Japanese invasion of 1937, they had never been able to recapture the life of professional commitment and family solidarity that they had known in their home near the Daxia campus. It is one of Lu Jie's deep regrets that her parents had to experience the Cultural Revolution in the last years of their lives.

*Lu Jie's father and mother at home
in Shanghai in the 1940s*

Educator in Socialist China

Lu Jie graduated from Nanjing Normal College in 1953, and was asked to stay on as a political instructor. Having joined the Communist underground in the late forties, she was one of the few with the necessary combination of political and academic qualifications for the task. Her husband was also a committed Communist Party member and held a leadership position in the university as head of the department of political science. Throughout the 1950s she worked as a political instructor and in the mid-1950s she was given a year and a half of training in Russian and Marxism-Leninism with Soviet scholars at Fudan University. She felt this gave her a strong foundation in classical texts of Marxism, which has stayed with her up till now. In some respects she feels China has not yet risen above the standards of knowledge and understanding represented in those works.

As for the influence of Soviet educational ideas at Nanjing Normal College, she observed this but was not directly involved, given her very specific responsibility for political education. Overall, she felt Soviet educational influences were beneficial, enabling China to develop many needed subjects and specialisms which supported economic development in a short time, and to open up learning opportunities to a wider range of students. She noted how Nanjing had had only three tertiary institutions before 1949, while there were already eight by 1953. She felt Kairov's ideas were widely accepted in the field of education because they were seen as both systematic and academically based. This was a welcome contrast to the eclectic range of educational theories introduced from the West, which were sometimes contradictory and confusing.

As for Soviet approaches to pedagogy, she felt they tended to be rather dogmatic, with Soviet experts insisting that course outlines be memorized and giving no opportunity for discussion or varying interpretations of texts. Sometimes it seems they were simply repeating what others had said rather than providing a helpful or liberating educational experience. In retrospect, Lu Jie felt the greatest problem with Soviet patterns lay in the fact that they tended to be a closed system, unable to reform themselves over time and not open to divergent views. In the end, this may have contributed to the collapse of the Soviet system, she believed.

Her perspective arose from her many years of exposure to progressive educational ideas, from her father and from her own early education. She noted how most Chinese professors had difficulty adapting to Soviet educational patterns, since they had been used to greater freedom for discussion and alternative views before 1949. Many had studied in the USA or Europe. By contrast, Chinese students welcomed Soviet patterns at the time, seeing them as a kind of "ideal kingdom", a set of patterns and ideas that would enable China to make rapid progress and become strong as a nation.

Lu Jie saw the Great Leap Forward of 1958, as a reaction to the intensity of Soviet influence. Mao Zedong had ideas of his own, and did not want to be simply a follower. His idea of "walking on two legs" and utilizing non-formal as well as formal approaches to educational expansion was unique to China and suited to the practical needs of the period, though it may have been applied too enthusiastically. This led to a problem of quality and sustainability in the many new non-formal institutions. Lu noted that two influential textbooks in educational studies (*jiaoyu xue*) were published in 1958, one by Liu Fonian, the leading educational theorist at East China Normal University, [42] and another by scholars at Nanjing Normal University. In other areas of the humanities, the well-known literary figure Zhou Yang had also developed new teaching materials. While the academic quality was not as high as that of the Soviet texts, Lu felt they were significant as an expression of Chinese ideas in education under the new socialist government.

Lu was greatly troubled, however, by the Anti-Rightist Movement of 1957. One of the main targets of criticism was Tao Xingzhi, the well-known progressive educator whom her father had studied with at Columbia. He had died in the 1940s, but his name was taken as a symbol of progressive education, a concept that was attacked as individualistic and associated with a capitalist economy. President Chen Heqin, who had been closely associated with Tao, was forced to step down and suffered a great deal in the nation-wide campaign to criticize his former friend and colleague. He had to leave Nanjing Normal College, and was only rehabilitated after 1978.

Many other older intellectuals also suffered at this time, and Lu Jie felt deeply for these scholars of her father's generation. For her, it was the beginning of a period of soul searching and a recurring sense of loss (*shiluo gan*). She found herself wishing that she had stayed in her original field of chemistry, or had chosen engineering like Wang Yongquan, rather than the complex and contested field of education.

In 1960, Lu was transferred from her work as a political instructor to the department of education where she took up teaching in educational theory and educational sociology. With the Sixty Articles promulgated in 1961, a strong framework for academic development was

---

[42] Chapter Eleven, pp.331-332.

*Lu Jie (far left, back row) with her parents and her brother
Lu Ping and his family in Beijing in the late 1950s*

established, which was firmly rooted in a Chinese rather than a Soviet approach to scholarship, Lu Jie felt. She was delighted with the quality of the four cohorts of students enrolled between 1960 and 1964, and felt this was a time she was able to throw herself energetically into teaching in the field of education. It is interesting to see the parallel here with Xie Xide's comments on her teaching and research work over this same period at Fudan University in Shanghai.[43]

The outbreak of the Cultural Revolution in 1966 was the beginning of a painful period in Lu Jie's life and that of her husband. At first she simply could not accept or believe, as a loyal member of the Communist party and political educator, that the revolution could take this kind of irrational direction. She found herself paralyzed in face of the early attacks of the rebel Red Guards, overcome with anxiety and incomeprehension. She thought there were certainly problems in the leadership that needed to be acknowledged, such as the abuse of power by cadres at the basic level. Yet those being attacked by the rebels were leaders of genuine integrity and commitment. Her own husband, who was head of the department of political science, was categorized as one of the "black line" (*heixian*) of reactionaries, and Lu found herself subject to attack because of her husband, even though she herself was an ordinary lecturer in the department of education at the time.

From the beginning, she refused to go along with the rebel group or to countenance their criticisms, even though this stance was to cause a

---

[43] Chapter Six, p.193.

great deal of suffering. Her ability to stand firm and refuse to bend was linked to the Western style of education she had experienced, she believed. She insisted on thinking independently and thinking for herself. She had a rebel streak of her own. Since she had always been somewhat critical of leaders whose style and approach she considered unhealthy, there may well have been an element of revenge in what was done to her, she felt.

She was in the first group who were forced to go down and work in the rural countryside in a remove area of Jiangsu province. She did not mind the arduous physical labor, but she was deeply distressed to see elderly professors of her father's generation subject to ruthless indignities and forced to endure outdoor work in bitter winter conditions. She spoke out against the way they were treated, when others dared not do so. As a result she was forced to go on innumerable parades and repeatedly subjected to public humiliation. She absolutely refused to admit that she was at fault, and was considered extremely stubborn by the rebel "authorities." Seven long years passed in this rural area, and she was unable to do any teaching or educational work.

What distressed her most of all was a particular meeting at which she was accused of being part of "an international spy network," because her father had spent some time in Hong Kong and Taiwan. Another incident, which she found extremely painful, was the experience of having Red Guards rampage through her home and demand that she hand over all of her personal letters. She refused to do so, as she felt privacy was a basic principle of her family and professional life. This resulted in one more experience of being severely criticized at a public meeting. In these kinds of circumstances, she noted, many other people found a measure of protection through turning to criticize others, and so contributing to the rebels' cause. This was something she absolutely refused to do. Particular pressure was put on her to criticize her husband publicly, but she firmly refused.

What enabled her to remain strong through this period of terror? Probably the same quiet rationalism that lay behind her firm decision in the late 1940s to turn away from the opportunity for study abroad, and join the revolution. As noted earlier, this was a decision she never regretted, in spite of the sufferings of the Cultural Revolution. As she tried to analyze the situation, she came to the conclusion that the Party itself had become deeply divided, between urban intellectuals like herself who had joined the underground in the 1940s, and rural Party enthusiasts who had grouped around Mao Zedong and the Gang of Four.

It was a bitter pill to be labeled a "traitor" after all she had sacrificed for her country. Yet she comforted herself with the thought that even China's President, Liu Shaoqi, had to swallow this pill. As she shared these recollections, one incident came to mind, which had somehow been a source of strength. One of the older cadres in the college administration, whom she greatly respected, made the following cryptic comment to her during the most difficult time: "Only you yourself have a clear understanding of your own personal affairs." (*Ziji de shiqing, ziji zui qingqu*).

Creating a Chinese Scholarship of Education after the Reforms of Deng Xiaoping

With the arrest of the Gang of Four in 1976 signaling the end of the Cultural Revolution, and the death of her father in 1977 and her mother in 1978, Lu Jie threw herself into the task of rebuilding Nanjing Normal College into a strong center of education. She wanted it to carry forward the rich progressive traditions which had nurtured her over so many years. In 1981, she became head of the department of education, and in 1982 head of the Institute for Educational Research. After the re-instatement of national university entry examinations in 1977-78, the department recruited 30-40 students each year. When these students began to graduate in 1982, she selected the best to stay on to teach and rebuild the field. With the development of graduate programs, many gained masters and doctoral degrees. Among them were three who spent time in Canada under our joint doctoral program, two as doctoral students, and another as a visiting scholar.

Over the subsequent years Lu wrote a number of prize-winning textbooks, which are widely used in normal universities. *The Study of Education* (Jiaoyuxue) was published in 1985 and awarded a first class prize at the national level, the Wu Yizhang prize. In *The Sociology of Education* (Jiaoyu shehuixue), co-edited with Wu Kangning and published in 1990, she wrote two major sections on education and the economic system, and education and culture. *A New Theory of Moral Education* (Deyu xinlun), another single-authored text, was published in 1988 and given a national award from the Ministry of Education.

In years since China's opened its doors under Deng Xiaoping's policies, Lu Jie commented that she felt she faced two major challenges – nurturing a new generation of scholars in the field of education, and re-building educational theory. On the human side, there have been many joys and successes, but also deep disappointments. Her greatest sadness lay in the fact that a large number of the young lecturers she had selected and nurtured, and for whom she arranged opportunities for study abroad, never returned. It was painful for her to try to come to terms with the difference in their mentality and outlook from her own. The gap between the choice she had made in the late forties, when China was torn by war, and the choice made by many in the new generation of China's youth was difficult to bridge.

Lu Jie with her husband in 1993

In terms of the building of theory, one of her areas of interest is in rural education. She is working to develop a theoretical understanding of the connections between education, labor and rural life. Every year she takes her students to visit rural schools and asks them to link what they are learning in educational theory to the realities of what they see in these schools. Like Li Bingde, she feels China's educational theory must be deeply rooted in its own culture and in its experience of social development.[44]

In the paper she wrote for our 1992 conference on Knowledge Across Cultures. Lu began by noting how China went through experiences of "total Westernization" and "total Sovietization" in the historical development of modern education. Given the rich heritage of China's own educational culture, this kind of borrowing is equivalent "to throwing away a large inheritance and begging in the streets," she went on to say.[45] Chinese pedagogy has finally come into its own in the 1980s,

---

[44] See Chapter Three, pp.103-104.
[45] Lu Jie, "On the Indigenousness of Chinese Pedagogy," in Ruth Hayhoe and Julia Pan (eds.), *Knowledge Across Cultures: A Contribution to Dialogue among*

as scholars have sought to analyze the complex educational developments of a country going through several social transformations simultaneously – from an agricultural to an industrialized society, and from an industrialized to a post-industrial society, somewhere between tradition and modernity, modernity and post-modernity.[46]

Although she did not experience the kinds of exposure to education in the Chinese classics that were common for an earlier generation such as Li Bingde[47] and Pan Maoyuan,[48] she feels that Confucianism forms a strong basis for Chinese education and finds herself constantly drawing upon China's rich classical literature. While filial piety is often thought to be a core value of Confucianism, emphasizing the respect owed by youth to an older generation, Lu points out that China has actual been a culture that has focused on children, with parents prepared to commit financial, human and time resources to their children which often go far beyond what they can afford. In a sense they see their children as the extension of their own lives. "This passionate commitment to education constitutes a dynamic force for educational development in China."[49]

One of the ways in which Lu Jie has sought to promote the building of educational theory that is rooted in Chinese culture and China's historical experience has been through a major conference organized in 1997 in Nanjing on the subject of Chinese education in the global community. To this event, she invited Chinese scholars from all parts of the world, and also included many non-Chinese who have had a research interest in Chinese education. In her introduction to the volume of conference papers, which she edited, she commented that this was a historic occasion, full of deep meaning. Chinese people constitute one quarter of humanity, and live in Mainland China, Taiwan, Hong Kong, Singapore, as well as many other parts of the world. She was motivated to hold this conference by the concept of "Cultural China," developed by Tu Wei-ming at Harvard, with its three circles reaching out around the world. The first circle involves societies that are mainly Chinese and are found in Asia, the second includes large groupings of Chinese immigrants in many different parts of the world, while the third embraces all

---

Civilizations (Hong Kong: Comparative Education Research Centre, The University of Hong Kong, 2001), p.251.

[46] *Ibid*. p.250.

[47] Chapter Three, pp.89-90.

[48] Chapter Five, p.153.

[49] Lu Jie, "On the Indigenousness of Chinese Pedagogy", p.250.

those who are interested in Chinese culture and have committed time to research on it.[50]

She notes the difference between *Hua ren* (people of Chinese culture) and *Zhongguo ren* (people of the Chinese nation) and makes the point that it is a cultural concept rather than a racially based one. Then she goes on to reflect on the ways in which the increasing pace of globalization is leading to a deep search for roots and a sense of belonging in many different societies. "Only when you are exposed to many different cultures, in a process of struggle and comparison, do you come to know how your own is different, and to ask the questions 'Who am I? Where do I come from? Where can I go?'"[51] She then points to the notion of "cultural consciousness," articulated by the famous Chinese sociologist, Fei Xiaotong, and notes how one of the tasks of education is helping people to become fully aware of their own cultural heritage and its possibilities.[52] Finally she comments on the various contributions to the volume, which bring ideas and concepts from philosophy, history, cultural anthropology, sociology and psychology, and include papers by Chinese scholars around the world as well as non-Chinese who have been drawn into the circle of cultural China.[53]

While Lu Jie has a profound commitment to a cultural understanding of China's educational thought and heritage, she also continues to develop an understanding of education in the Chinese context which builds upon classical Marxist theory in an open way and moves beyond some of the inflexibilities she noted in the Soviet approaches of the 1950s. An example of this can be found in a recent article published in the prestigious national journal *Educational Research* (Jiaoyu yanjiu) entitled "Education: The activities of practice involved in the construction of the human self." In this article, Lu begins by noting that the concept of practice in Marxist thought is usually associated with productive labor, and that Marxist theories of education have usually focused on the relationship between education and the economic base of societies, as well as education's relation to the political superstructure. "Now that we face the coming of a new century, can we not truly answer the question

---

[50] Lu Jie, "Qianyan" [Preface], in *Education of Chinese: The Global Prospect of National Cultural Tradition* [Huaren jiaoyu: minzu wenhua chuantong de quanqiu zhanwang] (Nanjing: Nanjing shifan daxue chubanshe, 1999), p.1.

[51] *Ibid.* p.2.

[52] *Ibid.*

[53] *Ibid.* p.3

of whether education is, or is not, a form of 'practice' and whether it is, in fact, an independent set of activities of practice? If we are not able to suggest that education is something in itself, then education is sure to lose itself in face of all the external forces, such as the economy and the market. Education would not be able to face the many challenges of the contemporary period."[54]

In this article, Lu Jie goes on to develop a concept of human subjectivity, and human ability to transform the world through the ongoing 'production of the self.' From there she considers the interaction between the role of the subjective self and the objective external world, and how that has changed in the early twenty-first century. Finally she considers education and makes the point that "in the past our theory of education took practice as the foundation in investigating education and human development, but it did not see human development as the result of the interaction between subjective and objective in the educational process."[55] Lu Jie concludes her paper by commenting that "contemporary human persons engaged in the development of the self commonly experience a sense of transcendence, and they fulfill a need for a conscious experience of development. Thus educational practice has already broken through its former closed boundaries, and entered into every aspect of life, and the notion of the "learning society" is already moving from an ideal to reality."[56]

In another recent article, written for a major two-volume work edited by the well known educational leader and policy maker Hao Keming, which includes essays by many leading thinkers in China, Lu Jie has presented some of her recent thinking on educational theory in a somewhat different way. She has linked it to classic debates in European philosophical thought and their interface with American pragmatism and the work of John Dewey. This essay is entitled "Human transformation: The Education theme of the new century." The essay begins with a discussion of globalization and how it is changing the context of human life, in terms of the sense of time and space and history. It then goes on to consider the new boundaries or definitions of the human self that reflect

---

[54] Lu Jie, "Jiaoyu: renzhi ziwo jiangou de shijian huodong" [Education: The activities of practice involved in the construction of the human self] in *Jiaoyu yanjiu* [Educational Research], No. 9, 1998, p.13.

[55] *Ibid.* p.18.

[56] *Ibid.*

this changed context. There was a consideration of the notion of the individual as an isolated self in European enlightenment thought, with reference to the philosophy of Kant, Hegel and Descartes, then challenges were posed by later thinkers such as Husserl and Heidigger. Lu Jie concludes this discussion with the comment, "To put it simply, what contemporary philosophy is concerned about is how each individual enters into the circle of other individuals, in order to attain to an integration between the self and the other."[57]

From here Lu Jie moves into a fascinating discussion of John Dewey's ideas of the individual, old and new, exploring in depth Dewey's notion that the "new individual" is constructed in interaction with human society and embraces collective participation in society and collective enjoyment of the benefits of this participation.[58] Lu's discussion of Deweyan communitarianism and how it responds to and supersedes European individualism has resonance with the work of the American philosophers, Roger Ames and David Hall, which is discussed in chapter one.[59] It leads to a fuller and more rounded concept of the person, as a person in relationship, rather than an isolated individual. Lu is concerned mainly with the moral and spiritual aspects of this idea in her article, while Ames and Hall explore its potential for a revitalized approach to democratic development in their important book on the subject.[60]

In the final section of this paper, Lu turns to the situation in China, and notes the contradictory demands for education in a situation where two transformations are taking place at once – from an agricultural to an industrial society for the rural masses, and from an industrial to a post-industrial society for urban inhabitants. She notes how vital it is that education nurture the fullest development of the independent individual in the context of rural transformation, while at the same time supporting the move from an isolated individual to a communitarian individual in

---

[57] Lu Jie, "Ren de zhuanrang: Shijixing de jiaoyu timu" [Human transformation: The Education theme of the new century] in Hao Keming (ed.) *Mianxiang ershiyi shiji: Wo de jiaoyu guan* [Toward the 21st Century: My View on Education] (Guangzhou: Guangdong jiaoyu chubanshe, 1999), p.393.

[58] *Ibid.* pp.393-394.

[59] Chapter One, p.37.

[60] David L. Hall and Roger T. Ames, *The Democracy of the Dead: Dewey, Confucius and the Hope for Democracy in China* (Chicago and Lasalle, Illinois: Open Court, 1999).

the case of urban young people. Chinese education thus has a complex dual role in the present period – "it must establish the independent individual personality, and stimulate the rich and varied development of the individual, while at the same time function as a kind of antidote to the unlimited development of individualism."[61] In the long term, education must nurture the kind of historic individual suited to a globalized society, who is able to absorb the richness of many human cultures, and develop into a fully inter-dependent moral person.

Lu Jie's vision for education is to nurture a kind of consciousness that includes concern for future generations, for environmental sustainability, and for the collective well-being of all of the human community. In this passionately-argued piece, we can see parallels with some of the ideas of Wang Fengxian on the unlimited potential of the subjective self in chapter seven, and of Li Bingde on the concept of quality education in chapter three.[62] We can also see how this way of thinking may be rooted in aspects of Daoist thought, especially as they were integrated within neo-Confucianism by Wang Yangming, leading him to a strong emphasis on the power of the subjective mind, and the value of practical personal knowledge.[63]

Finally, I turn to a profoundly moving personal document which Lu Jie gave me in manuscript form at the time of our second interview in March of 2000. It is entitled "A Choice which I never regretted" and is a reflection on her 43 years in educational work from her graduation from Nanjing Normal University at the age of 23 until she was sixty-six years old, in 1996. Part One of this essay addresses the question "what is a teacher?" The question is answered in a series of subtitles, which describe the nature of teachers' work. First, however, she points out the metaphor of a candle is often used for the teacher's life, giving the image of life being consumed in a process of self-sacrifice, and of students as a burden and responsibility. By contrast, she feels that her life with students has been one of mutual supportive interaction – with students' lives upholding her life, even as she sought to nurture theirs.

This leads to the first sub-title in her paper – "A kind of work that has eternal significance." She begins by recollecting a comment of her father to her mother, which she overheard as a child, "Human life is

---

[61] Lu Jie, "Ren de zhuanrang: Shijixing de jiaoyu timu" p.396.
[62] Chapter Seven, pp.221-223; Chapter Three, pp.103, 107.
[63] Chapter One, p.34.

never extinguished, since our genes are already present in our children and so our lives have a kind of eternity." Lu Jie goes on to reflect how her own sense of the heritage of thought and culture which she has passed on to her students, including the fourteen doctoral students who have worked closely with her, has connected her to eternity, as she has seen their accomplishments reach a higher level than her own. Of all the forms of life on earth, only human persons will ask "What is the meaning and purpose of our lives?" For the teacher, it is this giving of one's life of thought, of one's heritage of culture, to the next generation, a kind of sowing of seeds that will build up the nation.

"A kind of work that has developmental meaning" is the second sub-title of this paper. Under it, Lu Jie reflects on the notion of human development throughout the lifespan, and turns to Confucius' interpretation of the stages of his life, which has been discussed in chapter one of this book. She notes how he felt he came to know "Heaven's place for him" (*tianming*) at the age of 50, found his ears attuned to Heaven at the age of 60, and at 70 he could "give his heart and mind full rein, without overstepping the mark."[64] Lu Jie comments that this is an expression of social practice within human life, and that "at the same time as one transforms the objective world around one, one also transforms the self."[65] For teachers, self-transformation and the transformation of the world takes place through the interactive aspects of education. She notes how she has found her students to be the source of her spiritual strength. They force her to continue her pathway of human development, to stretch her mind to its limits in reaching out for deeper understanding, and exploring issues and questions ever more widely.

Her next subtitle, "A kind of work that involves the blending of genuine feelings," moves to the place of the human heart in teaching. The mind is not enough, as work with students requires engaging deep feelings. Simply stated, it calls for love. Here Lu Jie begins with an incident she observed while visiting the United States in 1986, which left an indelible memory. An elderly woman was celebrating her birthday all alone in a restaurant – with only the waiters to keep her company, not a single family member or friend. This made her realize how fortunate she was to be a teacher. She is surrounded by students who have become as

---

[64] Chapter One, p.21.

[65] Lu Jie, "Yifen wuhui de xuanze" [A Choice that I do not Regret], unpublished manuscript, March 2000, p.10.

close as family in the feelings that develop. The teacher's role involves shaping the very soul of others, and she describes her sense of holding and supporting each of her students within her heart. In return their feelings for her run very deep. When a doctoral student completes their thesis defense, there is happiness, but there are also tears – as the time for separation comes near.

Part Two of the essay is called "My outlook on Teaching." Its first sub-title is "Knowledge and Experience." Here she notes how it is relatively easy to pass on knowledge to students, but much more demanding to nurture them in ways where they develop their own viewpoints, based on the analysis of experience. She deplores what she sees as a widespread tendency in Chinese universities for students to simply absorb and work within Western theories, without developing viewpoints and perspectives of their own that are derived from a serious study of Chinese educational contexts. Then she describes how she organized a salon for doctoral students, to enable them to discuss, argue and debate their views, and formulate unique theoretical perspectives, which they are able to defend. Her description reminds us of Pan Maoyuan's Saturday evening salon for graduate students, which has been described earlier.[66]

Her second subtitle is called "Scholarship and Passion," and here she makes the point that scholarship must be linked to a purpose, a higher good, and that its pursuit will certainly involve deep feelings. "There is no such thing as a scholarship that is cold and detached, it must enter into the warmth of the human heart and spirit, and use this to transform the world and change the circumstances of human life."[67] Here we can see a deep-rooted Chinese philosophical perspective that true knowledge always involves action, and can in fact only be demonstrated through action. For the doctoral research in education which Lu Jie has guided over the years, she feels the broad purpose is clear and highly demanding – to raise the quality of human life in China, to develop a healthy life-path for young people, to reform the conditions of education, and improve the standards of education. If one hopes to succeed in this kind of demanding mission, it is not enough to apply rational thought; one must also invest one's emotions in the task. She goes on to describe her investigations of rural education together with students, and how

---

[66] Chapter Five, pp.145-146.
[67] Lu Jie, "Yifen wuhui de xuanze", p.26.

rural teachers remain as inhabitants in her heart and in the hearts of her students after each trip down to the countryside.

Conclusion: A Woman Educator of Principle and Passion

This chapter has told the story of a woman educator of standing, the circumstances of life that formed her, the heritage of her family, the ways in which a range of educational experiences influenced her, and her remarkable contributions to teaching and research through a scholarly career at Nanjing Normal University.

Lu Jie is the second woman to be portrayed in this volume, and it is natural to reflect on the similarities and differences between her life and that of Xie Xide, which has been described in chapter six. Both women grew up in relatively privileged family environments, where there was a natural integration of aspects of Western educational thought with Chinese culture and values. While Xie Xide went to the United States for higher study shortly after the war, Lu Jie was younger at the time, and felt impelled to stay in China and do what she could to join the political struggle for liberation.

Both began their professional careers in the early 1950s, and both were blessed by happy marriages with husbands who were professionals in related fields and had a shared political commitment. We have noted how Xie Xide's husband worked in an institute of the Chinese Academy of Sciences, while she was appointed to Jiaotong University, and then moved to Fudan University with the physics department in 1952. In Lu Jie's case, both husband and wife spent the whole of their professional careers at Nanjing Normal University. The suffering they shared during the painful decade of the Cultural Revolution has been described. After the reform and opening up, Lu Jie's husband served as party secretary at Nanjing Normal University for some years, and Lu Jie gives this as a main reason why she was not given any higher leadership appointment than those of department head and subsequently head of the educational research institute.

There was an occasion, she explained, when provincial education authorities came to the campus to do some background investigation relating to the appointment of new leaders, and they let her know she was

*Lu Jie enjoying a cruise on the
Li River in Guilin in 2003.*

under consideration. The main reason she was not given any higher appointment, she believes, was that it might have been misinterpreted, due to her husband's position. For her part, she was happy to be able to devote herself wholeheartedly to research and teaching after so many years of political upheaval. She was also relieved not to have to face the complexities of leadership in a Chinese institution where there are many difficult issues in dealing with people. At the same time, she knew she was perfectly capable of leading men, and had no lack of self-confidence, or sense of inferiority as a woman.

In some ways she felt this went back to her own education and her mother's independence of spirit. She remembers how disappointed her parents were when her older sister married on graduation from university in the mid 1940s, as she had excellent degrees in chemistry and economics and they felt she should have a career. She noted the expectation in those years that a woman who wanted a career should not marry, as was the case with such outstanding women leaders as Wu Yifang, the president of Ginling Women's College. Only after 1949 was it expected that all educated urban women should have professional work in the new socialist system, while those with lesser educational qualifications worked in factories or service positions. For rural women, however, Lu feels there are still many inequities and barriers. This may be one of the reasons she puts so much emphasis on the nurturing of individuality and independence in the transition from agricultural to industrial society, as noted above.

In all that she shared of her family background and life experience in the interviews which provided the information for this chapter, Lu Jie allowed us to see the unfolding of a life rooted in Chinese culture yet open to diverse external influences and deeply thoughtful in the face of the increasing integration of a globalized world. Through her theoretical essays and her personal reflections on the value of a teacher's life, she has also brought us into a rich interior world of thought, emotion and spirit.

Chapter Eleven

Liu Fonian and Ye Lan –
Influential Educators of Two Generations

This chapter presents portraits of influential educators of two generations. Professor Liu Fonian belongs to the same generation as Professors Wang Chengxu, Li Bingde and Zhu Jiusi. He was born in 1914, and had a distinguished career before 1949, including some years in England, France and Germany in the late 1930s. He was a member of the organizing committee for the founding of East China Normal University in the early 1950s, and served as its president from 1978 to 1984. Without doubt, he was one of China's most influential educational theorists between 1949 and the 1980s.

Liu was also a guide and mentor to Ye Lan, who was born in 1941, and grew up to become China's leading theorist in basic education and school reform. In September of 2001, Ye Lan was awarded a national level key base for her center on basic education reform and development, and her experimental educational projects have included an ever wider network of schools in different parts of China.

In my years of collaborative work with China, I was aware of Professor Liu Fonian's leading role in educational theory, but did not have the opportunity to get to know him personally. While working on this book project, a close colleague in my collaborative work over the years told me he felt it was important that Liu Fonian's story be included.[1] Since Professor Liu was already suffering from Alzheimer's disease at the time and was thus unable to take part in an interview, I had a talk with Professor Jin Yiming, who studied under Liu Fonian in

---

[1] This was Professor Ding Gang, Dean of the Faculty of Education, East China Normal University, and a participant in our collaborative project for joint doctoral study and educational research.

the 1950s, and worked at his side through much of his career.[2] Jin is also the author of the biography of Liu Fonian, which has been used to construct this portrait. Liu passed away on May 12, 2001, greatly mourned by his colleagues and the many younger educators whom he had nurtured over the years.

This chapter will thus begin by telling the story of Liu Fonian. Then it sketches out an overview of the history of the East China Normal University (ECNU), which was newly established after 1949, and profoundly influenced by Liu in its development. This in turn provides a setting for the story of Ye Lan, who was a student at ECNU in the 1950s, and has taught there throughout her career.

Ye Lan benefited greatly from the contributions of an earlier generation of educators, and Liu Fonian was a particularly important mentor in her professional development. Yet she grew up within the world of socialist China, and has personally forged her own unique framework of educational theory. It is rooted in the reality of China's schools and oriented towards a transformation of learning processes and educational contexts.

I have been privileged to meet Professor Ye Lan on a number of occasions both in Shanghai and Hong Kong. However, I have not had the opportunity of working closely with her in educational collaboration. This account of her life and thinking is thus based on two lengthy interviews, which I held with her in 2001.[3]

Ye Lan and Ruth Hayhoe after the interview with her in April of 2001 in Shanghai

---

[2] Interview with Jin Yiming, Shanghai, April 16, 2001.

[3] Interviews with Professor Ye Lan, February 14, 2001 in Hong Kong, and April 15, 2001 in Shanghai.

Liu Fonian – Leading Educator of Socialist China

Liu Fonian was born in the central province of Hunan, in 1914, the third of seven children. His father had been a teacher of mathematics in secondary school for a time, then joined the Revolution of 1911, and subsequently became a newspaper writer and editor. Given the political struggles of the time, this was an uncertain occupation, and there were numerous occasions when he and his family had to escape to rural areas, to avoid punitive action from conservative political authorities. In his later life, he worked for the provincial government of Hunan province, and after the Revolution of 1949 he worked in a museum of history and culture in Hunan.[4]

Liu felt that his father had an enormous influence on his life, particularly his desire to become a scholar and his love of reading and study. His father was a scholar and poet, who had a special interest in Buddhism. The first character in Liu's given name, Fo, is the word for the Buddha in Chinese, and Liu was to read many of the Buddhist classics under his father's guidance. He also read such Confucian classical texts as the *Four Books*, and many classical novels.

Liu's formal education, however, was in the modern primary schools, which were being established in China throughout the 1920s. His stepmother was a primary school teacher, and from the age of six he began to go to school with her, and listen to her classes. Later he completed primary schooling in a school in Changsha, the capital of Hunan province. The period of his primary education was in the years after the May 4th movement of 1919, when there was a strong atmosphere of patriotism.

Liu was also aware of American influences on his education from an early age. The famous Dalton Plan, which emphasized providing an environment for children to learn on their own, was used in the primary school where he studied.[5] When he later reflected on this experience, he felt he had not gained a strong foundation in basic knowledge of mathematics and language, due to an over-emphasis on freedom, and allowing the child to find its own way.

---

[4] Most of the information in this section is taken from Liu Fonian and Jin Yiming, *Liu Fonian xueshu* [The Scholarship of Liu Fonian] (Hangzhou: Zhejiang renmin chubanshe, 1999).

[5] Barry Keenan, *The Dewey Experiment in China* (Cambridge, Mass.: Council on East Asian Studies, Harvard University, 1977), p.85.

In 1925, Liu entered a famous secondary school in Changsha, the Mingde School, where he studied for four years. It was a time of political strife, and he experienced what he described as "white terror," with the school leaders being under the firm control of reactionary elements in the Guomindang party. On graduation in 1929, he went to Wuhan and joined the university preparatory class for Wuhan University, where he studied for two years before being accepted into the university program. Again he experienced a very conservative study atmosphere, with a strong emphasis on reading classical Chinese texts such as the *Book of Poetry*, the *Classic of Change*, the *Zuozhuan*, and the writings of the Daoist philosophers, Lao Zi and Zhuang Zi. He became deeply interested in philosophy in these two years, and began to read important Western philosophical works in translation, such as Plato's *Republic*, David Hume's *Treatise On Human Nature*, and works of Bertrand Russell.[6]

In 1931, five years earlier than Zhu Jiusi, whose story has been told in chapter four,[7] Li entered the Department of Education and Philosophy at Wuhan University. He noted how these two fields were combined in one department as a result of John Dewey's influence and reputation as both a philosopher and an educator. During his years as an undergraduate student, he was exposed to a systematic study of Western philosophy, including the work of Locke, Bacon, Hume, Kant, Hegel and others, also such Chinese classical philosophers as as Lao Zi and Zhuang Zi. He became deeply interested in concepts of causation, as presented in Hume's work, and his graduation thesis was on Hegel's logic.

On graduation in 1935, he had made up his mind to pursue a career in scholarship and was able to get a reference letter from a friend of his father, which enabled him to be accepted for higher studies in the famed Xuehai Academy in Guangdong. It was headed by an influential scholar of metaphysics, Zhang Junli, at the time. His intention was to focus on the study of Hegel's idea of the dialectic, also the works of Russell and A.N. Whitehead. However, his studies were soon interrupted by the Japanese invasion and impending war.

In January of 1937 he moved to Beijing and rented a room near the main library, where he could read. Then in September of that year he went to England to pursue further studies. After two months in London

---

[6] Russell had been in China from 1919 to 1921, the same period as John Dewey, See Bertrand Russell, *The Problem of China* (London: Allen & Unwin, 1972).

[7] Chapter Four, p.124.

he moved to Cambridge, where he benefited from lectures in logic from philosophers such as C.E. Moore and G.E. Broad.[8] He was impressed by the brilliance of their expositions of pure logic, yet felt there was no bridge to practice or action. During his year in England he also read a great deal of material from the British left, and joined some of their meetings, gaining insight into their understanding of dialectical materialism.

*Liu Fonian at Cambridge
in 1938*

After a year in England, he moved on to Paris in 1938, where he spent ten months at the University of Paris. From there he went on to Berlin for two months of study at the University of Berlin. In September of 1939 he returned to China, having exhausted his funds for study abroad.

His first teaching position on return to China in 1939 was at Northwest University in Xi'an, where he taught philosophy for half a year. He had expected there to be a strong spirit of nationalism and intense concern about national issues, given the wartime strug-gle underway. Instead he found many of his colleagues had short-term horizons and were only interested in how they could make extra money on the side. Given the university was firmly in the hands of admini-strators loyal to the Nationalist government, he was only allowed to teach French philosophy and it was not permitted to include any Marxist viewpoints or analysis in the courses.

For this reason, he moved on to Hunan in 1941, and taught for a year at the National Normal College (*Guoli shifan xueyuan*). He found a number of academically strong professors teaching there, but the control of administrators loyal to the Nationalist government meant there was little academic freedom. In this situation, he decided to focus on the philosophy of science, and ideas relating to science in service of the people, some of which were drawn from the leftist writings he had been exposed to in England. In 1943, he was relieved of his position at the National Normal College, due to suspicions about his leftist leanings on

---

[8] Liu Fonian and Jin Yiming, *Liu Fonian xueshu*, p.9.

the part of the Ministry of Education.

After two years as a secondary school teacher of English in Changsha, he was persuaded by friends to move to Shanghai and teach at Jinan University. He describes this move as a major turning point in his life. For the three years leading up to the Communist victory of 1949 he applied himself to the study of Marxism, and introduced Marxist ideas and texts into his philosophy courses at the university. Over the difficult years of the Civil War, he became more and more critical of the United States, given its support for the corrupt Nationalist government. He therefore began to develop a philosophical critique of American liberalism.

Three major articles published over these years expressed the ideas he was developing. The first was a broad-based critique of American cultural imperialism. The second focused specifically on the educational philosophy of John Dewey, which Liu had been exposed to since his own primary education. He argued that Dewey's confidence in education as a process able to bring about a transformation of society was misguided, since this view of education was itself a reflection of the capitalist economic relations of the society in which it was found.

The third article focused on the philosophy of Bertrand Russell. While affirming the validity of Russell's approach to logic, which was rooted in mathematics, Liu argued that his utopian view of a kind of socialism that focused on rural transformation through education reflected his aristocratic background. It was this, in turn, which accounted for his well-known appreciation of China's cultural traditions.[9]

Liu's philosophical studies, and attraction to Marxism over these years prepared him to play a leading role in educational theory after the Communist Revolution of 1949. He continued to teach at Jinan University for a short time, then became principal of the Shanghai Normal School, and a professor in Fudan University's education department. Meanwhile a planning committee had been set up with the mandate of establishing a leading national level normal university in Shanghai. Liu was appointed a member of this committee. The university was to be named the East China Normal University, and the next section of this chapter will tell its story. Since that story is closely intertwined with Liu's professional career after 1949, this overview of the development of his

---

[9] *Ibid.* pp.14-17.

educational ideas sheds some light on the university's development as well.

East China Normal University opened its doors in 1952, and Liu was appointed provost, working under the leadership of the first president, Professor Meng Xiancheng, a well-known educational sociologist. In his role as provost, Liu oversaw the implementation of a completely new academic system following the patterns of the Soviet Union, a similar role to that played by Pan Maoyuan in Xiamen University, as described in chapter five. He appreciated many aspects of the Soviet model yet was concerned by the tendency to a high degree of centralization in the unified curricula, and an over-emphasis on control. He noted, however, that academic standards were high.

Over these years, Liu prepared himself for membership in the Chinese Communist Party, joining the Party in 1956. He also wrote further articles criticizing pragmatist theories of education, and gave talks criticizing Dewey's ideas. At the same time he was troubled by inadequacies he had identified in the approach to teaching and learning that informed Ivan Kairov's text, *Pedagogy*, which had been translated into Chinese and was used as the core textbook in the field.[10] While it was supposed to represent a Marxist approach to education, Liu felt it was linear and one-sided. All the emphasis was on the responsibility of the state to manage education in a top down manner, and the role of teachers as experts dispensing knowledge to students within a formal education system. Liu felt its use in the Chinese context, which was so different from that of the Soviet Union, caused its inadequacies to be revealed.

With the Hundred Flowers movement of 1956, Liu had already begun to reflect on some of the problems of Kairov's text, which he saw as conceptually rooted in European rationalism. In 1957 he published an article identifying major contradictions that needed to be addressed in developing educational theory. The contradictions which he felt should be incorporated into a more flexible approach to educational theory were as follows: learning and thought, knowledge and action, unified truth and diverse viewpoints, the needs of society and the practical realities of students, the individual and the collective, specialist training and general education, need and possibility, independence and connectedness.[11]

---

[10] See Chapter Three, p.100.
[11] Liu Fonian and Jin Yiming, *Liu Fonian xueshu*, pp.19-20.

In that same year Liu was appointed vice-president of ECNU, and so was responsible for teaching and curricular developments during the Great Leap Forward of 1958, when there was a backlash against academic influences from the Soviet Union and great emphasis was placed on developing Chinese theories of education which were closely linked to practice. It was also a time when students were encouraged to play a leading role in knowledge development, and became involved in research projects and the writing of teaching materials based on local knowledge and experience. The guiding text for many of these activities was Mao Zedong's article "On Practice" which sets forth a three-step rhythm of knowledge development from practice to theory, then back to practice again. Liu noted how there were some positive aspects to this movement, but it had led to an unfortunate contempt for book knowledge and for the accumulated knowledge of human development over the centuries.

He wrote an article that year to explain why students could not take the lead in educational development, and the importance of the Communist Party's leadership, also respect for teachers and their authority, within certain constraints. He also led the development of draft materials for a new textbook, which was intended to replace Kairov's *Pedagogy*. It represented an effort to apply Mao Zedong's idea of the role of practice in learning, and through this to explore some of the contradictions which Liu had identified.

With the promulgation of the Sixty Articles for higher education reform in 1961,[12] and parallel movements for reform in the primary and secondary systems, there was an effort to develop a whole new set of teaching materials that would be academically rigorous yet distinct from the Soviet approach, which had dominated the early fifties. It was to take into account the Chinese context, and Chinese approaches to epistemology which were less linear than European rationalism, and more oriented to the concept of unfolding contradictions in the process of social change. Zhou Yang, the well known Marxist theorist and Minister of Propaganda had overall responsibility for the development of new teaching materials across the humanities and the social sciences. Liu notes how he was invited to edit a completely new text on educational

---

[12] Theodore Chen Hsi-en, *Chinese Education Since 1949: Academic and Revolutionary Models* (New York: Pergamon, 1981), pp.182-185.

theory, which was formally designated to replace Kairov's widely used *Pedagogy*.

At this time, Zhou Yang examined the draft textbook which Liu and the group of colleagues at ECNU and Nanjing Normal had put together during the Great Leap Forward, and commented that it was a collection of essays on educational policy, but not a systematic work of scholarship. He asked Liu to put together a textbook in educational theory which would give a complete overview of the field, would present Marxist perspectives but would also introduce other educational theories.

Liu was given just one year to complete the task and he organized a group of lecturers from both ECNU and Shanghai Normal University and put together twelve chapters which covered all the major topics. Liu felt some satisfaction with the way in which this volume presented an approach to educational theory based on the application of Marxist and Maoist thought to Chinese conditions. He felt it could be clearly differentiated from the approach of American pragmatism in Dewey's *Education and Democracy*, which had been widely used as a textbook before 1949, and from that of European rationalism in Kairov's *Pedagogy*, the standard text in education from 1950 to 1958. Once the draft was completed, Zhou Yang himself came to spend three days in discussion with Liu and his team of colleagues, making various suggestions for improvement. Then he asked them to have it ready for publication within a year. As it turned out, this text was not to be formally published until much later, though it was widely used for teaching in draft form.

To complement the use of this text, Liu organized a series of seminars to enable younger lecturers in the field to read the major classics of educational theory and have a good understanding of the different theoretical approaches. Although he was a busy vice-president, Liu always attended these discussion meetings himself, as he felt one of his main responsibilities was to nurture a younger generation of educational theorists and leaders.

Liu's biographer, Professor Jin Yiming, who graduated from ECNU in 1956, told me how tremendously valuable this experience was for him. During his undergraduate studies, from 1952 to 1956, he had only had access to the Soviet textbooks of the period until his graduation year, when he was allowed to read some of the educational classics in the teachers reference room. [13] With the Hundred Flowers of 1956, new

---

[13] Interview with Jin Yiming, Shanghai, April 16, 2001.

translations appeared of works by scholars such as Comenius, Spencer, Pestalozzi and Makarenko, which were available for discussion in these seminars organized by Liu at ECNU.[14] There was also considerable focus on reading and discussing core writings of John Dewey, though his theories were subject to rigorous criticism.

The outbreak of the Cultural Revolution in 1966 brought an end to all of this. Liu became a particular target of the Red Guards at ECNU, and was criticized as an academic authority, since he had been the chief editor of the new textbook of educational theory. In the large character posters spread all over the campus at the height of the revolutionary fervor he was called "China's Kairov." The new text on educational theory was pronounced a "poisonous weed," guilty of promoting philosophical dualism, since it had suggested that education might actually influence child development, and should not be seen only as a reflection of the economic base and class struggle. A further reason for it being criticized was that it had supported and built upon the ideas in the Sixty Articles of 1961, which were condemned as the educational policies of leaders within the Party who were taking the capitalist road.

For much of the Cultural Revolution decade Liu was kept under surveillance by Red Guards on campus, and subject to various indignities. He was required to write his own life-story in some detail, something he was reluctant to do, as a scholar who had always focused his attention on philosophical and theoretical questions. Jin Yiming noted, however, that this manuscript was invaluable later, as it provided important information for the writing of Liu's biography. In the end, nothing could be found in Liu's history or background that would incriminate him, and by the early 1970s he was made a leading member of a revolutionary education group at the university.

Since the Gang of Four were based in Shanghai, from time to time they would send messengers to the ECNU campus asking for materials on foreign education that could be useful to them. This gave Liu the opportunity to develop interesting research on education in six capitalist countries, including the USA, England, France, West Germany, Sweden and Japan, also on a variety of theories and philosophies of education. Since Liu was one of the few scholars with knowledge of several European languages, he played a key role in selecting and introducing

---

[14] See Chapter Two, pp.66-67 for a description of Wang Chengxu's contribution to this series of translations.

materials for this work. He had good reason for purchasing a considerable number of foreign books, and felt that the discussion and research done in this period was important in laying a foundation for the development of education as a science after the end of the Cultural Revolution.

In 1978, after the fall of the Gang of Four and the promulgation of Deng Xiaoping's policy on education and modernization, Liu was appointed president of the Shanghai Normal University, the name assigned to ECNU during the Cultural Revolution. He was deeply concerned about the huge shortage of teachers for the secondary schools, resulting from the drastic drop in enrolments during the Cultural Revolution decade, and also about the low quality of those that had graduated. A further concern was for the academic staff of ECNU, since many of the older professors had suffered greatly, while younger academics had been given no opportunity for scholarly development.

Liu thus had many concerns as he took up this new responsibility. His major focus was on conceptualizing the role that a normal university should play. Under the Soviet model of the 1950s, its main function had been to train secondary school teachers in the major academic disciplines. Liu felt this was important, but far from enough. He wrote an article entitled, somewhat provocatively, "How to run a keypoint normal university in a keypoint way," reflecting the dominant concern of the time with ways of regaining academic excellence. His vision included strengthening foundation programs in the disciplines, recruiting excellent students and building up graduate programs that could nurture future faculty. He also wanted to integrate research into all aspects of the university's work and encourage the development of new programs in fields not directly related to teacher education. A normal university should be seen to contribute to education broadly defined, not only the formation of teachers but also the nurturing of administrators and educational leaders, he felt.

By the time Liu had served as president of East China Normal University for six years, the university had grown to 14 departments and 25 undergraduate programs, 10 research institutes, 67 masters degree programs and 18 doctoral programs. It was on the way to being a leading university in the field.[15]

---

[15] Liu Fonian and Jin Yiming, *Liu Fonian xueshu*, pp.40-41.

In 1979, Liu had published an important article about the need for universities to have a greater degree of autonomy over the establishment of disciplines, research, programs for study abroad and international collaboration. He himself traveled widely in Europe, Japan and North America, promoting a wide range of exchanges and projects of research collaboration. By 1985, the year after he stepped down, China's State Education Commission promulgated an important reform document which specified considerable autonomy for universities in all of the areas that Professor Liu had argued for.[16]

In his capacity as president emeritus, Liu continued to play an active role in leading educational research, and was responsible for two major national-level projects for China's Sixth (1986-1990) and Seventh (1991-1995) Five-year Plans. The first dealt broadly with Marxist educational theory, and the second focused on the future of Chinese education, including reform of the educational structure, and a series of sub-themes, which were taken up by a number of young and middle-aged scholars at ECNU.

Liu himself became fascinated with a project carried out in Shanghai's Qingpu district to raise the effectiveness of children's learning of mathematics, and hoped to see it widely applied across China. He had arranged for the translation of Benjamin Bloom's famous taxonomy for learning, teaching and assessment, which he felt was relevant to this work. Afterwards he had invited Bloom to ECNU to discuss his ideas and their application in a Chinese context.[17]

The restoration of unified national entrance examinations had led to an ever intensifying hierarchy of schools by prestige and examination results, and huge pressures on children to study for examination success. Liu therefore became greatly concerned about both structural and classroom interventions which could support effective learning for all children. He encouraged an approach to teacher education that would involve all teachers in classroom-based research, and pioneered a number of experiments in the Shanghai context, which mitigated against the over-emphasis on examination achievement that was putting such great stress on children and young people.

---

[16] Ruth Hayhoe, *China's Universities 1895-1995: A Century of Cultural Conflict* (Hong Kong: Comparative Education Research Centre, The University of Hong Kong, 1999), p.119.

[17] Liu Fonian and Jin Yiming, *Liu Fonian xueshu*, p.48.

In summarizing the scholarly achievements and contributions of his respected mentor, Jin Yiming commented that Liu Fonian was a scholar who lived the scholar's life – refusing any of the perquisites that might go with a leadership position and focusing all of his energy on the development of scholarship.[18] He was wholly committed to forming and nurturing a new generation of younger scholars, and much of his time and energy, outside of his administrative leadership role, went into discussion with groups of younger scholars working in different areas. He encouraged them to read the classic texts of educational thought and theory carefully and thoroughly, and develop a soundly based critical understanding of them.

Since his focus was on nurturing scholarship in others, Liu himself only published one single-authored work, and two edited works, including his widely influential text on educational theory, which has been discussed earlier. The impact of these was enormous, however. Similarly the East China Normal University, the institution he had helped to found, and had led through the important years of reform from 1978 to 1984, became a nation-wide leader in educational theory.

Liu Fonian, China's most influential educator, in the 1980s.

As mentioned earlier, ECNU was one of the seven normal universities in China that partnered with the Ontario Institute for Studies in Education in our joint doctoral project.[19] Several influential younger

---

[18] Interview with Jin Yiming, Shanghai, April 16, 2001.
[19] Chapter Nine, pp.261-262.

academics spent time at OISE as doctoral students, postdoctoral fellows and visiting scholars. One of the earliest, Professor Shi Liangfang, came for the spring term of 1993, spending time in the department of curriculum, teaching and learning (CTL), which was close to his own area of research.

I will never forget the comment Shi made to me not long before returning to China that summer. "I was surprised and shocked to find there were some graduate students and professors in OISE's CTL department who had not read any of John Dewey's basic works." Shi was clearly one of those who had been influenced by Liu Fonian's insistence that all scholars at ECNU must have a thorough grounding in the most important works in educational theory of the 20th century. It continues to be an important legacy.

East China Normal University

The creation of the East China Normal University as a leading institution for the education of secondary school teachers in 1951 reflected very closely the model for a new socialist higher education system which was adopted in China under Soviet influence after 1949. Under this new system the country was divided up into six major geographical regions, with one leading center for higher education in each region. We have already noted how Wuhan was the center for higher education in the Central South Region, and Shanghai was the undisputed center for the East China Region, although there were major universities of importance in nearby Nanjing and Hangzhou, the provincial capitals of two economically dynamic provinces, Jiangsu and Zhejiang, as well as Shandong to the north, and Fujian to the south.

Under the Soviet model, higher education was organized sectorally, with three major types of university under the Ministry of Higher Education and all others under other specialist ministries. Under the Ministry of Higher Education were comprehensive universities like Beida and Fudan, polytechnical universities like Tsinghua and Zheda, and normal universities which had a full range of arts and science departments as well as a department of education. The fact that East China Normal University was established as a new university at a national level, located in Shanghai, the center of the East China Region, meant that it was given resources and a status well above Nanjing Normal University, in spite of the latter's remarkable heritage of scholarship in education.

The model for the national-level normal university had come from the Soviet Union, but its earlier antecedent was the Ecole Normal Supérieure of France, one of the important institutions founded just after the French Revolution.[20] It was Liu's understanding of this European context that enabled him to set forth a vision for ECNU to be a leading centre of educational scholarship, not merely a specialist institution playing the functional role of training secondary teachers within a specialized higher education system.

The beautiful garden campus that had belonged to the private Utopia (Daxia) University was given to ECNU on its founding in July of 1951.[21] This was the university where Lu Jie's father had served as professor of education and provost over a long period, and where Lu Jie had spent her childhood in the years before the Japanese invasion.[22] The other private university which also contributed to the foundation of ECNU was Guanghua (Light) University, which had been founded by a group of students and professors who left St John's University in protest after the May 30th Movement of 1925, including Meng Xiancheng.[23] Both universities had had their own attached secondary schools, and these schools were combined in the autumn of 1951 to form the attached secondary school of ECNU, as a locus for educational experimentation and research.[24] The departments established for the new university in 1951 included Chinese literature, foreign literature, education, history, geography, mathematics, physics, chemistry, biology, music and physical education, 11 in all, reflecting the major fields of knowledge taught in secondary schools, together with education.[25]

The first president of ECNU was the influential scholar of education, Meng Xiancheng, who had studied at Nanyang Gongxue and St John's University in Shanghai, had gone to the University of Washington in the US for a Master of Education in 1918, and on to England for further studies at the University of London Institute of Education, returning to

---

[20] Smith, Robert, *The Ecole Normale Supérieure and the Third Republic* (Albany, New York: State University of New York Press, 1982).

[21] Yuan Yunkai and Wong Tiexian (eds.) *Huadong shifan daxue xiaoshi 1951-2001* [An Institutional History of East China Normal University 1951-2001] (Shanghai: Huadong shida chubanshe, 2001), pp.2-3.

[22] See Chapter Ten, pp.303-305.

[23] Yuan and Wong, *Huadong shifan daxue xiaoshi*, p.3, pp.361-370.

[24] *Ibid.* pp.5-6.

[25] *Ibid.* p.7.

China in about 1923. He had taught at a number of different universities before 1949, including St. John's, Guanghua, Zhejiang University and Dongnan/National Central University, where he was dean of education. He had also translated several of John Dewey's works into Chinese, including "How We Think."

Liu Fonian was appointed provost and head of the department of education. With the nationwide reorganization of colleges and departments of 1952, ECNU gained many influential professors and departmental resources from other Shanghai universities, including the departments of education of Fudan University, Zhendan (Aurora) University, Hu Jiang University, and Datong University. The department of geography of Zhejiang University and a number of professors in the arts and sciences from Zheda, as well as the science departments of St John's University were also merged with ECNU. Between 1952 and 1953, academic staff numbers grew from 131 to 297, with the many scholars who moved there in the reorganization.[26]

The chapter outlining the first stage of ECNU's history from 1952 to 1957 is called "Initial Dimensions and Scope," and there is a detailed description of the reorganization of teaching and learning that took place under the Soviet influence, with numerous teaching and research groups responsible for developing detailed plans for each specialization.[27] There is also an interesting description of efforts to introduce oral examinations in place of written ones, following the Soviet model, and finally the decision to go back to written examinations.[28] Another section describes the six Soviet experts who were invited to teach at ECNU, one of them acting as an advisor to the Shanghai education bureau as well. There is also a discussion of the organizational work done to ensure that the work of the Soviet experts was valued and adapted to the university's needs.[29]

By 1954 over 200 research projects had been started up. Students were also encouraged to take part in educational research. In 1957 the first two research institutes were established, one in demography and the other in river delta studies, both led by famous scholars. This was the first time the national Ministry of Education had established research institutes in universities, and ECNU got two of the eighteen approved

---

[26] *Ibid.* pp.17-18.
[27] *Ibid.* pp.25-26.
[28] *Ibid.* p.29.
[29] *Ibid.* p.30.

that year. Between 1953 and 1957 several classes of graduate students were recruited, and programs established in areas of strength. This chapter has a lengthy section describing efforts to develop faculty, and also a section on political education work and efforts to implement the national policy on intellectuals, which was announced by Zhou Enlai in January of 1956, and emphasized the importance of according them respect. [30] Nothing is said, however, about the Hundred Flowers movement of 1956 and the Anti-Rightist Movement, which followed in 1957.

Chapter three, entitled "The Expansion and Development of Professional Work," covers the period from 1958 to 1960, beginning with the Great Leap Forward and the educational revolution that accompanied it. This is followed by a chapter on the period between 1961 and 1965, the implementation of the Sixty Articles for Higher Education.[31] We have seen earlier the important role played by Liu Fonian, then vice-president, in developing a body of educational theory which was academically rigorous yet rooted in the realities of China's educational system and educational thought, not simply a translation of Soviet theory, with its European roots. By the eve of the Cultural Revolution in 1966, the university had over 4,100 students, 912 academic staff and another 363 administrative staff.[32] Altogether 12,580 students had graduated since its founding in 1951, with most going into secondary schools as teachers.[33]

The Cultural Revolution, which broke out in 1966, had a particularly devastating impact on ECNU due to its location in Shanghai, an important base for the Gang of Four. Quite a lengthy chapter in the university history is devoted to telling this story. While only a few names of those who suffered most are told, it was clearly a painful time. At least 37 deaths among academic and administrative staff were directly linked to the violent activism of the Red Guards,[34] and many others suffered from longstanding health problems as a result of how they were treated. In 1971, Zhang Chunqiao, one of the Gang of Four, mandated a merger between ECNU and four other Shanghai-based educational institutions, under the umbrella name of Shanghai Normal University. Many

---

[30] Chapter Five, p.158.
[31] *Huadong shifan daxue xiaoshi 1951-2001*, pp.78-100.
[32] *Ibid.* p.101.
[33] *Ibid.* p.109.
[34] *Ibid.* p.103.

national-level institutions were brought under local control during this decade, so this reflected the times. It also had the effect of giving radical leaders greater unified control over education at all levels in Shanghai. It was to be 1980, before ECNU got back its original name, though the other institutions were separated out again in 1978.

We have already noted from Liu Fonian's story how he and other scholars found an opportunity to do research on education in various European countries and Japan in the later years of the Cultural Revolution, laying a foundation for the developments that were to come after 1978. Another initiative of the late Cultural Revolution period was a mission to help remote parts of the country. In 1974, 21 academic staff members took a study class in the Tibetan language and then went to Tibet to help establish a teachers' college. Two years later in 1976 a second group followed.[35]

The years from 1978 to 1984 under Liu Fonian's presidency were years in which academic programs were restored and expanded, from 11 to 14 academic departments. Also a whole range of new research initiatives were launched, anticipating the reform decision of 1985, which mandated universities to undertake research as well as teaching. In subsequent years ECNU grew from strength to strength, greatly expanding its curricular offerings. By 2001 it had 33 academic departments, organized within eleven colleges, and including new programs in areas like statistics, accounting, environmental science and technology, engineering management, information technology and law, as well as education and all the basic disciplines for teacher education.[36] The expansion in student numbers during the 1990s was dramatic, reflecting the move to mass higher education across the country, with total enrolments rising from about 12,000 in 1991 to close to 23,000 by the year 2000.[37]

The government's concern for the quality of education and of teachers was such that normal universities were excluded from the large-scale mergers taking place in the late 1990s, such as the experience of Zhejiang University described in chapter two.[38] However, East China Normal University was invited to take over three local educational

---

[35] *Ibid.* p.125.
[36] *Ibid.* pp.394-395.
[37] *Ibid.* pp.402-403.
[38] See Chapter Two, p.50.

institutions in 1997, including the first and second Shanghai education colleges, which had been responsible for in-service education of teachers over a long period, and the Shanghai institute for early childhood education. With strong support from the Shanghai municipal govern-ment, it was able to gain entry into the 21/1 project and receive consi-derable additional funding. In 1996 the establishment of a school of graduate studies was approved, reflecting the significant scope of its graduate studies, with student numbers having grown from 1062 in 1991 to 2415 by the year 2000.[39]

In 2000 and 2001 ECNU was the only university to be given two national key bases in education, one in curriculum and teaching, the other in basic education reform and development. The second was awarded to Ye Lan's research group, as noted in the introduction to this chapter.[40] This was a national initiative to support high level research in the humanities and social sciences, and there were only eight bases in education throughout the whole country.

Much more could be written about the contributions of the East China Normal University, but this overview is intended to provide a context for understanding the life-story and educational ideas of Ye Lan, the youngest educator to be portrayed in this volume. Ye Lan's personal history was closely connected to ECNU from its earliest years, as she was a student in its attached secondary school in the early 1950s, then entered its undergraduate program in 1958, and has spent her whole professional career there up to the present.

Growing Up in Shanghai at the Beginning of a New Era

Ye Lan was born in 1941, making her nearly thirty years younger than the oldest of the influential educators portrayed earlier in this volume, and eleven years younger than the youngest. Her father was from Fujian and her mother from Shanghai. Her father had left his father when he was quite young, and enrolled in the Jimei Normal School near Xiamen, one of the network of schools established by the philanthropist Chen Jiagen, which has been described in chapter five.[41] This was because his

---

[39] *Ibid.* pp.289-290, 403.

[40] *www.moe.edu.cn/wreports.*

[41] See Chapter Five, pp.146-147.

grandfather was authoritarian, supportive of the warlord regime, and very harsh towards his children.

Once her father had enrolled in the Jimei Normal School he secretly joined the Communist Youth League, and subsequently joined the underground Communist party. As a result he was expelled from the school in 1924 because of his revolutionary commitment. He left Xiamen and moved north to Shanghai, where he enrolled in the Shanghai School of the Arts (*Shanghai Meishu zhuanke xuexiao*), and studied under the famous artist, Liu Haishu, who was principal of the school. While studying in Shanghai, her father got to know her mother, the youngest of a large landlord family in the Pudong area, which had fallen on hard times as a result of the older generation's involvement in opium smoking and gambling.[42] Her mother had been sent to primary school and on graduation she made up her mind to find a factory job in Shanghai in order to be independent of the family. The factory's hostel, where she lived, was close to the art school, and so she got to know Ye Lan's father and they married after his graduation. Her parents protested her marriage to someone from Fujian, but in the end they gave their permission.

Nine children were born to the couple, but only six survived. Ye Lan was fourth, having two older surviving siblings and three younger. Her father taught in a primary school and the family lived in a small two-room apartment. It was a crowded yet a happy home, as Ye Lan remembers it. She had a particularly close relationship with her father, and at the age of four and a half she began to go with him to school every day. He was a lover of books, and she remembered borrowing books from the school

Ye Lan with her parents and younger brother in Shanghai in 1947

---

[42] Ye Lan noted that her mother's family were treated as poor peasants after the revolution, rather than landlords, because the family had fallen on hard times.

library every week, and immersing herself in reading from an early age.

Although her young years were spent under the shadow of the Japanese occupation of Shanghai, she has little memory of that. She does remember how her father's friends were of two very different types – artists and art teachers on the one hand, and leftwing activists on the other. Since her father had joined the Communist Party very early, he was trusted by Party members and she remembers how they came to see him always one at a time, for safety reasons. Those were the difficult days of the Civil War before the Communist victory of 1949.

Ye Lan has very happy memories of her early schooling. She loved going to school with her father and was proud to be a teacher's daughter. From an early age she had made up her own mind that she would become a teacher. She particularly enjoyed studying Chinese literature, reading many traditional stories as well as contemporary fiction. Mathematics had less appeal for her, given that it was taught as a subject that must be memorized. Ye Lan studied in her father's school up to the end of primary school. She also has vivid memories of a home where there were always paintings hanging on the walls, and her father supplemented his meager salary by selling some of his paintings. Her mother remained independent in spirit, in spite of the demanding family responsibilities, and encouraged her to make her own decisions and find her own way.

After the Liberation in 1949 Ye Lan's father got a job teachng fine arts in Gezhi zhongxue, an excellent secondary school. She herself wanted very much to get into a good secondary school, feeling the local school was not appealing. However, her parents did not open doors for her. They simply suggested that she go to talk with one of their friends from the Communist underground who had become a secondary school principal after Liberation. She took her courage in both hands, and went to talk with him. She was accepted into this excellent school, yet she did not do well. Before long the principal came to visit her parents, to find out why she was a trouble-maker and took little interest in her studies. This situation continued until her third year of secondary school. Then she suddenly decided to change her ways and take school seriously. In 1955 she took the examinations for entry to the upper secondary school of the East China Normal University, and was accepted.

In reflecting on those years of early secondary schooling, Ye Lan feels that her lack of interest in study resulted from the fact that she was a lively child, who wanted to speak out and express her own views. But she found herself in an atmosphere where this kind of behavior was not encouraged. The class teacher tended to scold students a lot and did not encourage active participation in learning. The result was that she developed a spirit of rebellion. On one occasion he asked her, "How will you manage students, if you become a teacher?" Her reply was quick and to the point: "If I become a teacher, I won't be like you!" She now realizes how hurtful this outburst must have been to the teacher in question.

The upper secondary school attached to ECNU had belonged to the private Guanghua University before 1949 and had excellent standards. A number of its teaching staff had previously taught in the university. She found a genuine atmosphere of scholarship there, as well as a rich cultural environment. All of the students were disciplined and serious, and the influence of these peers upon her was particularly important. She was soon aware of being behind most of them, and determined to work hard in order to catch up. This was also the time when she made up her mind to become a teacher. On graduation in 1958 she made application for university studies, with strong support from both her father and her mother. Her first choice was the department of education at East China Normal University.

She was successful in gaining entry to ECNU, and found herself one of the youngest in the class. It was an exciting time to be beginning university studies, as Mao Zedong had called for a Great Leap Forward, and a revolution in education was underway. The goal was for China to catch up with England within ten years, and many believed that the superiority of the communist system would ensure that this happened with minimal effort. Students were encouraged to organize discussion groups and to visualize the nature of the future society that would be created. The group she belonged to called itself "the electric button group," since they believed a rapid technological revolution would make everything available effortlessly, and there would be no need for work in future. Another group of students called themselves, "the labor group," and put more emphasis on physical effort in the change process.

It was an exhilarating time, but also a troubling time, with the famine that was to follow. Along with fellow students, she spent lengthy periods in the countryside, participating directly in manual labor, carrying out literacy work, and working on the building of a railway. The positive aspect of this experience was the emphasis on young people thinking for themselves and expressing themselves, not just accepting what was written in the textbook. The great debates that took place were exciting events in which they gained confidence in public speaking. Labor was a training of the will, she felt, as enormous hardships had to be overcome, and there was real experience of the difficult life of working people in the rural areas. "We had none of the arrogance of city children nowadays, including my own child," she said.

The negative aspect of the experience was the fact that they were caught up in criticism of works of scholarship which they had never had the opportunity to learn or understand – it was a reactive kind of criticism, based on a simplistic, literal interpretation of Mao thought, not an informed or thoughtful criticism. Overall, so much time was spent in labor and in activism, that genuine learning and study had to suffer. "The cost was too high, even though there were some positive aspects to the experience."

From 1960, the whole atmosphere changed, as much greater emphasis was placed on academic standards and the development of a curriculum that encouraged systematic and in-depth learning. She had been an avid reader since her years in primary and secondary school, reading huge amounts of both Russian and Western literature in translation. This gave her a definite advantage academically, and she noted how in the undergraduate class in the education department in her year, the 40 students had come from different backgrounds. There were 20 from regular academic secondary schools, like herself. The rest had been admitted from primary teacher training schools, or special schools that

Ye Lan on graduation from East China Normal University in 1962

offered a second chance to workers. She was the youngest in the class, yet her strong secondary education had given her a definite advantage over most others.

At the end of the four years, only two students were given appointments as assistant lecturers at ECNU, and she was one of them. In reflecting on this situation from an educator's perspective, much later, she realized how important her secondary education had been to laying the cultural foundations for a scholarly career, and how difficult it was for young people to catch up, if they did not have the foundation in reading and critical thinking developed at the secondary level. Her ability for theoretical analysis had its roots in her secondary education, yet depended mainly on her university studies in education, she felt.

Career as a Young Socialist Educator

Ye Lan was delighted to be given a job assignment in a teaching and research group on primary education within the Department of Education from which she had graduated in 1962. This was a reflection of her academic results on graduation. The fact that she had excellent Putonghua or Mandarin was also important, as huge efforts were being made to universalize Putonghua as the language of education and media communication, as well as government. She was quite ambitious, and had made an application for graduate studies at Beijing Normal University. However, the leaders at ECNU who had appointed her saw this as unnecessary, since she already had a lifetime appointment in ECNU. On the advice of a senior administrator in her department, she simply did not attend the graduate entry examination, which she had applied to take. There was not much freedom of choice for a young person at the time, she explained. One was expected to accept the job assignment given to one on graduation.

Her first assignment as a young lecturer was to spend two years teaching in ECNU's attached school to gain real experience at the school level.[43] She expected this to be easy, but in fact it turned out to be extremely difficult. She was assigned a primary level class famous for being extremely boisterous. They had already gone through four class teachers, and she found her month of field experience in her undergraduate program had not prepared her for the difficulties she now faced. Her youth and liveliness seemed to encourage the students to get more and more out of control, and she had to ask other more experienced teachers for help. Her frustration was so great at times, that it brought tears to her eyes. In the second year, however, the situation improved. She was given a lower secondary class, and by this time she had accumulated some experience, which helped her to deal with the students. She was nevertheless exhausted at the end of every day, and had little time for reflecting on her experience.

In 1964 she went back to the department of education at ECNU, leaving behind "the bitter sea" of school based experience, yet more and

---

[43] This was similar to Gu Mingyuan's experience, see Chapter Nine, p.280.

more aware of how important it had been to have spent this time in primary and secondary classrooms. "Few people understand how demanding the job is; it is harder than being a medical doctor," she commented. There was little chance, however, to reflect on this experience, since the "Four Clean-Ups Campaign" (*Si Qing*) was launched in that year, and she had to go to Anhui and participate in rural labor with a production brigade for a year. She returned to ECNU in 1965. That year she was assigned to teach Putonghua and written Chinese to the first group of overseas students from Vietnam. They had been sent by the Vietnamese Communist Party and were a very serious and hardworking group of students.

With the outbreak of the Cultural Revolution in 1966, Ye Lan faced a new set of challenges. What troubled her most was her father's distress in being labeled a "traitor". He had, in fact, been an early member of the underground Communist Party, but his fellow party members had cut off all communication with him, when he was briefly arrested, for the sake of their own safety. After 1949, he had applied several times for a restoration of his membership, but had failed to find a witness who could verify his claim to membership. With the excesses of the Cultural Revolution, he was to suffer greatly as a result of this aspect of his past. There were a number of struggle sessions against him at the school where he taught, though his students never turned against him. Somehow he lived through the difficulties, to be rehabilitated in 1976, after the arrest of the Gang of Four.

For Ye Lan, her father's painful experience sowed doubts in her mind for the very first time. In 1970 she applied to go to ECNU's May 7th cadre school in northern Jiangsu. There she spent a year and a half growing vegetables, raising pigs, and experiencing the life of rural people. There were no students at ECNU at the time, since all classes had been put on hold to allow time and space for revolutionary activism. In 1972, she returned to Shanghai from northern Jiangsu, and began to teach the first group of "worker-peasant-soldier" students, who had been recruited through a process of recommendation rather than unified examination. By this time she had moved from the primary education research group to the teaching and learning group. She remembers how much time was spent criticizing the Soviet educator, Kairov, a particular focus at ECNU where the leading educational theorist, Professor Liu Fonian, had been labeled "China's Kairov."[44]

In 1974, Ye Lan decided to volunteer for a new and exciting assignment – to join the first group of ECNU lecturers to go to Tibet and establish a school for training primary teachers. Her only child was six years old and her husband, who was teaching in the far Northeastern province of Heilongjiang on a three month assignment, did not want her to go so far away. However, when his mother offered to take care of their child, he agreed. Why did she choose this difficult assignment? "I felt I was young and strong, and when I saw the notice I thought I might as well do this sooner, rather than later. Also I really wanted to do something for others, and felt it would be very meaningful to help Tibet develop. Thirdly, I was still somewhat romantic, and felt it would be fascinating to go to a place as different as Tibet, and learn about the culture."

The two years in Tibet, from 1974 to 1976, proved to be extremely interesting. "There was a great deal to do. Since I was the only one in education, I often left Llasa and went to visit schools in rural areas. I went to such remote rural villages as Lingzhi, Sannan and Liemai, and learned a great deal about the needs, poverty and backwardness of rural schools. We also appreciated the cultural sites we were able to visit and the dramatic mountain scenery that surrounded us."

The teacher training school which Ye Lan helped to pioneer has now become the University of Tibet and Ye Lan feels great pride and satisfaction in its achievements. Many of the teachers whom she helped to train still keep in touch, writing to her often, and seeking her out when they visit Shanghai. In many ways she feels her Tibet experience has been fundamental to her present work in basic education, where her focus has been on schools with the greatest need, rather than on excellent urban schools.

In August of 1976, Ye Lan returned to Shanghai from Tibet after two years away. It was a time of great change for China, with several important leaders passing away during that year – Zhou Enlai in January, Zhu De in July and Mao Zedong in September. One month later, the infamous group of radical leaders, nicknamed the Gang of Four, fell from power, and a whole new phase of Chinese history began under Deng Xiaoping.

---

[44] See p.333.

How did Ye Lan feel in this time of drastic political and social change? "The whole thing was deeply upsetting to me at first. I had always believed in what our leaders told us, and now it was a shock to discover how many evil things had been going on behind the scenes. I felt a sense of hopelessness, since it seemed we had gone through all of these struggles to establish our professional work for nothing. This was my first real life experience of politics."

The next two years, 1978 and 1979, were a time of reflection and forms of criticism that were of an entirely different type from the revolutionary movements of the past. There was criticism of the Gang of Four, of course. There was also a reconsideration of the Soviet educator Kairov and great effort was made to proceed on a foundation of broad understanding and careful analysis. Three different editions of Kairov's works were read and discussed, and Ye felt she was able to get to know his ideas in an entirely new way. She came to understand their roots in European thought, the way they had changed over time in the Soviet educational context, and the problems with their application to the very different cultural and educational environment of China.

Everyone in the discussion group she took part in agreed that Kairov's educational theories were far superior to those of the Gang of Four, which they now saw as weapons of ideological struggle. Nevertheless, they felt it was not appropriate to simply go back to Kairov and depend on his work for their courses in education. Rather they needed to raise educational theory to a higher level, and to take into account educational ideas and developments in Western countries, which they had been cut off from for so long. This was a time of new openness, and there were many opportunities for academics and administrators to join study tours abroad or to participate in longer term programs of educational exchange.

Ye Lan was given a unique opportunity in these changing circumstances. She was selected to go to Yugoslavia for a two-year study period. This meant studying the Serbian language before departure. Although it was a surprising assignment, she welcomed it with an open heart, feeling that it would be interesting to spend time in a country which was socialist, but which had chosen a very different kind of socialism from that of the Soviet Union. In the spring of 1979, she attended a three-month language study program in Nanning, Guangxi, where 60 Chinese scholars from all parts of China studied Serbian under three Serbian professors. Then in the summer of that year she went to Yugoslavia and spent two years as a visiting scholar in the department of education and philosophy of the University of Zagreb. She was attached to a senior professor of educational theory, and attended his classes regularly, as well as reading and doing research. Less than two years later, in June of 1982, she returned to China and to ECNU.

What did she gain from this experience in Yugoslavia? "My greatest gain was an understanding of human development through education, and of the independence and self-awareness of each human being. I realized that different perspectives and different ways of thinking would lead to different assessments of similar phenomena. There was a much stronger sense of individuality than anything I had experienced in Chinese education up till then. It was also extremely valuable to be able to see that there are many different models of socialism, not just that of the Soviet Union. Furthermore, I felt a strong sense of the contrast between Yugoslavia's socialist experience and what I had lived through in China. Yugoslavia never had a Cultural Revolution, so it was far ahead of us in living standards."

She returned to China greatly enriched, feeling that only after she had been abroad, did she truly know she was Chinese. It was a time for rediscovering her own cultural heritage and facing the many questions that arose as a result of living in a culture so different from her own. She had been exposed to a lot of new theories in education, which stimulated her mind, and caused her to re-think the theoretical approaches to Chinese education with which she had been familiar. She also felt a strong sense of responsibility and a wish to do something useful on her return. One of her contributions was to translate into Chinese a book on educational theory written by her Serbian professor. In doing this, she found she was re-thinking the familiar educational theories she had learned in China, and seeing them through different eyes. It was her first experience of a deep self-reflection on the professional knowledge she had built up since graduating from university.

Shortly after her return, Ye Lan was called in for a talk by Liu Fonian, who was then president of ECNU. He was eager to hear all about her experience in Yugoslavia and what she had learned. His questions were so deep and probing, that it gave her an immediate sense of the wisdom that lay behind them. He also called in younger scholars who had been in France, Japan and other countries to hear about their experiences. Then he organized a seminar in the Yellow Mountains, a beautiful resort area in Anhui province, with the specific purpose of having all of the returned scholars share their ideas with one another, and prepare reports to communicate what they had learned to their colleagues. She was invited to chair one of the groups, and was responsible for writing the report. The whole activity turned out to be extremely valuable, enabling them to focus on new problems emerging from their experience and observations. Ye Lan noted that this was her first experience of presenting her own educational views before a large group, and it prepared her for the next phase of her professional development in important ways.

Over many years, Ye Lan had felt the enormous influence Liu Fonian had had on her and on many other younger scholars of her generation. He was always ready to listen carefully and seriously, and one could ask him any question, without restraint, and communicate any idea without fear of being misunderstood. Ye felt that he was instrumental in bringing ECNU into the international community, through his invitations to influential scholars such as Benjamin Bloom to come to Shanghai, through the way he encouraged those who had returned to share what they had learned and apply it, and through his often repeated insistence that they should read classic works of education from around the world with care and attention. When she asked him on one occasion how she might prepare herself professionally to be able to make a serious contribution to educational theory, his reply was that she should select a small number of great educational thinkers, who had had a continuing historical influence, and read their works thoroughly and systematically until she understood them in depth. This could provide a kind of foundation for her to build her own theoretical approach and contributions to education.

She also noted how Liu had taken a great deal of interest in educational practice and school reform. Before going to Yugoslavia she had worked under him on an experiment to link up all the levels of schooling, from primary through lower and upper secondary in ECNU's attached schools. She had been involved at the primary three level. Efforts were made to adapt the teaching and learning process to the different interests and talents of different students. Later these efforts influenced other schools in Shanghai, and were found to have positive outcomes for students' learning. Then she realized how Liu's leadership had had an enormous impact on the educational reforms of the 1980s and 1990s in different ways and at different times.

When Ye Lan was appointed vice president of the East China Normal University from 1994 to 1996, Liu gave her good advice. "Only attend the meetings that are necessary, and be sure to keep some time for reflection and reading. Don't allow administrative work to interfere with your scholarship." After serving a relatively short period of two and a half years, she stepped down in order to be able to concentrate all of her energy on a burgeoning research project, which encompassed an ambitious vision for the improvement of basic education. In the final section of this chapter, the story of how this approach to research grew from strength to strength will be told. It is based on Ye Lan's own account of the three phases that had evolved up to the spring of 2001, when I was privileged to interview her in Shanghai.

A Vision for the Transformation of Basic Education in China

The beginning of Ye Lan's vision for a new approach to understanding educational theory and basic education in China came with the assignment to teach a course on educational concepts (*jiaoyu gailun*) for all undergraduate students in ECNU's department of education in 1983, not long after she had returned from Yugoslavia. She decided that she needed to make a completely new start for this task, not relying on past textbooks in educational theory. Her starting point was the recognition that education is a complex system that must be understood in a dynamic interactive way. Her first chapter introduced this concept, and later chapters added topics which she felt had been neglected in the past, such as education and population studies, education and culture.

To some degree her approach was a kind of reaction to what she felt had been missing in Kairov's pedagogy and the Marxist emphasis on labor in education. Kairov had stressed three main factors – the genetic heritage, which is given, the environment which has a determining effect, and education which can be no more than a "helping factor" in relation to the other two. This framework had been widely influential in China. By contrast, Ye gave enormous importance to human potential, and to the human ability to know the self (*ziwo renshi*) and the human desire to develop the self (*ziwo fazhan*). While human beings are part of the collective, as individuals they have the possibility of choosing among alternatives and developing themselves. For labor to be a learning experience, there must be interaction between student and teacher – it cannot happen in a mechanical way.

Her interactive model stressed the fact that the genetic heritage actually offers many possibilities, and it depends on the person how they will develop them. It also suggested that the environment has less and less determining influence over time, as the child comes to understand and transform it. All learning takes place through interaction among human beings, and this changes at different stages of life, from childhood to old age. Ye Lan found herself deeply attracted to a post-Newtonian scientific framework in reflecting on the natural environment and read the work of Ilya Prigogine and others. She also strongly emphasized the need for a holistic framework of thought for understanding education, and the interlinking circles from macrocosm to microcosm.

Was she influenced by Confucian traditions in her thinking? Was there an element of feminism in her attempt to see education in a holistic and interactive way, rather than a more linear, determinative way? Ye Lan replied that she was sure Confucianism had had some influence, though she does not make explicit reference to it in her work. As for feminism, she responded with a laugh, "I have not thought about it from that perspective." At a later point, she noted that she had worked with five women scholars and teachers over a ten-year period in developing her research on basic education and school reform. "They do seem to be more holistic in their thinking, and to have tremendous strength in carrying their projects through." She also noted how easily women communicate with one another, and their shared sense of life as the basis of education.[45]

Ye Lan's book, *Jiaoyu gailun* [Educational concepts], has been widely used as an undergraduate textbook in normal universities throughout China.[46] She feels its most important contribution lies in the emphasis on the potential of the individual and the possibility of self knowledge and knowledge of the other through education.

Only after she had developed her own systematic approach to understanding education, based on years of wide reading in philosophy, psychology and sociology, as well as her lifelong love of literature, did Ye Lan begin to do school-based research. Her first research project was developed in response to a request from educational leaders at the district level in a relatively backward school district of Shanghai. They

---

[45] Interview with Ye Lan, July 18, 2004, Shanghai.
[46] Ye Lan, *Jiaoyu gailun* [Educational concepts] (Beijing: People's Education Press, 1990).

had noted remarkable improvements in the schools of one sub-sector of the district, and wanted to find out what had brought this about. Together with a colleague and several students Ye Lan carried out an empirical investigation of the schools, using a range of research methods, including classroom observation, focus group discussions, interviews and the collection of documents.

From this experience she felt she learned "the wisdom of practice," since the success of these schools was not a matter of theory being applied to practice, but rather of practice or action giving rise to theoretical understanding. This experience made her see in a new way the interaction between practice and theory, and she came to feel that theory was somewhat like an "x-ray" process, which made it possible to see and understand practice.

In the three years spent studying this case of successful reform, she made many discoveries. In past analyses of educational reform, there was an assumption that at some point a breakthrough took place which affected the whole reform process, and the researcher needed to identify this breakthrough. What Ye Lan and her team discovered in this case, however, was what she described as a "system of breakthrough points" [*tupokou de xitong*], many of them in interaction with one another, which made possible the effectiveness of the reform. Through a series of reform measures, many of the schools in this district had achieved significant improvement in educational quality. They were clear about what they had done, and what changes had come about, but they could not explain the overall rationale for what had happened.

The first breakthrough point was an awareness of the importance of how the school looked, the need for the outside to be cleaned up to give an orderly appearance, for a gate to be put in place so that outsiders would not freely enter to use the facilities irresponsibly, and for a high level of maintenance. The second breakthrough point had come with the restoration of classroom discipline and a sense of classroom pride, with teachers always being on time, dressing appropriately, and preparing well for their lessons.

The third breakthrough point related to raising the quality of the teaching process itself. The strategy which had been used here was to select the subject which most needed improvement, yet which was also limited in its scope and in the resources needed for change. Improvement could then take place quickly and in a way that was evident to everyone. The subject chosen was English, which most students took only twice a week; the number of teachers involved was thus limited. The standards in the teaching of English were impossibly poor and in huge need of improvement. Significant resources were therefore given to support the development of the teachers, the transformation of teaching methods and the overall environment for learning English. This soon became evident to everyone and constituted a stimulus and challenge for improvement in other subject areas.

Ye Lan and her team published an influential report, coming out of this research project, entitled "Climbing out of a Deep Gully" [*Zouchu digu*]. She highlighted several points in her report. One was that reform should begin with changes that are highly visible and also with changes that are relatively easy to bring about in a short time. This results in rising morale and excitement about the possibilities of change. She also introduced her idea of a system of breakthrough points which interact with one another, resulting in a multi-faceted transformation.

The second major project built on the relationships established in the first one, and set new goals for improvement. The proposal focused on students' self-education and the nurturing of students' ability. Her intention was to try out some of the concepts developed in the textbook described earlier, particularly with regard to the development of self-knowledge and the ability to gain increasing understanding of and control over one's environment. The basic problem identified was the tendency for students to be extremely passive in their learning, responding only to pressure from parents and teachers for examination success.

This was an action research project, which emphasized giving children control over their own environment and observing how this changed their learning experience. Children were organized in groups, and each week they were given 45 minutes of time in which they could organize their own learning experience. There were only two rules: all children in the group had to participate in what was organized, and they were not allowed to ask their teacher what they should do. The results of this experiment were quite remarkable. Children loved the sense of responsibility they were given, and organized many interesting learning activities, which enabled them to get to know themselves and one another better. They took a practical approach to solving many kinds of problems. An example which Ye Lan gave was the case where the father of one of the children was in hospital, and the children very much wanted to visit him. After discussing how they might do this, and realizing the complications involved, they decided to prepare a tape recording from all of them, and send it to the hospital instead of visiting.

This second project was carried out systematically over a three-year period, with experimental and control groups. At the end of the three years, the most striking difference between the two groups was the fact that all of the children participating in the experimental group were much more pro-active in learning. They had a greater interest in reading, and therefore their knowledge was broadened, and their academic results improved. By contrast, there were much greater gaps between those children who did well in their studies and those who did poorly in the control group. Other findings of this study pointed to the importance of teachers being involved in the research and understanding it fully. The results were published in 1994, and awarded a scientific research prize by the Ministry of Education.

A third study, started in 1994, was entitled "Exploratory Research for a New Basic Education" [*Xinjichu jiaoyu tansuo yanjiu*]. Far more ambitious than the earlier ones, it attempted a systematic study of primary and lower secondary education, and reached out to an ever widening network of schools which wanted to get involved. Three subjects were studied, language, mathematics and moral education, and all participating teachers were given training. The project ran from 1994 to 1999, with successful results for most of the children participating. A particularly encouraging result was the change in attitude of parents. Originally highly concerned about the examination results of their children, many were suspicious of self-initiated learning projects which took time away from examination preparation, especially at the secondary level. Their change of attitude became evident when a group of form three students, in the last year of lower secondary and preparing to compete for entrance to the best schools at the upper secondary level, wanted to organize an activity during the crucial spring time period. Their parents agreed and supported the activity, as they appreciated so much the change they had seen in their children under the experimental learning conditions.[47]

As I was meeting with Ye Lan in April of 2001, to learn about her influential theoretical and experimental work in education, she was

---

[47] The project and its results are described in detail in Ye Lan (ed), *Xin Jichu jiaoyu lilun* [Theory for a New Foundation in Education] (Shanghai: Sanlian shudian, 1999).

deeply absorbed in planning the next project, which was reaching out nationwide to involve schools in different parts of China. Her office in the East China Normal University was a hub of activity, with students and colleagues dropping by for advice, the telephone ringing constantly, and a sense of energy and dynamism pervading her surroundings. I felt privileged to be able to have two hours of her time, in which she explained her vision, and how it had carried her forward since she began working on her textbook on Educational Concepts, and was subsequently drawn into school-based experimental work.

Ye Lan with her husband in Guangxi in 2004

In closing this chapter of the book, I hesitate to add anything of my own to the dynamic portrait that has emerged above of one of China's most influential contemporary educators. Suffice it to say that Ye Lan is conscious of standing on the shoulders of giants, such as Professor Liu Fonian, who was an important mentor throughout her career. She is also deeply aware of the wealth of her own cultural and philosophical heritage, which she began to explore at her father's side in her earliest experiences of schooling. In many ways, her experimental work reminds one of the work of scholars such as Li Bingde, Tao Xingzhi, and Liang Shuming, who sought to transform schools, districts and counties through their wide-ranging experimental methods. Finally, her emphasis on theory arising out of practice, knowledge out of action takes one back to the ideas of Wang Yangming, who integrated aspects of both Daoism and Buddhism into his neo-Confucian philosophy of the mind and heart.

Chapter Twelve

Comparative Reflections on the Portraits

The eleven portraits of influential educators and their institutions, which have been presented in this book, give us a sense of the diversity and richness of the Confucian educational tradition. The lives and ideas of these educators do not conform to either of the stereotypes of Confucianism that have been dominant in Western educational thought – that of a closed hierarchical social order that encouraged subordination and conformity and was antithetical to modernization, on the one hand, or that of an instrumentalist ethos of self-discipline, community cohesion and nationalist loyalty which produced the "East Asian economic miracle" on the other. Rather they take us back to de Bary's sensitive depiction of Confucian learning, which has been noted in chapter one: "a sense of self-worth and self-respect not to be sacrificed for any short-term utilitarian purpose; a sense of place in the world not to be surrendered to any state or party; a sense of how one could cultivate one's individual powers to meet the social responsibilities that the enjoyment of learning always brought ... ; a sense of educational process through discursive learning in dialogue among teachers and students which allowed different understandings of traditional teachings to emerge."[1]

This final chapter to the book is intended to be brief, and its purpose is to reflect comparatively on the life experiences and educational ideas of the eleven scholars. How far are we able to get a better understanding of enduring Confucian values through their life

---

[1] William Theodore de Bary, "Confucian Education in Premodern Asia," in Tu Wei-ming (ed.), *Confucian Traditions in East Asian Modernity* (Cambridge: Harvard University Press, 1996), p.33.

experiences and ideas? What lessons do they have for the global community in a period of dialogue among civilizations?

Education within the Family

Perhaps we could begin by a consideration of education within the family. We see a great diversity in experiences among the eleven educators, reflecting the different time periods in which they lived, the different regions where they grew up and the different kinds of family background they came from. What is common to all, however, is the intense concern of parents, even those with very limited education and means, with their children's education, both at home and in school.

In chapter ten, Lu Jie pointed to the fact that Chinese culture has focused on children to a remarkable degree, and suggested that this is the other, less noticed, side of filial piety. Yet, we see a remarkable degree of freedom given to young people to make their own choices and find their own way in these life-stories. We see Li Bingde striking out for Henan University's attached school in Kaifeng at the age of 16; we see Zhu Jiusi choosing his preferred secondary school and later rejecting his father's choice of National Central University for Wuhan University; we see Lu Jie deciding to leave home and move to Nanjing for tertiary study; we see Xie Xide overturning her father's objection to her fiancé, and choosing a life path entirely contrary to her father's wishes and hopes.

We also see the close relationship of siblings, Li Bingde and Wang Chengxu taking serious responsibility for the education of their younger brothers; Xie Xide having close ties to step-siblings; Pan Maoyuan and Wang Fengxian understanding their self-development in comparison to older siblings who did not share their opportunities for education. The self was definitely a self in relation, to parents, siblings, children, and the wider family. Yet it was also a self that balanced freedom and responsibility, independence and interdependence.

This comes across also in the relationship of the educators to their children. Li Bingde could set out for higher studies in Switzerland, leaving his wife and four young children in a China torn by Civil War. Xie Xide could move from Shanghai to Beijing for two years of intensive research in physics, leaving her infant son in the care of her husband. Ye Lan could set out for two years of pioneering educational work in Tibet, leaving her young son in the care of his paternal grandparents. These were not individuals stifled and controlled by rigid familial rules, but individuals with a rich understanding of the need to seek a balance between their personal development and the demands of their family. Confucian learning was a learning for the self, as both Tu Wei-ming and William Theodore de Bary pointed out, but it was for a self in relationship, a "flowing stream" rather than "an island."[2]

The ways in which that balance was achieved, in historical circumstances of extreme difficulty and deprivation, may be one of the valuable lessons of this book. We have noted Benjamin Schwartz's interpretation of Confucian society as a macrocosm of the family and Wang Yangming's carefully thought-through choice of family and service to government over the monastic life in chapter one. This did not mean that the full development of the individual's potential was sacrificed; rather that one could only understand the development of the individual as an individual in relationship to family and community.

This may be a valuable lesson for a Western world, where the individual's satisfaction and fulfillment has tended to be given priority over family solidarity and community benefit. The individual has rights that transcend and often over-ride responsibilities for family and community. The resulting costs to society in terms of social fragmentation, alienation and loneliness are very real.

Gender and Education

Since family responsibility has tended to be a particular constraint upon women's development, it may be useful to consider the gender angle of these life-stories at this point. What differences can we see in the educational experiences and ideas of the three women, as against the eight men? Perhaps the most notable differences lies in their family backgrounds, with all three having well educated fathers, Xie Xide's and Lu Jie's fathers being professors, Ye Lan's being a teacher. They had thus been brought up in families dedicated to education, and had been encouraged to pursue a higher education from their earliest years.

---

[2] Tu Wei-ming, "Beyond the Enlightenment Mentality," in Mary Evelyn Tucker and John Berthwrong (eds.) *Confucianism and Ecology: The Interrelation of Heaven, Earth and Humans* (Cambridge, Mass.: Centre for the Study of World Religions, Harvard University, 1998), p.13. Of course, one cannot help but think of John Donne's "No man is an island" when reflecting on this quotation.

None of the three was strongly feminist in outlook. The difficulties they faced in developing their careers had been related to political movements rather than gender prejudice. Once the barriers to women's education in China had been removed in the early part of the 20th century, Chinese women were quick to take advantage of modern education. The life-stories of these three influential educators suggest that there was little to prevent them from aspiring to equal participation with men at all levels of education, and from taking up leadership roles, when the opportunity arose.

The experience of all three draws attention to a fascinating paradox in Chinese tradition, which has been noted by Ames and Hall. While Confucian social structures had rigidly excluded women from public life, Confucian epistemology was far more consonant with women's ways of knowing than the linear and mechanistic patterns of the epistemology associated with modern science in the West.[3]

School Education

If we turn from education in the family to education in school, further interesting comparisons emerge. For the older educators, particularly those born between 1912 and 1916, school education included exposure to the traditional classroom as well as modern forms of schooling. The latter were typically primary schools influenced by Deweyan ideas of progressive pedagogy in the 1920s. For those educated later, exposure to classical learning came from family or informal educational experiences, while modern school education was the dominant influence on their development. Here again we see a great diversity of responses and experiences.

Liu Fonian found progressive pedagogy inadequate in laying the foundations of knowledge, and was drawn towards more systematic approaches to curriculum. Lu Jie, by contrast, felt fortunate to have experienced both progressive pedagogy, in an American-influenced pre-school and primary school setting, and more traditional European style pedagogy, in a Catholic secondary school.

---

[3] David L. Hall and Roger T. Ames, "Chinese Sexism," in *Thinking from the Han: Self, Truth and Transcendence in Chinese and Western Culture* (Albany: State University of New York Press, 1998), pp.79-100.

Pan Maoyuan saw the classical learning he had gained in a traditional primary school as the foundation of his love for literature, yet he was later to embrace Deweyan progressive ideas with great enthusiasm, and to apply them in teaching and school leadership. Subsequently he came to see the value of the systematic way in which knowledge was organized under Soviet influence. Of all the educators, he was the most appreciative of the contribution these patterns made to China in the 1950s. Thus, he could jokingly state his admiration for all three forms of education labeled by radicals as feudal, capitalistic and revisionist (*feng, zi, xiu*) during the Cultural Revolution.

Zhu Jiusi was so impressed by the excellent quality of his academic secondary school, led by a principal who was a member of the Nationalist Party, that this became his model for rebuilding his university after the turmoil of the Cultural Revolution in a completely different socio-political setting.

Wang Chengxu was so inspired by the teachers and textbooks he encountered in lower secondary education that he found a way to continue his studies in a normal school for primary teachers, which charged no fees. Thus a village boy ventured into a world of educational thought and theory that was to motivate him to reach for the highest possible academic opportunities, and take him eventually to the University of London.

Wang Yongquan looked back on his secondary schooling in wartime with great appreciation for the quality of the teachers. Retrospectively, however, it was less important in his overall development than his two years in the "school of life," caring for a dying mother.

Li Bingde became convinced of the need for an experimental approach to understanding the way in which children learned from his own school experiences. As soon as it became possible, he visited and observed three distinctive experiments, those of Liang Shuming, Yan Yangchu and Tao Xingzhi. This direct experience led him to see Tao's approach as the soundest, since it integrated the best of Chinese tradition and Western progressivism in pedagogy.

In the schooling experiences of our influential educators, we do not see the stereotype of passive learners being molded into conformity by the inculcation of set patterns of knowledge under the instruction of authoritarian teachers. Rather we see individuals who had a lively and critical experience of interaction with their teachers, whose diverse experiences resulted in flexible and open minds, and who were able to make critical judgments about what they felt was best suited to the needs around them in a later era.

We also see a very high degree of awareness and remarkable powers of observation and memory. This meant that early school experiences became a treasure house of resources for meeting later educational challenges. The ability to observe at a deep level, to have a high degree of awareness of one's surroundings, and to store up one's experiences for later use may well be linked to both the traditions of Confucianism and of Buddhism. We have noted the name given to Zhu Jiusi by his father – "think on nine things (*jiu si*)." The first two things were "clear seeing and distinct hearing." Likewise, Liu Fonian was given a name that means "the year of the Buddha" (*fo nian*) and nurtured by his father in the Buddhist value of awareness.

In a West where we are educated to solve problems, to project and promote our individual interests, and to ensure that our voices are heard in the cacophony of a media-drenched society, this type of educational experience is often neglected. When are we taught to listen, with concentration and sustained attention? How do we learn to observe the ways in which our classrooms are organized and our knowledge is acquired? When do we study the expressions on the faces of those around us and seek to understand the feelings that lie behind them? The quality of awareness and the ability to find a quiet place within the self, from which to observe one's surroundings with deep perception and understanding, may be a second important lesson which Chinese education can bring into the global community.

The Educators and their Institutions, Regions and Nation

A third area for interesting comparison lies in the relationship between the educators and the higher institutions where they studied, and where they taught. In the socialist patterns put in place after 1949, most individuals stayed for a whole lifetime in one institution, with the most talented members of each graduating class being kept as young teachers in their home institution. This pattern is thus not surprising in the case of those whose studies spanned the 1949 Revolution, including Gu Mingyuan, Lu Jie, Wang Fengxian and Ye Lan. Most of the others had the experience of studying in one institution and teaching in another, and some, such as Liu Fonian, had the experience of studying and teaching in several institutions as a result of war-time disruption.

It is interesting, however, to note the diverse roles they took up within their institutions. For some, such as Zhu Jiusi and Liu Fonian, leading their institution and shaping its transformation, was the foremost focus and task. Its achievement led to a scholarship of practice that had a national impact. For others, leadership was accepted as an important responsibility at one period of their career, but set aside for a focus on scholarship subsequently. This was the case for Pan Maoyuan, and two decades later for Ye Lan, who gave up her role as vice-president to devote herself to research that would transform basic education around the nation.

In several cases, political movements led to unjustified attacks upon those who had studied abroad, or were regarded as politically suspect for other reasons. Here it is remarkable to see the ability to forget and forgive, and the willingness to take up the demands and responsibilities of leadership in spite of the severe depredation that had been suffered. The most striking case is Xie Xide, who became vice-president and then president of Fudan, just a few years after being locked up in her own laboratory by rampaging Red Guards. Likewise Li Bingde took on the presidency of Northwest Normal in 1980, after having been under a cloud ever since the Anti-Rightist Movement of 1957.

Some have been primarily institutional leaders, while others have been primarily scholars. One or two have succeeded in balancing the two roles over a long period of time, as is the case with Gu Mingyuan, who served as vice-president and dean of the graduate school while leading a remarkable research program. Yet all of the influential educators have had a relationship of depth and intensity with their university.

To some extent their identity has been shaped by its destiny, both its geographical location, in the southeast or northwest, in a major city such as Beijing and Shanghai, or a provincial capital, such as Lanzhou, Nanjing, Hangzhou or Changchun, and its curricular focus as a national comprehensive university, a polytechnic university or a normal university. In all cases, the institutions take pride in the reputation and influence of their educators, while the educators have a special sense of responsibility for their institution, as well as a sense of belonging and shared identity. The institution is not a platform on which they perform, nor is it a work unit that controls them. It is a dynamic organism which their work has contributed to shaping, and which has shaped them in return. It is a place of shared struggles, shared memories, shared pain and shared achievements.

This may take us back to the discussion of Confucius' sense of being "no longer of two minds" when he reached forty, and knowing "Heaven's place for him" at the age of fifty. Hall and Ames write about "growing into a kind of focus on those fields of possibility where one can engage in the fullest and most fruitful way with society," in contrast to the Western notion of making choices which shape one's destiny. They also talk about the fully-developed person as both "a source of continuity and a ground for creativity."[4] The understanding Confucius had of his life at age fifty was less an awareness of destiny or the mandate of heaven, than a sense of confluence between the natural and human worlds, suggest Hall and Ames. Confucius was finally able to see and understand how life had to unfold.

This kind of awareness seems to be evident in many of the portraits. Lu Jie spoke about the fact that she had no choice in the late 1940s, but to stay in China and support the revolution, even though her father had found her a scholarship in the USA. Nor was there any regret at a later time, in spite of the betrayal she experienced during the Cultural Revolution. Rather she retained a strong sense of the rightness of her decision and its inevitability, due to her early experience of political maturity under conditions of national crisis.

Neither Li Bingde nor Wang Chengxu saw the question of their return to China after completing their studies in Europe as a matter of a choice, over which they agonized. Rather it was a determination that arose naturally out of love for their country. They both had a sense of the rightness of return. In the case of Xie Xide, returning was a matter of going against her father's wishes, and finding a way around the constraints arising from US-China relations in the early 1950s. But again she saw it less as a choice, than the natural and necessary next step in her personal and professional life pathway.

Probably it was because each of them felt such a strong sense of the inter-relationship between the self and their institution, their region and their nation, that they were able to devote their energy to education in remarkable ways. This can be seen in the building up of new institutions, such as Zhu Jiusi's work at HUST, Liu Fonian's leadership at ECNU, Wang Yongquan's creation of an institute of higher education at Beida, Gu Mingyuan's efforts in building the field of comparative education

---

[4] David Hall and Roger Ames, *Thinking Through Confucius* (Albany: State University of New York Press, 1987), p.192.

nationwide and Pan Maoyuan's commitment to creating a new discipline of higher education. It can also be seen in visionary research projects at the national level, from basic education to moral education and higher education.

Those leading these initiatives knew, at a deep level, who they were. They had a sense of the meaning of their lives in the period of China's development that followed on Deng Xiaoping's reform program. Thus they moved very quickly into the space Deng had created and made remarkable contributions into their old age.

What are the lessons for the world community in these experiences? I sense they are quite profound, though not easy to elucidate. How far does Western education serve to root us in the values of our civilization and the sense of the destiny of our community and nation? To what extent does it emphasize so much the value of freedom of choice, and the calculation of the outcomes of different choices, that we are unlikely to probe deeply into our heritage, and understand the self in relation to that heritage?

External Influences

With regard to their views on the many external influences and ideas, which influenced China over the century, we again see a diversity of responses. Li Bingde wrote about the fact that China had been copying for over one hundred years, and needed to develop theories of its own, based on experimental work in China. Lu Jie took students regularly to rural schools in China in order to develop an indigenous Chinese pedagogy. Wang Chengxu made an effort to translate a series of classical European texts in education, so as to lay a foundation for a critical understanding of the many theories that had been introduced from both the capitalist and the socialist West.

None of the educators was satisfied by the over-simplistic formulae provided by their political leaders, such as "socialism with Chinese characteristics" or "Marxism-Leninism-Mao Zedong thought." Chinese theories of education, and Chinese approaches to moral education, to higher education and to comparative education had to be developed gradually, through close attention to the realities of the Chinese context.

Gu Mingyuan was in many ways the pioneer, with his careful comparative analysis of education for modernization gradually developing into a call for the concept of modernization itself to be re-thought, and the claim that this concept could not be fully understood until China's experience of modernization was incorporated within it. Gu's investigation into Chinese cultural traditions led to a focus on aspects of Confucian thought which supported general trends of global development, such as its capacity to accommodate and absorb ideas from outside, and its tendency to integration. It also opened up space for a new consideration of the subjective self, and the notion of education as learning for the development of the self, not only as an instrument for the economic and social transformation of society.

Lu Jie organized an international conference, to bring together members of the Chinese diaspora with the purpose of challenging them to formulate an indigenous Chinese pedagogy. She herself developed an analysis of the dual requirements of education in a Chinese context that was seeing multiple transitions, from an agricultural to an industrial society in rural areas, and from an industrial to a post-industrial society in urban areas. The full development of the independent individual was crucial in rural settings, she felt, while the nurturing of the communitarian individual should be the focus in urban settings. The long-term aim was to shape fully inter-dependent moral persons who would be capable of action in the global community.

Ye Lan saw the Soviet-style pedagogy, which had been so widely disseminated through Kairov's text in the 1950s, as superior to the radical rhetoric of Cultural Revolution activists, yet fundamentally unsuited to the Chinese context. Thus she developed her basic text in Educational Concepts for students of teacher education with a conscious sense of the limitations of Kairov's approach. In contrast to his three dimensions (genetic heritage, the environment and education), she created a picture of education as a complex system at the heart of which are individuals exploring the many different possibilities of their genetic heritage and coming to understand the social and natural environments in such a way as to be able to transform them.

A strong emphasis on the subjective self is evident in Ye Lan's work, and she has launched wide-ranging experiments with the intention of empowering children to stretch the limits of their creativity. On the basis of experimental research, she has also developed concepts such as a system of breakthrough points making possible effective reform, and educational theory as a kind of x-ray through which to see and understand educational practice.

Pan Maoyuan saw the opportunity for China to develop a discipline from the ground up in the field of higher education, since there was not yet an extensive international literature at the time he began his research in China. He laid out two broad arenas for theory development. The first was to look at the function of higher education in relationship to the economy, the political system and society. The second was to consider the inter-relationships within higher education systems among scholarship and professionalism, general education and specialist formation, research and teaching. He suggested that Chinese scholars will have important roles in developing the field in future, given several factors. The first is the historic foundation of China's scholarly culture and the past influence of this culture in Asia. The second is the tremendous size of China's contemporary higher education system, and the rapid and dramatic changes it is undergoing in response to economic change. The third is the large and flexible nature of the body of scholars devoting themselves to higher education research in China.

Wang Chengxu wanted Chinese scholars of education to have access to influential books in comparative and higher education of the contemporary period, as well as the Western classics in education. His selection of titles to translate was remarkable in its scope and quality. However, he was also committed to supporting the development of a Chinese historical framework for understanding global education comparatively, as is evident in the three-volume history of education around the world he edited, which integrates global developments into this Chinese historical framework.

Overall, we see a strong concern on the part of all of these influential educators to develop theories of education rooted in China's own social and cultural realities, and reflecting Chinese patterns of thinking. These are more fluid and dialectical than the rationalist linearity of the European academic tradition.

Western educational theories had been introduced and applied in China for more than a hundred years, without being able to take deep root. The most recent had been the ideas of Ivan Kairov, which dominated pedagogy in the 1950s. In his comparative essay on teachers and teaching, Gu Mingyuan gives a thoughtful overview of the pedagogical ideas of Johannes Herbart, which placed the teacher at the center of the learning process and emphasized the inculcation of systematic knowledge. He also notes how influential these ideas were around the world, including in the Soviet Union, where they combined well with Russian tradition and the authority structure of the Soviet State.

Gu suggests that Herbart's approach to teaching reflected the historical context of a Germany that was ambivalent about the revolutionary changes coming about through industrialization. By contrast, John Dewey's ideas reflected the modern era of a century later, when the inherent ability of children to learn through activity and experience was understood and contributed to a remarkable release of creativity. While suggesting the need for caution and discrimination, Gu endorsed many aspects of the Deweyan approach as suited to the demands of modernization.

Liu Fonian had been highly critical of Dewey, yet he also felt there were serious limitations to Kairov's pedagogy. His efforts to develop an educational text that could replace Kairov gives insight into a resilient bipolarity in Chinese educational thought. He identified a series of fundamental contradictions: between knowledge and action, unified truth and diverse viewpoints, the needs of society and the practical realities of students, individual and collective, specialist training and general education, independence and connectedness. This approach to knowledge and this way of understanding the process of education was certainly closer to American pragmatism than European rationalism, in spite of Liu's reservations about Dewey.

Most of the educators had come across Deweyan progressivism in one way or another before 1949, and all had been required to get to know the ideas of Kairov rather well during the 1950s. Overall, one gets the sense that the former was somehow more consonant with their thinking than the latter. This brings us back to the point made by Ames and Hall in their provocative book, *The Democracy of the Dead: Dewey, Confucius and the Hope for Democracy in China*. They drew attention to the parallels between Confucian ideas of the individual in community and those of Dewey. They described Confucianism as "the continuing narrative of a specific community of people, the center of an ongoing way of thinking and living," rather than a firmly fixed belief structure. This they saw as having a certain degree of consonance with Dewey's vision of the individual as particular but not discrete, and his view that "interactive participatory behavior is the mark of a viable democratic community and ... the context within which an individual is constituted."[5]

Conclusion: The Confucian Word Made Flesh

In an interesting comparative reflection on Christianity and Confucianism, Chinese philosopher Chen Kuide asked the following question: "How should the vitality of Chinese culture be coordinated with the general modernized framework of the world?" He then commented that "the basic question in Chinese culture is how can the Word (*Dao*) become flesh?"[6]

In bringing this book to a close, I would like to suggest that the life-stories of these eleven influential educators might well be understood as the Confucian word become flesh. Their lives are a kind of living book, which reveals the rich humanity and diverse contributions to society and nation of a group of individuals who are all deeply rooted in China's cultural soil.

---

[5] David L. Hall and Roger T. Ames, *The Democracy of the Dead: Dewey, Confucius and the Hope for Democracy in China* (Chicago and Lasalle, Illinois: Open Court, 1999), p.31.

[6] Chen Kuide, "Zhongguo de wenhua weiji yu jiazhi chongjian wenti," [Crisis in Chinese Culture and Reestablishment of Values" in *Dangdai Zhongguo yanjiu* [Modern China Studies], Nos. 4 & 5, 1995, p.117.

Bibliography

Abe, Hiroshi, "Borrowing from Japan: China's First Modern Education System," in Ruth Hayhoe and Marianne Bastid (eds.), *China's Education and the Industrialized World: Studies in Cultural Transfer* (New York: M.E. Sharpe, 1987), pp.57-80.

Ayers, William, *Chang Chih-tung and Educational Reform in China* (Cambridge, Mass.: Harvard University Press, 1971).

Bai, Limin, *Shaping the Ideal Child: Children and their Primers in Late Imperial China* (Hong Kong: Chinese University of Hong Kong Press, 2005).

Beijing shifan daxue xiaoshi xiezu (ed.), *Beijing shifan daxue xiaoshi* [An Institutional History of Beijing Normal University] (Beijing: Beijing shifan daxue chubanshe, 1982).

Birge, Bettine, "Chu Hsi and Women's Education," in William Theodore de Bary and John Chaffee (eds.), *Neo-Confucian Education: The Formative Stage* (Berkeley: University of California Press, 1989), pp.325-367.

Bullock, Mary Brown, *An American Transplant: The Rockefeller Foundation and Peking Union Medical College* (Berkeley: University of California Press, 1980).

Cai Yuanpei, *Cai Yuanpei xuanji* [Selected Writings of Cai Yuanpei] (Beijing: Zhongguo shuju, 1959).

Chen Hsi-en, Theodore, *Chinese Education Since 1949: Academic and Revolutionary Models* (New York: Pergamon, 1981).

Chen Jingpan, *Confucius as a Teacher – Philosophy of Confucius with Special Reference to Its Educational Implications* (Beijing: Foreign Languages Press, 1990).

Chen Wangdao, *Chen Wangdao Wenji* [Selected writings of Chen Wangdao], Vol. I (Shanghai: Renmin Chubanshe, 1979).

Cheng, Joseph, *The May Fourth Movement in Shanghai,* (London: E.J. Brill, 1971).

Ching, Julia, To *Acquire Wisdom – The Way of Wang Yang-ming* (New York and London: Columbia University Press, 1976).

Chuan Mu, Min Zi, Gao Wei (eds.), *Wo Guan Beida* (My View of Beida) (Beijing: Wenhua yishu chubanshe, 1998).

Chuang Tzu: Taoist Philosopher and Chinese Mystic (Trans. Herbert Giles) (London: Unwin Paperbacks, 1980).

Clandinin, Jean and Connelly, Michael F., *Narrative Inquiry: Experience and Story in Qualitative Research* (San Francisco: Jossey-Bass Inc., 2000).

Cody, Jeffrey W., *Building in China: Henry K. Murphy's Adaptive Architecture* (Hong Kong and Seattle: Chinese University Press and University of Washington Press, 2001).

Da Zuoling (ed.) *Nanjing shifan daxue zhi 1993-2002* [History of Nanjing Normal University 1993-2002] (Nanjing: Nanjing shifan daxue chubanshe, 2002).

de Bary, William Theodore, Chan, Wing-Tsit and Watson, Burton (eds.), *Sources of Chinese Tradition* (New York: Columbia University Press, 1960)

de Bary, William Theodore, *East Asian Civilizations – A Dialogue in Five Stages* (Cambridge, Mass.: Harvard University Press, 1988).

de Bary, William Theodore, "Confucian Education in Premodern Asia," in Tu Wei-ming (ed.), *Confucian Traditions in East Asian Modernity* (Cambridge: Harvard University Press, 1996), pp.21-37.

Ding Gang, "The Shuyuan and the Development of Chinese Universities in the Early Twentieth Century," in Ruth Hayhoe and Julia Pan (eds.), *East-West Dialogue in Knowledge and Higher Education* (New York: M.E. Sharpe, 1996), pp.226-244.

Dongbei daxue xiaoshi bianji weiyuanhui, *Dongbei shifan daxue xiaoshi 1946-1986* [An Institutional History of Northeast Normal University 1946-1986] (Changchun: Dongbei shifan daxue chubanshe, 1986).

Du Qin & Sui Xingyan, *Beijing daxue xuezhi yangai* [The Evolution of Peking University's Academic System] (Beijing: Beijing daxue chubanshe, 1998).

Duiker, William, *Ts'ai Yuan-p'ei: Educator of Modern China* (University Park and London: University of Pennsylvania Press, 1977).

Fenn, William Purviance, *Christian Higher Education in Changing China 1880-1950* (Grand Rapids: William B. Eerdmans Publishing Co., 1976).

Feng Shichang (ed.) *Nanjing shifan daxue zhi 1902-1992* [History of Nanjing Normal University 1902-1992] (Nanjing: Nanjing shifan daxue chubanshe, 2002).

Fu Xianqing (ed.), *Fujian gaodeng jiaoyu fazhan yanjiu* [Research into the Development of Higher Education in Fujian] (Fuzhou: Fujian jiaoyu chubanshe, 1997).

Fudan daxue xiaoshi bianxiezu (ed.), *Fudan daxue zhi 1905-1949* [Fudan University History] Vol. 1, (Shanghai: Fudan daxue chubanshe, 1985).

Gardner, John, "Study and Criticism: The Voice of Shanghai Radicalism," in Howe, Christopher (ed.), *Shanghai: Revolution and Development in an Asian Metropolis* (Cambridge: Cambridge University Press, 1981), pp.326-347.

Garner, Karen, *Precious Fire: Maud Russell and the Chinese Revolution* (Amherst and Boston: University of Massachusetts Press, 2003).

Goldman, Rene. "The Rectification Campaign at Peking University May-June, 1957," in *China Quarterly*, No. 12, (October-December, 1964).

Gu Mingyuan, *Shijie jiaoyu fazhan de qishi* [What can be learned from World Educational Trends] (Chengdu: Sichuan jiaoyu chubanshe, 1989).

Gu Mingyuan et al, *Bijiao jiaoyu daolun* [A Guide to Comparative Education] (Beijing: renmin jiaoyu chubanshe, 1996).

Gu Mingyuan, *Education in China and Abroad: Perspectives from a Lifetime in Comparative Education* (Hong Kong: Comparative Education Research

Centre, The University of Hong Kong, 2001).

Guo Ge, "Li Bingde xiansheng de jiaoyu sixiang" [Li Bingde's educational thought] in *Jiaoyu yanjiu* [Educational Research], No. 8, 1997.

Hall, David and Ames, Roger, *Thinking Through Confucius* (Albany: State University of New York Press, 1987).

Hall, David and Ames, Roger, *Anticipating China: Thinking Through the Narratives of Chinese and Western Culture* (Albany, State University of New York Press, 1995).

Hall, David, and Ames, Roger, *The Democracy of the Dead: Dewey, Confucius and the Hope for Democracy in China* (Chicago and Lasalle, Illinois: Open Court, 1999).

Hangzhou daxue xiaoshi bianji weiyuanhui, *Hangzhou daxue xiaoshi 1897-1997 [An Institutional History of Hangzhou University]* (Published by Hangzhou University, 1997).

Hayford, Charles, *To the People: James Yen and Village China* (New York: Columbia University Press, 1990).

Hayhoe, Ruth, "Towards the Forging of a Chinese University Ethos: Zhendan and Fudan 1903-1919," in *China Quarterly*, No. 94 (June, 1983).

Hayhoe, Ruth, "A Chinese Catholic Philosophy of Higher Education in Republican China," in *Tripod*, No. 48, 1988, pp.49-60.

Hayhoe, Ruth, *China's Universities and the Open Door* (Toronto: OISE Press, New York: M.E.Sharpe, 1989).

Hayhoe, Ruth, "The Confucian Ethic and the Spirit of Capitalism," in *Curriculum Inquiry*, Vol. 22, No. 4, Winter, 1992, pp.425-431.

Hayhoe, Ruth "Chinese Universities and the Social Sciences," in *Minerva*, Vol. XXXI, No. 4 (Winter, 1993), pp.478-503.

Hayhoe, Ruth, *China's Universities 1895-1995: A Century of Cultural Conflict* (New York: Garland, 1996, Hong Kong: Comparative Education Research Centre, The University of Hong Kong, 1999).

Hayhoe, Ruth, *Full Circle: A Life with Hong Kong and China* (Toronto: Women's Press, Hong Kong: Comparative Education Research Centre, The University of Hong Kong, 2004).

Hayhoe, Ruth, "Sino-American Educational Interaction from the Microcosm of Fudan's Early Years," in Cheng Li (ed.), *Bridges Across the Pacific: Sino-American Educational Relations.* (Lanham, Maryland: Lexington Press, 2005), pp.25-47.

Hayhoe, Ruth and Pan, Julia (eds.), *Knowledge Across Cultures: A Contribution to Dialogue Among Civilizations* (Hong Kong: Hong Kong: Comparative Education Research Centre, The University of Hong Kong, 2001)

Henan daxue xiaoshi [An Institutional History of Henan University] (Kaifeng: Henan daxue xiaoshi bianji shi, 1985).

Hong Yonghong, *Xiamen daxue xiaoshi diyizhuan* [An Institutional History of Xiamen University Volume 1] (Xiamen: Xiamen daxue chubanshe, 1990).

Hsia, Ronald, "The Intellectual and Public Life of Ma Yin-ch'u" in *China Quarterly*, No. 6, (April-June, 1961), pp.53-63.

Huntington, Samuel, "The Clash of Civilizations?" in *Foreign Affairs*, Vol. 72, No. 3, 1993), pp.22-49.

Huang Shiqi, "Contemporary Educational Relations with the Industrialized World: A Chinese View," in R. Hayhoe and M. Bastid (eds.), *China's Education and the Industrialized World: Studies in Cultural Transfer* (New York: M.E. Sharpe, 1976) pp.225-251.

Israel, John, *Lianda: A Chinese University in War and Revolution* (Stanford: Stanford University Press, 1996).

Ji Quansheng (ed.), *Fudan yishi* [Fudan Anecdotes], (Shenyang: Liaoning chubanshe, 1998).

Keenan, Barry, *The Dewey Experiment in China* (Cambridge, Mass.: Council on East Asian Studies, Harvard University, 1977).

Ko, Dorothy, *Teachers of the Inner Chambers: Women and Culture in Seventeenth Century China* (Stanford: Stanford University Press, 1994).

Lao Tzu, *Tao Te Ching* (Trans. D.C. Lau) (Harmondsworth: Penguin Books, 1982).

Levine, Steven I., *Anvil of Victory: The Communist Revolution in Manchuria 1945-1948* (New York: Columbia University Press, 1987).

Li Bingde, *Jiaoxuelun* [The Theory of Teaching and Learning] (Beijing: Renmin jiaoyu chubanshe, 1991)

Li Bingde, *Jiaoyu kexue yanjiu fangfa* [Research Methodology in Education Science] (Beijing: Renmin jiaoyu chubanshe, 1986).

Li Bingde, *Li Bingde jiaoyu wenxuan* [Selected education essays by Li Bingde] (Beijing: Jiaoyu kexue chubanshe, 1997).

Li Bingde, "Hongyang Zhongguo zhishifenzi de youliang chuantong danfu qi jinri jiaoyu gongzuozhe de zeren," [Promote the excellent tradition of Chinese intellectuals as a resource for contemporary educational workers in taking up their responsibility] in *Xibei shida xuebao (shehui kexueban)* [The Journal of Northwest Normal University (Social Sciences Section)] Vol. 36, No. 2 (March, 1999).

Li Bingde, "A Brief Overview of Sino-Western Exchange Past and Present," in Ruth Hayhoe and Julia Pan (eds.), *Knowledge Across Cultures: A Contribution to Dialogue among Civilizations* (Hong Kong: Comparative Education Research Centre, The University of Hong Kong, 2001), pp.289-294.

Li Bingde, "Yige laonian jiaoshi de xinsheng" [The heart-cry of a senior teacher] in *Jiaoyu yanjiu* [Educational Research] No. 8, 2002, pp.48-54.

Li Zehou, *Lunyu jindu* [Contemporary Reading of the Analects] (Hefei: Anhui Art Press, 1998).

Linden, Allen B., "Politics and Education in Nationalist China: The Case of the University Council 1927-1928," in *The Journal of Asian Studies*, Vol. XXVII, No. 4, (August, 1968), pp.763-776.

Liu Fonian and Jin Yiming, *Liu Fonian xueshu* [The Scholarship of Liu Fonian] (Hangzhou: Zhejiang renmin chubanshe, 1999).

Liu Haifeng and Zhuang Mingshui, *Fujian jiaoyushi* [The History of Education in Fujian] (Fuzhou:Fujian jiaoyu chubanshe, 1996).

Liu Junning (ed.) *Ziyou zhuyi de xiansheng: Beida chuantong yu jindai Zhongguo* [The first voice of Liberalism: The Beida tradition and recent Chinese history] (Beijing:Zhongguo renshi chubanshe, 1998).

Liu Zhengkun, Yang Juqing, Zheng Wenjing (eds.), *Xiamen daxue yuanxi guansuo jianshi* [A brief history of Xiamen University's colleges, departments, centers and institutes] (Xiamen: Xiamen daxue chubanshe, 1990).

Lu Jie, "Jiaoyu: renzhi ziwo jiangou de shijian huodong" [Education: The activities of practice involved in the construction of the human self] in *Jiaoyu yanjiu* [Educational Research], No. 9, 1998, pp.13-18.

Lu Jie (ed.) *Education of Chinese: The Global Prospect of National Cultural Tradition* [Huaren jiaoyu: minzu wenhua chuantong de quanqiu zhanwang] (Nanjing: Nanjing shifan daxue chubanshe, 1999).

Lu Jie, "Ren de zhuanrang: Shijixing de jiaoyu timu" [Human transformation: The Education theme of the new century] in Hao Keming (ed.) *Mianxiang ershiyi shiji: Wo de jiaoyu guan* [Toward the 21st Century: My View on Education] (Guangzhou: Guangdong jiaoyu chubanshe, 1999), pp.389-398.

Lu Jie, "On the Indigenousness of Chinese Pedagogy," in Ruth Hayhoe and Julia Pan (eds.), *Knowledge Across Cultures: A Contribution to Dialogue among Civilizations* (Hong Kong: Comparative Education Research Centre, The University of Hong Kong, 2001), pp.249-253.

Lu Yongling, "Standing Between Two Worlds: Ma Xiangbo's Educational Thought and Practice" in Ruth Hayhoe and Yongling Lu, *Ma Xiangbo and the Mind of Modern China* (New York: M.E. Sharpe, 1996), pp.143-203.

Lutz, Jessie, *China and the Christian Colleges 1850-1950* (Ithaca and London: Cornell University Press, 1971).

MacIntyre, Alasdair, *After Virtue: A Study in Moral Theory* (Notre Dame, Indiana: University of Indiana press, 1984).

McCormack, Gavin, *Chang Tso-lin in Northeast China 1911-1928: China, Japan and the Manchurian Idea* (Stanford: Stanford University Press, 1977).

Ng, Peter, *Changing Paradigms of Christian Higher Education in China (1888-1950)* (Lewiston: The Edwin Mellen Press, 2002).

Pan Maoyuan, *Pan Maoyuan lun gaodeng jiaoyu* [Pan Maoyuan's Higher Education Theories] (Fuzhou; Fujian jiaoyu chubanshe, 2000).

Pan Suyan, "How Higher Educational Institutions Cope with Social Change: The Case of Tsinghua University, China," Unpublished Ph.D. thesis, The University of Hong Kong, 2004.

Polkinghorne, Donald E., *Narrative Knowing and the Human Sciences* (Albany: State University of New York Press, 1988).

Russell, Bertrand, *The Problem of China* (London: Allen & Unwin, 1972).

Schwartz, Benjamin, *In Search of Wealth and Power: Yen Fu and the West* (London: England, and Cambridge, Mass.: The Belknap Press of Harvard University Press, 1964, 1983).

Schwartz, Benjamin I., *The World of Thought in Ancient China* (Cambridge, Mass.: The Bellknap Press of Harvard University Press, 1985).

Smith, Robert, *The Ecole Normale Supérieure and the Third Republic* (Albany, New York: State University of New York Press, 1982).

The Four Books, with Original Chinese Text, English translation and Notes by James Legge (New York: Paragon Book Reprint Corp., 1966).

Tsai, Kathryn, "The Chinese Buddhist Monastic Order for Women: The First Two Centuries," in Richard Guisso and Stanley Johannesen (eds.) *Women in China: Current Directions in Historical Research* (Lewiston, New York: Edwin Mellen Press, 1982), pp.1-20.

Tsinghua daxue xiaoshi bianxie zu (ed.) *Tsinghua daxue xiaoshi gao* [Draft History of Tsinghua University] (Beijing: Zhonghua shuju, 1981).

Tu Wei-ming, *Neo-Confucian Thought in Action: Wang Yang-ming's Youth (1472-1509)* (Berkeley: University of California Press, 1976).

Tu Wei-ming, *Confucian Thought: Selfhood as Creative Transformation* (Albany: State University of New York Press, 1985).

Tu Wei-Ming, "Beyond the Enlightenment Mentality," in Mary Evelyn Tucker and John Berthrong (eds.) *Confucianism and Ecology: The Interrelation of Heaven, Earth and Humans* (Cambridge, Mass.: Centre for the Study of World Religions, Harvard University, 1998), pp.3-21.

Vogel, Ezra, *The Four Little Dragons: The Spread of Industrialization in East Asia* (Cambridge, Mass.: Harvard University Press, 1991).

Waley, Arthur, *Three Ways of Thought in Ancient China* (Stanford: Stanford University Press, 1982).

Wang Chengxu, Zhu Bo, Gu Mingyuan (eds.) *Bijiao jiaoyu* [Comparative Education] (Beijing: People's Education press, 1982).

Wang Fengxian, "Dui jiaoyu youxian fazhan zhanlue de zai renshi" [A Reconsideration of the strategy of giving priority to education in development] in *Zhongguo jiaoyu xuekan* [Chinese Education journal], No. 1, 1998, pp.8-11.

Wang Fengxian, "Jixu jiefang sixiang, wei chuangzao yiren weiben de weilai shijie peiyang yi daidai chuangzaoxing xinren" [Continue to liberate our thinking and nurture one generation after another of new creative individuals in order to fashion a future society where human beings are the foundation] in Zhongguo jiaoyu xue, Zhongguo gaodeng jiaoyu xue hui (eds.), *Zhongguo jiaoyu gaige fazhan ershinian* [Twenty Years of Chinese Education Reform and Development] (Beijing: Beijing shifan daxue chubanshe, 1999), pp.434-447.

Wang Fengxian, "Meeting Points of Trans-cultural Exchange – A Chinese View," in R. Hayhoe and Julia Pan, *Knowledge Across Cultures: A Contribution to*

Dialogue Among Civilizations (Hong Kong: Comparative Education Research Centre, The University of Hong Kong, 2001), pp.295-300.

Wang Minghan, Heng Jun (eds.), *Xibei shifan daxue xiaoshi 1939-1989* [An Institutional History of Northwest Normal University] (Xining: Qinghai People's Press, 1989).

Wang, Ting, "Propaganda and political Struggle: a Preliminary Case Study of Hsueh-hsi yu P'i-p'an", in *Issues and Studies*, Vol. XIII, No.6, June 1977, pp.1-14.

Wang Yingjie, "A New University Model for the New Century: from Perspectives of Chinese Philosophy," Paper prepared for the Learning Conference 2003 organized by the Institute of Education, University of London, held on July 15 – 18, 2003, in London, U.K.

Wang Yongquan and Li Manli, "The Concept of General Education in Chinese Higher Education," in Ruth Hayhoe and Julia Pan (eds.) *Knowledge Across Cultures: A Contribution to Dialogue Among Civilizations* (Hong Kong: Comparative Education Research Centre, The University of Hong Kong, 2001), pp.311-322.

Wang Yongquan, "Waiguo gaodeng jiaoyu jiegou de bijiao" [A Comparison of the Structure of Foreign Higher Education] in *Jiaoyu yanjiu* [Educational research] No. 2, 1988, pp.3-13.

Weerasinghe, Henry, *Education for Peace: The Buddha's Way* (Ratmalana, Sri Lanka: Aarvodaya Book Publishing Services, 1992).

Weston, Timothy B. *The Power of Position: Beijing University, Intellectuals and Chinese Political Culture 1898-1929* (Berkeley: University of California Press, 2004).

West, Philip, *Yenching University and Sino-Western Relations, 1916-1952* (Cambridge, Mass.: Harvard University Press, 1976).

Wu Yigu (ed.) *Wuhan daxue xiaoshi 1893-1993* [An Institutional History of Wuhan University 1893-1993] (Wuhan: Wuhan daxue chubanshe, 1993).

Wang Zengfan, *Xie Xide* [A Biography of Xie Xide] (Fuzhou: Fujian kexue jishu chubanshe, 1993).

Xiao Chaoran et al, *Beijing daxue xiaoshi 1898-1949* [An Institutional History of Peking University 1898-1949] (Beijing: Beijing daxue chubanshe, 1988).

Xie Xide, *Xie Xide Wenxuan* [Selected Works of Xie Xide] (Shanghai: Shanghai Scientific and Technical Publishers, 1988).

Yao Qihe (ed.) *Huazhong ligong daxue de sishinian* [The forty years of Central China University of Science and Technology] (Wuhan: Huazhong ligong daxue chubanshe, 1993).

Yang, Rui and Au Yeung, King Hau, "China's Plan to Promote Research in the Humanities and Social Sciences," in *International Higher Education*, 27 (Spring, 2002), pp.20-21.

Ye Lan, *Jiaoyu gailun* [Educational concepts] (Beijing: People's Education Press, 1990).

Ye Lan (ed), *Xin Jichu jiaoyu lilun* [Theory for a New Foundation in Education] (Shanghai: Sanlian shudian, 1999).

Yuan Yunkai and Wong Tiexian (eds.) *Huadong shifan daxue xiaoshi 1951-2001* [An Institutional History of East China Normal University 1951-2001] (Shanghai: Huadong shida chubanshe, 2001).

Xin Fuliang (ed.) *Dangdai Zhonguo gaodeng jiaoyu jia* [Contemporary Chinese Higher Education Specialists] (Shanghai: Shanghai Jiaotong daxue chubanshe, 1995).

Zhang Liuquan, *Zhongguo shuyuan shihua* [The Evolution of Academies in China] (Beijing jiaoyu kexue chubanshe, 1982).

Zhang Ruifan and Wang Chengxu (eds.) *Zhongwai jiaoyu bijiaoshi gang* [An Outline of Comparative Chinese and Western History of Education] (Jinan: Shandong Education Press, 1997.) Three volumes.

Zhao Junming, "The Making of a Chinese University: An Insider's View of an Educational Danwei," Ph.D. Thesis, McGill University, Montreal, October, 1998.

Zhejiang daxue xiaoshi bianxiezu, *Zhejiang daxue jianshi* [A Brief History of Zhejiang University], (Hangzhou: Zhejiang daxue chubanshe, 1996).

Zhong Ningsha and Ruth Hayhoe, "University Autonomy in Twentieth Century China," in Glen Peterson, Ruth Hayhoe and Yongling Lu (eds.), *Education, Culture and Identity in Twentieth Century China* (Ann Arbor: University of Michigan Press, 2001), pp.265-296.

Zhou Enlai, "On the Question of Intellectuals," *New China News Agency*, January 29, 1956, in Robert Bowie and John Fairbank (eds.) *Communist China 1955-1959: Policy Documents with Analysis* (Cambridge, Mass: Harvard University Press, 1962), pp.128-144.

Zhu Jiusi, *Gaodeng jiaoyu sanlun* [Essays on Higher Education] (Wuhan: Huazhong ligong daxue chubanshe, 1990).

Zhu Jiusi, "Lishi de huigu" [A Retrospect on History] in *Gaodeng jiaoyu yanjiu*, No. 4, 1992, pp.1-13.

Zhu Jiusi, *Jingzheng yu zhuanhua* [Struggle and Transformation] (Wuhan: Huazhong keji daxue chubanshe, 2000).

Index